MW01148958

AIR COMMANDO ONE

AIR COMMANDO ONE

HEINIE ADERHOLT AND AMERICA'S SECRET AIR WARS

WARREN A. TREST

SMITHSONIAN INSTITUTION PRESS
Washington and London

Copy editor: Lise Rodgers
Production editor: Robert A. Poarch
Designer: Janice Wheeler

Library of Congress Cataloging-in-Publication Data
Trest, Warren A.
    Air Commando One : Heinie Aderholt and America's secret air wars / Warren A. Trest.
      p. cm.
    Includes bibliographical references and index.
    ISBN 1-56098-807-X
    1. Aderholt, Harry C. 2. United States. Air Force—Biography. 3. Generals—United
    States—Biography. 4. Special operations (Military science) I. Title.
    UG626.2.A335 T74 2000
    358.4′0092—dc21
    [B]   99-053643

British Library Cataloguing-in-Publication Data is available

Manufactured in the United States of America
05 04 03 02 01 00 5 4 3 2 1

∞ The paper used in this publication meets the minimum requirements of the American National
Standard for Information Sciences—Permanence of Paper for Printed Library Materials ANSI
Z39.48-1984.

The photographs appearing in this book are from the collection of the author. The Smithsonian
Institution Press does not retain reproduction rights for these illustrations individually, or maintain a file of addresses for photo sources.

To "all those guys who flew away and did not return . . . men who will forever live in our memories."

CONTENTS

PREFACE

I first met Brigadier General Heinie Aderholt in 1967 when he was a colonel commanding the 56th Air Commando Wing at Nakhon Phanom, Thailand. The air staff wanted a special report on the wing's operations, and I had gone to the remote base with another historian to do the research. We flew there from Udorn in the backseats of two A-1E Skyraiders (known by their call sign as Sandys), which were used as escort aircraft for rescue missions. After a short flight we climbed down from the cockpits at Nakhon Phanom and stepped back into the past. The rows of other propeller-driven warplanes, the pierced steel-planking runway, and the austere wooden-frame buildings still undergoing construction on the friendly side of the Mekong River were vintage "Terry and the Pirates." We half expected a young Steve Canyon, Flip Corkin, or the Dragon Lady to come out from the shadows to greet us.

We were met instead by an unforgettable cast of real people: Colonel Heinie Aderholt and his spirited air commandos—unsung heroes who were as boldly adventurous and as colorful as any of the timeless characters who fired Milton Caniff's imagination. I never ran into a more proud or more committed force during my two years at Seventh Air Force, while serving on a team of historians with Project CHECO (Contemporary Historical Evaluation of Combat Operations).Whether they were flying missions against the Ho Chi Minh Trail in Laos, making shot-up planes whole again, patrolling the perimeter, paying a voucher, treating a patient, training Thai aircrews, or whatever, the men loved what they were doing and it showed. The camaraderie between the commander and his men was electric. Putting us up in the trailer next to his, Aderholt said with a grin that he was not trying to give us special treatment but wanted to keep an eye on us.

It was not unusual to be roused out of bed after midnight to attend a mission briefing or to debrief returning pilots, because that's the way our host did things. He wanted us to see it all. We were given total access. Going through the well-weeded command section files, I came across a letter that had obviously been crumpled and thrown into the wastebasket, then retrieved, smoothed out, and filed away. The missive was an angry reminder from the Seventh Air Commander that he was running the air war, and that Colonel Aderholt was not to recommend improvements in air operations to anyone else but his headquarters. To avoid intruding upon the story in chapter 8, "The Tigers of Nakhon Phanom," all that needs saying here is that after discussing the crumpled letter with Colonel Aderholt, I knew there was a serious "disconnect" between the two commanders over how to interdict the Ho Chi Minh Trail and, indeed, how the war as a whole should be fought.

That crash course in Special Operations 101 gave me a new way of looking at the Vietnam War. Although I studied the U.S. Air Force (USAF) in Southeast Asia for several more years, I never looked at the war or at air operations quite the same way again. This biography of General Aderholt tells why. I left Nakhon Phanom knowing there was far more to the story of this remarkable man and his elite force than was covered in our CHECO report. Thirty years would go by before I had an opportunity to expand on the theme. Renewing my acquaintance with Heinie Aderholt and the brotherhood of air commandos has made the waiting worthwhile.

The legend of *Air Commando One* could not have been written without the unstinting support of the many Air Commando Association members who gave freely of their time and assistance in piecing together the story of General Aderholt's distinctive military career. Their recollections and those of others who served with him—consisting of interviews, audiotapes, and letters—were indispensable to me in writing the biography. Special thanks are due Warren Aderholt, James Baginski, Frank Blum, Lynn Bollinger, Robert Brewer, Robert Cardenas, Jim Cherry, Carlos Christian, Drexel Cochran, John Doonan, Walter Forbes, Robert Gleason, Michael Haas, Lester Hansen, James Hildreth, Joe Holden, Clyde Howard, Jimmy Ifland, Charles Jones, Bill Keeler, Benjamin King, Joseph Kittinger, Roland Lutz, LeRoy Manor, Sid Marshall, Joe Norrell, Arthur Overton, Paul Pettigrew, Lawrence Ropka, Richard Secord, Ed Smith, William Sullivan, Leroy Svendsen, Saras Taverrungsenykl, James Taylor, Tom Temple, William Thomas, William Toomey, Lee Volet, Robert White, James Wilson, Carl Zeigler, and Robert Zimmerman. I would also like to thank Professor William M. Leary, University of Georgia, for the encouragement and help he gave General Aderholt in gathering documentation.

Within General Aderholt's office I am indebted to Rose Dykes for her steadfast support and encouragement. A special tribute is owed the staff at the Air Force Historical Research Agency, Maxwell AFB, Alabama, for their sustained support over the past two years. The tireless and timely responses of Joseph Caver, Edward Cummings, Hugh Ahmann, and Edward Russell to my many requests for assistance were clearly above and beyond the call. I would also like to thank Douglas Bagley, Donna Billingsley, Faye Davis, Archie Difante, Essie Roberts, Hezekiah Smith, and Margaret Tolbert for their help in researching documents and accessioning General Aderholt's personal papers into their collection. I am indebted to Lloyd Cornett, Frank Futrell, John Huston, Dan Mortensen, Wayne Thompson, and Jay Wurts for reviewing the draft manuscript. Special thanks to Mark Gatlin and Robert Poarch, Smithsonian Institution Press, and to Lise Rodgers for helping to make *Air Commando One* a better book.

AIR COMMANDO ONE

PROLOGUE
The Man and the Mission

The gathering of a rare breed of American fighting men each year at Fort Walton Beach, Florida, keeps alive the spirit and tradition of the United States Air Force's legendary air commandos and their half century of special operations. These highly decorated combat veterans belong to the Air Commando Association, a brotherhood of warriors past and present that was formed at Fort Walton Beach (home to Hurlburt Field and the Air Force Special Operations Command) in the twilight of U.S. military involvement in the Vietnam War. The charter members had all fought in the war, most had served more than one combat tour, and some were there to the bitter end. Among those staying the course in the protracted conflict was the Air Commando Association's founder, Brigadier General Harry C. "Heinie"Aderholt—a dynamic, fearless, and charismatic leader who had flown and fought in three wars and whose remarkable military career was cloaked in mystery because of his years of clandestine operations with the Central Intelligence Agency. Other members of this elite group know him as Air Commando One. His story is their story—an epic American journey through the perilous skies of the Cold War.

General Aderholt's career is a case study in military leadership, courage, and conviction. In today's technocratic military culture, it is hard to picture anyone pinning on stars who has never attended college or an equivalent military school. When asked if this had been a handicap to him, Aderholt smiled wryly and fired back that the Air Force today "is overeducated." He had joined the Army Air Forces aviation cadet program in World War II and remained on active duty when the war was over. "At that time people stayed in the Air Force to fly airplanes," he said. "Today they stay in the Air Force to go to school."[1]

1

Officers and NCOs who served under Aderholt's command learned by example that integrity and dedication to the mission—that is, taking care of your people and getting the job done—are paramount.

Growing up in Birmingham, Alabama, during the hard times of the Great Depression, Aderholt learned family values and the work ethic at an early age. He lost his father, a railroad fireman who was killed in a train crash in 1929, when he was nine years old and, along with six brothers and sisters, helped his mother support the family. To emphasize the family's closeness, he recalled there was a saying in Birmingham: "If you get in a fight with an Aderholt, you've got to whip all seven of them."[2]

Aderholt's mathematics teacher at Woodlawn High School described him as a friendly, industrious, and outgoing student, who was popular with both pupils and teachers. She recalled that he quit school when he was sixteen years old "to get a job and help his widowed mother of seven make ends meet." The high school principal convinced him to return to Woodlawn and complete his high school education. The principal took the teenager a hand-me-down suit and pair of shoes. Aderholt said years later that the pants were patched, but wearable, and the coat was the first he had ever owned.[3]

Aderholt showed leadership ability at an early age, according to his teacher. Weighing about 140 pounds, the scrappy youngster was a good athlete who lettered in football and baseball at Woodlawn High. He played left halfback on the football team and shortstop on the baseball team. In a tribute to Aderholt's football prowess, a Birmingham newspaper described him as "Woodlawn's 'howitzer-armed' little Heinie Aderholt . . . who stacks up as one of the Big Five's top-ranking pass-throwers."[4]

After high school, Aderholt tried out at the University of Alabama, when Paul "Bear" Bryant was a freshman coach there, but he was too small for college football. In 1940 he coached the Gate City American Legion baseball team to the state championship and to third-place finish in the South. The players hitchhiked to and from their games. Few people owned cars, and those who did used them for commuting to work. He was working and playing semiprofessional baseball with a steel mill in Birmingham when he and his four brothers responded to the call to serve their country after the Japanese attacked Pearl Harbor. They would eventually serve eight combat tours in three wars.

The family traits of pride, loyalty, and tenacity carried over into Aderholt's military life. As a commander, the general demanded the best from his people but always looked after their best interests and stood by them "come hell or high water." He could be hard-nosed and exacting toward those who were dishonest, disloyal, or made a career of screwing up, yet warm, kind, and generous to a fault with those he found deserving. In an appraisal of combat leadership in Southeast Asia, Colonel Joseph W. Kittinger Jr.—a returning Air Force hero and F-4 squadron commander who was shot down late in the war and interned by the North Vietnamese—put Aderholt (described by Kittinger as "a fantastic leader") in a class by himself. Colonel Kittinger had served three combat tours in Southeast Asia, one of those with Aderholt's 56th Air Commando Wing operating out of Nakhon Phanom, Thailand. "Heinie Aderholt has the personality and the leadership ability and the guts and the courage that everybody just admires and loves," Kittinger said. "He is the only Air Force leader that I have known in my twenty-four years in the Air Force who could pick up the phone and by his own personality get three thousand or four thousand guys that would go with him anytime, anyplace."[5]

Another beribboned combat commander, Major General James R. Hildreth, said there was "not a more gung ho outfit" in the war than Aderholt's air commandos, and that this standing was "maintained solely by superior leadership." "One cannot fake leadership in combat," Hildreth said. "You must demonstrate the courage and integrity that inspires your men to follow you through hell if necessary, and Heinie did."[6] Lieutenant General LeRoy J. Manor, who led the famed Son Tay raid deep inside North Vietnam in 1970 to attempt the rescue of American prisoners of war, described Aderholt as an intrepid aviator whose "leadership in combat inspired others to superior achievement."[7] In his book, *Honored and Betrayed*, Major General Richard V. Secord said the best combat commander he ever worked for was Heinie Aderholt.[8]

On a discordant note Joe Kittinger recalled an ugly confrontation with General William W. Momyer, Seventh Air Force commander, that cost Aderholt his command in 1967 and nearly ruined his career.[9] The run-in with Momyer (who was a WWII fighter ace and full colonel at the age of twenty-six) underscored the deep philosophical differences between the two men and what they stood for. A hard-charging commander like Aderholt (who epitomized the air commando mystique and had never flown high-performance jet fighters) was antithetical to the Momyers of the Air Force—the architects of "higher and faster" tactical air power calculated to respond to any level of hostilities. The tactical air planners were unmoved by criticism that the USAF's century-series fighter-bombers had been designed for nuclear strike operations and were, therefore, ill suited for low-intensity combat in the jungles of Vietnam. They modified their tactical nuclear workhorses (the F-100 Super Sabre and the F-105 Thunderchief) to deliver conventional ordnance, and procured U.S. Navy–developed F-4 Phantoms for the air superiority role. The tactical air leaders were convinced that high-performance jet fighters could perform effectively across the spectrum of armed conflict. They looked upon counterinsurgency in the Vietnam War as an aberration and upon air commandos as throwbacks to a bygone era.

A no-nonsense, autocratic commander, General Momyer (called "Spike," but only by his peers) ruled by the book in Vietnam and brooked no argument from subordinates. The Air Force had sent him to Vietnam in mid 1966 to guarantee doctrinal unity in command and control of the massive buildup of first-line combat aircraft and their employment in Southeast Asia. Years later Lieutenant General Elwood R. Quesada, the great WWII tactical air commander, said to Momyer that he was picked for the Seventh Air Force commander's post because the transition from a backwater counterinsurgency (COIN) effort to a full-blown U.S. commitment needed "somebody there who [understood] the use of air power and [didn't] give a goddamn about getting along." Quesada said that Momyer was the right man for the job because it required "conviction and also a personality and enough arrogance—if you don't mind my calling it that—to stand up."[10]

In his book *Air Power in Three Wars* Momyer admits that senior airmen "questioned the investment" the Air Force had made in COIN forces. It was common knowledge that he believed the funds could have been better spent on modern jet fighters. Momyer was dogmatic in his views on the command of air power, but his two-year quest to bring all air operations in the war under the Air Force's doctrine of centralized control, with decentralized execution, was not a shining success. In his dual capacity as the deputy commander for Air Operations, Military Assistance Command, Vietnam (MACV), Momyer never controlled the Army's aircraft or the Air Force's B-52s, for that matter, and even when Marine Corps fighters were centrally tasked (fragged) after Khe Sanh and the Tet Offensive of 1968, the Marines claimed this was a temporary arrangement and did not constitute operational control by the MACV air component.[11]

Another unresolved doctrinal bias during Momyer's tenure was the control that Ambassador William H. Sullivan exercised over air operations in the secret war in northern Laos. An able and experienced career foreign-service officer who was the ambassador during 1964–69, Sullivan directed the secret war through the embassy's military attaches and the CIA in Vientiane. Because Aderholt worked closely with the country team in Vientiane, the ambassador was well briefed on the superior support he received from the air commandos and their devastating results on the Ho Chi Minh Trail. Sullivan probably surmised that he was indirectly responsible for the Seventh Air Force commander taking out his frustrations on Aderholt, since bullying a subordinate does not run the risk of quid pro quo. When later asked his opinion about Aderholt's promotion to general officer rank, Sullivan said emphatically that he "deserved stars." He briefly described the special caliber of the man: "He was a colorful character, who eschewed the traditional martinet role of an Air Force commander. He often wore no insignia (in fact no recognizable uniform), he flew missions sometimes as a wingman, he swore and drank and arm-wrestled with his troops and never seemed concerned with the perquisites of his office, except one—he made sure everyone knew he was the boss."[12]

Prelude to the Vietnam War

An examination of General Aderholt's military records yields no conclusive evidence as to whether his back channels to the CIA helped or hindered his Air Force career. The truth is probably somewhere in between—that it was a little of both. He first became involved with clandestine operations and the CIA as a young captain commanding a special air missions detachment in the Korean War. During World War II he had flown B-17s and C-47s in North Africa and Italy but had seen little of what he defined as "real combat." He sought to remedy this when the Korean War broke out by volunteering for fighters but was told that his extensive multiengine experience was sorely needed in Korea. This fatefully led to his initial assignment with special operations—a mission environment that, henceforth, would guide his Air Force career.[13]

During the brutal battles raging up and down the Korean peninsula in 1950–51, Aderholt's detachment of C-47 Gooney Birds flew a punishing schedule of special airlift missions in support of the United Nations ground campaign. These included parachute drops into the thick of combat and perilous low-level night penetrations as far north as Manchuria to airdrop Korean partisans and secret agents behind enemy lines. Code-named "Rabbits," these intrepid men and women became a vital source of human intelligence during this critical phase of the war.[14]

As one of the detachment's satisfied "customers," the CIA was impressed with the daring and innovative work by Aderholt and his pilots and recruited them for assignments with the air section in its Washington headquarters. The introductory tour with CIA headquarters, however, was not as challenging or as exciting as Aderholt had been led to expect. Nearly two years (1951–53) working undercover in Washington and down on the Farm (secret CIA training installation at Williamsburg, Virginia) proved to be a tedious orientation into the shadowy world of paramilitary operations. He worked hard setting up the CIA's air training school at the Farm and developed strong operational bonds within the agency, but the tedium of the training routine bored him.[15]

Colonel Aderholt in the
cockpit of an AT-28 at
Nakhon Phanom,
Thailand.

Promoted to major while in Korea, Aderholt sought greater responsibility
and grew restless to return to a more demanding Air Force assignment, prefer-
ably within special operations. He soon learned, however, that the armed forces
were in a state of flux coming out of the Korean War and had no room in their
contingency plans or in their inventories for unconventional operations and
special forces. Three air resupply and communications wings established during the Korean War to perform psychological and unconventional warfare missions were downgraded to groups in 1953 and were deactivated in 1956. There
was little concern even for conventional force readiness since the post-Korea
national security strategy tilted the Pentagon's war planning almost exclusively
toward nuclear deterrence. The consequences for the fledgling field of special
air warfare were more debilitating than post-WWII retrenchment, which had
wiped out the famous air commando units that were born during the war.[16]

Frustrating tours on the heaquarters staffs of Eighteenth Air Force (Donaldson AFB, South Carolina) and United States Air Forces in Europe (Wiesbaden
AB, Germany) over the next four years were stark reminders of the neglected
role of special air warfare. These were years of exceptional growth for the Air
Force, but programs other than Strategic Air Command (SAC) received a beg-

gar's share of the defense budget. Critics had accused the Air Force of building up strategic air power at the expense of other programs when it became a separate service in 1947. That disparity became even more lopsided during the prime of Dwight D. Eisenhower's two presidential terms.[17]

After keeping a campaign pledge to end Korean hostilities in the summer of 1953, the new president enunciated a doctrine of massive retaliation that promised no more Koreas. Essential elements of the Eisenhower Doctrine entailed building a strong nuclear posture to deter Communist aggression, while equipping and training smaller allied nations to defend themselves under the global protection of the U.S. nuclear umbrella. In the long term, however, massive retaliation not only fostered a nuclear arms race between the two superpowers, the United States and the Soviet Union, but exacerbated interservice rivalries at home over who would develop and employ weapons of mass destruction. Belatedly, some strategic planners would decry the fact that overreliance on nuclear deterrence had encouraged Communist insurgencies and so-called wars of national liberation, while depriving U.S. and allied arsenals of the special forces needed to fight these brushfire wars.

Within this disparate defense environment Aderholt turned back to the CIA in the autumn of 1957 as the provisional guardian of special operations. This second tour, which entailed working with the CIA's light aircraft development program, lasted through the end of the 1950s, when agency officials called on their blue-suit troubleshooter to take command of a problem-ridden covert detachment operating out of Kadena, Okinawa. Among other clandestine activities, the Okinawa-based detachment was flying highly sensitive missions in support of Tibetan partisans fighting for their freedom on "the roof of the world." The assignment provided an opportunity for Aderholt to field-test a light, short takeoff and landing (STOL) aircraft, which he had taken the lead in procuring, in the hostile wilds of Laos. The unmarked C-130s—newly developed four-engine turboprop transport aircraft destined to become a mainstay of tactical airlift—flying the Tibetan airlift staged through Takhli, Thailand, where the CIA had bare-base facilities supporting covert activities in Laos and elsewhere in the region. Aderholt deployed to Okinawa in January 1960, at the start of a decade portending great change for the armed forces and for the nation.[18]

A Renaissance for the Air Commandos

President John F. Kennedy's inauguration in January 1961 breathed new life into the air commandos and other special forces. During Eisenhower's second term warning shots such as the launching of the USSR's *Sputnik* satellite in

1957, simultaneous crises in the Taiwan strait and Lebanon in 1958, and Fidel Castro's galling Communist toehold on America's doorstep in 1959 punched holes in the nuclear umbrella concept and caused some military strategists to rethink massive retaliation. Soviet Premier Nikita Khrushchev's "wars of national liberation" speech two weeks before Kennedy took office put the new president on notice that world Communism was a threat to the peace at any level of aggression, from insurgencies to all-out nuclear war. In the months ahead Castro's support for leftist guerrillas in Central America, the Bay of Pigs fiasco, and heightened insurgent activity in Southeast Asia convinced the administration that the only viable military strategy was flexible response, which retired Army chief of staff General Maxwell D. Taylor had proposed in his book *The Uncertain Trumpet*. Since Aderholt was one of the few active-duty airmen who had expertise in special air warfare, he became a prized resource in the spring of 1961 when President Kennedy ordered the urgent development of counterinsurgency capabilities to defeat mounting Communist guerrilla activity.

When he finally pinned on silver leaves in August 1961, Aderholt had gone ten years without a promotion.This lengthy hiatus was not unusual in the SAC-dominated Air Force, since the nerve center for massive retaliation at Offutt AFB, Nebraska, not only had an iron grip on air resources and the purse strings but monopolized the promotion system as well. The promotion to lieutenant colonel was the icing on one of Aderholt's most rewarding tours. He had hit the ground running on Okinawa and had not slowed since. "We had more things going than you could shake a stick at," he later recalled. "It wasn't a big detachment, but I made sure it was fully committed by seeking new missions."[19]

As the tour unfolded, he found more and more of his time and energy taken up with CIA activities in Laos, where Communist Pathet Lao forces and North Vietnamese intruders threatened to topple the United States–backed government in Vientiane. From the CIA facilities (nicknamed the Ranch) on Takhli, Aderholt controlled covert C-46 airlift operations supporting General Vang Pao and his Hmong hill tribesmen defending against the Pathet Lao on the Plaine des Jarres. To facilitate these covert activities, he teamed up with the CIA's James William "Bill" Lair, Air America pilot Ron Sutphin, and Vang Pao in developing the initial rudimentary airfields throughout the embattled country. These airstrips, known as Lima sites, later served as forward staging bases for rescue and recovery operations in Laos and North Vietnam.[20]

During this same period Aderholt sent pilots on temporary duty from the detachment to assist the Cuban task force forming in Guatemala for the assault on the Bay of Pigs. The CIA rushed Aderholt back at one point to accompany senior agency officials to Managua to negotiate with Nicaragua's dictator, Anastasio Somoza, for departure bases. Earlier, while stationed in Washington, he had been involved in identifying the Alabama Air National Guard to train Cuban aircrews for the invasion. There was no intent to use the guard pilots in combat. A proposal Aderholt assisted in developing, which called for more bombers and sustained airstrikes against Cuban airfields and other military targets, was scrubbed in Washington. The disastrous defeat at the Bay of Pigs caused the administration to cancel B-26 strike missions (Operation Mill Pond) that Aderholt and the CIA had planned against the Pathet Lao on the Plaine des Jarres in Laos.[21]

Meanwhile the Air Force had halfheartedly begun to carry out the president's order to develop counterinsurgency capabilities. While the Army augmented its special forces capabilities at Fort Bragg, North Carolina, the Air Force activated a squadron at Eglin AFB, Florida, as part of Operation Jungle Jim to train special air warfare forces. Both services deployed special forces to Vietnam in late 1961—the Army sending the Green Berets and the Air Force its Farm Gate detachment of AT-28s, B-26s, and C-47s. They ostensibly were there to train the South Vietnamese in COIN warfare but inevitably were drawn into combat against the Viet Cong. [22]

One of the Farm Gate detachment commanders, Colonel Robert L. Gleason, recalled a lengthy visit he had with Aderholt in 1962 at Takhli. Gleason said that during their extensive discussions on counterinsurgency concepts, Aderholt "was extremely critical" of special operations in South Vietnam because they "emphasized the more glamorous role of combat operations." "Heinie held that the U.S. counterinsurgency effort should be almost entirely that of supplying local forces with food and other supplies necessary to resist and continue to exist," Gleason said. Although Gleason "defended the primacy of the combat role," he said they were in full agreement that the host country had primary responsibility for counterinsurgency operations and that the U.S. effort "should be ancillary and supportive in nature." "There was no place for B-52s, battleships, and large-scale U.S. conventional forces in this type of operation," he added. "I often ponder how the Vietnam conflict would have evolved had that philosophy prevailed."[23]

A few months later, in August 1962, Lieutenant Colonel Aderholt reported to the new U.S. Air Force Special Air Warfare Center at Eglin as assistant director of operations. He was promoted to colonel in January 1964 and assumed command of the famed 1st Air CommandoWing at nearby Hurlburt Field in February. Although he was not a fighter pilot, the new commander had an aggressive, gung ho style of leadership, proved expertise, and a passion for special operations, all of which captured the imagination and respect of the younger air commandos. Never would he forget the magnificent élan of these men. Many years later he recalled his first muster of the pilots and crews, not knowing what to expect when he told them "to get rid of their golf clubs" because he was there to prepare them "to go to war." "I was told there were a bunch of fighter jocks here who were looking for a place to die," he said, "and I know that place and I am here to lead you to it." The response was deafening, as the men threw their caps into the air and roared their approval. "It was love at first sight for me," Aderholt recalled, "and we went on to do many good things."[24]

One of those "good things" was to deploy a covert detachment of air commandos from the wing to Udorn, Thailand, for the purpose of training Lao, Thai, and Hmong pilots to fly AT-28s in combat. Deployed in March 1964 under the code name "Water Pump," the detachment remained and eventually was integrated into the force buildup in Thailand. Back at Hurlburt an incoming colonel who outranked Aderholt replaced him as wing commander. This occurred in the summer of 1964, and Aderholt stayed on as vice commander until the following summer, when he departed for an assignment at Clark AB, in the Philippines. En route, he stopped for an orientation in Hawaii, where he met with General Hunter Harris, the commander in chief, Pacific Air Forces (CINCPACAF). Harris later assured him that he would be given command of a combat wing at the first opportunity.[25]

The American role in the Vietnam War had changed with the assassination of President Kennedy in November 1963. The axiom that "a great country can have no such thing as a little war," attributed to the Duke of Wellington in 1815, was coming true in Southeast Asia.[26] From the Philippines, Aderholt observed firsthand the massive buildup of American air power following the Gulf of Tonkin incident in August 1964, the Flaming Dart retaliatory strikes against North Vietnam a few months later, and the start of the Rolling Thunder bombing campaign soon thereafter. Even at this juncture it was obvious that escalation and Americanization of the war were calculated to wrest the initiative from the enemy by changing the nature of the conflict, from counterinsurgency to limited war. As Aderholt later reflected, how different the outcome might have been had the war for the hearts and minds of the people—a canon of counterinsurgency warfare—not been sacrificed to the gods of massive military intervention.[27]

Aderholt's first brush with General Momyer occurred while he was in Saigon on special assignment from the Philippines. While working with the Army's battle-hardened General John Singlaub and MACV's top secret Studies and Observations Group (SOG), Aderholt conceived and activated the Joint

Personnel Recovery Center (JPRC) and served as the chief from July to December 1966. The JPRC was a joint service activity that was responsible for collecting and disseminating information on missing or captured U.S. personnel, and for recommending and coordinating operations to liberate them, when feasible. Aderholt's criticism of Seventh Air Force operations—when the JPRC could not get dedicated airlift, and a rescue attempt went tragically wrong because the centralized airlift system did not get raiding parties to a rendezvous point on schedule—did not sit well with Momyer. To make matters worse, Aderholt complained that he had requested propeller-driven A-ls for close air support of the operation, but Seventh Air Force had instead sent F-100 jet aircraft, which could not get below the overcast to deliver their ordnance. He recalled that Momyer was indignant, telling him in no uncertain terms, "You lay on the requirement, and we will tell you what you need."[28]

In December, General Harris kept his promise and gave Aderholt command of the 56th Air Commando Wing, which was organized following his arrival at Nakhon Phanom, an austere hinterland base near Thailand's border with Laos. He apparently took the assignment against Momyer's wishes, since the general called him in and tried to dissuade him from going.[29] The inspiring leadership and the wing's unrivaled combat record under Aderholt's command are well documented in official histories and studies. Ambassador Sullivan called Aderholt "a splendid leader of men" and "one of the most imaginative and resourceful Air Force officers" he had ever known. The ambassador also said that Aderholt's wing "had the finest morale of any Air Force unit" he had visited.[30] This assertion was backed up by others, including Lieutenant General Benjamin O. Davis Jr., the famed Tuskegee airman who served as Thirteenth Air Force commander in the Philippines during this period.[31]

From the outset, however, Momyer showed his dislike for Aderholt by excluding him from Seventh Air Force conferences routinely attended by other wing commanders from Thailand and Vietnam. While Aderholt's wing had a dynamic civic action program, its combat operations in Laos were what really concerned the Seventh Air Force commander. Odd command arrangements for the Air Force's Thailand-based units placed them under the administrative control of Thirteenth Air Force, with Seventh Air Force exercising operational control. Flying propeller-driven T-28s and A-26s, the wing supported Vang Pao's irregulars and bore the brunt of night interdiction against the Ho Chi Minh Trail in Laos and North Vietnam. The wing's night attacks against the trail were so successful, they provoked a "propeller versus jet" debate that resounded throughout the halls of the Pentagon and Seventh Air Force headquarters. The debate and the flaunting of the wing's success enraged General

Momyer, resulting in the transfer of operational control to a special Steel Tiger task force at Nakhon Phanom in advance of Aderholt's scheduled departure.[32]

For Aderholt there was no debate. He knew that once you took politics—the divisive roles and missions polemic with the Army over air-ground capabilities and budget battles for future force requirements—off the table, there remained the simple fact that jet and prop aircraft had distinctive characteristics making them both useful in combat. As for survivability over the Ho Chi Minh Trail, the boundaries between permissive and nonpermissive target environments kept shifting in the protracted war, as did tactics, but there were always countermeasures available, just as there had been in the high-threat areas of North Vietnam. The air commandos traditionally had used whatever capabilities were available to get the job done, and when the needed capabilities were not there, they improvised.

"My God, we are in trouble if we think that jet technology and high-performance fighters have made less advanced capabilities obsolete," Aderholt exclaimed. "That's the kind of arrogance that not only led us to believe the atomic bomb had made us safe from lesser wars, but got us so deeply into the Vietnam War in the first place."[33] In a 1986 interview General David C. Jones—former Air Force chief of staff (CSAF) and chairman, Joint Chiefs of Staff (JCS)—said the question was "How in the world did we get ourselves involved in a land war in Southeast Asia where we tried to fight the war rather than let the Vietnamese fight the war and we support them?"[34]Aderholt believed that U.S. military involvement could and should have been limited to a COIN advisory effort, an option that was more palatable if and when a host government did not prevail. "That nonsensical business of graduated response, for instance, came right out of 1950s nuclear doctrine," he said, "and obviously made no sense whatsoever in a jungle war like the one in Southeast Asia."[35]

"Air power could not win or lose the war, given its political and strategic context," he continued, "so laying our first-line forces on the line the way we did was unforgivable." He realized that it was not the Air Force's decision to make, but he also knew Air Force leaders had the responsibility to explain air power, its capabilities, and its limitations to the decision makers—to help shape their understanding and their policies for the use of military force. This responsibility, of course, extended to the other service leaders and to the joint application of air, ground, and sea power. "The Vietnam War reaffirmed that, while we must have sound air power doctrine," Aderholt said, "we don't need dogma to suppress the very flexibility our doctrine provides."[36]

In January 1968 Colonel Aderholt returned to the Special Air Warfare Center (SAWC)—redesignated the USAF Special Operations Force (SOF) in July 1968—as deputy chief of staff for operations. The SOF commander, Brigadier General Robert L. Cardenas, recalled they were doing "many wonderful things" in special operations, until "one dark day General Momyer was assigned as commander of Tactical Air Command (TAC)." Momyer made an orientation visit to subordinate organizations at Eglin not long after his return from Vietnam in August 1968. Cardenas said that "Heinie gave Momyer an outstanding briefing wherein he held nothing back." Afterward the general "asked questions that indicated his lack of understanding [of special operations] while he had been in command in Vietnam" and, when he was alone with Cardenas, expressed displeasure that Aderholt was there. Momyer warned Cardenas, "He is going to get you and SOF in trouble." When Cardenas defended Aderholt, Momyer said, "Okay, keep him, but if he screws up you are both gone."[37]

While he was TAC commander, Momyer showed his disdain for the "nickel and dime forces" used to fight "so-called wars of national liberation." He said it was doubtful that "wars of liberation" had "much credibility for the future, if they ever did, with what has transpired in Southeast Asia." He stated that the countries involved should be the ones "to fight the wars of liberation," whereas the U.S. role should be limited to "airlift of people, medicine, community development, and this sort of thing where the elements of open shooting have not developed." "Where there is shooting," he said, "I don't believe the USAF should be involved with 'so-called' low performance aircraft delivering firepower." In a statement reminiscent of force modernization trends during the 1950s, Momyer concluded: "If decision is made to enter the conflict, we go in with our tactical forces, which are structured to fight regardless of the level of firepower. If we aren't prepared to go in under these circumstances, I believe we should stay out altogether with full appreciation the country may be lost. It seems to me our strategy can't straddle this fence."[38]

Aderholt continued to fight for the development of special air warfare capabilities, and when Cardenas left Eglin in July 1969, after only a year as commander, Momyer replaced him with a brigadier general from TAC headquarters who pressured Aderholt to retire. Word was out that General Momyer suspected him of being a CIA agent who had infiltrated the Air Force. When he learned of this, Aderholt exploded, "What kind of paranoia is that? The bastards actually thought I was a CIA spy." In June 1970, wearying of the constant harassment, he returned to Thailand for a two-year tour as chief of the Air Force Advisory Group in Bangkok, then came back to Eglin and retired from active duty in December 1972.[39]

Vindication

The two years in Bangkok were enjoyable ones for Colonel Aderholt and his wife, Jessie. The colonel had established good rapport with the Thai military and government leaders during his earlier tours, and he and Jessie were greeted with friendliness and warmth. What made a choice assignment a truly great one was that it was the first time in a long while that Jessie was able to accompany him on an overseas tour. They had met and married in 1946 while he was stationed at Maxwell AFB, Alabama, after World War II. During the 1950s she had accompanied him to Germany, where they had adopted their two children, George and Janet; and in later years the family had gone with him to Okinawa and to the Philippines but rarely saw him because he was away for long periods doing what air commandos do. The Bangkok assignment let them be together more often, while giving Colonel Aderholt ample opportunity to work with the U.S. and Thai military commanders, and to keep his hand in the war. When the Aderholts left Bangkok in 1972, they had no expectations of ever returning.

Aderholt and some of the other "old-timers" had organized the Air Commando Association during his previous tour at Eglin. He remained actively involved as founder and later president when he came back in 1972. During the short time at Eglin before he retired, the Air Force assigned him to an air rescue group rather than to special operations. The SOF commander sent word through an intermediary that he was not welcome at SOF headquarters or subordinate activities such as the special operations school.[40] His detractors appeared determined to make the colonel's fall from grace an object lesson within the institution he had done so much to help build. At this point no one in Tactical Air Command would have taken odds on Heinie Aderholt being in the Air Force beyond General Momyer's tenure as TAC commander, much less bet on him advancing beyond the rank of colonel.

That seemed to be the safe call when General Momyer stayed on active duty nearly a year after Aderholt's retirement in December 1972. A TAC commander as powerful as Momyer was not someone you wanted for an enemy at any time, but especially not when tactical aviation—after years of neglect and subordination to SAC—had risen to a position of predominance within the Air Force. The general's contributions and influence would be felt in TAC and in the halls of the Pentagon long after he retired from active duty in September 1973—at a time when so-called Vietnamization of the war was taking hold and there was still faint hope that America's great sacrifice in blood, honor, and treasure would not have been in vain.

At the same time, however, the troubling onrush of events near the end of U.S. intervention in Southeast Asia vindicated Heinie Aderholt and men like him who had understood the war better than many of their compatriots. In October 1973, the month after Momyer retired, the Department of Defense (DOD) recalled Heinie Aderholt to active duty and returned him to Bangkok as deputy commander of the American Military Assistance Command in Thailand (MACTHAI). The secretary of defense promoted him to brigadier general in May 1974. Later made the commander of MACTHAI and the Joint U.S. Military Advisory Group (JUSMAG), Thailand, he was deeply involved in closing out the U.S. presence in the war, which included planning and coordinating with the Thai high command on Thai-based air support for the besieged Khmer Republic and rescuing indigenous patriots, such as General Vang Pao and the Hmong, whose lives were imperiled because they had been partners with the United States.[41]

In the summer of 1976, just over a year after Saigon fell to the North Vietnamese, Brigadier General Aderholt came home. He was the last American general officer to leave Southeast Asia when the war was over. His ties to the region have remained strong in the years since. He has retained business interests in Thailand, he has been a compassionate adviser to the Hmong community now resettled in the United States, and he has tirelessly helped look into legitimate leads about POWs left behind. He and the Air Commando Association have been active in helping World Medical Relief and other charities alleviate suffering around the world. Here at home he is still a dynamo in business and community affairs, a friend to any veteran down on his luck, and a passionate spokesman for the Air Force and its air commandos—two institutions he has served faithfully and truly loves.[42]

If you are ever in Fort Walton Beach, drive down Miracle Strip Parkway and check out Far East Interiors, sitting across from the chamber of commerce. The store's owner, who manages a variety of enterprises from his office there, is none other than retired Brigadier General Heinie Aderholt. Having celebrated his eightieth birthday on January 6, 2000, he has aged like the fighter he has always been. He is white-haired and weathered but is still 160 pounds of restless energy wound up in a tough, athletic frame (five feet, six inches), ready to spring into action. This ramrod Air Force maverick who persisted in doing things his way is the first inductee into the Air Commando Hall of Fame. The ensuing narrative—beginning with his wartime exploits over the "Frozen Chosen"—tells why.

1. THE CALL TO ARMS

When the Korean War broke out in late June 1950, Captain Aderholt was in the Canadian backwoods vacationing with his wife and mother-in-law. They had driven leisurely up from Alabama to Ontario's scenic Algonquin Park to enjoy the great outdoors and fish the freshwater lakes for perch and trout. Upon returning to their cabin at dusk one evening, he turned on a shortwave radio and heard the news that the North Korean Communists had invaded South Korea. General Douglas MacArthur's Far East Command headquarters in Tokyo had deployed a holding force to engage the aggressors, while politicians at home negotiated a combined military response under the flag of the United Nations. The captain told his family to pack their bags. "I've got to report back to Maxwell Field," he said. "And we'd better step on it, or the war will be over before I can get there."[1]

The rush home in the Aderholt's 1949 Ford contrasted sharply with the relaxed twelve-hundred-mile drive the family had made a few days earlier. They stopped only for brief rest periods, once in Tennessee to purchase and eat a watermelon alongside the road, and arrived back at Maxwell Field the following night. After a few hours' sleep and an early-morning run, the refreshed captain reported for duty and volunteered for an immediate combat assignment flying P-51 fighters. Like most Americans, he believed the war would end quickly when the mighty armed forces of the United States stormed ashore on the Korean peninsula.[2] Few people realized the extent of the postwar drawdown in U.S. military might, or foresaw the ramifications of a limited war being fought under the auspices of the United Nations. It was to be a wake-up call for the nation and for its unprepared fighting men who slogged through that first year of bitter combat on the Korean peninsula.

A few days after Captain Aderholt's return to duty, a personnel officer called to inform him that a combat tour in fighters was out of the question because of an overage in fighter-qualified volunteers and to alert him that a quota for transport aircrews was on its way. Near the end of July, he received orders to form a crew (comprising a copilot, a navigator, a flight engineer, and a radio operator) and to pilot a C-47 Skytrain (the indomitable "Gooney Bird") to the West Coast, where the plane would be modified with eight one-hundred-gallon internal tanks before departing on a transoceanic flight to the Far East. Disappointed at having missed another opportunity to fly fighters, Aderholt consoled himself with the reality that he had "to play with the hand that was dealt him." He looked forward to the challenge of combat in Korea, but was nostalgic about leaving. Over the coming months, his thoughts would return often to the years at Maxwell Field and their influence in his life.[3]

Interlude at Maxwell Field

The nearly five years that he was stationed at Maxwell Field were formative ones for the young captain. Upon coming home from Italy in the summer of 1945, he was uncertain about pursuing a military career but was in no hurry to return to civilian life. When Captain Edward "Eddie" Rickenbacker, the famous World War I ace, approached returning "military pilots with Gooney Bird time" about going to work for his Eastern Airlines, Aderholt turned him down. With the war over in Europe, he longed to get into the fray in the Pacific before it ended. So he volunteered for any combat assignment flying the B-29 Superfortress. "I knew damned well I couldn't get a fighter job this late in the war," he said, "but I figured they would lose enough B-29s that I might get in those." In August he was in B-17 instructor training at Lockbourne Field, outside Columbus, Ohio, awaiting a B-29 assignment, when the war's two most historic Superfortresses, the *Enola Gay* and *Bock's Car,* dropped atomic bombs on Hiroshima and Nagasaki, and the Japanese surrendered.[4]

Upon completing B-17 instructor training in September, Captain Aderholt transferred to Maxwell Field as a staff pilot with the Army Air Forces Eastern Flying Training Command. The assignment to Maxwell, which was only one hundred miles from his hometown of Birmingham, soon convinced the Alabama native that he had "found a home" in military aviation. "The pay was good and I loved to fly," Aderholt recalled in later years. "When I got to

Maxwell, there were more than one hundred airplanes (a B-17, B-25s, B-26s, C-45s, a couple of C-47s, a C-46, a couple of T-6s) on the ramp. I flew them all. Often on local flights I flew the B-17 alone. It was great. I loved it." Now that he knew he wanted to stay in the Air Force, however, he was faced with the problem of postwar retrenchment having drastically reduced career opportunities in all branches of the armed forces.[5]

In the young captain's favor, he was well liked and admired at Maxwell and had won the backing of senior officers there. In addition to serving as the assistant base operations officer and running the instrument school, he comanaged Maxwell's world-champion baseball team. Sports had been his first love and he had briefly been player-manager of a semipro baseball team before joining the Army Air Forces in 1942. All of his fellow officers knew him as Heinie, the nickname he had answered to since his glory days of football and baseball at Woodlawn High. Near the end of the 1946 baseball season, the base commander (Colonel William E. Covington) called and told him that Maxwell was facing drastic manpower cuts and would lose a lot of pilots. The colonel advised him that he had "to get a real important job," if he wanted to stay in the Air Force. "Have you ever handled black people?" Covington asked. "Hell, I grew up with them," Aderholt replied. The colonel then explained that he was having "all kinds of problems" with the black squadron on base. Assuring the colonel that he could resolve those problems, Aderholt became the new squadron commander in September 1946, the same month that the Air University was established at Maxwell Field.[6]

Meanwhile, Aderholt's military career got a boost from another direction. Explaining how this came about, Aderholt recalled that he "was a pretty good drinker" in those days. He and other junior officers used to "hang out" with a line officer who was greatly admired at Maxwell. That officer was Colonel John M. Price, who was known to the men as "Big Jack" and described by Aderholt as "an All-American, a West Pointer [class of 1932], and a legend." When they were holding forth at the officers' club bar one evening, Big Jack suggested that he should think about applying for a Regular commission. "I have no college education," Aderholt replied. "I haven't a chance." Big Jack grinned and said, "I'm going to be on the board. You've got a good chance."[7]

Soon after submitting his application to the board, presided over by Colonel Price at nearby Fort Benning, Georgia, Aderholt married Jessie Reid of Montgomery in December 1946, adding a new sense of purpose and direction to his career plans. The popular newlyweds were overjoyed the following October when he was awarded his appointment in the Regular Army. The news was timely because the appointment coincided with the transfer of the Army's aviation resources to the newly established United States Air Force, created in September by the National Security Act of 1947. From this point in time, there was never any doubt about Aderholt's resolve to be a career Air Force officer. Two of his brothers also became career military men: Warren, an Air Force fighter pilot who also flew and fought in three wars, and Robert, who was a chief petty officer in the Navy.[8]

Warren had gone through flying training a year after his older brother and joined a fighter group in Italy while he was there. "My younger brother comes over as a hot-shot fighter pilot, and there I was driving B-17s and air transports around in noncombat roles," Aderholt said, laughing. He recalled that on Warren's twenty-third combat mission, his P-51 experienced a vapor lock over the Po Valley and he had landed on a German airfield rather than bailing out and exposing himself to enemy fire. Intentionally overshooting and sliding his crippled fighter down to the end of the runway, Warren jumped from the plane and escaped into tall grass surrounding the airfield. Italian partisans reached him before the Nazis did, and he made his way back to the American lines. He returned to a sector that was controlled by the famed Japanese-American unit, the 442d Regimental Combat Team. When a sentry asked where he had come from, Warren pointed to an open area behind them. The sentry exclaimed, "Goda'mighty, Lieutenant, you just walked through our minefield!"

The brothers spent a few days in Naples together before Warren returned to his group. A "canned" message that Aderholt sent to his mother informing her that Warren was alive and well arrived two days before she received official notification that her son was missing in action. "The war ended, he went back to his unit, and I caught a boat home," Aderholt recalled, proud of the way his brother stood up to the rigors of combat. There was a tinge of envy in his voice when he said, "I had served twenty-one months over there . . . mostly flying and not getting shot at a hell of a lot. That was my only regret . . . that I didn't go over there and shoot somebody or drop bombs on them."

Aderholt's "tough, but caring and fair" brand of military leadership—tempered by the challenges and the camaraderie of war—had a telling effect on Squadron F at Maxwell. The inroads that the segregated black squadron made under his command remained a source of great pride and satisfaction throughout his life. He often said that he had "really learned more there about leadership and about people" than at any other time in his career. The squadron consisted of himself, an adjutant, and five hundred black troops who were completely demoralized by the government's failure to redress their plight as second-class citizens in the aftermath of World War II. Not only denied equal opportunity and treatment, black troops throughout the armed forces lived in segregated conditions both on and off base and were assigned to perform only menial tasks. Aderholt recalled that Squadron F's men were used "as nothing but service troops," worked in the motor pool as "drivers" and "tire changers," and "did all the janitorial work" for the Air University after it started classes at Maxwell. He said his superior officers just wanted him to keep the black troops satisified, to keep them on their side of the base, and to keep them from causing trouble. But the troops wanted more, and Aderholt wanted more for and from them.[9]

Determined to make a difference as the squadron commander, Aderholt set about trying to improve his troops' military performance and their quality of life on the segregated base. He had not anticipated that his greatest obstacle would be the squadron's black first sergeant, who stood between him and the troops and resisted efforts aimed at improving the situation. "The first shirt had been there forever but made a bad mistake when he told me that commanders come and commanders go, but he stayed put," Aderholt said. "He implied that he was there when I came and he would be there when I was gone." After looking into the situation, Aderholt learned that the first sergeant (who had nearly thirty years' service) was using his position for personal gain. Among other schemes, he was in charge of slot machines in the club and split the profits with owners downtown. Aderholt confronted him. "Sergeant, I'm asking you to volunteer for reassignment, and if you don't, I'm going to court-martial you," Aderholt said. "He went. I stayed."

"I replaced him with a Tuskegee graduate named Earl Garrett, a fantastic first soldier," Aderholt continued. Garrett said, "Captain, you tell me what you want and we will get it done." Aderholt said the first priority was "to establish control" of the squadron, to get "discipline straightened out," to instill military pride in the men, and to motivate and move them in the right direction. As squadron commander, he had the authority to appoint duty NCOs and give them spot promotions. He asked Garrett to pick out six or eight men to be appointed as duty NCOs. "I want you to get the best soldiers in the outfit, the best dressed, the best disciplined," he said, "and I want you to issue them a nightstick and give them three stripes. Explain the rules and the dress regulations, and I want you to start implementing them."

That the root problems of segregation between black and white America precluded a full measure of reconciliation at military installations was true throughout the postwar armed forces, however. Mutinous riots by some black servicemen—the largest occurring at MacDill AFB near Tampa, Florida, the month after Aderholt became squadron commander at Maxwell—created fears that racial unrest might spread to military installations nationwide. The base

Captain Aderholt at his desk in 1946 while commanding Squadron F at Maxwell AFB, Ala. Aderholt described the black squadron as the first and one of the best USAF units he ever commanded.

commander raised the subject at his weekly staff meeting, and Aderholt assured him there was no problem with his squadron. Late that evening First Sergeant Garrett called and said, "Captain, you'd better come down here. We've got a riot."[10]

Aderholt and his adjutant Lieutenant Harold Poole drove to the orderly room, where Sergeant Garrett and the duty NCOs were waiting. Retrieving a Colt .45 from his office safe, he turned on the floodlights in the squadron area, then strode to a line of unlit barracks with First Sergeant Garrett at his side. Their demeanor suggested a great deal of mutual trust and respect between the young white captain and the older black first sergeant, whose impeccable military record showed in his bearing and in the firm set of his jaw. Stopping at the entrance to the first barracks, the captain barked, "We're coming in, and if any son of a bitch has his head above the covers, I'm going to shoot him right between the eyes." He later admitted he was not that good a shot, but it seemed like the right thing to say at the time. The way he recalled the event, "We kicked open the door . . . it was summertime . . . and I flipped the light switch. There were sixty-four sheets up over sixty-four heads. We went right on through—it was the same in each barracks." The night was eerily quiet as they completed the walk-through and departed the squadron area.[11]

At muster the following morning, the commander reassured the troops that no official action would be taken against them, individually or collectively, for any unruliness the evening before. He promised to deal quickly and severely with any future refractions, however. When he told the men that if any of them wanted out of the service, they should just tell him and he would have them out "in a very short time," Aderholt said there were "no takers." Then vowing to do all within his power to address their grievances, he said, "I want to know what the hell your problems are. You can speak off the record. Nobody is going to do anything against you."[12]

Over the ensuing months the commander worked against the grain to improve the living and working conditions of his troops. He gained the confidence of the base commander and the troops for his efforts, but deep down he knew the real solutions were "above his pay grade." Some of the white officers at Maxwell were supportive of his actions; others were not. He received helpful insights from Colonel Noel Parrish, who had been a wartime commander at Tuskegee and was one of the few senior white officers advocating integration of the armed forces. In a thesis submitted to the Air Command and Staff College in May 1947, Parrish recognized that segregation not only was morally indefensible, but "was the prime cause of low morale among blacks."[13]

Help finally came from above in the spring and summer of 1948. The Air Force was concerned "about the impact of segregation upon its own effectiveness" and announced a decision to integrate during the spring. This was followed in July by President Truman's Executive Order 9981 to foster equal opportunity in the armed services. Well before then Aderholt had begun to instill pride in the squadron by insisting on their inclusion in base activities. "We started molding that place over," he recalled proudly. "We won every damned parade. Every time we had a review, Squadron F won it hands down."[14]

He fought to include black athletes in Maxwell's sports programs while commanding the squadron. When he took charge, the black troops were not allowed to play on white baseball teams, so he organized and managed a team that played against other black teams. He was the only white person at these games. The squadron faced similar discriminatory practices when basketball season came around, but Aderholt overcame opposition from white players to schedule his team against others at Maxwell and nearby Gunter Air Station. He met with the base commander and said, "I'm going to have a basketball team, and I want us to play in the league." The other teams threatened to withdraw from league play, but he called their bluff, telling the airmen in charge to schedule the squadron against the best team on base. "We went up there, and we just kicked the living hell out of them," he said. "We never lost a game, and we played all year."[15]

He recalled with a thin smile "the unenviable task of integrating the Maxwell USO Club there in the heart of the Confederacy." The top men in the squadron were singled out and groomed for the task. They were bused to the USO on Saturday evening with orders not "to get drunk," but to be on their best behavior. "When the black airmen went in, all the Montgomery belles went out," Aderholt recalled. They eventually trickled back when the shock wore off and when the squadron continued to send its airmen to the USO weekend after weekend. Pride in this "grassroots" involvement toward racial equality sparkled whenever he discussed the early days of integrating the Air Force. Laughing, he told about using the experience, years later, to punctuate his remarks on the Air Force's rejection of counterinsurgency warfare in Vietnam. "You think it is hard to get the United States Air Force to accept its role in counterinsurgency, low-intensity warfare," he said at an Air University dining-in in the late 1960s. "You ought to try to integrate the blacks into Montgomery society at the USO club on the base here. Hell, it is nothing compared to that."[16]

The distinguished black leader of the Tuskegee Airmen, Colonel Benjamin O. Davis, reported to the Air War College as a student in 1949. The assignment of a black student to the Air War College—unthinkable when the Air University was established at Maxwell three years earlier—was a first step toward breaking down the color barrier to professional military education within the Air Force. Davis had endured exceptional racial prejudice as the U.S. Military Academy's first black graduate of the twentieth century, but rose above bigotry and discriminatory treatment to become the Air Force's first black three-star general. He was proud that the Air Force took the lead in integration in 1948 and reassigned the men formerly "grouped on predominantly white bases in all-black 'F squadrons' . . . worldwide into white units." He spoke less favorably of the year spent as a War College student at Maxwell, however, observing that the base "was guilty of some of the worst foot-dragging" on integration. The only black officer on Maxwell at the time, Colonel Davis said he and his wife "had no social life of any kind off base, and Montgomery was like a foreign country."[17]

Aderholt remembered Davis being at the Air War College as a colonel and described him as "a real gentleman." He later served under Davis, who assumed command of Thirteenth Air Force in the Philippines while Aderholt led the Air Commando Wing at Nakhon Phanom in 1967. General William W. Momyer, the Saigon-based Seventh Air Force commander whose heavy-handed leadership style made life miserable for Aderholt and the air commandos at Nakhon Phanom, also studied at the Air War College in 1949, staying on as a faculty member after graduation. Ironically, while commanding the 33d Fighter Group in North Africa during World War II, Momyer filed a report rebuking the performance of the group's 99th Fighter Squadron—the famed Tuskegee Airmen led by Benjamin Davis. Momyer recommended the squadron's removal from combat. Davis successfully refuted the allegations, and after receiving the new P-51 long-range fighters, the black airmen went on to compile one of the most impressive combat records of the war. No bomber formation escorted by the black pilots ever lost a plane to enemy fighters.[18]

As a company grade officer who was not part of the Air University faculty, Aderholt did not interact socially or professionally with either Colonel Davis or Colonel Momyer while they were at Maxwell. He had no way of knowing the contrasting roles that both men would play in his life nearly two decades later in the Vietnam War. Meanwhile, his forceful and fair-minded leadership while commanding the black squadron at Maxwell caught the attention of his superiors. His efficiency report for the period highlighted his special qualities "as a commander of men," describing him as "a morale builder, firm in his convictions, and respected by officers and men alike."[19]

In his final days at Maxwell, he did a favor for a senior officer who would become an important influence on his career. Aderholt and the newly formed crew were getting ready to leave for California when Colonel Cecil H. Childre, a chief instructor at Air Command and Staff College, came to them and said he was told they were on their way to Korea and had a layover in San Bernardino. "Captain, I'd like for you to take my dog to San Bernardino," the colonel said, explaining that he would be following them to Korea in a few weeks and that his wife was staying in California while he was gone. Aderholt described Childre as "one helluva good guy," whom he had known slightly at the officers' club and elsewhere on base. He did not think twice about taking the family's pet dog to San Bernardino, an act that unwittingly stood him in good stead with the man who would be his new boss in Korea.[20]

To Korea with the Kyushu Gypsies

The runway was steaming when Captain Aderholt and his crew lifted off from Maxwell Field in late July. Their flight suits were drenched but would dry as they climbed to cruising altitude and leveled off. Jessie and the other wives were at the flight line to bid them Godspeed. Viewed from the cockpit and the windows of the C-47, the waving arms of the well-wishers faded rapidly into the vaporous landscape below. A popular country-and-western tune—"I'm Moving On," by Canadian recording star Hank Snow, destined to be a Korean War classic—crackled through the static on the plane's radio. Aderholt smiled. They were on their way.

The ground patterns below were as familiar as his reflection in the windshield. He had flown religiously while at Maxwell. After completing his tour as Squadron F commander in August 1948, he had gone on temporary duty to Tyndall AFB, Florida, as a student at the Air Tactical School—the only formal classes of his career other than pilot training. Returning to Maxwell in December, he was assigned to base operations managing a variety of activities, including flying training, the instrument training school, the checkout program, and flying safety. He was current in at least six airplanes at Maxwell and often flew alone. He said that flying the large multiengine planes with no one else on board "got lonesome," but he loved it. "I was having a helluva good time," he recalled.[21]

Making two refueling stops in Texas (Fort Worth and El Paso), the C-47 touched down at San Bernardino late the same day. Colonel Childre's wife met them at base operations to take the canine passenger off their hands. Captain Aderholt and the crew "twiddled their thumbs" for nearly a week at San Bernardino, waiting for their plane to undergo engine maintenance and have eight one-hundred-gallon fuel tanks installed in the fuselage. Then on a balmy southern California morning, the captain and his crew departed for Hawaii, the first and longest leg on their flight across the Pacific. They were carrying sixteen hundred gallons of fuel, enough to last them twenty-three or twenty-four hours in the air, more than sufficient for the Hawaii leg, which took about nineteen to twenty hours.[22] It was a long, wearing journey, wrapped in a Plexiglas cocoon of flight instruments, sky, and ocean.

Just past midnight, a light appearing in the darkness ahead broke the monotony. Only Aderholt was awake, flying the plane on automatic pilot. Seeing the light grow larger, he rubbed his eyes and nudged the sleeping copilot. "Is that light another plane, or what?" he asked. "Jesus Christ, I think that's an airplane," the half-awake copilot responded. They were surprised to be overtaking another plane, since the Gooney Bird was on cruise control with a zero wind factor and was "going along at about 110 or 115 miles per hour." They crept up on the other craft, flying at the same altitude, and slowly flew past what they recognized as a Martin PB2M Mars, a mammoth four-engine seaplane the Navy had acquired for transporting cargo in World War II. Cruising at about 105 miles per hour, the lumbering behemoth was on a milk run between Alameda and Honolulu.[23]

Arriving at daybreak, Aderholt and his crew stayed at Hickam AFB overnight and departed for Johnson Island the following morning. From Johnston they flew to Kwajalein, to Guam, and on to Tachikawa Air Base, on the outskirts of Tokyo. "Everywhere we went we spent the night," Aderholt said. "It didn't seem like anybody was in a big hurry." The aura of Mount Fuji—a great oriental shrine breaking through the clouds—rose to greet them as they turned for the descent into Tachikawa. Reporting to the 374th Troop Carrier Wing, they were put on crew rest awaiting further orders. Nearly a week had gone by since they left California, and they "sat and waited" another week at Tachikawa.[24]

Just after the Korean War erupted, Far East Air Forces (FEAF) beefed up the 374th Wing's two squadrons of C-54 transports at Tachikawa by stationing a squadron equipped with C-47s at Ashiya Air Base in southern Japan. The rugged Gooney Bird was ideal for airlift operations supporting the hard-pressed U.S. and South Korean defenders because the small, unimproved airstrips on the war-torn peninsula would not accommodate heavier planes. The squadron initially flew some C-46s into Korea but discontinued using them because the runways could not support their landing weight. The initial buildup of C-47s at Ashiya was accomplished with planes borrowed from other FEAF bases—a temporary measure until additional C-47s arrived from the United States. The planes were assigned to the 21st Troop Carrier Squadron, better known as the Kyushu Gypsies, a former C-54 unit that had moved sans aircraft from the Philippines to Ashiya in early July.[25]

Because Kyushu was the southernmost of the main islands, Ashiya and its neighboring installation, Itazuki, were two of the more strategically situated bases available to FEAF at this desperate stage of the ground war. When the North Korean onslaught drove defending forces back to the southern tip of the war-ravaged peninsula in July, General MacArthur ordered Eighth Army Commanding General Walton H. Walker to hold the Pusan perimeter at all costs. MacArthur did not want another Dunkirk on his hands, and preserving a foothold on the peninsula was vital to his plans for an amphibious assault on South Korea's waistline at Inchon. His daring maneuver to cut off the enemy's main line of advance and drive the aggressors back across the thirty-eighth parallel was contingent upon the arrival of essential reinforcements by September. Meanwhile, the C-47s flying out of Ashiya, sitting across the narrow strait from the Pusan perimeter, were a primary source of resupply and emergency evacuation for General Walker's besieged Eighth Army. Similarly, the 8th Fighter Bomber Group and other fighter units at nearby Itazuke assured Eighth Army of readily available tactical air support.[26]

Impatient to end the delay and join the airlift action into Korea, Captain Aderholt exploded in frustration when finally told why they were being held over at Tachikawa. The 374th Wing would not let him fly the C-47 to Ashiya because local procedures prohibited pilots from operating in Japanese airspace unless they were flight-checked and qualified by Fifth Air Force. "Boy, was I pissed," Aderholt said. "Here we were ready to go to war, and they made us sit on our hands at Tachikawa." There was no one else available to fly the C-47. The group had only C-54 pilots assigned at Tachikawa, so Aderholt and his crew had to wait for a "qualified" pilot to arrive. "It was Catch-22," he recalled. "They sent us a second lieutenant who had a total of about seven hundred hours in the air. He got us to Ashiya all right, but then taxied my perfectly good airplane that I'd nursed across the Pacific into a damned utility pole and tore the right wingtip off. That was my introduction to Far East Air Forces."[27]

The squadron singled out Aderholt to be operations officer, but he begged off with the explanation that he had come there "to fly." So he started "flying the line" into Korea, night and day. The airlift of cargo into Korea was a continuous operation. Base operations scheduled the flights. "The planes were all lined up in a single row," he explained. "They were ready to go, and you just took the first aircraft in line and flew to Korea. When you got to Korea and somebody wanted you to do something, they sent you around. When you decided you'd had enough, you came home. You put your airplane at the end of the line, and they checked it. It was pretty well organized." The aircrews, consisting of a copilot, flight engineer, and radio operator, were never the same people. "Since we had pretty good nondirectional beacons, we didn't really need a navigator," Aderholt noted. He recalled that he spent most of his time in Korea. "They always kept one or two planes in Korea," he said, "and we often stayed two or three days before returning to Ashiya. When we couldn't find a bunk, we slept in the planes."[28]

The squadron's name, the Kyushu Gypsies, was an appropriate one. "We were gypsies," he recalled. "It wasn't like being in a squadron. We never saw anybody. We just flew. We did a hell of a lot of flying. The guys who wanted to fly got to fly, and those who didn't push didn't have to do too much." The squadron airlifted thousands of tons of urgently needed arms, ammunition, rations, and supplies from Ashiya to Eighth Army units through early September, while transporting endless manifests of passengers, including the evacuation of wounded troops to hospitals in Japan. Aderholt started flying with the squadron in early August, and by the end of the month he had chalked up seventy-two sorties and nearly two hundred flying hours—a feat that put him in the top 10 percent of the 130 pilots assigned to the squadron at that time.[29]

Recounting these early missions, he said there was "such a confused front when we had the Pusan perimeter" that pilots never had a clear picture of the ground battle. When Army troops were being resupplied, they normally laid out panels and the pilots dropped on those panels. Many times the pilots had to land on airfields that were under attack, and these missions "could get hairy." Flying emergency resupplies into Pohang (K-3) when the field was under siege was one such mission. "We were flying ammunition in, and the artillery was all around the perimeter," Aderholt said. "I just taxied around and off-loaded it where the artillerymen were firing." They were "shooting it up" as fast as the pilots could bring it in. "We spent two days doing nothing but hauling ammo from Taegu (K-2) to Pohang," he said. He also recalled that the enemy was on "the hill above Taegu (K-2) and stayed there" until the North Korean forces withdrew from the Pusan perimeter. "We didn't know whether the field would still be ours when we came in some nights," he said, adding, "Some people don't know how close we came to getting our ass kicked off that peninsula."[30]

While Aderholt was away in early September, his squadron moved from Ashiya to nearby Brady Field. The mission did not change, but the squadron came under operational control of the newly formed FEAF Combat Cargo Command after relocating to Brady. The move was part of a larger realignment to centralize all theater air transport under Major General William H. Tunner (architect of "Over the Hump" airlift in World War II and the Berlin Airlift) initially as commander of FEAF Combat Cargo Command, later of the 315th Air Division. Colonel Cecil Childre arrived in the theater about the same time and became deputy commander of the 21st Squadron's parent unit, the 374th Wing at Tachikawa. In October, Childre moved to FEAF's forward headquarters in Seoul and established the air terminal units of the Combat Cargo Command. On the first of the month, Aderholt activated a special air missions detachment in Korea, operating briefly out of Taegu (K-2) and then from Kimpo (K-14) on the outskirts of Seoul. Upon relocating to Kimpo, the detachment worked for and got its instructions from Colonel Childre, a rugged, soft-spoken Texan who rose to three-star rank after the war and took a personal interest in Aderholt's career.[31]

The shake-up in combat airlift coincided with MacArthur's amphibious assault at Inchon in mid September where Marine landing forces "backed by devastating naval and air bombardment . . . readily defeated the weak, stunned North Korean defenders." The enemy's main invasion force had advanced south of the thirty-seventh parallel, well below Seoul, where it stalled because of Eighth Army's stubborn defense of the Pusan perimeter. The North Koreans' "long, exposed lines of communications" were overextended and under constant attack by air and naval fire. Their "logistical problems worsened daily." On the heels of the Marine landing, the Army's 7th Division came ashore and struck south toward Suwon, helping to facilitate Eighth Army's breakout at Pusan. By the twentieth, the Marines had taken Kimpo airfield and "were pounding at the gates of Seoul." Nine days later Seoul had been recaptured and the North Korean Army's withdrawal "had turned into a rout."[32]

During preparations for the Inchon landings, pilots from the 21st Squadron were brought to Tokyo for training in airborne operations. MacArthur's headquarters planned to drop the 187th Airborne Regimental Combat Team into Korea at the time of the Inchon landings. The 21st was designated as one of the squadrons to support the airborne assault. Having flown paratroopers in training at Fort Benning and in Sicily, Aderholt was one of the few pilots in the squadron who had airborne experience. All of the pilots needed to hone their skills in formation flying. After completing the training, they were told that the airborne assault had been put off because the 187th RCT would not arrive in Japan in time for the Inchon landings. Aderholt learned that he was going to establish the special missions detachment working for Colonel Childre in Korea when he returned to the squadron with the other pilots.[33]

"Our mission was a little bit of everything . . . strictly combat support and combat operations," he said, "and we supported nearly everybody . . . Fifth Air Force, Far East Command, Army G2, and anybody else that needed us." When the detachment moved from Taegu to Kimpo, Aderholt asked Colonel Childre what he wanted him to do. The colonel's matter-of-fact response: "Your job is to keep everybody in Korea off my back." The detachment never had more than a dozen pilots available to fly five or six planes, and they flew night and day. "We flew all kinds of missions, even taking the frag order around at night," Aderholt said. "It was terrible for the pilots. We just flew the pilots into the ground." When not flying, they lived in conditions that were "about as primitive as they could get." "We had about sixteen to eighteen officers crammed into a quonset hut," he said. "No toilet facilities. No bath facilities." Then he paused for a moment and reflected, "But we had it better than those poor bastards slugging it out on the ground."[34]

Participating in the long-delayed airdrop of the 187th RCT, which had shipped to Korea and was in GHQ Reserve around Kimpo, afforded a break in the routine. In October, after President Truman and the UN Security Council assented, General Walker's reinforced Eighth Army and other UNC forces launched an all-out drive across the thirty-eighth parallel (including an amphibious assault at Wonsan) to punish the retreating aggressors and to take North Korea. When Eighth Army troops captured Pyongyang on the nineteenth, MacArthur ordered the airdrop of the 187th the next day near the towns of Sukchon and Sunchon to entrap the North Koreans and keep them from fleeing across the Yalu River to Manchuria. Approximately fifty C-47s from the 21st Troop Carrier Squadron, and an equal number of C-119s of the 314th Troop Carrier Group, carried out the airdrop. Aderholt flew deputy lead to the 21st Squadron commander, Lieutenant Colonel Phil Cage. "It was just another day at the office," he said. "We had total air superiority and got no flak from the North Koreans."[35]

All hell was about to break loose "in the Land of the Morning Calm," but nobody believed it. General MacArthur reported that the airborne landing of the 187th had been a complete surprise and spelled the end for the North Koreans. From Tokyo he confidently predicted the war would be "coming to an end shortly." "The troops thought they'd be home for Christmas," Aderholt recalled. This optimism faded quickly, however, when U.S. and ROK forces clashed with Chinese troops below the Yalu River at the Changjin Reservoir and at Onjong in late October and early November. While UNC forces were engaged in defeating the North Korean Army, intelligence reports estimated that as many as 180,000 Chinese troops had crossed the border undetected. The Chinese abruptly broke off the encounter on 6 November, allowing UNC forces to fall back and regroup. Although the enemy's intentions were unclear at this point, it would soon be evident that the fog of war settling back over the ravaged land was the harbinger of a harsh and savage winter.[36]

Flying the Dark of the Moon

The threat of Chinese intervention changed the outlook of the war, imposing urgent new mission requirements on Aderholt's detachment. Around the time U.S. and Chinese forces first clashed near the end of October, Colonel Childre called to tell Aderholt he was sending an Army captain out to see him. "Whatever this guy wants, give it to him," Childre said. The Army captain was Bob Brewer, a case officer assigned to special intelligence within Far East Command's forward headquarters. He was responsible for collecting "essential elements of information" about opposing military forces, a highly classified project involving clandestine operations deep inside North Korea. Brewer was one of three case officers charged with collecting and analyzing this information, known in the trade as human intelligence (HUMINT). He had gone to Colonel Childre seeking Fifth Air Force's help airdropping agents over the north.[37]

Constraints imposed by MacArthur's headquarters prior to the Inchon landing had limited Brewer's project to using boats for inserting agents behind the lines—an option that he found "unsatisfactory." Meanwhile, he prepared for the eventuality of parachuting agents into the north, by carefully choosing seven (three women and four men) of his "best Korean spies," training them "in a safe house how to jump out of an airplane," and keeping them in good physical condition. After successfully parachuting these operatives into North Korea at the time of the Inchon landing, Brewer developed a continuing program of insertions by air and gained approval to implement it. When he ran into problems finding regular, qualified air support for the project, he turned to Colonel Childre. "You go out to Kimpo and talk to Captain Aderholt," Childre said. "He is the man you are looking for."[38]

Despite Childre's assurances, Brewer's disappointing experience with earlier air support had him primed "to expect a little trouble convincing my Air Force counterparts to fly the kind of mission that would get the job done." For such clandestine missions to be successful, the agents had to be dropped with pinpoint accuracy without being detected by the enemy. This meant that the supporting aircraft had to penetrate at low altitude and at night, "flying by the dark of the moon and below the rim of the mountains wherever possible," to avoid detection and to navigate with precision to the objective. If radar tracked the plane's penetration, the enemy could plot the probable drop zone and zero in on the agent. Likewise, an agent who landed outside the zone had to move through unfamiliar territory to the objective and was susceptible to capture. It was a mission demanding "the utmost in skill and guts" by all concerned.[39]

Brewer was pleasantly surprised when he got to Kimpo and found that "Aderholt and some of his assistants were all ready for me." Aderholt looked back on the meeting as the start of "a lifetime friendship with Bob Brewer." He recalled Brewer explaining his mission and complaining that he "had all these agents to drop and the Air Force hadn't given him any qualified flying crews." "Well, you just tell us what you want us to do, and we'll take care of that," Aderholt told him. Brewer agreed that they "immediately hit it off" and became the best of friends. He noted that Aderholt's strong points—"the ability to innovate and to communicate"—were ideally suited for the heat of combat and the exceptional risks of clandestine operations. "He communicated with everybody and everybody knew exactly where he stood," Brewer said.[40]

Aderholt's terse account of the detachment's first flight supporting Brewer's operation could not mask his thrill in the mission:

He had about eighteen or twenty Korean agents all parachuted up and a big map on the wall, and he pointed out where we were going. I looked where he was pointing, and we were going up on the Yalu River. I remember thinking, What in the hell are we going up there for? We got on the airplane, and he became the damned navigator. He took my ass all the way on the deck up to the Yalu River and down the Yalu River, and we were dropping these poor sons of bitches out. My navigator was this second lieutenant, just commissioned, and he kept saying, You are going to let this Army captain get us killed. When we got back, that was the last time we ever saw the navigator. He went back to the squadron in Japan and he never returned.[41]

The operatives they dropped that night were part of a growing pool of trained Korean spies known as "Rabbits" in the intelligence community. "These guys looked tough, and they were tough," Aderholt said. Some were North Korean refugees "who had a score to settle with the Communists." They parachuted into the heart of enemy territory, carried out the assigned mission, and made their way back to prearranged rendezvous points inside friendly lines. Often allowing themselves to be captured and interned by friendly forces, agents then used prearranged signals to gain release from prisoner of war (POW) cages. Intelligence officers immediately debriefed them and reported the information obtained from their mission.[42]

Taken on as a recurring mission, the detachment's support for Brewer's operation grew in importance. Entailing more than just airdropping the agents, the mission included monitoring signals by some agents and resupplying them when required. The Office of Strategic Services (OSS) had developed radios and other equipment for clandestine work during World War II, but these items were not available in Korea. Some agents carried heavy SCR-300 backpack infantry radios and relayed information to a detachment aircraft orbiting overhead. Aderholt's radio operator, Staff Sergeant Robert Gross, rigged "a long coaxial reception antenna trailing behind the aircraft," where he could communicate with agents on the ground ten miles away. As operations progressed, they developed other innovative means of communicating with the agents. Brewer emphasized how important communications were to the success of a mission. "When you told agents you would be back the next night at a certain hour and they could hear that plane wandering around the sky, they would break their backs for you," he said, "but you could kiss the mission good-bye if you failed to keep your word or they thought you didn't care."[43]

According to Brewer, during the ten months or so that he and Aderholt's detachment worked together, they averaged about twenty missions a month for Far East Command—all at night and many of them flown "in the dark of the moon." They airdropped approximately one thousand agents in all, with over seven hundred of them either returning on time or coming up over the radio on time. Brewer interpreted a delay of more than two days to mean an agent had been compromised. He claimed their success rate of above 70 percent far exceeded that of other wars. "It was because we were accurate," he said. "We put people in exactly where we said they were going to go, and once they were on the ground, they knew where to go and carry out their mission."[44]

Meanwhile, the detachment continued to carry out its regular air transport tasks, providing routine and emergency airlift, flying the ambassador and other VIPs around, and making the frag run each night to a growing family of Allied bases. Another part of its regular mission was psychological warfare, which included aerial broadcasting of loudspeaker messages and "wide-ranging leaflet drops urging Chinese and North Korean soldiers to surrender or face inevitable death." Always innovative and willing to try new ideas, Aderholt decided that because they were flying over enemy-held terrain anyway and nearly always spotted tempting targets, they might as well make the most of the opportunity. In the saga of what has been described as the first and last C-47 "Bomber," the detachment rigged some of its planes to hold "two seventy-five-gallon napalm bombs under the transport's belly." The C-47 had paracontainer racks underneath that were used to drop bundles. Aderholt's crews screwed aerodelivery shackles into the racks and hung napalm canisters the same way it was done on fighters. When the last agent had parachuted from the plane, Aderholt and his crews flew "armed reconnaissance," dropping the napalm canisters on trucks and other lucrative targets on their way home.[45]

Aderholt and Captain Lou Droste made the first C-47 napalm drop against a target that Fifth Air Force intelligence had identified as an enemy headquarters. On Christmas Eve they made a reconnaissance run over the target, observing a large barnlike structure sitting in the open with tracks leading through the snow into the building. "At dawn the following morning, flying at minimum altitude, fifty feet off the ground, we delivered a Christmas present—two napalm canisters crashing through the front door at the same time," Aderholt recalled. "The building erupted in flames. Nobody got out." That was the first time the 21st Troop Carrier Squadron's planes had dropped napalm and was believed to have been the first napalm dropped in combat from a transport aircraft.[46]

The detachment believed higher headquarters was unaware of its midnight bombing runs until Colonel Childre called and said, "I know you have been dropping napalm." Hesitantly, Aderholt answered, "Yes." "Well, officially I've got to tell you not to do it," Childre said, "but I know you are going to do it anyway." Months later, as Aderholt was nearing the end of his tour in Korea,

Childre called and asked him to come to Tokyo. The colonel had left Korea in February 1951 to become deputy commander of the 315th Air Division at Tachikawa. He explained that the division was planning a napalm saturation mission using C-119s and could benefit from the detachment's experience. Aderholt flew to Tachikawa and briefed Childre and his staff. The division subsequently massed a large formation of C-119s loaded with fifty-five-gallon drums of napalm. Their target was a hill where heavily fortified enemy troops persisted in beating back attacks from exposed UNC positions below. After the C-119s saturated the hill with napalm, fighters roared in and ignited the fire. Aderholt learned later that they burned off the hill, but enemy troops were well dug in, and most survived the firestorm.[47]

As the detachment's reputation in flying special missions grew, more agencies asked for support. Already lean in resources, the unit got a few more men and planes for the increased workload, but mostly "sucked it up" with what was already available. "Aircraft were hard to come by, and my outfit had so few people," Aderholt said. "Nobody wanted to fly with us when they could live in Tokyo." Bringing to mind the lieutenant who never returned, he said the detachment's C-47s rarely had navigators. "Navigators were hard to come by, and none of them wanted to fly with us," he said. Pilots like Droste, Jack Nabors, and John McDonald (captains at the time) who flew the hard missions and were always there when you needed them "had balls of steel" and were crucial to detachment operations.[48]

Among the detachment's new missions were more daring penetrations deep into North Korea in support of Fifth Air Force intelligence and the Central Intelligence Agency, the latter having far-reaching implications for Aderholt's career. These missions did not begin until January 1951, however, amid perhaps the harshest winter endured by American fighting men since Valley Forge and the "Winter of Despair" nearly two centuries earlier. The convulsion of the bitter Korean winter of 1950–51 into a hellish struggle for survival might have been averted had General MacArthur and his staff heeded intelligence gleaned from prisoner interrogations and partisans dropped into North Korea by Aderholt's detachment.[49]

Autumn's Fury, Winter's Storm

While the heavy Chinese probes against UNC forces during late October and early November were defined after the fact as "their First Phase Offensive," Army historians concluded that intelligence experts in MacArthur's headquarters misread their meaning at the time. The chief of intelligence Major General

(Left to right) Captain Robert W. Smith and Captain Aderholt at Kimpo, Korea, in 1950 before dropping paratroopers near North Korean capital of Pyongyang.

Charles A.Willoughby and his analysts could not agree on whether the Chinese were bluffing, merely saving face, or warning of greater risks to come. Intelligence estimates of enemy infiltration varied greatly as MacArthur's commanders laid plans to launch an all-out offensive after Thanksgiving to finish the job of defeating the North Koreans. All Willoughby's office was prepared to say with certainty was that an unknown number of well-trained and well-organized troops, infiltrating at night and maintaining strict discipline, had entered Korea, while "Chinese armies had massed in great strength along the Yalu in Manchuria, disposed for early action in Korea if the signal came." The UNC ground forces were exposed mostly to guerrilla activity during this brief interlude, but airmen flying near the Yalu increasingly drew antiaircraft fire from the other side of the river and encountered MiG-15s rising to challenge them from bases in Manchuria.[50]

There was ample military intelligence pointing to massive intervention by Chinese forces if the Allies persisted in taking all of North Korea. Information gleaned from freed American captives, Chinese prisoners, partisan agents, and other sources corroborated this. One of Captain Brewer's "most productive agents" sat for days unobserved near a main bridge across the Yalu counting trucks and recording their bumper numbers. From this agent's reports, Brewer arrived at an estimate of five hundred thousand Chinese infiltrators and submitted Report No. 100, containing unit names and commanders to General Willoughby's office. Brewer predicted "that the Chinese were going to reinforce and attack in huge numbers . . . between Thanksgiving and Christmas."[51] Later analyses confirmed that the Chinese Communists threw approximately three hundred thousand troops against the advancing allied forces starting on 27 November.

Brewer recalled asking his boss, Lieutenant Colonel James C. Tarkington, what he made of the five-hundred-thousand estimate and said Tarkington "just shook his head." Willoughby's office pulled the agent out of Korea and flew him to Tokyo for debriefing but must have believed he was lying or exaggerating. Even if the agent had exaggerated, Brewer noted, a force half that size posed a serious threat—as UNC forces soon found out. An official Army history concluded that during the third week in November, General Walker and his G-2 Colonel Tarkington (and by inference, Generals MacArthur and Willoughby) "apparently shared the view . . . that the Chinese in Korea numbered only a few divisions . . . and that China would not enter the war." Admitting that others were skeptical of this assessment, the official history simply notes that "the controlling . . . viewpoint . . . seems to have been that China would not intervene with major forces."[52]

For whatever reason General MacArthur ordered the resumption of the November offensive on the twenty-fourth—whether calling what he believed to be a Chinese bluff, testing their resolve, or goading President Truman and the JCS into stronger action—it could not have come at a worse time for the soldiers and Marines deployed in the far reaches of North Korea. MacArthur had hoped to take North Korea before winter set in, but wintry weather struck early "with violent force and subzero temperatures" on 10 November, sending freezing winds of thirty to thirty-five miles an hour velocity across northernmost positions. On the Koto-ri plateau at the southern tip of the Chosin Reservoir, the 7th Marines reported that during the afternoon and night "the temperature dropped forty degrees to eight below zero." The weather later became much colder, dropping in some areas to twenty to thirty degrees below zero.[53] The Marines in the Changjin Reservoir area had cold-weather gear, but when Aderholt and his pilots had made airdrops to the Army's 2d Infantry Division during the advance northward, he recalled "those guys were in summer uniform" at the time. "Can you imagine what it was like going from hotter than hell to freezing your ass off and not being ready when winter came?" he asked.[54]

"Soon thereafter we were airdropping winter clothes to them because they had not been issued winter clothing," he recalled. Three weeks later they were trapped in subfreezing temperatures. Aderholt remembered getting an urgent requirement at one point to drop sleeping bags to the 2d Infantry Division. After completing the mission, he heard later that the division commander had confiscated the sleeping bags. Apparently the North Koreans had adopted a tactic of slipping into the camps and bayoneting the soldiers in their sleeping bags. "We weren't nearly prepared for that war," he said.[55]

Throughout November the C-47s from Aderholt's detachment had dropped supplies to the forward allied columns. The urgency and frequency of these drops increased dramatically after advancing forces were stopped in their tracks by the massive Chinese offensive on the twenty-seventh. At the same time, there had been no letup in the detachment's support for special mission activities. As demands for intelligence intensified during this period, Aderholt and his pilots flew every night they could, winging their way over hostile terrain either dropping agents or monitoring their signals. Hardly a night passed without spotting enemy convoys and troop movements, precipitating the detachment's innovative bombing runs with napalm.

"The Chinese had real discipline," Aderholt recalled. "You could fly right over the sons of bitches, and they normally would not fire at you at night." Staging out of the fallen North Korean capital of Pyongyang one "cold as hell" November night, Aderholt was flying "low and slow" dropping agents at five hundred feet when he spotted miles of Chinese troops pouring in from Manchuria. He had gone to Pyongyang to pick up Captain Bob Williams, a P-51 pilot and friend from Maxwell who now served with the advanced echelon of Fifth Air Force. Williams went along for the ride and helped navigate to the drop points. They flew to the Yalu and followed the orderly Chinese procession southward. The lines extended "thirty or forty miles" into North Korea, "wagon after wagon, truck after truck." The convoys were blacked out, but were easy targets because there was a full moon and a blanket of snow. "That was the damnedest thing I had ever seen," Aderholt said. "Thousands and thousands of troops. I flew right down over the bastards and turned my landing lights on, but they wouldn't fire at us." He could only conclude that the Chinese soldiers had been ordered not to fire on any airplane at night. "Talk about fire discipline," he said in awe.[56]

When they arrived back at Pyongyang, Aderholt and Williams reported their sightings to Fifth Air Force. "The whole goddamned Chinese Army is coming across the Yalu, moving south," they told an incredulous duty officer. "Don't worry about it," the duty officer responded. "The B-26s will get them." They learned later that the B-26s did not "get them" because the bombers were not staging out of Kimpo that night. They were weathered in at their home base of Komaki, Japan. "I don't think Fifth Air Force believed our report," Aderholt said. Two days later, just after dark, the Chinese forces in the west struck suddenly and hard at the Eighth Army front north of Pyongyang, forcing withdrawal of the 2d Infantry Division from Kunu-ri. To the northeast, the Chinese overran 7th Infantry Division and ROK forward positions near the Yalu and drove south toward the 1st Marines at the Changjin (Chosin) Reservoir.[57]

While noting that his C-47s frequently drew ground fire when overflying the north, Aderholt reemphasized the strict fire discipline observed by Chinese convoys, saying that he had seen this more than once. He recalled another occasion when he and Brewer spotted Chinese troop movements near Wonsan. "We saw the same thing, horsedrawn carts and trucks blacked out for miles and they didn't fire at us," he said. "I turned the landing lights on and flew low enough to cut their heads off and still could not get them to open fire." He thought about this years later going up against the North Vietnamese gunners on the Ho Chi Minh Trail. "There were times when I wished those bastards were more like their Chinese cousins," he said.[58]

By December the Chinese onslaught had UNC forces in full retreat. The Allies started withdrawing from Pyongyang on 4 December. The historic evacuation of the Army and Marine units cut off by the Chinese around the Changjin Reservoir began four days later. A total of 350 Air Force transports (313 C-119s and 37 C-47s) flew in support of the evacuation. Aderholt's detachment did not have a large role in the operation but was called on to augment its parent unit, the 21st TCSq, for three or four days. Aderholt flew multiple sorties into Hagaru-ri, where Marine bulldozers had cut out a rocky two-thousand-foot airstrip on the frozen bank of the reservoir. "We were carrying thirty-five to forty evacuees in the Gooney Bird," he recalled. "The 21st TCSq and our detachment's transports flew out about forty-eight hundred Marines altogether." What really stuck in his mind was the large number of Marines who had frozen feet and hands. He would not soon forget "the god-awful cold . . . below zero in the daytime and dropping to thirty to forty degrees below at night."[59]

The Marines prepared another landing strip at Koto-ri on the southern end of the reservoir that was too short for liftoff by heavily laden transports. The 21st TCSq commander Lieutenant Colonel Cage landed at Koto-ri and "had a hell of a time getting out." Aderholt recalled that the Marines brought in some "old torpedo bombers" and made a few "carrier landings" on the rugged strip— hauling some wounded troops out in their bomb bays. "They had everything under control, and I really wasn't needed there," Aderholt said, so he returned to Kimpo to handle the detachment's heavy night schedule. "We were dropping agents all over the place trying to get a fix on the enemy's order of battle," he explained. "Everybody was retreating so fast, they lost contact with the enemy."[60]

When Allied forces withdrew below the thirty-eighth parallel in December, the Chinese moved into Pyongyang but did not follow up Eighth Army's withdrawal "as closely as had been expected." The front lines were temporarily separated by a sprawling "No Man's Land." General Walker announced he would hold Seoul as long as possible but might have to retreat southward toward the old Pusan perimeter. The general stood a better chance of defending against the Chinese offensive if he knew where the brunt of attack was coming from. A few days before Christmas, he tasked the intelligence staff to find out where the Chinese were concentrating their forces and where they were going to attack. He gave them seventy-two hours to collect and report the information.[61]

The general's tasking sent Captain Brewer's operation into a tailspin. "How in the hell was he going to answer Walker in seventy-two hours?" Brewer wondered. "It not only was in the realm of the impossible, but was a suicide mission." Then he thought of the Northwest Youth Association, a hardened group of refugees from the North Korean town of Sinuiju who "had revenge in their hearts" and had volunteered their services. "The Communists had killed their wives, daughters, and sisters," Brewer said, "and all they wanted to do was kill Communists." Since he was not in the business of assassination and sabotage, Brewer had used this group sparingly in the past because he was afraid their thirst for revenge might jeopardize the intelligence mission. Now he needed their services.[62]

Brewer contacted Aderholt and explained his problem. They did not have "decent radios" available, so Brewer had serious communications problems even if he decided to use the Sinuiju avengers. Colonel Childre called and told Aderholt they had to find a way to get this job done. "No sweat," Aderholt told them. "I'll get back to you." Mulling through the problem and "kicking it around" with his best people, he came right back with the solution. He explained that the detachment would paint the special mission C-47s with "huge black and white" invasion stripes, similar to those used in Overlord during World War II, around the fuselage and underneath the wings so they could be readily identified by Brewer's agents. The agents would be given different-colored smoke grenades and dropped at strategic points across the waist of the enemy's advance. The C-47s would go up each morning and afternoon at prearranged times, and the agents would set off combinations of yellow, green, or red smoke grenades to signal information on enemy forces in their locales.[63]

Brewer marveled at the simplicity and ingenuity of the concept. "It worked like a charm," he said. "We put these bloodthirsty guys on the tops of mountains across the waist of Korea, and they did the job for us." They inserted "twelve teams of two in two lines" across the enemy's front. Brewer noted that he had not expected many of the agents to survive the mission. They were parachuting onto rocky, precipitous mountaintops right in the heart of advancing enemy troops. He said they had been given enough grenades to last for three days. To Brewer's surprise, all of the agents eventually trickled back to the Allied lines. He briefly described the procedures they used in the operation:

> Most of the roads in Korea run north and south . . . below the ridgelines. The men we inserted scouted out the areas on both sides of the mountains . . . going down to the roads and finding out from the people there what kind of enemy had been through or were there. Then they climbed back on the mountains and waited for the specially marked plane to come and popped their smoke grenades in various combinations to tell us where the Chinese were. The combinations of signals were kept simple because we didn't want any mix-ups. They popped the grenades when first spotting the planes so the smoke would billow out before we got there. It's hard to read these things after you've flown over them. We did get our messages three days in a row. I was able to give General Walker the information . . . that the bulk of the Chinese were in the West sector at that time.[64]

Not a man to condone failure, Walker would have expected no less from his intelligence people. Known as the "stand or die" defender of the Pusan perimeter, Walker was a "hard and demanding" leader who reportedly "told one general he did not want to see him back from the front again unless it was in a coffin." He was also a "hands-on" commander who spent most of his days visiting combat units at the front. During one of these visits on the morning of 23 December, Walker was killed in a jeep accident north of Seoul near Uijongbu. The enemy meanwhile had massed for an attack across a wide front, with the greatest strength of the Chinese armies assembled in the west poised to strike down the Yongchon-Uijongbu-Seoul axis at the heart of Eighth Army.[65]

When General Matthew B. Ridgway arrived in Korea to replace Walker on 27 December, he had MacArthur's permission to attack and regain lost ground. Ridgway put off attacking when he found that major commanders and his Eighth Army staff were not "offensive minded." The Communists, on the other hand, did not delay once their troops were in position for a general offensive. Opening an all-out attack on New Year's Eve, the enemy struck fast and hard toward Seoul and captured the city four days later. Ridgway abandoned Seoul on 3 January and pulled Allied forces back to a defensive line running from about twenty-five miles below Seoul across the peninsula.[66]

Fifth Air Force had prepared for the loss of airfields at Seoul, Kimpo, and Suwon and moved some units from these bases in December. The remaining units pulled out at the beginning of January when Ridgway ordered the withdrawal from Seoul. Aderholt's detachment moved back to K-2 at Taegu for two weeks, then relocated across town at K-37. Aderholt recalled that his Gooney Bird was the next-to-the-last aircraft to leave Kimpo before it fell. "Not because we wanted to be heroes," he swore gently. "We started the right engine, but the starter was out in the left engine. We couldn't get the goddamned thing started." He credited the crew chief with "saving our bacon," noting that the chief jumped down from the plane, yelling, "Don't worry, we'll jump-start it with a rope." "What in the hell do you mean?" Aderholt shouted back, not believing the sergeant was serious about using a rope to crank a twelve-hundred-horsepower airplane engine. "Well, I was wrong," he said with a laugh. "The crew chief wrapped the tie-down rope around the propeller shaft and secured it to a jeep. I got up in the cockpit and set the throttle and mixture. He revved the jeep, roared off, and that spun the propeller to start the left engine." They lifted off and flew to Taegu as if nothing had happened.[67]

On the way they flew over South Korea's bleak snow-covered landscape of frozen rice paddies; barren, burned, and cratered hills; and mangled roads that "were jammed all the way down with civilian refugees and military units." Many of the refugees carried all their worldly possessions in large bundles balanced on their heads, in carts, or on A-frames strapped to their backs. The long gray ribbon of human misery unwinding through the fields of snow beneath them evoked nightmarish images of howling arctic winds sweeping across the desolate wasteland to the far north, already erasing traces of the carnage and suffering inflicted there in November and December. "My God," Aderholt thought. "And winter hasn't really started yet."[68]

Daughters of the Morning Calm

The question of just who would be left to rebuild the "Land of the Morning Calm" when this "godforsaken war" was over intruded on his thoughts as the droning engines lumbered toward Taegu. The mornings, afternoons, and nights had been "anything but calm" since his arrival five months ago. His thoughts turned to the Korean agents they dropped nightly onto the dark and forbidding mountains of the enemy. He saw hope in their burning patriotism, purpose, and courage. These intrepid men and women were doers and survivors. They were South Korea's future. He wondered whether any of them were in that wretched procession below.

Captain Aderholt cared for the Korean people, and it showed in the way they reacted to him. Brewer talked about how much the Asians loved his friend. They trusted him with their lives. When asked if the Korean agents were patriots, Aderholt said, "Damn right. You couldn't pay people enough to do their job." Brewer noted that the male agents were at greater risk than the female agents, because all able-bodied men were supposed to be in uniform. He said the women had truly excelled in a man's profession and were much admired by the Koreans. Most of them were recruited personally by Madame Francesca Donner Rhee, Austrian-born wife of South Korea's president Syngman Rhee. No older than the Rhee's own two daughters, Madame Rhee's "little girl patriots" were in a sense the daughters of her adopted land. "They were the artists, the starlets, the musicians, accomplished people, the very best," Aderholt recalled. Brewer chuckled when he thought about the cultural divide. When he first proposed to insert female agents behind the lines, he "had to go all the way to Washington for approval." He said it was worth the trouble because the women came back with some of the best intelligence in the war.[69]

The Korean agents did not have the realistic parachute training that was available to airborne troops in the United States. Aderholt recalled that Brewer "trained them off the back of an Army truck," many times having to "crash" train agents who were "going in the next night." Looking back on the airdrops, Aderholt said it was hard to believe the female agents "did what they did." "Bob put them out where the temperature was forty or fifty degrees below zero," he recalled. "They would go out in little cotton-padded shoes and a cotton-padded suit, and you would think they didn't weigh enough to get them to the ground." The agents did not have reserve chutes because at five hundred feet they would have been of no use. "How about that for on-the-job training?" he asked.[70]

The detachment's insertion of agents went back into operation immediately after that bitterly cold day when Aderholt and his crew finally lifted off from Kimpo and limped into K-2. Their arrival completed the detachment's evacuation, and they wasted no time going into action. Colonel Childre and Captain Brewer were already on the phone to him scheduling missions. The withdrawal was just another crisis in a rapidly shifting war, and General Ridgway was not one to stay on the defensive when time came to counterattack. The general needed good intelligence, and he needed it yesterday. While increased support for Eighth Army carried priority, the detachment took on an even greater mission workload beginning in January. After moving over to K-37 at midmonth, Aderholt and his people began flying special missions for the CIA while increasing other mission activities such as pyschological warfare, supporting

Fifth Air Force intelligence, and air transport. The detachment continued to fly VIPs, including Korean president Rhee and Ambassador Muccio, and was assigned responsibility for a plush B-17 that General Ridgway had refurbished for his use. Aderholt said they gave the detachment six more planes, but not "a hell of a lot of more people." "We were flying our butts off," he said.[71]

Conceding air superiority over the battlefield and leaving extended lines of communication open to attack—although keeping MiG Alley hot—the Communist advance stalled in mid January. General Ridgway went on the offensive, advancing in a slow, bruising drive to the Han River that steadily ground up the Chinese and North Korean armies and inched them back across the thirty-eighth parallel. The Allies reoccupied Seoul on 14 March without a fight. The months of April and May were more of the same, with Ridgway's revitalized forces gaining the advantage in a brutal and hard-fought exchange. By June the Allies had stopped a short distance inside North Korea after a Communist spring offensive sputtered and died. Truce talks began in July, while the two sides dug in and faced each other just north of the thirty-eighth parallel.[72] A different kind of war lay over the horizon.

A tragic accident in February brought home the imperative role that discipline had in military operations. Brigadier General John P. Henebry replaced Tunner as 315th Air Division commander in February when Eighth Army was in the early stages of its advance toward the thirty-eighth parallel. Colonel Childre became Henebry's deputy. To support the front lines north of Chungju, the engineers carved out a two-thousand-foot airstrip near the Han River at General Henebry's urging so transport aircraft could haul sorely needed supplies to troops at the front. Aderholt received an urgent message to fly to the airstrip and employ his C-47 as a "control tower" for approximately twenty-five C-46s airlifting supplies from Japan. Parachute drops from C-119s had drifted too far afield, so Henebry had decided to use the 437th Troop Carrier Wing's C-46s to haul supplies into the emergency strip. The 437th was a mobilized Reserve wing from Chicago that entered active service in July, trained in South Carolina for several weeks, and then started flying into Korea out of southern Japan in November.[73]

The dirt airstrip near Chungju was frozen solid in the mornings and could bear the landing weight of the C-46s but had to be closed to traffic when the sun came out and thawed the ice. Aderholt flew up early the next morning and parked his C-47 about four hundred feet down the runway to control the C-46 landings. The Army engineers had worked on the strip the night before to make it as smooth as possible, but there were still rough spots. In Aderholt's instructions to the pilots, he cautioned them to maintain strict radio silence. "Do not talk on the radio," he told them, explaining that he had no other means of communicating with approaching aircraft if they got into trouble. "We will call you in the sequence you come in," he stated. "We can only have three airplanes on the ground at any one time. When one takes off, we will call the next one in."[74]

Aderholt said he had no sooner got the words out of his mouth when a C-46 came in too low, striking frozen dirt and debris piled at the end of the strip. The plane's right landing gear "went sailing off," and Aderholt yelled over the radio to the pilot that he had lost his gear and to "pull up and go around." But the pilot did not hear the instructions. The radio frequency was cluttered with chatter between the other planes, blocking the transmission. Aderholt described what happened next: "The guy never got my go around, go around. We fired the flare, and he touched down. When he did, the C-46 veered and hit another airplane head-on and killed everybody on the plane." Aderholt got back on the radio and told the pilots what had happened, chewed "their ass," and demanded they stay off the air. "There wasn't another word," he said, "but we had killed four people."[75]

"That was one of the worst breaches of discipline I've ever seen," he said. "And it cost four people their lives." He reported the incident to Colonel Childre and said "the Reserve outfit really needed shaking up." He had mellowed considerably when looking back on the incident forty years later. "That is just an indication of a Reserve unit that wasn't too well disciplined," he said. "It could have happened to anybody." But he repeated the thought that discipline has always been a distinction of military life, and always would be. "Military discipline is the glue that holds all else together," he said. "Any military unit without it eventually comes apart at the seams."[76]

The detachment's clandestine operations played a small but vital role in support of General Ridgway's offensive strategy that winter and spring of 1951. The special intelligence apparatus had proved its worth during the vicious battles up north and got better with experience. The female agents had become aces at carrying out their missions by this time, and Brewer put more trust in them. He pointed out that all of the women had carried out more than one mission in enemy territory, and some had completed as many as four missions. The information one of these agents brought back got General Ridgway's attention and might have been "the best intelligence mission of the war." She had been airdropped behind enemy lines with a group of other women agents after the detachment moved to Taegu. Their mission was to fan out and collect intelligence on the enemy order of battle, with a special requirement to pinpoint the location of an entire Chinese corps that had mysteriously disappeared from the Seoul front.[77]

The successful agent bailed out onto a mountainside, buried her parachute, brushed herself off, went down to the nearest main supply route, and began thumbing for a ride as she had been told. A Chinese colonel came by at daybreak and picked her up. She passed herself off as a refugee, and the colonel took her back to camp. She shared his tent long enough to collect the intelligence she came for, then slipped away and returned to Allied lines on the central front. Retrieving the agent from a POW cage, Aderholt and Brewer flew her to Tokyo without delay to be debriefed. She had come back with the whole enemy order of battle and reported that the missing Chinese corps had sideslipped from the Seoul front over to the central sector at Chunchon, where it was massed for an attack against the U.S. 2d Division. Armed with this information, General Ridgway moved the 1st Marine Division up from the Pusan line to reinforce the sector and block the Chinese advance. The little agent in the padded suit and padded shoes was the unsung heroine.[78]

Warring in the shadows and not getting recognized for one's accomplishments, not even masterstrokes, are sine qua nons of clandestine operations. Operating outside the mainstream military structure tends to isolate clandestine forces, often puts them on the spot explaining what might appear to the establishment as heresy, and has stunted many promising careers. A story that another legendary Air Commando brigadier general, Benjamin H. King, tells about the first time he met Heinie Aderholt helps illustrate the different worlds in which regular and special forces sometimes lived and worked. It also captures early traces of Aderholt's wit and compassion, and the lengths that he would go to take care of his people.[79]

The incident occurred in late 1950 when the detachment was at Kimpo. Aderholt had taken off that night on a drop mission with fifteen or sixteen female agents on board. When they got to the drop zone over North Korea, heavy fog had rolled in, making the parachute jumps too dangerous. There was zero visibility. He aborted the mission and returned to find Kimpo socked in. He raised the tower and was told that the weather at Taegu was marginal. When they arrived over K-2, the fog had beat them there. After going to Pusan and finding out that "the whole damned peninsula was fogged in," he took the C-47 out over the water and let down to about two hundred feet, but still did not break out of the weather. He had two choices. He could attempt an ADF (automatic direction finder) approach to Pusan (K-1), where the weather was zero-zero, or divert to Itazuke, the nearest base in Japan.[80]

There was one small problem. "We had strict orders never to take Koreans into Japan without approval from higher authority, which we occasionally had when flying hot agents to Tokyo for debriefing," he said. This restriction was in political deference to the Japanese government. "Screw them," he thought as they let down over the "hallelujah" runway lights at Itazuke. It was pitch dark, it was cold, and they were worn to a frazzle. His first thought was "to get the people fed." He got a flight-line vehicle, took the Koreans over to the mess hall, and told the mess sergeant they were on official business and had to be fed. "Who are you?" the sergeant asked. Aderholt showed his ID card and said, "It doesn't matter who I am. I'm a captain in the United States Air Force, and I want these people fed." "They aren't eligible to eat in the mess hall," the sergeant said. Aderholt could not say much else without revealing that the agents were Korean nationals who were not supposed to be in Japan. "Get your commander," he told the sergeant. "One damned way or the other you are going to feed these people."[81]

Across the mess hall Lieutenant Colonel Ben King (a fighter ace in World War II who now commanded a squadron in the 8th Fighter-Bomber Wing) sat alone having an early breakfast before leading the predawn takeoff that morning. "About halfway through my breakfast, I heard a commotion at the other end of the mess hall," King recalled. He looked up and saw the sergeant talking to some people dressed in heavy winter GI coats and parkas. He could not tell "who they were or what they were" because they were wearing no insignia. After an animated discussion with the apparent leader of the group, the sergeant came over to King's table, explained the situation, and asked what he should do. King had no control over the mess hall, but he was a field grade officer and the only one having breakfast that early in the morning. King told the sergeant to have the person who seemed to be in charge come back and discuss it with him.[82]

"So this individual comes back and tells me that he has these people who have been out on a mission, and they needed to eat," King recalled. When he asked what mission they had been on, the individual said it was classified and he couldn't tell him. "Well, who are you?" King asked. "What are you doing here?" The person responded, "It's classified and I can't tell you." After more of the same, King said he told the individual that "by God if he couldn't identify himself and tell me who he was and where he was going and what he was doing, then I thought the best thing to do was to get the air police and have them throw the whole bunch out of the mess hall." At that point King said he was told "the damnedest tale" a fighter pilot could absorb sober at that hour of the morning:

> He introduced himself as Captain Heinie Aderholt. Of course, I had never heard of Captain Heinie Aderholt. He told me he was on a classified mission out of southern Korea and the people with him were South Korean women

who were agents of the United States government working on a classified mission. Their mission was to fly up over North Korea. These women were to bail out behind the enemy lines, and then work their way back across the lines to the American troops in a period of about six weeks to two months. He said they were infected with every known venereal disease, and their whole mission was to infect the North Koreans with venereal disease. Then they were to get back across the lines and get cured before anything happened to them.[83]

Ben King said he sat and listened to Aderholt embellish the story as only he could, finding it extremely interesting and entertaining. "I had never heard of such a mission," King said, "but I had heard that the North Koreans accused us of germ warfare, and I thought to myself that this is germ warfare at its basics." Repeating that he "had never heard . . . such a fantastic story," King shook his head and "called the sergeant over and told him to feed the group . . . which made Aderholt happy." "But I thought to myself that fellow can sure tell a big tale," King recalled. He had not forgotten the captain or the "tall tale" when they met again "at another time, in another war" a decade later.[84]

Where Legends Are Born

The irony of the chance encounter between Heinie Aderholt and Ben King is in the knowledge that they would become two of the best-known air commandos of the Vietnam War. King was a top-gun fighter pilot in Korea and became a "helluva" air commando a decade later when he led the Farm Gate special air warfare detachment to Vietnam. Aderholt was "a frustrated fighter pilot at heart" who found his calling in special operations as commander of the maverick C-47 detachment flying clandestine missions in Korea. He had become a special air warfare convert and would pursue this offbeat career field rather than the grind of military airlift when his combat tour came to a close. This put him ten years ahead of his contemporaries when the legendary air commandos of World War II were reborn in the Vietnam War. It was not planned that way when he left Maxwell Field the year before, but unconventional warfare was the Grail he unknowingly sought, and it had found him in the perilous skies over North Korea.

Colonel Childre had been his sponsor and the detachment's sponsor. Childre was quick to see the value in supporting Captain Brewer's orphan endeavors and knew Aderholt was the man to do the job. He gave his blessing to the detachment's special missions over the north and protected them from "colonels with blinders" who viewed the unit's aircraft and crews as theater airlift resources only. Aderholt said the detachment had no priority within the theater because Tunner "hated the C-47s" and "all he wanted to do was run a Berlin Airlift into Korea with C- 119s." He recalled flying Tunner to the front lines on two occasions, taking "him into some real short dirt strips." The general said, "I want all you guys to have DFCs (Distinguished Flying Crosses) just for flying up here," but that was the last anyone heard about it. Aderholt was blunt in his belief that the Air Force needed more creative leaders like Colonel Childre, whose egos were not larger than the people they commanded.[85]

Aderholt called Brewer "the best case officer I've ever known, by far" and "the man who taught me everything I knew" about shadow operations in Korea. Working with Brewer prepared him for supporting the CIA when an agent named Fritz Larkin contacted the detachment for assistance in January 1951. After Allied forces withdrew from North Korea in December, the CIA developed plans for covert operations in the north, including setting up a guerrilla force in the vicinity of the Changjin Reservoir. When spring arrived, the detachment began flying clandestine airdrops to insert CIA operatives below the Yalu and to keep them resupplied.[86]

It was becoming increasingly obvious to everyone that the Allies would not attempt another all-out drive to defeat North Korea. Any remaining doubts faded when President Truman relieved General MacArthur in April. When General Ridgway replaced MacArthur on the fourteenth, Lieutenant General James A. Van Fleet took over Eighth Army with orders to hold the line after moving back across the thirty-eighth parallel. With the two sides stalemated on the battlefield and at the truce table, the concept of friendly guerrilla forces operating behind enemy lines became more appealing. "We started dropping people way up north," Aderholt said. "We would fly eight-hour missions in a C-47, dropping people all over." The flights did not cross into Manchuria, but he occasionally flew along the Yalu at seven thousand to eight thousand feet to see if the Chinese gunners were awake.[87]

During the late spring Lieutenant Colonel George W. Haney (an Air Force officer who headed the CIA's air section in Washington) visited Korea and observed firsthand the job that Aderholt and his people were doing for the agency. He told Aderholt that the CIA was impressed with the support he had given the agency and asked him to join his office to set up a training program for covert air operations when the tour in Korea was up. Aderholt accepted the offer on the spot, with the understanding that he could recruit key people like Brewer, Droste, Nabors, and McDonald when he returned to Washington. Haney assured him that "would be no problem."[88]

Aderholt had pinned on major's leaves in February, although he did not wear them on missions over the north. He wanted to continue the work he had been doing in Korea and knew the opportunities were limited. The Air Force had shown renewed interest in unconventional warfare capabilities in February by activating the Air Resupply and Communications Service for global application, but Aderholt had no connection to the new organization and was not fully briefed on its mission. Haney told him that the CIA planned to expand its support for guerrilla and counterguerrilla operations around the globe and hinted that an experienced airman could write his own ticket. It was an offer he could not refuse. Colonel Childre agreed.[89]

When Major Aderholt entered the pipeline to return stateside on the first of September, he sensed that he would not be coming back to Korea. While heavy fighting for position near the thirty-eighth parallel dragged on just short of two more years, the brutal war of attrition essentially ended with that first bloody year. One day on the flight line, he saw a young soldier sitting on his duffel bag waiting for a plane out. He was strumming a guitar and softly singing the "Bugout Boogie" to the tune of the country-and-western hit, "I'm Moving On." The improvised lyrics obviously referred to the Allied retreat from North Korea the previous winter. Aderholt looked closely at the soldier. He was wearing the combat infantryman badge, a cluster of ribbons, and on his shoulder the Indian-head emblem of the 2d Infantry Division. "God hit a homerun when he made the American GI," Aderholt said to himself—then added as an afterthought, "With the bases loaded," as he walked away humming the tune.

Aderholt was proud of the detachment's airmen and what they had done in the past year. Tragically, two unarmed planes went down with their brave aircrews (including Staff Sergeant Robert Gross, who was on the initial crew from Maxwell)—always the heaviest loss—but a surprisingly low number considering their missions and where they were flying. Substantially more sustained hits from ground fire. Aderholt was quick to agree that at least one more Gooney Bird might have been damaged or destroyed one terribly cold night in November had the Chinese not been such disciplined soldiers. After moving to Taegu in January, the detachment averaged 115 special mission sorties monthly, all flown behind enemy lines dropping leaflets, broadcasting to enemy troops, dropping agents and resupplying them, or intercepting radio transmissions. These were in addition to the grueling schedule of transporting VIPs, flying the frag order circuit, and other airlift missions routinely imposed by higher headquarters. They had flown "damned near every night and every day," but Aderholt had no regrets about pushing himself or pushing his people. As one wise old top sergeant who mastered in esprit de corps expressed it, "You can keep troops busy, but you'd better not keep them bored."[90]

He had come to Korea to fly airplanes and he had flown airplanes. He had no regrets about that either. He had turned down the job as operations officer at Ashiya, and had refused other offers. That might be where the next promotion came from, but he was just not cut out to fly a desk up to the next lieutenant colonel's list. Somebody had to do those jobs. His place was in the cockpit and out there on the flight line with the men, leading them, working with them, and caring for them. He had never felt better than when planning and flying those "in-your-face" secret missions in the skies over North Korea. "Hell, those skies are what the Air Force is all about," he said.[91] Never would he have given it a thought, much less said it, but those skies are also where heroes die and where legends are born.

2. ON ASSIGNMENT WITH THE CIA

On the long flight home "via Wake Island and Hawaii, autopilot out," Major Aderholt reflected on the highs and lows of his combat tour in Korea. As special missions detachment commander, he had been the point man in Korea for covert air operations against the enemy. Time and again Colonel Childre had entrusted the detachment with "the most dangerous and difficult covert missions," because he knew that Aderholt and his pilots would carry them out "if humanly possible." Childre's trust and the detachment's guts, perseverance, and ingenuity had sustained UNC clandestine air operations when conditions were at their worst in the war. For Aderholt and his aircrews, however, the unit's selfless dedication to the mission could not be reconciled with what they perceived to be a lack of support and recognition for covert operations by higher echelons.[1]

The USAF's failure to provide special aircraft and equipment for performing clandestine missions encumbered the detachment's operations and imperiled the aircrews. Aderholt had improvised to get the job done. Before leaving the Far East, he reemphasized the urgent need for equipping the detachment with aircraft specially configured for covert operations during a debriefing to Colonel Childre in Tokyo. Childre consistently supported the detachment's requirements, but the top brass had not been forthcoming. Aderholt did not know at the time that the Air Force had activated a highly classified organization, the Air Resupply and Communications Service (ARCS), in Washington to build up unconventional air capabilities around the globe. The new service had already begun secretly grooming and deploying these capabilities to the Far East for use in the war against North Korea and Communist China. Aderholt later learned that "the very aircraft we so urgently needed were en route to the theater" to augment the special missions detachment as he packed his B-4 bag and winged his way homeward. He applauded the effort, but it was "too little too late" as far as he was concerned.[2]

Thoughts of the war faded into the background when he landed in California and hitched a ride aboard a SAC bomber to Maxwell Field and a long-awaited reunion with his lovely wife, Jessie. He spent two idyllic weeks at home, including visits with family and friends in Birmingham and Montgomery. Missing from the reunion was his brother Warren who had been recalled to active duty and was flying F-80s in Germany. Aderholt was anxious to get back to work, however, and "was pulling at the traces" by the time he and Jessie left for Washington to report to the 1007th Air Intelligence Service Group, an Air Force unit attached to CIA Headquarters.[3]

The Aderholts arrived in the nation's capital in early autumn, a seasonal hiatus when Congress was not in session, when the tourist rush had gone, when trees wore khaki, and when the thud of Redskin leather replaced the crack of Senators bats in the cool Potomac nights. They stayed with friends, A. M. "Red" Jones and his wife, Carrie, in their basement apartment until he knew where he would be working with the CIA. Red was an Air Force civilian assigned to Operations in the Pentagon but was better known for his gridiron prowess. General Curtis LeMay had picked Red to recruit a championship service football team while the newly formed Air Force Academy brought its athletic program "up to speed." Red was also "a nationally known pool artist and billiards player," whose pool-hall skills and derring-do—laughingly described as "sure signs of a misspent youth"—added unexpected adventure to the Aderholts' stay in Washington.[4]

Major Aderholt's orientation to CIA headquarters was reminiscent of the "hurry up and wait" treatment he had encountered en route to Ashiya the year before. A letter from the agency before leaving Korea had advised that nothing could be revealed to him about the assignment until after he reported to Washington and obtained a security clearance to the agency. He was told only that the job entailed wearing civilian clothes, an anomaly for him but a trend in the making for post-WWII military personnel working in Washington. Not knowing what lay in store for him made Aderholt even more eager to get started. When he reported for duty in late October, however, he was denied access to agency operations because his security clearance had not been processed. As an interim measure, the agency placed him on temporary-duty status with the seven-month-old Air Resupply and Communications Service headquarters on Wisconsin Avenue.[5]

Aderholt spent a "useful, informative month" with the ARCS planners and operators on Wisconsin Avenue. "They really opened my eyes to what was happening worldwide in special air operations," he said.[6] Their mission was to develop unconventional and psychological warfare capabilities to help contain the global spread of Communism. The headquarters was in the process of creating three huge flying wings equipped with modified B-29s, twin-engine SA-16 amphibians, C-119 and C-54 transports, and H-19 helicopters for deployment to strategically located bases overseas. Former members of the 492d Bombardment Group, the "Carpetbaggers," who flew clandestine missions in Europe during World War II for the Office of Strategic Services (the CIA's predecessor) could have provided a pool of experienced personnel to man the wings, but there was no Air Force Specialty Code identifier to earmark their prior service in special operations. With the exception of their commander, Brigadier General Monro MacCloskey, and a few other senior officers, most of the people assigned had no special-operations experience.[7]

Although much of the past had been forgotten, the future had never looked brighter for the Air Force's special air warfare capabilities. The first unconventional warfare wing, the 581st ARCWg, was activated at Mountain Home AFB, Idaho, in July, and immediately deployed to Clark Air Base in the Philippines. It was now flying clandestine missions in the Korean War. Another wing, the 580th, activated soon after and deployed to Wheelus Air Base, Libya. Plans called for activating a third wing the next year to deploy to an RAF base at Molesworth, England. There were to be four wings altogether. "It was impressive," Aderholt recalled. "We had the greatest capability to conduct clandestine air operations in the history of our country." The bright future soon faded, however. Much like the decline in special air capabilities after World War II, the Air Force's support for covert operations declined after a cease-fire was attained in Korea. The huge wings with close ties to the CIA were downgraded to groups in 1953 and were inactivated three years later.[8] While saluting the concept, Aderholt observed that the overstaffed headquarters on Wisconsin Avenue was in a sense the father of its own demise. "They were deep into building up a big, bureaucratic system that was too large and cumbersome for the brushfire wars we became involved with in the third world countries," he explained.[9]

Aderholt identified with the air resupply and communications wings while they lasted. After obtaining his security clearance to the agency and taking charge in his new assignment, he visited Mountain Home to pass on his Korean

Unshaven Captain Aderholt
during the Korean War.

War experiences to the ARC wings and later to the Air Guard's special operations squadrons. He also trained the CIA case officers who were sent overseas
to work with the wings. He never served directly with the operation, however,
except for his brief stint while waiting to be cleared by the CIA during the fall
of 1951.[10]

When the temporary duty assignment ended in November, the agency notified him to report to a WWII temporary building near the Reflecting Pool for
further instructions. To his dismay Aderholt arrived at the designated duty station the following morning to find that he was enrolled in an advanced Russian
language class. "I didn't know one damned word of Russian," he said. "It was
all gibberish." At the noon break, "escorted through every door," he tracked
down Lieutenant Colonel Haney (the head of the Air Training Branch), who
had recruited him in Korea. He found Haney's office and told him about the
"Mickey Mouse" treatment he had received. "I told him that I had had it, that I
had come to Washington believing there was an urgent requirement for an experienced covert air operations officer, but if I had known then what I knew
now, I would have stayed where the action was," Aderholt recalled. "He told
me to go home, and he would call me." Haney called the next day and told him

to report back to the office so he could meet the people he would be working with as chief of field training.[11]

Haney briefed Aderholt on his new duties, explaining that he would be responsible primarily for establishing and running a clandestine air training program at Camp Perry, a secret CIA training base dubbed the Farm, located on the outskirts of Williamsburg, Virginia. Among agency standouts Haney introduced that morning was Chick Barquin, a man Aderholt described as "one of the most dedicated, energetic, smartest, and experienced case officers in the business." Barquin was a balloon expert who had earned his credentials with a highly secret project "floating balloons across Russia." "I learned a lot from Chick Barquin," he said. "We worked together many times through the years."[12]

Another member of the Haney air section was Pop Milligan, an NCO who had served with OSS light air operations in Burma during World War II and who worked with Barquin in the CIA's balloon program. "Pop was a grand old guy," Aderholt said. "He was a great logistics and maintenance man, but a little short on the experience end of flying." An amusing incident that occurred before Aderholt's arrival made his point: "Pop had lifted off from the Kellogg Plant in Michigan on a balloon cross-country test run when he misread the altimeter and ascended to five hundred feet, instead of five thousand feet. He had taken off after dark, and was unaware that he was too low until the gondola hung up on a telephone line. Unable to get loose at that hour of the night, he let himself down on a lift line, found a barn, and went to sleep. Shortly after dawn, he was rudely awakened by farmers with pitchforks who ignored his protestations and moved him off to the pokey. They thought he was a Russian spy."[13]

Haney also kept the promise he had made to support Aderholt in recruiting the top covert operations people he had worked with in Korea. At Aderholt's urging the agency persuaded the Army to issue orders for Captain Bob Brewer to report to the newly created air training branch at the Farm after graduating from the Armored School at Fort Knox, Kentucky, in the spring of 1952. The Army was reluctant to let Brewer go. Besides his outstanding record with Eighth Army intelligence in Korea, Brewer was an experienced combat paratrooper who had evaded the Germans and returned to friendly lines after being severely wounded in World War II. He had the attributes the Army needed and was in an elite class with two famous military sons, Captains John Eisenhower and George S. Patton IV, at the Armored School.[14]

Three top pilots (Captains John McDonald, Louis Droste, and Jack Nabors) in Aderholt's detachment in Korea joined the team at the Farm when their combat tours were up. These were "super pilots" who had volunteered "to stay the whole year in Korea in combat" instead of spending thirty days TDY from their unit in Japan like other pilots. "All flew more than one hundred night drops at low level over some of the most rugged terrain in the world," Aderholt said. They did not hesitate when he asked them to join him at the Farm. Although leadership came naturally to Aderholt, war taught him that good leaders are made by good troops and not the other way around. "Get the best people, demand the best from them, and do the best for them" was a sermon he preached throughout his military career.[15]

Aderholt and the men he brought to the Farm were readily accepted by their CIA counterparts, and readily assimilated into the agency's unique culture of high risk and low visibility. Dispensing with formality, Aderholt was soon known throughout the agency by his irrepressible nickname, Heinie. When talking about his first assignment with the CIA, he rarely transitioned to life at the Farm until the story of his off-duty adventure with Red Jones, pool shark extraordinaire, was told. Admitting that he might have embellished the story over time, Aderholt relished telling it and swore it really happened. Red, who passed away in December 1997 at age eighty-three, confirmed the story through the years.

Red Jones and the Soldier Boy

As he remembered the episode, one morning while still awaiting his CIA security clearance, Major Aderholt received a call from Red Jones asking him to get together after work, and to bring two hundred dollars with him. When they met that afternoon, Jones explained that an Army sergeant who was a Korean War veteran and now worked in the Pentagon had been cheated out of two hundred dollars by "a bunch of rednecks" in a pool hall out at Seven Corners, Virginia, which was little more than a country crossroads outside Washington in those days. The pool hall was a converted garage. Local hustlers had conned the young sergeant into a game of pool and took all his money. He told Red Jones what had happened, and Red said he would get his money back with interest. "Of course, I would finance Red with the last two hundred bucks I had to my name," Aderholt said with a laugh.[16]

After dark the two friends drove to Seven Corners and parked down the highway from the pool hall. Wearing his uniform, Major Aderholt entered the establishment first according to plan, showing no sign of recognition when Jones came in later. "Red told me beforehand that he planned to have me hold the bets," Aderholt said. "And when he gave me the high sign, I was to amble out of the establishment, then run like hell and wait for him at the car." When

Red walked in, he was wearing a Texaco service uniform and cap, with a chew of Beechnut tobacco in one cheek. After being coaxed into playing for small wagers, Red began "flashing a large bankroll of ones with a hundred-dollar bill on top," saying that he had "sold this service station in Alabama and was en route to New York to have a fling."[17]

"The pool hustlers were sure they had a pigeon," Aderholt said. "Red was shooting left-handed and looked like a pushover. Despite the handicap, they managed to let him win a few bets, and then told him they wanted to play for big money." Red pretended to resist larger stakes, while continuing "to flash his roll and crow that he was headed for the bright lights of New York, insisting that he couldn't hang around." He finally agreed to a no-limit, winner-take-all game with the local billiard artist who had taken the sergeant's money. A large crowd of onlookers had gathered, hoping to get part of the action. Red covered all the bets he could, and the money was stuffed into a bystander's hat. When asked whom he wanted to hold the money, Red said he knew no one there, then looked around and pointed to Aderholt. "Give it to that soldier boy over there," he said. "He looks like he can take care of it."[18]

They were playing rotational pool. Red's opponent asked him who should break. Red told him to go ahead and break because he wouldn't get another shot. There was an audible buzz among the bystanders in response to Red's comment, but the local champion just smirked. He broke and ran the first three balls, then missed the fourth. With a thin smile Red leaned over the table with the cue in his left hand, then flipped it to his right hand and centered on his little finger. A wizened bystander who appeared to be in his eighties yelled, "Look, he's a slicker!" Red turned, looked him in the eye, and said, "You're damned right." He turned back and slammed the four ball into the corner pocket. "When he sank the eight ball, that was my cue to slip out with the money, nearly five hundred bucks, and hightail it back to the car," Aderholt said.[19]

When Red failed to show after about ten minutes, Aderholt located a telephone and called the police. As he feared, the local toughs had jumped Red after he ran the table and tried to leave. A squad car finally arrived in response to Aderholt's call and rescued Red from the angry crowd. "Those crooks had already given Red a bad beating," Aderholt said, "but the cops probably saved him from a lynching." In the excitement of having to rescue Red and get back to friendly surroundings, he forgot to retrieve his two hundred dollars from the kitty. "The next day Red gave the GI the whole wad of over four hundred dollars, including my money," Aderholt said, laughing. "That's my buddy, Red. We stayed so long in their apartment, I used to rib him about the funny way he had of collecting rent." He said events of that night convinced him life might be healthier down on the Farm.[20]

Ploughing Air Tactics Down on the Farm

Life at the Farm was the opposite of bureaucratic Washington. Aderholt could not abide administrative red tape, so there was none in the air training program he developed and ran at Camp Perry. In November 1951 he and Jessie drove down to Williamsburg and rented a small house near the camp. A few months later they moved into base quarters. "Williamsburg is a beautiful place and the people were great," he said, "but we were so isolated, so preoccupied in our work, that we didn't mix a lot with the local community." Upon arrival he immediately set about building the air training program—"getting our runways completed, our jump towers up, our training aids, and our faculty in place." He acquired a C-47 to conduct air training and obtained surplus aircraft to serve as sabotage training aids. Soon after his arrival, he was joined by Droste, McDonald, and Nabors, with Brewer reporting in the spring from Fort Knox.[21]

The three Air Force officers not only were "great pilots," but were experts in the tactics and techniques of special air operations, such as penetrating hostile airspace at night, maneuvering low over unfamiliar terrain to evade radar and visual sighting. Brewer, who was not a pilot, was well versed in all aspects of clandestine operations and, according to Aderholt, was "the dynamo behind our training efforts at the Farm." "We were training CIA agents, not pilots," he explained. Through a vigorous recruitment program on the nation's top college campuses, the CIA (as part of the Truman administration's Cold War policy to contain Communist aggression) had begun rebuilding its depleted wartime force of skilled operatives. The secret training activities at Camp Perry were an integral part of this effort.[22]

Training new CIA case officers for their future roles in clandestine air operations was just part of the curriculum at Camp Perry. "The agency put these men through a brutal academic and physical fitness program," Aderholt said. "The initial class completed airborne training at Fort Benning before coming to us." Relatively small, the classes consisted of twenty-five to thirty case officer trainees. Aderholt and his instructors taught the trainees those air aspects of covert operations that were required to make them successful case officers in any part of the world. "They had to learn basic things such as understanding aircraft capabilities, selecting landing zones, lighting up the drop zones, jumping behind enemy lines, communicating, and receiving their supplies," he explained.[23]

Field training was the acid test for students at the Farm. Each case officer trainee planned and carried out a realistic exercise covering every phase of covert air infiltration and resupply activity. The exercise required that trainees navigate some three hundred miles through the mountains of Virginia, West Virginia, and North Carolina. They packed resupply bundles and dropped them over predetermined targets to reception teams on the ground. "It was a fantastic training operation," Aderholt said, "and it would be repeated many times in actual combat." The trainees were put through a variety of other realistic combat situations such as border crossings, survival training, and so on. Emphasizing the toughness of the training, Aderholt noted that one student suffered a broken back and was paralyzed for life. Another was seriously wounded when accidently shot point-blank by an M-1 rifle loaded with blank ammunition.[24]

"The upshot was that our graduates were ready for the full range of covert missions and the perils awaiting them when they reported overseas," Aderholt said. He reemphasized the "high caliber and dedication" of most graduates, adding that the school "put through all the guys" he would work with later in the Vietnam conflict. The initial class included Pat Landry, Tony Poe, Jack Shirley, and Tom Fosmire, who all became deeply involved in CIA operations in Laos. Richard Fecteau and John Downey, who were also in the first class at the Farm, were shot down over China shortly after they graduated from the school in 1952. At one point the agency ran a modified course at the Farm for King Hussein of Jordan to prepare for potential air-supported guerrilla activities should his nation be overrun. Some classes were so sensitive, Aderholt noted, that the agency did not tell the instructors whom they were training.[25]

When not training agents, Aderholt and his instructors were busy developing and refining tactics, equipment, and techniques for use in clandestine air operations. While experimenting with the recovery of agents and downed pilots, he met and established a lifelong friendship with Robert Fulton, great grandson and namesake of the famous inventor of the steamship. A successful inventor in his own right, the younger Fulton was under contract with the CIA to develop an aerial recovery system that could be used to retrieve agents. Called the "Skyhook," Fulton's system was used by the CIA and the top-secret Studies and Operations Group during the Vietnam War years. Aderholt described Robert Fulton as one of the most memorable people he had ever met, "a fantastic individual" who made "a lasting, great impression" on his life.[26]

The airmen at the Farm also conducted special exercises along the East Coast to evaluate Air Defense Command's warning capabilities against low penetrating aircraft at night or in bad weather. Using low-level tactics that the detachment had perfected in Korea, the airmen proved they could penetrate the nation's elaborate air defense system "with all its sophisticated equipment" without being detected. Aderholt recalled that the preplanned route for the "hostile" aircraft was from Kitty Hawk, North Carolina, over Norfolk,Virginia, up the Potomac to the primary target, the White House. Then the planes flew simulated attacks against nearby Andrews AFB, against steel mills in Pennsylvania, against research facilities in New York, and against Boston Harbor, Cape Cod, and Mitchel Field, New York. The planes landed at Mitchel Field after five grueling hours in the air undetected by radar.[27]

Aderholt and his crews also demonstrated that by flying low at night with lights out they could breach Strategic Air Command's defenses without warning. General LeMay had personally asked for the mission to assist in identifying and plugging any holes in SAC's defense systems. Brewer, who was flying with Aderholt and Droste on one of the ADC exercises, recalled that mission controllers became so frustrated at one point, they asked the pilot "to come up to altitude so their fighters could make a practice run against us." Even then the intruders were able to elude attacking fighter aircraft. "We came up to between five thousand to ten thousand feet, and the fighters came in on us," Brewer said. "Droste was flying about 130 knots, and every time that fighter came toward us, Droste throttled back to 80 knots and made a sharp turn. The fighters couldn't make an effective run on us."[28]

Aderholt recalled the panic Brewer and Droste had caused on another occasion when they simulated a Soviet air attack over the plane's intercom system. Colonel Haney had come up to New York to fly the aircraft back to the Farm after one of these exercise missions. "I was working the radio in the cockpit when Brewer and Droste, who were directly behind us in the plane's radio room, came on the air identifying themselves as the New York Control Center and declaring a Red alert," Aderholt said. "They announced that atomic attacks were being carried out against New York, Philadelphia, and Washington, and instructed all aircraft to maintain radio silence and land at the nearest airfield."[29]

Colonel Haney made a high-speed descent and was on final approach to Baltimore Friendship Airport when Aderholt told him there was no Soviet attack, that it was a hoax carried out directly behind him by Brewer and Droste. "At first he didn't believe me and continued the approach," Aderholt recalled. "When he finally realized he'd been had, he was furious. Of course, I don't blame him, but it was a moment of fun and relief after a very wearying operational test."[30] He emphasized how fortunate the training branch had been to have someone of Haney's experience and supportiveness in the Washington office. Unfortunately, Haney left the agency about a year after Aderholt established the air training program at the Farm, and was replaced by a staff officer "who had absolutely no experience in special air operations." Aderholt explained that the replacement was "a nice enough guy," but having never "been particularly fond of professional staff officers," he could see they were on a natural collision course. Aderholt's drive and enthusiasm were already cramped from eighteen months of training routine, but a clash with his headquarters counterpart over special effects at a demonstration for Washington dignitaries might have spurred his efforts to leave the Farm in the spring of 1953.[31]

He and Brewer had put together a demonstration of clandestine air capabilities for the new CIA director, Allen W. Dulles, and other high-level Washington officials. Dulles became the first civilian head of the CIA (replacing General Walter Bedell Smith) soon after President Dwight D. Eisenhower's inauguration in January 1953. Colonel Haney's replacement in the air section agreed to host the demonstration and to narrate the schedule of events for the spectators. The Farm had provided a script beforehand for the air section's review. The scenario for the event was a simulated infiltration mission, opening with a low-level airdrop of four agents who would land and set up receiving parties for subsequent resupply drops. Unknown to the narrator, however, Aderholt and Brewer had devised special effects for the occasion that were not in the script.[32]

"We should jerk their chain to get their attention," Aderholt told Brewer in the days before the demonstration. Together they worked out a scheme to substitute a "rope-head dummy" with a defective parachute for one of the four agents to be dropped. The parachute was rigged to fail, and when it streamed, a small explosive charge opened the reserve chute, which also failed. When the dignitaries were all seated, the narrator started reading the script, and a black C-47 stripped of all markings began its approach over the drop zone directly in front of the stands. When the plane arrived over the target, the narrator began counting as the agents descended. "One . . . two . . . three . . . oh my God," he shouted when the fourth parachute failed to open and the dummy agent plummeted to the ground before the stunned spectators. With sirens wailing, an ambulance sped to the scene and two medics jumped out, threw the dummy onto a stretcher and into the ambulance, and off they roared.[33]

"It was goddamn terrifying," Aderholt recalled with a roar of laughter. "The stands were in shock until they realized it was only a dummy." The narrator was "visibly shaken" but regained his composure as the demonstration continued without further interruption. "Allen Dulles thought it was great after he got over the scare," Aderholt said. He gained a lot of respect for Dulles and got to know the director better during a second tour with the agency. For the time being, however, he had made up his mind to seek a more challenging assignment, and his days at the Farm were numbered.[34]

Once in Training, Always in Training

Aderholt left the Farm in June 1953, a month before the shooting stopped in Korea. Earlier, he had gone to CIA headquarters to see the head of training, Colonel Matthew Baird, about transferring to an operations assignment within the agency. Aderholt respected Baird, whom he described as "a real gentleman" and "a true CIA friend." Baird denied the request for a transfer, however, on the grounds that air training had become vital to the agency's operations and Aderholt was needed at the Farm to supervise the program he had established.[35]

Aderholt explained that he had "the best damn people in the business" doing the training at the Farm, that the school was up and running, and that nothing was left there for him to do. "Hell, the training practically runs itself," he said. "I need to be out in the real world with the people we've been training, somewhere running operations in the field." "Look, son. Once in training, always in training," Baird replied, protectively. "You might as well get used to the fact that you are in this training business through your whole career. We are not releasing anybody to the operations Mafia."[36]

"Well, if that's the way things are, it's time to be moving on," Aderholt mumbled as he left Baird's office. He felt "perfectly at home" working with the agency and had been given a free hand at the Farm in developing tactics, techniques, and equipment for clandestine air operations. "But damned if I was going to make a career out of training," he said. "I figured I might as well be in a troop carrier outfit." He also thought that "maybe some day the Air Force would wake up and fully support its special operations."[37]

Reluctantly, he called and talked the situation over with Colonel Childre, who had returned in February from Far East Air Forces to become the deputy chief of staff for operations at Eighteenth Air Force, Donaldson AFB, South Carolina. "Colonel Childre was one of the finest officers I've ever known," Aderholt said. "He did not think I should leave but was glad to get me back if that was what I wanted." After their conversation Childre arranged for his immediate transfer to operations at Eighteenth Air Force headquarters. He was elated to be going back to work for Colonel Childre but had misgivings about the future status of Air Force special operations. Although his heart bet on "the long shot" that special operations would win greater acceptance within the Air Force, his head warned of the infinite odds that were against him and that would dog his career every step of the way. "Those odds sure made the going tough at times," he said. "It sometimes seemed like we were standing way too close to the prop wash, pissing against the wind."[38]

3. COLD WAR RITUALS

W hen Major Aderholt left the CIA and went to Eighteenth Air Force in 1953, a reappraisal of national military strategy was under way in Washington that did not bode well for his Air Force career or for the advocacy of special air warfare. After using the threat of nuclear strikes to end hostilities in Korea that summer, President Eisenhower ordered the Joint Chiefs of Staff to take a "new look at military capabilities in light of global commitments." The strategic thinking behind the new look at force objectives crystallized the following January when Secretary of State John Foster Dulles warned that U.S. forces would respond to Communist aggression with "massive retaliation" by nuclear arms. This transition in strategy was a turning point in Cold War history that primed the Pentagon for a shake-up in the force structure and a sharp refocusing of fiscal priorities in favor of nuclear deterrence. Heavy cuts in conventional and special warfare capabilities were a foregone conclusion.

A contemporaneous National Security Council policy statement approved by the president proposed to halt Communist expansion by arming and training allied nations under the military assistance program (MAP) to deal with insurgencies and to fight their own brushfire wars, while the United States unfurled a global nuclear umbrella to deter wider aggression. The president punctuated this policy with his decision not to intervene militarily in Indochina in the spring of 1954 when Ho Chi Minh's guerrilla army defeated the French at Dienbienphu. Ironically, the ensuing Geneva agreements partitioning Vietnam and granting Laos and Cambodia their independence would draw U.S. forces a decade later into a protracted low-intensity war they were unprepared to fight.[1]

The force structure implications of massive retaliation and questions about the dominant role of strategic air power overshadowed Senate confirmation hearings in June on Eisenhower's nominees to head the Joint Chiefs of Staff and to lead the Army, the Navy, and the Air Force. During Ike's first term, the new USAF chief of staff, General Nàthan F. Twining, presided over an emergent nuclear air posture developed around Strategic Air Command's atomic strike capabilities. The nuclear deterrence mission was centered in SAC's growing fleet of B-52 bombers after they entered the inventory in 1955, evolving by decade's end into a strategic triad of manned bombers, land-based ballistic missiles, and the Navy's nuclear-capable submarines.[2]

As the fist for flexing America's nuclear muscle, SAC was in its heyday during Eisenhower's two terms in the White House. The Air Force got the lion's share of the defense budget—earmarked mainly for SAC and nuclear weapons research and development—while the other services vied for larger strategic roles and appropriations. In the scramble for dwindling defense dollars, the Pentagon became a hotbed of interservice rivalry. The Army fought a losing battle to maintain a strong conventional presence overseas to deter small wars and to meet limited aggression with nonnuclear force if necessary. Ground commanders were not alone in their struggle because a large number of seasoned airmen, Major Aderholt included, agreed with repeated warnings in the mid-1950s by the top tactical air commander, General Otto P. Weyland, that nuclear deterrence made small wars more likely and the USAF should be prepared to fight them with weapons other than nuclear bombs. These warriors would be proved right in the long run, but meanwhile the Air Force neglected all but nuclear roles and missions, and in so doing created a void in tactical air support that the Army was only too willing to try to fill.[3]

In this "time of nuclear plenty," the Air Force deprived a whole generation of airmen of much-needed experience and growth in other than the strategic applications of air warfare—a neglect for which combat forces would pay dearly a decade later in Vietnam. Although all nonstrategic forces were slighted (that is, underfunded, undermanned, undertrained, and underpromoted) to some degree during this period, the unconventional and special air warfare elements were all but wiped out. Capabilities in the field, including the ARC wings, were stripped to their bare threads, leaving only small clusters of airmen and planes supporting the CIA's clandestine operations against Communist insurgencies around the world. Unconventional warfare planning in air command headquarters at home and abroad was relegated to a desk at the back of the room. This was where Major Aderholt landed after leaving the CIA in 1953—

amid the frustrations of two successive headquarters assignments, Eighteenth
Air Force at Donaldson and United States Air Forces in Europe at Lindsey Air
Station in Wiesbaden, Germany.[4]

And Now He Was One

"For years I accused headquarters staff officers of being candy asses, and now
I was one," Aderholt remarked, referring to his voluntary reassignment to
Eighteenth Air Force. Adding to his frustration, the Eighteenth was strictly a
troop carrier operation, with no special missions like the ones he had commanded in Korea. Activated two years earlier under Tactical Air Command, the
Eighteenth flew troop carrier support for other Air Force commands and carried out joint operations with land and amphibious forces. Aderholt's job as an
operations staff officer dealt primarily with airborne tactics flown by the command's eight wings of C-119s and C-124s. He was also the readiness officer.
The headquarters routine was "ho-hum," but he was glad to be working for
Colonel Childre again and met new friends who made the assignment worthwhile. One of these was Lieutenant Colonel Otis E. Wynn, who had "tremendous background with the invasions and airborne operations in Europe" during
World War II and who later made general. "I learned a lot about the troop carrier business working with him," Aderholt said.[5]

His opinion of the Eighteenth's airborne expertise was less flattering, however. He soon found that tactical airlift did not enjoy a high priority in TAC because of the command's predominant fighter pilot orientation and its budding
subordinate role in nuclear deterrence. As a consequence, "troop carrier command had slipped a lot as far as airborne operations were concerned."[6] Flying
airborne support for the Army was only one of several missions laid on the
troop carrier wings and their dwindling resources. This and the fact that the
wings were poorly equipped and trained to perform airborne operations made
them easy targets for disgruntled Army field commanders who wanted their
own organic air support. Nagging roles and missions squabbles between the
Army and the Air Force during the Korean conflict had poisoned the working
relationship with airborne commanders, a problem that was exacerbated by ex-
cessive controls imposed upon troop carrier operations from above. At one
point the Eighteenth's irate commander, Major General Robert W. Douglass
Jr., complained that he was getting more help than was needed from TAC headquarters. "If TAC has enough people to run my job, they have too many,"
Douglas wrote to the commanding general, John K. Cannon, suggesting that

"ranking air force officers must be reoriented to the great historical fact that no headquarters ever won a war."[7]

A spate of incidents where C-119s or C-124s dropped paratroopers dangerously short of their designated drop zones supported Aderholt's view that airborne operations had "slipped" since his previous involvement in Korea. The Army threatened a board of inquiry, while the Eighteenth wrestled with the problem.[8] "There was a lot of finger pointing by both sides, and there was plenty of blame to go around," Aderholt recalled. "In the operations shop, we believed the crux of the problem involved the qualifications of pilots flying the lead aircraft in airborne formations." Aderholt discussed with Colonel Childre that during larger airborne exercises at Fort Bragg, he had made a note of wing commanders flying lead even though they had not flown airdrop missions regularly and their skills were not as sharp as they should have been. He urged that all pilots flying lead aircraft be required to take additional training to stay proficient in airborne operations.[9]

Matters came to a head in March 1954 when another mishap at Fort Bragg ended in tragedy. Two paratroopers were killed in the jump and many others were injured.[10] A C-119 stalled out, crash-landed, hit a deer, and exploded. Aderholt described the tragedy: "We had C-119s from six wings participating in a large-scale training maneuver. The 464th from Columbus, Georgia, was the lead formation, and the wing commander was flying lead. They arrived at the turning point early, and he slowed down to make up the time as he approached. When he cut the power, approximately 150 planes behind him started stacking up and stalling out. Strings of paratroopers made their jumps early and were cut up badly when they bailed out through the props of following aircraft. It was a real fiasco."[11]

In the aftermath of this tragedy, Aderholt told investigating officers that previous exercises had identified problems with wing commanders flying lead aircraft when they were not qualified to do so. Subsequent changes to the operations manual included a requirement that pilots had to meet stringent training criteria before they were allowed to fly lead. Putting an exclamation point on the tragedy, a few days later another C-119 lost an engine on takeoff and crashed into the mess hall at Fort Bragg. The plane exploded, killing the crew and demolishing the mess hall. Fortunately, the crash occurred after the last call for breakfast, when the building was empty.[12]

Frustrated by the Eighteenth's poor record of airborne support and anxious to get back into special operations, Aderholt asked to leave after only eighteen months at Donaldson. He might have stayed had Colonel Childre not left in

Helio Courier on civic action visit to a remote Thai village without landing field.

August 1954 to command the 463d Troop Carrier Wing based at Ardmore, Oklahoma. Childre had been in charge of operations in the Eighteenth since early 1953, having reported to the headquarters upon returning from the Far East. He was promoted to brigadier general two months after moving to Ardmore. Childre asked Aderholt to go with him as the operations officer, but he declined. "I didn't want to be an imposition, although I wanted badly to leave the Eighteenth. I was spinning my wheels there," he explained. "A USAFE unconventional warfare vacancy came open at Lindsey Air Force Station in Wiesbaden, Germany, and Colonel Childre helped me get the job." Although the tour at Donaldson had its drawbacks, he emphasized that the experience was more useful to him than "any military service school." He and Jessie made the move to Germany in October 1954.[13]

Stacking BBs in a Garden of Nukes

Most officers considered USAFE a plum assignment, but the tour was not the challenge Aderholt had expected. "It was a miserable goddamned assignment," he said. "The only thing good coming out of it was that Jessie and I adopted our two children, Janet and George, while we were in Germany." When asked about the career-broadening aspects of the assignment, he shrugged off his three years in the headquarters, saying, "Working in USAFE during that period added nothing to my understanding of special air warfare or any other kind of warfare. The only weapons that counted were nukes. The rest of us might as well have been stacking BBs."[14]

Although USAFE was the front line of NATO air power, its weapons alone were no match for the Soviet bloc air forces. The command flew an array of combat aircraft (including first-generation jet fighters and light bombers, and a gaggle of support planes), but the forces at center stage were those standing nuclear alert. The first B-45s and F-84s modified to carry atomic weapons had entered the USAFE inventory in 1952. Four years later the arrival of F-100Cs, the first of the century-series aircraft, modernized the command's tactical nuclear capabilities. Back home, TAC had organized its atomic-capable composite air strike forces to deal with regional hostilities overseas. The real forward nuclear punch supporting NATO Europe at that time, however, was provided by the rotational strike forces that SAC had deployed to bases in the United Kingdom and North Africa since the early days of the Korean War. The SAC posture in Europe grew by 1957 to include newly constructed bases in Spain.[15]

Aderholt recalled that fighter pilots were dumbfounded when the Air Force appointed Lieutenant General William H. Tunner to command USAFE in 1953 and were even more surprised that he stayed in the job through the years of the nuclear buildup into the summer of 1957. Having an airlift general's hands on the controls implied that the airlift mission was king, and it kept USAFE planners on their toes anticipating another Berlin crisis. "The fighter jocks were shell-shocked," Aderholt said. "Never in their wildest dreams had they imagined working for a 'trash hauler,' not even a big-shot airlifter like Tunner."[16]

When Tunner commanded airlift in the Korean War, he had shown little interest in the clandestine missions flown by Aderholt's detachment, and there was a similar lack of interest while he was the USAFE commander in chief. "He didn't know a damned thing about fighting a war," Aderholt said. "He only knew how to load up transports and fly them from point A to point B." The Air Force had downgraded the Air Resupply and Communications wings to groups in 1953 and deactivated them three years later. The two groups that were based in Libya and the United Kingdom were supporting CIA operations but were assigned to USAFE. During Tunner's tenure in USAFE, the Air Force stripped the groups of their transport aircraft, returning them to regular airlift operations. After the groups were deactivated in 1956, a special troop carrier squadron, the 42nd, flew some clandestine missions from the United Kingdom before it too was deactivated in 1957. The Cold War's special air operations in Europe died with the 42nd's deactivation.[17]

During his first year in USAFE, Aderholt served as an unconventional warfare officer in the special activities branch at Lindsey and represented USAFE on the Special Operations Task Force Europe (SOTFE), located in the former German Gestapo headquarters in Paris, just off the Champs Élysées. "It was a hectic year," he recalled. "Jessie and I lived out of a suitcase in a German hotel for six months until Air Force housing became available, and I was away in Paris much of the time." Unlike the covert operations in World War II and Korea, the focus of the special activities branch was on psychological warfare. "My boss was a good guy, but the only thing he knew about special ops was psywar," he said. "USAFE had no plans to penetrate the iron curtain to supply partisans or to infiltrate intelligence teams like the Carpetbaggers had done in World War II and we had done in Korea. All covert missions came under the CIA and the ARC wings."[18]

After a year with the special activities branch, he moved to the USAFE plans office when his unconventional warfare and SOTFE liaison responsibilities were assumed by plans during a headquarters reorganization. "They put me back in a corner," he stated. "Nobody knew anything about special air warfare, and nobody wanted to know anything about it." It was soon obvious that unconventional warfare plans were the least of his duties. One of his most demanding tasks was rewriting the massive Berlin airlift plan, which had not been touched since the airlift ended in 1949. "Updating that plan was the most tedious job I ever had," he recalled. "I never saw so many damned chapters and annexes. It put Ma Bell's yellow pages to shame. It was a helluva volume, but like most plans we never had to use it." The experience taught him that his time at Eighteenth Air Force had not been wasted, because he got a lot of "good training" in writing plans there. "I think every officer ought to have to write plans for at least one year," he said.[19]

"That plan was General Tunner's baby," he stated, but noted that the USAFE commander "had been a son of a bitch to deal with." Not once had Tunner shown any sign of recognizing Major Aderholt as one of his former combat commanders in Korea or having flown with him over the front lines. "He was only concerned with what you were doing for him today," Aderholt said, but hastened to add that "even working for a son of a bitch like Tunner had its moments."[20] A decade later he and Brigadier General Albert W. Schinz, chief of the Air Force's Advisory Group in Vietnam, would share a laugh over one of those moments.

Not long after Aderholt arrived in USAFE, Schinz had reported to the headquarters as the new director of operations and training. Word had preceded

Schinz—a gregarious fighter pilot commanding the 50th Fighter Bomber Group at Wheelus—that he had been dragooned into the director's job against his will. As the story went, General Tunner had visited Wheelus, where he dropped into the officers' club unannounced and overheard Schinz "holding forth at the bar about what a bunch of lousy bastards they had at USAFE headquarters . . . and how they didn't know their asses from a hole in the ground about the fighter business." Schinz felt a tap on his shoulder, turned around, and there stood General Tunner asking, "Who are you?" When he told Tunner his name, the general snapped, "Go pack your bags, Schinz. You've just been transferred to my headquarters," and he walked out.[21]

Another story that Aderholt relished telling involved his participation in a USAFE operational readiness inspection (ORI) of the 48th Fighter Bomber Wing at Chaumont Air Base in France. The wing commander was Colonel Albert P. Clark, a rising star in the Air Force who was on the brigadier general's list and slated to become the next chief of staff at USAFE headquarters. "My boss, Lieutenant Colonel Bob [Robert O.] Fricks, headed the inspection team. He said he wanted to really catch them with their skirts down," Aderholt recalled. "I was piloting the plane, a C-47, with the IG team on board, so I suggested we file for Paris, then report an engine out over Chaumont, make an emergency landing there, and surprise them with an early-morning ORI." Fricks agreed. Just outside Chaumont he cut an engine and called the tower for permission to make an emergency landing. The C-47 sputtered onto the runway to be met by screaming fire trucks, crash vehicles, and a nervous base operations officer. When they were on the ground, he started the engine, taxied across the runway, and parked. Fricks stepped down from the airplane and said, "This is an ORI," much to the consternation of the officer meeting them.[22]

"It was the biggest screw-up you've ever seen," Aderholt said. "We went to wing headquarters, and the officer of the day couldn't get the safe open to retrieve the emergency recall plan. It took three hours just to get all the people back on base. Everything was screwed up." As the morning wore on, however, after being briefed by his people and calling USAFE headquarters, the wing commander, Colonel Clark, told the inspection team he was canceling the ORI and ordered them off his base. The team got back on the C-47 and returned to Weisbaden. "I didn't get my ass chewed, although I came up with the ruse to surprise the wing," Aderholt said. "Bob Fricks caught hell from Tunner, though, and we never did anything like that again." Instead the headquarters devised a plan to notify units a few days before they were to have a "no-notice" inspection. "To me that was bullshit," he stated, adding an afterthought that the Chaumont fiasco had been worth it just to get to know A. P. Clark. "What a great guy he is," Aderholt said.[23]

Low on the Pecking Order, High on the Hit List

During the final months of his tour in USAFE, Aderholt took a hard look at career options and did not like what he saw. He was thirty-seven years old, had been a major for six years, and the prospects for promotion did not look good. His rating officer had recommended him for the Armed Forces Staff College following his USAFE tour, but he was not selected. Although still on flying status and proficient in several multiengine planes, he was not jet-qualified in an era when modern jet bombers and fighters, long-range missiles, and nuclear warheads ruled the Pentagon. In the aftermath of the Korean conflict, special operations had been left "to die on the vine" by Cold War doctrine preoccupied with nuclear deterrence and the arms race between the superpowers. "Everybody but SAC was taking hits, but unconventional warfare was at the bottom of the pecking order when it came to resources and promotions, and at the top of the hit list when it came to cuts," Aderholt said.[24]

After weighing the options, he chose the only door to special operations that remained open to him. With the help of a friend in the agency, Chick Barquin, and General Childre, who had become director of operations at HQ TAC, he managed a second assignment with the 1007th Air Intelligence Service Group in Washington, D.C., reporting to CIA headquarters in September 1957 as a special warfare staff officer. "We stayed with Red and Carrie again for a few days until we could get settled," he said, adding, "but only after Red swore not to slick me into the middle of another pool-hall shootout like the one at Seven Corners."[25]

The timing of the assignment was right, for a change. "Hell, if you wanted to fight Communists in those days, the CIA was the place to do it," he recalled.[26] Under Allen Dulles, younger brother of Secretary of State John Foster Dulles (architect of both the domino theory and massive retaliation), the CIA had become not only the last refuge for covert military operations, but the progenitor of shadow wars that stemmed the spread of Communism among emerging nations. As a former OSS officer in charge of clandestine operations in Europe during World War II, Allen Dulles had developed a special fondness for paramilitary activities. Covert operations by the CIA thrived under his direction.[27]

During the Dulles era the CIA aided counterinsurgency campaigns against Communist guerrillas in some countries, and sponsored guerrilla warfare against leftist governments in others. Successful intrigues included the ouster of a Communist prime minister in Iran in 1953, and the overthrow of a leftist government in Guatemala in 1954. When Aderholt rejoined the CIA in 1957, the Communists had stepped up their support for Third World insurgencies in Asia, Africa, and the American hemisphere. By 1960 the final year of Eisenhower's second term, low-intensity armed struggles were brewing the world over, the Geneva agreements were becoming unraveled in Southeast Asia, and Fidel Castro's pesky Red menace was camped on America's doorstep.[28]

The Pentagon, meanwhile, had experienced a backlash against putting all its warfare options into the nuclear basket. General Maxwell D. Taylor, who became the Army chief of staff in 1955, had led vigorous opposition to "the Eisenhower Administration's reliance on massive nuclear retaliation, arguing that there was a continuing need for strong ground forces capable of fighting a conventional war." In 1959, after his retirement, Taylor published *The Uncertain Trumpet,* a book forcibly making the case for a range of Army capabilities to respond to all levels of Communist aggression. Taylor argued primarily for stronger conventional ground forces, but his book greatly influenced President John F. Kennedy's broader strategic thinking when he took office in 1961 — helping to shape the new president's strategy of flexible response and a renaissance in unconventional warfare.[29]

The armed forces had learned in two different deployments in 1958 — during the Lebanon and Taiwan Strait crises — they were unprepared for the contingencies that were most likely to be thrust upon them. This was illustrated in Lebanon, a situation clearly calling for conventional arms, when the Army landed with Honest John missiles in lieu of artillery and the Air Force's fighter pilots were trained only in nuclear weapons delivery. Questions about when to use nuclear weapons also hounded tactical forces that were subsequently deployed to Taiwan. As evidenced by President Charles de Gaulle's refusal in 1959 to allow the storage of atomic weapons on French soil, the European allies were beginning to have second thoughts about a forward U.S. posture that made their countries a potential nuclear battleground.[30]

The Air Force still clung stubbornly to its dominant role in massive retaliation, however, even though the Army had built up a fourth air force (in addition to the Navy and Marines), was planning to develop an air cavalry of helicopters, and openly challenged the Air Force's ability to fulfill its responsibilities in close air support and airlift to ground forces. Adhering to traditional doctrine that "an airplane is an airplane is an airplane," the Air Force steadfastly refused to develop special aircraft for ground support, arguing that the century-series fighters designed to deliver tactical "nukes" were fully capable of supporting the Army in a conventional war. The USAF opposed building up its own special air warfare capabilities and only minimally supported the CIA's paramilitary operations, yet did not want the agency to develop its own unique support planes or to build an organic air force.[31]

In this highly charged environment, Aderholt's return to the CIA opened a new and exciting chapter in his career. He spent the next two years at CIA headquarters developing and testing special light aircraft for covert operations, formulating tactics and training requirements for aircrews flying secret missions, and developing plans for tactical air support of paramilitary actions such as the Bay of Pigs invasion carried out later. They were full, fast-paced, and productive years, leading in January 1960 to his appointment as commander of a secret Okinawa-based group that planned and directed covert air operations supporting friendly guerrilla activities throughout Asia.[32] An Air Force officer who was with him on Okinawa recalled that Aderholt had inherited a haphazardly run, lackadaisical outfit and turned it into a buzz saw. The officer marveled at the changes in unit pride, esprit de corps, and mission performance that took place under Aderholt's command, reaffirming it was a story that needs telling.[33]

4. SHADOW WARS AND THE TIBETAN AIRLIFT

eturning to the CIA in the fall of 1957 brought Major Aderholt back
into the heart of unconventional warfare. He reported to the same unit,
the 1007th Air Intelligence Service Group (renamed the 1040th USAF Field
Activity Squadron in 1959), that he belonged to when developing tactics and
training case officers at the Farm in Williamsburg. The new assignment was
more his style, however, because it directly involved him in the gamut of paramilitary plans and operations. The CIA responded to Aderholt's expertise in
special operations and gung ho approach to the mission by giving him far more
latitude and responsibility than he could have expected from an equivalent Air
Force assignment.[1]

While with the CIA in Washington, he worked in the Air Branch, the operations element overseeing all covert air activity for the agency. His tireless efforts there and his firsthand knowledge of covert operations soon came to the
attention of Allen Dulles and two of his trusted lieutenants, Richard M. Bissell
and Richard M. Helms. Bissell had been the director's special assistant since
1954 guiding such high-profile projects as the top secret U-2 reconnaissance
program, which became headline news when Gary Powers was shot down over
the Soviet Union in 1960. Dulles made Bissell the deputy director of plans in
1959, putting him in charge of all CIA covert operations. Richard Helms, who
was second to Bissell, replaced him in 1962 after the Bay of Pigs debacle.
Helms became the CIA director four years later.[2]

The agency's clandestine activities, nurtured by Dulles, had grown in size
and scope since Aderholt left in 1953 and were now the dominant CIA mission.
When Aderholt came back in 1957, the paramilitary headquarters was still

housed in an office building on Eighth Street in downtown Washington, but the agency had lobbied successfully for a single structure to house its myriad activities and was slated to move into a new facility at Langley, Virginia, starting in 1961.[3] Aderholt had already transferred to Okinawa but, being an avid sports fan, considered himself fortunate to have been in Washington for a couple of baseball seasons before the Senators franchise moved to Minneapolis–St. Paul in 1961 and became the Minnesota Twins.[4]

Forthright, Frugal, and Utterly Fearless

The important work Aderholt was doing for the CIA finally won a well-deserved promotion to lieutenant colonel in March 1961, after he had been back with the agency for over three years and running covert air operations out of Okinawa and Thailand. His strong ties to covert operations and the Air Force's lack of interest in unconventional warfare were obvious reasons why he was not promoted earlier. Tensions between the CIA and DOD during the mid-to-late 1950s had turned detached service with the agency's covert operations into a career killer for many military officers. That his major's leaves were frayed from ten long years of waiting eclipsed any illusions Aderholt might have had about his promotion potential in the Air Force. He later stated that he "would never have gotten promoted without the war in Vietnam."[5] He never let up, however, for "the long dry spell" had not blunted his enthusiasm, tireless energy, or unabashed patriotism.

The fact that he had not attended college or equivalent military school had been another liability during the technocratic fifties. Since the cease-fire in Korea, the pursuit of higher education and so-called "square-filling" (or, in barracks language, "looking good in the shower") increasingly competed with mission performance as criteria for promotions. Major Aderholt followed a different track by becoming a "self-made" warrior. He threw himself totally into the mission, "working hard and playing hard," while engaging consistently in self-study and self-improvement. He read profusely, broadening his depth of knowledge in the fields of contemporary military history and unconventional warfare.

A senior officer's endorsement to his USAFE effectiveness report (OER) stated that Major Aderholt would make "an excellent squadron commander" in troop carrier operations.[6] He wanted a command assignment, but even if he was assured of one, the Air Force had no unconventional warfare units at the time, and he was not interested in a routine airlift job. In any event, he was back in his element working with the CIA's paramilitary operations, an arena where he identified with every aspect of the mission and believed he could best make a difference in fighting Communist aggression. Good friends such as Chick Barquin in the Air Branch and Bob Brewer and the "old gang" at the Farm made the tour even more rewarding.[7]

His OERs at Eighteenth Air Force and USAFE described Major Aderholt as an "extremely likable" officer who was practical, resourceful, and committed to the mission. The reports stated that he was "strong-minded," "extremely frank," and "intensely devoted to duty"—traits sometimes precluding "diplomacy" on his part. They portrayed a man who had "strong courage in his convictions" and invariably got results.[8] What the OERs do not reveal, but those who knew him best have stated, is that he was a charismatic military leader who had "great bureaucratic courage," "a huge, compassionate heart," and "a knack for cutting through the bureaucratic red tape to get the job done"—attributes that a fellow officer believed were "rare, almost nonexistent, in contemporary military society." "Heinie truly cared about people, especially if they were the underdog, and he was always sensitive to their needs," the officer said. "Throughout his career, he badgered his superiors for his causes, more often for his people." That is why he was known warmly as Heinie by warriors of all ranks throughout the Air Force and the CIA.[9]

Another officer who fought "the desk wars" with him in USAFE headquarters recalled that Aderholt was out of his element amid the "mounds of paperwork and paper clips." Having flown with the 1st Air Commando Group against the Japanese in Burma during World War II, the officer compared Aderholt to the group commander, Lieutenant Colonel Philip G. Cochran, the renowned model for one of Milton Caniff's comic-strip characters in "Terry and the Pirates." He said, "Phil Cochran, like Heinie, didn't give a damn about paperwork. Just get the aircraft in the air and get the job done."[10]

Those who worked closely with Aderholt also knew that he was "extraordinarily frugal with government resources," another rare commodity during the years when high technology and costly arms development ruled national defense. He was "utterly frank and frugal" in combating government wastefulness.[11] Because of the hardships he faced while growing up during the Great Depression, he knew the value of a dollar. His mother had not remarried when his father died in a train crash in 1929. She took in washing to raise her seven children. "I worked all my life," he said. "My family has always worked." He recalled earning five dollars a week in his first job. "There was never enough change left to burn a hole in your pocket," he said, laughing.[12] His frugality and his advocacy of low-cost, specially designed aircraft for covert operations were what sparked his enthusiasm for developing and procuring the "helioplane" (helio, for short) for CIA infiltration missions and as a light utility aircraft to support paramilitary activities in rugged, undeveloped areas of the world.

Helioplane: Flying the Light Fantastic

When Richard Bissell became head of the CIA's covert operations in 1959, he took a personal interest in Aderholt's career, urging that he be promoted ahead of his contemporaries. Aderholt was occupying a lieutenant colonel's position at the time. Bissell stated that he was an outstanding officer who had "handled and accomplished projects on his own," which normally required the work of a whole team of officers.[13] For the remainder of his tour with the CIA, Aderholt's evaluations were endorsed by either Bissell or Helms. One of the key projects that impressed the agency's top people was his work on the helioplane.

He had become interested in the helioplane during his previous tour with the agency and pursued the project more vigorously when he returned in 1957. The CIA was looking for ways to exfiltrate downed aircrews from hostile territory, and he had tested a variety of aircraft, including an inflatable rubber plane, for that mission. The agency also needed special aircraft to support partisans operating in remote areas. Aderholt realized that a more substantial aircraft with short-takeoff-and-landing capabilities was required. He had read about the helioplane, a light utility aircraft developed by Lynn L. Bollinger and Otto Kaplan at the Massachusetts Institute of Technology in the early 1940s, and arranged with Larry Montgomery (a missionary who had flown the plane off dirt strips in Ecuador) for a demonstration at Baltimore Friendship Airport. After an orientation ride Aderholt flew the helio and was convinced that, with some upgrades, he had found the solution to the CIA's unique air support requirements.[14]

Lynn Bollinger recalled that Aderholt "fought for the helioplane like a regiment of soldiers."[15] After briefing Allen Dulles on how the craft's special capabilities could support the agency's field operations, Aderholt offered the director a demonstration flight. Dulles accepted. Aderholt met the director at Washington National Airport and flew him in a borrowed helioplane to the Farm at Williamsburg. Familiar with the farmland between Washington and Williamsburg, he made three touch-and-go landings in pastures along the route to demonstrate how the helioplane's performance characteristics could support the CIA mission. "When it was lightly configured, you could land the helio in about 50 feet and take off in about 150 feet," he said, recalling that "Dulles really thought that was something." He added: "That was one time I had the director alone for an hour, so I pounded his ear about all the uses I thought we could put the light-plane concept to in the overseas areas, and why the helio was right for the job." Dulles authorized the purchase on the spot and subsequently approved funding for developing and procuring a turboprop helio and a twin-engine helio.[16]

The agency's initial purchase of five single-engine helios made Aderholt a one-man air force until he could get other pilots trained. He was the only officer in the Air Branch who could fly the plane. The craft was named the Helio Courier. The military version was designated the L-28. A few years later, in early 1962, the Air Force purchased similar aircraft (designated the U-10) for test and evaluation in Vietnam by air commandos deployed from Eglin AFB, Florida. The Helio Aircraft Corporation of Norwood, Massachusetts, modified the CIA planes according to Aderholt's specifications, including installing a more powerful engine, a three-bladed propeller, and greater fuel capacity for longer range. "I put enough tanks in there so we could go twenty-two hundred miles without refueling," he said. On one occasion he flew a helio around the country for twenty-two hours without having to refuel, "just to see how far the thing would go." Another time the Air Force transported a dismantled helio to Europe in a C-124, reassembled it at Wiesbaden Air Base, Germany, where a Polish pilot flew north to an island in the Baltic Sea and penetrated the Lithuanian coast, flying low at night, without being detected. Aderholt concluded from earlier experiments when he was at the Farm that he could penetrate Soviet airspace.[17]

When he procured the helio, Aderholt was involved with an agency project to insert telemetric devices in eastern Europe for monitoring air activity at three strategic Soviet bases. He trained Polish pilots to fly the helio at night without lights so they could penetrate Murmansk and other Soviet locales from Norway to insert the listening devices. The Polish pilots became proficient in the helio by making cross-country practice flights at night, while Aderholt "rested his eyes" lying in the back of the plane on an old rubber mattress. Because the missions to plant the telemetric devices required that pilots go in over water and set down off the Soviet coast, he arranged for the helio to be fitted with floats by the Edo Float Company of New York. A trip that he, Chick Barquin, and a crew chief made to New York to have floats put on the helio nearly got them thrown in a New York jail.[18]

Aderholt had landed the helio at the Flushing, New York, airport intending to disassemble the aircraft and truck it to the Edo Company on Long Island Sound. After going to the Edo compound and finding a cinder-covered yard that was 125 feet wide and clear of obstructions, he decided to save time by flying the helio there instead of sending it by truck. They downloaded the aircraft of all excess equipment, put ten gallons of gas in each wing tank, and, with Barquin standing at the approach end of the compound, Aderholt flew a STOL approach and dropped the aircraft into the yard, using less than the 125 feet and coming to a stop in the cinders. They were in the office with Edo's chief engineer, Si Flynn, congratulating each other when an angry policeman from the New York Port Authority walked in and placed them under arrest for landing in a populated area without prior approval. Aderholt used his one phone call to reach the CIA contact in the Pentagon. A few minutes later the head of the port authority called and told the policeman to forget the incident.[19]

"The aircraft was converted to floats and flown out the next day," Aderholt recalled, "but not without problems." They had reloaded their equipment on the helio for a trip on to northern Maine where the Polish pilots were to be trained, but he had never flown with floats before and could not get the plane airborne. After several takeoff attempts failed, the crew chief recalled from earlier in his career that you had to put seaplanes on a step or they would not take off. This was accomplished by applying full power and pushing the stick forward to raise the aft portion of the float out of the water. Because of the delays, they arrived over Millinocket Lake, Maine, after dark. "We made a poor landing on the lake because we had no landing lights," Aderholt said, "but we survived to fly another day."[20]

He shipped one of the helios to Okinawa for use in Laos, but contract pilots with Civil Air Transport (renamed Air America in 1959) who were being checked out in the helio kept cracking it up. "CAT had these great transport pilots . . . old Asian hands who had flown supplies into the doomed French garrison at Dienbienphu," Aderholt said. "They didn't want to fly the helio." He learned later that pilots preferred not to fly single-engine planes over Laos because they had no survival kits or search and rescue capabilities at that time. He was able to resolve this problem while he was running CIA air operations out of Okinawa and Thailand.[21]

In addition to working with the helio, Aderholt along with other pilots had tested a variety of special aircraft for the agency and experimented with ways to extend the range of aircraft. They succeeded in extending the range of the L-20, a light plane that the CIA had used to drop agents in the 1950s, by towing it with a B-26. "A full feathering prop was installed on the L-20 and hooked onto a B-26 in the air," he explained. "Lou Droste feathered the engine, and the B-26 towed the L-20 for three to four hundred miles before it dropped off and went on about its business." A similar experiment was carried out using a balloon to tow an L-19 from Duke Field, Alabama, to North Carolina, where the plane dropped off and landed using little fuel.[22]

In 1958 Aderholt renewed his friendship with Bob Fulton, who had put the finishing touches to the Skyhook aerial retrieval system and was preparing for live tests with naval aircraft. Fulton's contacts with the CIA (where Aderholt met and worked with him at the Farm) in the early 1950s had resulted in a development contract. The CIA, envisioning the system as a replacement for the antiquated All American system that was rushed into service to rescue downed pilots in World War II, sponsored Fulton's work on the Skyhook. Aderholt recommended the Skyhook aerial retrieval system for use by the air commandos, and later with the Studies and Observations Group in Vietnam.[23]

In his work with the Air Branch in Washington, Aderholt participated in planning and organizing air support for paramilitary operations. His initiation came a few weeks after rejoining the CIA when the National Security Council ordered the agency to aid rebel Indonesian colonels plotting to overthrow President Achmed Sukarno, who "was moving away from democracy towards a personal dictatorship." The CIA armed the rebels, provided paramilitary assistance, and based a small force of unmarked warplanes at the rebel stronghold of Menado in the Northern Celebes. Making up this rebel air force was a handful of B-26 Invaders taken out of storage at Clark AB in the Philippines and flown by CAT civilian pilots. The colonels waited until President Sukarno was away on a visit to Japan in February 1958 to proclaim a rebel government and to launch their attack. The government forces on Java remained loyal to Sukarno, however, and staved off the attack—eventually defeating the outnumbered rebel army and strengthening Sukarno's hold on power.[24]

For several weeks before the CIA closed down operations at Menado in late May, the few marauding rebel warplanes ranged over the islands attacking government airfields and ports and disrupting commercial shipping. The State Department, walking a political tightrope over the Indonesian situation, became less enthusiastic about supporting the rebels when allied ships were bombed and strafed along with those sailing under Communist colors. The rebel air raids were carried out with impunity until the final mission on 18 May. Aderholt recalled that two B-26s had launched from Menado when an urgent call came in from the State Department "to call off the mission." The CIA tried desperately to have the planes recalled, but to no avail. The pilots had turned off their departure frequencies and were starting their runs on the targets. One of the planes went down after bombing and strafing the Indonesian port of Amboina. The Indonesians captured the Florida-born pilot, Allen L. Pope, after he broke his right leg bailing out and parachuting onto a coral reef. They fished his wireless operator, an Indonesian rebel, out of the harbor. Both men were thrown into prison.[25]

There were differing accounts of how Pope got shot down. One version, portraying Pope as a hot pilot with "venom in his blood," said he was shot out of the sky because he stayed too long in the target area pressing the attack against Indonesian gunboats. Another report stated that Pope's B-26 was crippled by naval gunfire, making him an easy target for Indonesian Air Force fighters. A P-51 flown by Captain Ignatius Dewanto was credited with finishing him off.[26] Aderholt recalled that "a P-51 crawled up old Al's ass and shot him down," but said Pope and the other CAT pilots knew the risks. "They were all great pilots and thought they were bulletproof," he said. The Indonesian government threatened to execute Pope but did not go through with it.[27]

Aderholt knew the pilots supporting the Indonesian rebels and worked with them later in Thailand and Laos. One was William H. Beale Jr., who survived the hostile skies over Indonesia, only to be killed on takeoff in an L-20 light aircraft on a mountaintop in Laos. Another was Ronald J. Sutphin, the only Air America pilot in Southeast Asia that Aderholt would admit could fly the helio better than Aderholt himself. In late 1960, after he had gone to Okinawa, the Air Branch alerted him to plan to rescue Al Pope if the Indonesians acted to carry out the death sentence. The agency sent the Skyhook retrieval system and an RB-69 (USAF version of the Navy's P-3 four-engine reconnaissance plane), piloted by Major Frank "Beanie" Beard, to Okinawa, where he trained the CAT crew for the rescue. The prison break was never made because President Sukarno bartered with the U.S. government for the imprisoned pilot's release rather than execute him. Later the pilot that Beard trained was shot down in Laos flying a C-46 supply mission.[28]

The CIA used unmarked RB-69s for other clandestine missions, including peripheral electronic surveillance over mainland China. Manned by Chinese aircrews, the surveillance planes flew out of Taipei, Taiwan, landed at Kunsan Air Base, Korea, overflew China, and recovered in Thailand. "They played a little cat-and-mouse game with signal intelligence," Aderholt explained. He was not involved with the project, which was monitored by another section of the Air Branch, or with the U-2 reconnaissance program. Everyone in the Air Branch felt the reverberations, however, when the Soviets shot down the U-2 piloted by Gary Powers. When asked about the U-2 incident and what he thought about Gary Powers not swallowing a cyanide pill the CIA had given him, Aderholt responded that when he later ran agency flights out of Thailand, all of his CAT aircrews carried cyanide pills in case they went down over China, but he did not believe any of the crew members would have taken them. "I know I wouldn't," he said.[29]

Before leaving for Okinawa, Aderholt worked on the air portion of a CIA plan to invade Cuba, employing Nationalists who fled their homeland after Fidel Castro came to power. The generally favorable reaction Americans had to Castro's overthrow of corrupt dictator Fulgencio Batista in January 1959 faded as the year unfolded, and Castro revealed his true colors by seizing U.S. property, purging the government of nonrevolutionaries, exporting his revolution to neighboring countries, and embracing Soviet-style Communism. Before the year was out, the CIA was convinced of the need to get rid of Castro and had begun plotting his overthrow. The agency recruited pilots from the Alabama National Guard to assist in training Cuban fliers for the planned invasion. Aderholt knew the pilots well. His brother Warren had served with the Alabama unit before being recalled to active duty during the Korean War. An earlier air plan for the invasion envisioned a far greater use of air power, including the destruction of Castro's air force, than was finally approved and made available to the invading forces.[30]

Early in 1961, after President Kennedy's inauguration, Aderholt was called back to Washington for a few days to help prepare for the invasion. He believes to this day that the Bay of Pigs landing had a good chance of succeeding if the invaders had been given the air support recommended in the earlier plan, and if Navy fighter cover had been provided to the Alabama Guard pilots as promised. Meanwhile, however, management problems had come to a head in the CIA's clandestine airlift supporting Tibetan partisans in late 1959, and the head of the Air Branch, Colonel Stanley W. Beerli, "a real fine operations staff officer," asked Aderholt to go to Okinawa to take command of the unit that was responsible for the operation. Agency officials planned to upgrade the unit from a squadron serving under the Air Force to Detachment 2, 1045th Operational Evaluation Training Group, reporting directly to CIA headquarters. They wanted him to straighten out the problem-ridden Tibetan project and to expand the detachment's operations in Thailand, to include air support for burgeoning CIA activities in neighboring Laos.[31]

Colonel Beerli was last in a line of "great bosses" Aderholt had in the Air Branch. Relating a story about the first OER he received after coming back from Europe, Aderholt said he was working for a retired Army colonel, Lucius O. Rucker Jr., who lived up to his former service's reputation for not "firewalling" officer evaluations. He said Rucker was "a fantastic guy" but had given him one of those "Spartan evaluations that damn you for what it doesn't say." He went to Rucker and told him, "Lou, you've killed me." Rucker's terse response was, "If you don't like it, from now on write your own." "Needless to say, for the next two years, I was faster than a speeding bullet and walked on water," Aderholt quipped.[32] Actually, that was the first and last OER he got from Rucker. One thing Rucker apparently had in common with Beerli and other supervisors in the Air Branch was recognizing Aderholt's expertise in unconventional warfare and giving him free rein to take on projects and pursue objectives, without looking over his shoulder.

Shaking Up the Okinawa Operation

Aderholt was at his best when taking charge. He proved this with the black squadron at Maxwell after World War II, with the special air missions detachment in the Korean War, with the CIA's air training school at the Farm, and with special projects in the Air Branch. He was ready to prove it again with the CIA operation on Okinawa, but there was one catch. When he and Jessie applied for their adopted children to become naturalized citizens, they were advised there was a five-year residency requirement. They had resided in the United States for only two years. He went to Beerli and said, "Colonel, I can't go to Okinawa and keep those kids from getting their citizenship." Colonel Beerli answered, "No problem." The CIA got the State Department to waive the requirement, arranging for the Aderholts to complete the naturalization process before leaving Washington.

As they were preparing to leave, another obstacle came up. Aderholt knew the job would demand that he be away more often than he would be home and was concerned when he learned that the housing office at Kadena had a long waiting list for quarters on base. He did not want to leave the family in Washington or to repeat their first year in Germany, where Jessie was left alone off base for extended periods. Agency officials told him not to worry about housing, they would take care of it. They arranged a layover in Tokyo so the CIA office there could brief him on the Tibetan operation. While there, he was issued a new set of orders showing that he had served three years at Tachikawa before being transferred to Kadena. This gave him theater longevity for housing purposes, moving him to the top of the housing list at Kadena and making on-base quarters available upon arrival. "If the CIA has a leg up on the military's way of doing things, it is because they can cut through the mountains of bureaucracy and red tape that always plague the armed forces," Aderholt stated. "Nobody said they were perfect, but if the CIA people I knew had a job to do, they did not get wrapped up in regulations and restrictions, but cut straight to the objective, doing whatever was necessary to get the job done."[33]

From reports coming into the Air Branch, Aderholt surmised that many of the complaints coming out of Okinawa stemmed from differences in the way the Air Force and the CIA operated. This was not uncommon because the field expediency essential to effective clandestine operations often flew in the face of military regulations. A young navigator in the outfit said there was friction between "old-timers" and newly assigned pilots who had difficulty adjusting to the irregularity of covert operations. While "the old troops would do what it took to get the job done," new pilots coming from the Military Air Transport Service (forerunner to the Military Airlift Command) were used to "flying by the book." The friction between the two factions lowered morale and threatened the mission. Weak management and a wall of secrecy shutting the Air Force crews off from the missions they were supporting had exacerbated the situation.[34]

Forewarned about the problems he could expect to find on Okinawa, Aderholt sent Captain Donald J. Mercer (a colleague from Korean War days) to Kadena in advance to look things over and report to him upon arrival. Two of "the old troops," Captain Ed Smith and 1st Lieutenant Lawrence Ropka, remembered Mercer being at Kadena, but said that despite the group's small size (approximately seventy-five officers and enlisted men, two C-118 aircraft, and three C-54s), no one knew he was Aderholt's spy. When Aderholt arrived from Tokyo on a commercial flight, Mercer met the plane at the Naha airport and briefed him on "the troublemakers and deadwood, the good guys and ball-breakers, and where the skeletons were buried." Armed with this information and what he had learned on his layover in Tokyo, Aderholt called a meeting to explain the new ground rules. Then, after coordinating with Major General John R. Sutherland, the 313th Air Division commander at Kadena, he started transferring people who were not doing their job. "It was January 1960, and we started the new year with fireworks," he explained.[35]

One of the junior officers at the meeting was Lieutenant Robert White. He recalled Aderholt telling them that first morning he was going to expand operations and do a lot of new things. "It is going to be exciting," he said. "If you are not ready to be part of it, now is the time to raise your hand and get out." Then he met with the wives and told them their husbands had to call him "Major Aderholt" but they could call him "Heinie." "This of course endeared him to all the ladies," White said. The unit's facilities consisted of two quonset huts, one for an office and one for supplies, down near the flight line. Aderholt had the supply room renovated and turned it into a dayroom with a pool table, a Ping-Pong table, and a snack bar. "He always took care of the troops," White said. "He didn't ask the civil engineers or anybody. He just went ahead and got it done. That's the way Heinie did things."[36] "What the hell did we need sup-

Ron Sutphin, whom Aderholt called one of the best of the legendary Civil Air Transport and Air America pilots.

plies for at Kadena?" Aderholt said. "We were going to spend all of our time in Thailand and Laos."[37]

The so-called old-timers in the unit were mostly junior officers in their twenties who had joined the Air Force because they wanted to serve their country and were looking for more out of life than a nine-to-five job downtown. They were looking for a leader, and they found one in Major Heinie Aderholt. At forty, he had lost none of the fire or fighting edge he had at their age. He was still spring-loaded with energy, rising before daybreak, exercising religiously, always on the go, seeming to be everywhere at once. "We suddenly saw a take-charge man walking in there and taking charge," White recalled. "Those of us who stayed realized this was a go-getter, and we wanted to work for him." White also noted that the new boss took a special interest in the younger officers and gave them room to grow. He said Aderholt gave them opportunities and responsibilities most junior officers never had.[38]

Larry Ropka, who became a protégé and lifelong friend, described "the absolutely idyllic life" in the unit before Heinie's arrival. Ropka had been with the unit (which was the vestigial remains of the former 581st ARC Wg) since mid-1957. He had completed navigator training after being commissioned in 1954 and flew with MATS for a while before volunteering for an assignment to an air rescue squadron in northern Japan. "The squadron deactivated the day I got there," he stated, adding wryly, "Another example of good Air Force planning." Ropka said he stumbled into the job supporting CIA operations by accident, after he was sent to Okinawa and was told by the personnel office at Kadena they had an overage of navigators and he would have to go out to the units and find himself a job. Before Aderholt's arrival it was just another peacetime overseas assignment. "It was a fun outfit," Ropka said. "We had all these airplanes and not a heck of a lot to do." This changed overnight when Aderholt came.[39]

He got authority before leaving Washington to reorganize the outfit at Kadena to improve unity and efficiency, and to remove the wall of secrecy built into the old squadron structure. Previously, only the commander and one other officer in the unit were detailed to the CIA, allowing them to be "cleared and witting"—an agency term meaning they were fully briefed on the mission and had access to all communications. The bulk of the personnel were assigned to the Air Force and denied access to all CIA message traffic and information about the mission. In such a small operation, this awkward arrangement stifled people's interest and initiative in supporting a mission they knew nothing about. "It made no damned sense. How in the hell could you expect troops to take pride in their work if they didn't know why they were doing it?" Aderholt said. "I felt we couldn't run an effective covert operation unless everybody was witting." He immediately arranged for the entire organization to be detailed to the CIA and had the agency send a security officer to Okinawa to clear everyone who was assigned. A change in attitude was readily apparent.[40]

The new commander recognized that supporting the Tibetan airlift was not as glamorous as actually flying the covert missions but wanted his pilots and crews to know their jobs were just as important and could be just as exciting. The aircrews making the airdrops over Tibet were all civilians hired by Civil Air Transport. Each month they flew into Kadena from Tokyo or Taiwan a few days before a moon phase or mission cycle and deployed to Takhli about 130 miles north of Bangkok in two or three C-130s (depending on the size of the mission) furnished by the 21st Troop Carrier Squadron, Aderholt's old Korean War outfit now part of the 315th Air Division at Tachikawa. The squadron had dedicated a small flight of C-130s at Naha to support Detachment 2. Pilots from the squadron flew to Takhli with the CAT crews to give them monthly currency checks required by regulations. One of Aderholt's planes then flew the troop carrier pilots to Bangkok, where they waited until the CAT pilots completed the mission cycle and were ready to return to Okinawa. At Takhli the C-130s were sheep-dipped (had their markings removed) before the CAT pilots flew the secret airlift missions. Aderholt had troops on standby at Dacca or other airfields in East Pakistan (renamed Bangladesh in 1971), in case the CAT crews had to make an emergency landing.[41] Life would become more exciting for the troops when he expanded operations at Takhli to support secret CIA activities in Laos and to field-test the Helio Courier in the extremely rugged conditions there.

Larry Ropka and Ed Smith were away when Aderholt first took over. They were back in Baltimore picking up an overhauled C-118 and returned after he had fired some of the officers and "shook up the place." Aderholt met the plane and gave them the rest of the week off to spend with their families. On Sunday morning Ropka went to the Kadena officers' club to get a copy of *Pacific Stars & Stripes* when he met his new boss coming out of the club. They spoke in passing, then Aderholt wheeled around and said, "You work for me, don't you?" "I think so," stammered Ropka, having heard about the officers being fired. "Come with me," Aderholt said.[42]

They went down to the unit's quonset hut, and Aderholt handed Ropka a yellow pad. "You start writing, and I will start dictating," he said. He started dictating an entire operations order while Ropka, with great trepidation because he had never written or typed anything over two pages long, began writing it down. This went on through lunch, and the pages piled up. When they finished the operations order, he started dictating the annexes, the communications annex, the logistics annex, and so on. "It is now late and the sun's gone down," Ropka recalled. "My hand's falling off. I have stacks of these papers, and I figured I would retire before I ever got this thing typed." When the ordeal was finally over, he asked innocently, "What do I do with this?"

"Put it in the safe," Aderholt said.

"What do we do then?" Ropka asked, scratching his head. "Doesn't it have to be typed or anything?"

"No. We just go do what we've just written," Aderholt said.

"Then why in the world did we do it?" asked Ropka.

"Because now there's two sons of bitches in this outfit who know what we are going to do," Aderholt said, exasperated.

That was Ropka's introduction to his new boss, and he never forgot the experience. He could not recall ever seeing the operations order again. "It was never typed," he said, "and I don't know if it was ever taken out of the safe again." As he later realized, however, the blueprint for what the group was going to do, how it was going to be done, and the authority for doing it were locked in that safe if ever needed.[43] What he did not know right away was that Major Aderholt had already gone over every inch of the detachment's turf, including the forward staging and recovery base at Takhli, and was "totally shocked" by what he had seen.[44]

Partly for security reasons, but mostly because of the haphazard way things were done, the unit had no plan or support element for operating at Takhli. Aderholt knew this, but conditions at Takhli were so bad that he was still surprised by what he found there. The only quarters for the troops was a small run-down hangar isolated on the opposite side of the base from the Royal Thai Air Force's facilities. "We slept in the hangar and did our maintenance in the hangar," Aderholt said. "We ate in a little two-story building for Thai visiting officers. The food was bought on the local market, and the Thais cooked it. It was the most god-awful mess I'd ever seen." There was no transportation, and people had to walk wherever they went. "Talk about a junkyard operation," he said. "We had primitive conditions in Korea, but we were in a goddamn war."[45]

When he dictated the plan to Ropka, Aderholt had already started reshaping the outfit into an active support element at Takhli. From then on, they would spend more time at Takhli than at Kadena. To solve the transportation problem, Aderholt flew to Saigon the first month he was there and bought fifty bicycles for eight dollars apiece so all of the troops would have wheels. He got authorization from CIA headquarters to purchase a Volkswagen van and flew it down on a C-130. Later they got a second van. "That's what we used to ferry the crews," he said. "Before then, a C-141 would come in and park two miles from our hangar, and the troops had to walk all the way down there to meet the plane."[46]

Aderholt had personal-care items for the troops brought in from Okinawa, because there were no base exchange facilities at Takhli. He set up a mess support operation to keep the troops from having to eat local cooking. When he asked the base commander at Kadena for help in getting a cook assigned to Takhli, he was surprised when they sent him a major. He went to the base commander and said, "I need a cook, not a major." The colonel responded, "Keep the major. He can cook, and he's not worth a shit for anything else anyway." Aderholt said that was one unhappy major, but the troops liked his cooking.[47]

There were no bath facilities at Takhli until much later, when he got new buildings authorized. The only system available at Takhli was to drain rain water off the roofs into storage tanks the way the Thais did. Aderholt had the water in the storage tanks tested by sending a sample back to Tokyo. When the test results came back, the message identified a serious health problem using technical terms that nobody on Takhli understood. Aderholt sent back a message asking, "What in the hell is that?" The response was: "You have shit in your water." They drained the tanks and found everything from sewage to dead rats in them. Needless to say, everyone waited until they returned to Okinawa to take a bath.[48]

"You keep a low profile when you're running a sheep-dip operation halfway around the world," Aderholt said. "But you don't forget you are in the military. You take care of business. You take care of your people." Back on Okinawa, he had arranged for Major General Sutherland to be "cleared and witting" so the division commander could be briefed on their mission and "what they were doing on his air patch." Sutherland was surprised to learn the extent of the detachment's operations. He said that he had "no idea anything like this was going on" and assured Aderholt of his full support. He told Aderholt to invoke his name if necessary. Aderholt said the detachment got fantastic support from Sutherland, and they became good friends.[49]

As a military man, Aderholt knew that simplicity was the key to a successful operation. The more complicated an operation became, the more likely it would "get screwed up." On his first run through a mission cycle at Takhli, he concluded that dual command and control had unnecessarily complicated planning and directing the Tibetan airlift. A procedure in place before his time required that an Air Force major from the Tokyo office deploy to Okinawa at the start of each monthly moon phase to command the airlift. Aderholt's first trip to Takhli was in the company of the major who had flown in from Tokyo the previous day. He was shocked not only by the conditions at Takhli, but by the shoddy way the whole operation was run. The crews flying the airlift were not being briefed properly before missions, had inadequate survival kits and training, and endured squalid living conditions while at Takhli.[50]

When he returned to Okinawa, Aderholt was fuming. He sent a message to Washington explaining that two on-scene commanders were not needed at Takhli. It only complicated what was already a badly run operation, he argued. His boss responded that a procedural change at this time was premature. After stewing for a couple of days, Aderholt said he was about ready to send another message that either he be given full command authority or they could find someone else to run the detachment, when he received a message from Tokyo that the major would miss the next moon phase because he had broken his leg in a skiing accident. "I didn't wish the major any bad luck, but that skiing accident probably saved me from making a rash decision," Aderholt concluded. "They probably would have told me to pack my bags." Thereafter, he was single manager for the Tibetan airlift.[51]

Commanding the Tibetan Airlift

When Aderholt took command of the Okinawa detachment, the CIA had been conducting the Tibetan airlift for just over two years. A resistance movement by a warrior caste of Khamba tribesmen had been active in Tibet since the early 1950s, after Chinese Communist forces invaded the remote mountain kingdom and took over the government. When the Communists tightened their control, the partisan forces, consisting of several thousand Khamba horsemen, banded together to form the National Volunteer Defense Army of Tibet, sworn to serve and protect the Dalai Lama. The CIA became involved in supporting the armed resistance, and in the fall of 1957, a CAT-owned B-17 flew over the snowcapped Himalayas on a moonlit night and made the initial airdrop of partisan warriors. The CIA had trained the warriors at a secret base on Saipan and was returning the men to the high barren plateaus of their homeland.[52]

To sustain the airlift, the CIA called on the special missions squadron (later Detachment 2) at Kadena to support the operation with C-118 aircraft. Although CAT crews manned the unmarked planes making airdrops into Tibet, the squadron flew missions picking up and transporting exfiltrated Tibetan resistance fighters to and from Saipan (later Camp Hale, Colorado) for training. The CIA moved the training to Camp Hale, located in the Rocky Mountains near the resort town of Vail, when they found that Tibetans returning home "could not transition from sea level to the mountains very well." When the partisans came out of Tibet for training, they trekked down from the Himalayas and crossed Nepal into India, where CIA case officers bused them from Darjeeling to Dacca in East Pakistan (Bangladesh). From Dacca a C-118 out of Okinawa flew them to their training destination. When the Tibetans completed training, a C-118 flew them back to the staging base for the trip home.[53]

Some of Aderholt's young officers had flown the mountain warriors to and from their CIA training bases since the start of Detachment 2's involvement. Ropka described the Khamba tribesmen as being larger than most Asians and the fiercest warriors he'd ever seen. "They never went anywhere without carrying their rifles," he said. "It was eerie. They had never seen an airplane, and they would sit under the wing, twirl their prayer wheels, and chant before coming on board." On his first flight with the warriors, Ropka said there were a couple of cases of C-rations in the back of the C-118, and he showed them how to use a small GI can opener if they got hungry. He said he went to the cockpit for a few minutes, and when he returned, "they had opened every damned can back there . . . and had two hundred or more cans scattered all over that plane." On another occasion a crew member had to extinguish a small cooking fire the

Tibetans had started inside the plane. "A CIA case officer always accompanied the passengers, but we still never knew what to expect," Ropka explained.[54]

Transporting the Tibetan trainees was done in utmost secrecy. Because the planes were traversing friendly skies, there was no need to remove Air Force markings, as this would only have made them more conspicuous. When on the ground at Petersen Field, Colorado, which was the usual destination, or anywhere else, the plane was parked away from prying eyes, guards stood on alert, and the curtains were tightly drawn on the plane's windows. The buses taking the passengers to and from Camp Hale were also blacked out. The CIA went to great lengths to keep the Tibetans' presence in the United States from leaking.[55]

As part of their training, the Tibetan partisans were taught a rudimentary code for communicating with secret CIA teams operating out of India or Nepal. Using simple, prearranged signals, they reported vital information on weather conditions and the ground situation before the start of each monthly mission cycle, and continued reporting at established intervals until the planes were in the air. The CIA teams passed the information to Washington, where the headquarters started a countdown with the on-scene airlift commander. Packed with pallets of weapons and supplies, often accompanied by returning partisans, the masked planes stood by until given the go-ahead signal. With propellers churning, they lumbered down the runway and rose with a low groan into the evening air. Once over the target, the CAT crews dropped their passengers and cargo on a lighted signal from the ground, then turned their wings homeward.[56]

In the spring of 1959, after the Dalai Lama fled to India, the Eisenhower administration approved an accelerated program to train and resupply the partisans. To meet the increased requirements, the CIA needed aircraft with greater power and load capacity. The C-118s were not built to operate fully loaded in extreme weather conditions and high altitudes like those over the Himilayas. The Air Force responded by establishing the special flight of C-130As at Naha to support the airlift. At this juncture, after the C-130s had flown only a few missions and were not getting the results expected from them, the CIA sent Major Aderholt to Okinawa to take charge of the airlift.[57]

The C-130 operations out of Takhli had made slow progress because of poor planning, gross weight restrictions, and equipment failures. One urgent problem Aderholt faced when he got to Okinawa was to find out why the APN-59 radars in the C-130s were malfunctioning and what could be done to fix them. "The radars were essential navigation equipment for the perilous routes they were flying," Aderholt said, "and an unacceptable number of C-130 missions had aborted because their sets failed after takeoff." He contacted Warner Robins AFB, Georgia, and complained to the air materiel people about "the lousy spares" they were sending him. They told him to bench-test the radar spares when they arrived to make sure they were operational. He coordinated with the 21st TCSq commander to arrange for his own CIA communications experts to go to Naha and inspect the sets. They tested all the radar sets in the planes and in supply and found that they were all working properly. The problem was in the installed components, which were an integral part of the aircraft. The CIA communicators discovered that some of these components were malfunctioning and shorting out the radar when the plane's wheels retracted. They were given the numbers of the planes used in the airlift, and they fixed them. "This is another example of why you can't get bottled up in the military system when things break down in a time-sensitive operation," he said. "It takes forever, and you've got to have it now. You must have people who can be Johnny on the spot." To emphasize the point, he said, "We never had to abort another mission because a radar set went out."[58]

To increase economy and efficiency, Aderholt was determined to get the most he could out of the C-130's lift capacity. It did not make sense to him for the CAT crews to be risking their lives when the loads of ammunition and supplies were less than the planes were capable of carrying. A substantial increase in tonnage for each mission not only reduced overall costs, but in the long run meant that fewer planes and crews were put to risk in the night skies over Tibet. Ropka recalls Aderholt demanding that all nonessential equipment taking up loading space be removed from the C-130s. "We built some huge wire cages, and filled them with railings and stuff coming out of the C-130s," Ropka said. "We upped the payloads immensely."[59]

Aderholt also got the C-130 pilots to look into maximum takeoff weight restrictions, and how he could work around them to carry heavier loads. One of these pilots was a young lieutenant named James I. Baginski, known to his friends and fellow officers as "Bags." Aderholt saw great promise in Baginski, and later got the 315th Air Division commander, Brigadier General Theodore G. Kershaw, to place the lieutenant on temporary duty with the detachment to help out in Laos. Known as "Press-On" Kershaw, the general was a longtime airlifter who had served initially as an Army Air Corps pursuit pilot after completing flying training in 1930. He was the inspector general for 18th Air Force when Aderholt was there in 1953–54. Fourteen years later, when Aderholt was in charge of the MAAG in Thailand, he asked that Colonel Baginski, who was commanding the 374th Tactical Airlift Wing at Clark AB in the Philippines, be put in charge of the Cambodian airlift. Baginski stood out for the way he handled the Cambodian airlift, and rose to the rank of major general three years after U.S. forces pulled out of Southeast Asia.[60]

Through Baginski and the other C-130 pilots, Aderholt learned that a maximum takeoff weight of 125,000 pounds was imposed on the transports not because they were incapable of carrying heavier loads, but because of stress on the landing gears when the aircraft was taxiing. He rationalized that by keeping the planes flying the Tibetan airlift from making turns on the ground at Takhli, the gross weight restriction would not apply. Under emergency wartime planning, operators of the C-130A could request a waiver to raise the maximum takeoff weight to 135,000 pounds. Aderholt took it on his own to raise the weight to the emergency wartime planning level without obtaining a waiver. Ropka said Aderholt also had them line up the C-130s hours before each mission, put burlap bags on top of the wings, and spray them down with a fire hose all day long for shrinkage. Just before takeoff they removed the fuel caps and pumped gas in the tanks until they overflowed. These actions let them double the payload from approximately twelve thousand pounds to twenty-four or twenty-five thousand pounds for each aircraft making the thirteen-hour run to Tibet and back.[61]

Aderholt's gutsy way of doing things awed the younger pilots until they got used to it. Most became quickly acclimated, however, because they respected him as a leader and knew he accepted full responsibility if their actions failed. Ed Smith, who became his operations officer at Takhli, smiled when he recalled Aderholt coming into the detachment "like a tornado," getting everyone's attention and respect. "We respected him because he was a tough guy, but he was always fair," Smith said.[62] Bob White stated that a new pilot, who came in after Aderholt had been there a while, made a mistake by boasting that he had four thousand hours in the C-118 and did not want anybody telling him how to fly the airplane. One day when Aderholt was going to Takhli, the new pilot was flying the plane. After everyone boarded, the plane sat on the apron for several minutes while the pilot went through the checkoff list. Aderholt went up to the cockpit and asked what was causing the delay. The pilot said he was doing the checklist. "Shove that checklist up your ass and let's get this goddamn airplane in the air," Aderholt growled. After they were airborne, the plane made an unexpected bank, sending the commander back to the cockpit to find out what had happened. "What in the hell are you doing?" he asked. The pilot said he was going around a cloud. "Goddamit, the shortest distance between two points is straight ahead," Aderholt said. "I don't have time for you to be going around clouds." White laughed. "It was interesting how fast the new pilots could learn," he said.[63]

The fully loaded flights went smoothly until a returning C-130 Hercules arrived back over Takhli in deteriorating weather one night low on fuel. The jet stream had changed on the pilot after it was too late to use the recovery base in East Pakistan. As he flew into strong headwinds, his ground speed dropped, causing his fuel to run low. When he arrived over Takhli, a ground fog had settled in, obscuring the runway lights. The C-130 made two or three passes and was running out of fuel. Aderholt radioed that he was going to the end of the runway and shoot flares. He told the pilot to come by where he was shooting the flares and touch down. The pilot followed the instructions and landed safely. It so happened, however, that Aderholt had invited the 21st TCSq commander to Takhli to observe operations. Upon returning to his squadron, he reported to Brigadier General Kershaw at Tachikawa that the detachment was running "a cowboy operation" in Thailand. Aderholt said he got more exposure out of that visit than he had intended.[64]

Another C-130 had a similar experience with the jet stream during the next moon cycle, but the problem arose early enough on the return leg to reach the abandoned airport used for recovery operations in East Pakistan. Aderholt had sent White to the recovery base along with a communications team from the Philippines to monitor the mission and to assist in an emergency. Receiving word that one of the C-130s would recover at the airport, the team put out flare pots to mark the runway. Minutes after the team reported clear weather, the night turned ugly when a monsoon roared through the area. Heavy winds blew horizontally across the runway, extinguishing the flare pots. The entire area around the airport was blacked out. The team changed the weather report, but it was too late. They heard the plane coming in and drawing closer but could not see it and were unable to make radio contact. One of the communicators took his shirt off, dipped it into kerosene, and tried to set it afire to signal the plane. The soaked shirt would not burn. A flash of lightning revealed the plane descending toward a village nearby. The pilot saw the runway when the lightning flashed and was able to adjust his descent to make a safe landing. White had arranged to get fuel from the Pakistanis. After the monsoon lifted, they refueled the plane and headed back to Takhli.[65]

A few days after General Kershaw heard from his squadron commander about the first incident, he brought a team of C-130 experts out of HQ Pacific Air Forces in Hawaii to Takhli to investigate how his planes were being used. Ropka said they grilled him thoroughly on how he computed fuel for the missions, resulting in a directed cutback in tonnage to half what they were carrying. The team's presence was a distraction because Aderholt and his troops were busy launching a mission at the time. "We were jumping through our ass, and here they were sitting over at this little hut where everybody ate," Aderholt said. "We had the CAT pilots sleeping, everybody jammed on top of one another, and these guys from Tachikawa and PACAF were going to take our space." He came running in about the time the planes were launching, and General Kershaw asked him if there wasn't something they could be doing. "Yes, General, you can get out of here and go down to Bangkok and get laid," Aderholt answered. "I don't have time to show you around." Kershaw thought that was a good idea, so the group went to Bangkok until the mission cycle was over.[66]

When the team was leaving to go back to Tachikawa, the general told Aderholt they were doing a great job, but said the PACAF inspectors were concerned that he had junior officers doing jobs that SAC and other commands had colonels doing. "General, we're doing things most colonels never get a chance to do," Aderholt said. Kershaw smiled and nodded. "I suspect you're right," he replied. When they were ready to board the plane, Kershaw asked if they had some surplus rice he could take back to Tachikawa. "How much do you want, General?" Aderholt asked. Kershaw said, "Whatever you can afford." Aderholt said, "We've got lots of rice stored up at Okinawa. What do you want it for?" Kershaw explained that he wanted to help the Japanese civilians working for him at Tachikawa because prices were so high on the local economy. "When I get back to Kadena, I'll see if we can't help you out," Aderholt said, "but we are going to need an airplane." The general said, "No sweat, just call my people over at Naha."[67]

When Aderholt got back to Okinawa, he borrowed a C-130 from Naha and loaded ten one-ton pallets of rice on the plane at Kadena. He flew with the pilot and crew as they lifted off and headed toward Tokyo. Several miles out of Tachikawa, he had the pilot radio ahead with a message for General Kershaw to please meet the plane, that Lieutenant Colonel Aderholt was on board with supplies for the general. When they touched down at Tachikawa, the general was standing by his car on the ramp. "We didn't stop. We taxied by, opened the back, shoved ten tons of rice out, went to the end of the runway, took off, and returned to Kadena," Aderholt explained. When he got back, the phone was ringing. "General Kershaw was on the phone laughing his head off," Aderholt said. "All he said was, 'You son of a bitch, you really put one over on me.' He thanked me and hung up the phone."[68]

General Kershaw was ready to help Aderholt's operations any way he could, but the Tibetan airlift had already started to wind down. This was the summer of 1961, after Aderholt had been promoted to lieutenant colonel in March. Ropka said they were at Takhli when a message arrived saying Aderholt had been promoted. "We painted his major's leaves with silver paint we had lying around," Ropka recalled. "It hadn't dried when we pinned the leaves on, so we had silver paint all over him and me and everybody else." When asked how the news affected him, Aderholt said it was the best promotion he ever got. "But it didn't change a goddamn thing," he said. "When you're dead and they bring you back to life, you're still numb and humbled by it all."[69]

Aderholt thought he had put his career on the line after signing for fifty thousand dollars in gold sovereigns to aid the survival of contract aircrews in case their plane went down. He broke the coins down into individual packages so each crew member had five thousand dollars in gold coins. The first time he issued the sovereigns, a famous CAT pilot, "Doc" Johnson, signed for the packages for the entire crew as he was going out to the end of the runway to check the load on the aircraft. He laid the packages down on top of the bales, then inspected the plane, climbed into the cockpit, and took off. When the mission was over, Aderholt asked for the gold. Doc's face fell. The gold had been dropped with the load. "I don't know if the agency ever believed our story about dumping that gold over the Himalayas," Aderholt said. "It's amusing now, but I sure wasn't amused at the time."[70]

Larry Ropka had made captain that past November and was transferred to the Air Branch back at CIA headquarters not long after General Kershaw's visit. "Heinie arranged that," Ropka said. "I was only a captain, but he got me assigned to headquarters I guess so he would have somebody up there who knew what was going on out at Takhli." Ropka's new duties were planning and coordinating air support for unconventional warfare operations in Southeast Asia. Working for Aderholt had been a learning experience that he would not have traded for anything in the world. The experience convinced him that unconventional warfare forces were an essential arm of national security, and he wanted to be part of it.[71]

The Tibetan airlift was tapering off before Ropka's reassignment in July 1961. The U-2 incident over the Soviet Union in May 1960 had made President Eisenhower more sensitive to the political ramifications associated with covert operations. His administration now questioned whether U.S. support might be doing more harm to the Tibetan freedom fighters than good. After the Chinese Communists became more brutal in suppressing the resistance movement—slaying hundreds of thousands of Khamba tribesmen and loyal followers of the Dalai Lama—the Tibetan airlift eventually petered out. "We supported the Tibetans for several years, and when the Chinese army moved in and started this wholesale slaughter, we didn't say a damn word," Aderholt stated. "We just withdrew quietly and forgot about them." He called it "criminal and disgraceful" to "encourage an insurgency," then abandon it when the going gets tough.[72]

Aderholt did not blame the CIA for this, because the decisions were made at a higher level. He had only praise for the way the CIA organized the secret airlift and for the CAT mercenaries who flew the missions. He stated they were "probably the most remarkable pilots and crews in the history of aviation." Contrary to popular opinion, the CAT pilots were not highly paid for their services. Aderholt attempted to get extra pay for missions that were more hazardous than others, but CAT turned him down. He also praised his young officers and troops, saying that he would not have made it without them. Proof of their success was in the fact that a perilous covert airlift was sustained over the most unforgiving terrain in the world without losing a single aircraft or crew.[73] Now that the airlift had lost momentum, Aderholt and his hard-charging troops at Takhli could devote even more time and energy to helping protect U.S. interests in a steadily deteriorating political and military situation in neighboring Laos.

5. THE SECRET WAR IN LAOS

The CIA needed Major Aderholt at Takhli for reasons other than just the Tibetan airlift. As the agency's senior air adviser in Southeast Asia, he had an integral role to play in expanding support for paramilitary operations in neighboring Laos. A high priority was getting the Helio Courier in service to Laos's rugged jungle outposts where Air America's large transports could not land. The Geneva Accords of 1954 envisioned Laos as a neutral buffer zone between North Vietnam and Thailand, but the myth of neutrality was shattered when civil war broke out in the Land of a Million Elephants and the White Parasol in the summer of 1959. The outbreak of hostilities flared during the summer monsoons when Communist Pathet Lao forces, reinforced by the People's Army of Vietnam, attacked thinly spread elements of the Royal Lao army in the northeast provinces of Sam Neua and Phongsaly. The crisis was short-lived but set off a chain of events that eventually brought more U.S. forces into the troubled region and raised the level of CIA paramilitary activity. In this volatile milieu Major Aderholt and his detachment's covert operations out of Takhli became the vanguard for special air warfare in Southeast Asia.[1]

Only a few uniformed Americans were serving in Thailand in 1959. Most of these were members of the joint U.S. military advisory group established in Bangkok in the early 1950s. The two countries were partners in the Southeast Asia Treaty Organization (SEATO)—a collective security alliance formed in 1954 as a shield against Communist aggression in the region. Although Laos, South Vietnam, and Cambodia were not members of the alliance, they came under SEATO's protection when the eight signatory powers pledged to support their "security and independence" at a meeting in 1955.[2]

99

Southeast Asia (Courtesy HQ USAF Graphics)

The crisis tested SEATO solidarity and brought Laos to the brink of anarchy. The Pathet Lao rebelled against the strong anti-Communist regime of Phoui Sananikone, which had risen to power in 1958 and acted to bring all of Laos under control of the Royal government. When the rebellion started, Phoui incarcerated Prince Souphanouvong (known as the "Red Prince") and other Communist political leaders at Phone Kheng prison, outside Vientiane. He sidestepped any question of U.S. military intervention by appealing to the United Nations (of which Laos was a member) rather than SEATO for help. The UN defused the immediate crisis, but a military coup led by Brigadier General Phoumi Nosovan in December foreshadowed the years of political instability that lay ahead. More ominous, the outbreak of hostilities in 1959 struck the first sparks of a long and costly war in the jungles of Southeast Asia.[3]

Viewed retrospectively, the crisis revealed basic flaws in U.S. contingency planning for Southeast Asia. The military response to the crisis, up and down the chain of command, demonstrated an early misunderstanding of the budding regional war and how to deal with it. The makeup of the joint task force that U.S. commanders planned to send to Laos was essentially the same as the ones deployed to Taiwan and Lebanon in 1958, and those planned for any other contingency short of general war. To assuage interservice rivalries, joint planning assured all four services of integral roles in task force deployment whether they were needed or not. Even so, the contingency plan for supporting Laos ran the gauntlet of interservice bickering on its way up the chain of command to the Joint Chiefs of Staff, back down to component commanders in the Pacific.[4]

Despite the lessons of the Lebanon and Taiwan crises, the Air Force was adamant about bombers and fighters designed for nuclear war being capable of fulfilling mission requirements at all levels of conflict. The Air Force chief of staff, General Thomas D. White, carried the position to its extreme in 1959, suggesting that nuclear bombs might be used to destroy insurgent forces and their supplies in northeastern Laos and northwestern North Vietnam. The Air Force withdrew the proposal after the JCS rejected it, but people familiar with the region and its lack of clear battle lines were astounded that it was ever made.[5]

"We were going to drop nuclear bombs in the jungles of Laos and North Vietnam . . . and hit what?" Aderholt asked. There was no unconventional warfare option in General White's proposal, because the Air Force did not have one. Reflecting on the Pentagon's nuclear mind-set during the fifties, Aderholt decried the thinking that "every pitch was going to be a fastball no matter what the batting order was." He blasted "the technocrats who spent a king's ransom developing weapons that would never be fired in anger, while begrudging

(Left to right)
Hmong leader
Vang Pao and
Aderholt at
Bangkok in
1962.

every cent for special forces we needed to fight the dirty little wars stirred up by the Kremlin."[6]

In higher military circles, only a few mavericks like Brigadier General Edward Lansdale projected either the vision or the patience to see the budding Southeast Asia conflict for what it was—a long, bloody counterinsurgency to be won or lost by indigenous forces. We could arm them and train them to fight an unconventional war, but we could not win it for them. "Lansdale did not have all the answers, obviously. Nobody does," Aderholt said. "But he knew what kind of war it was." Aderholt did not know Lansdale personally but had heard him lecture and knew about his success against the Huk guerrillas in the Philippines. "One thing we learned about our shows of force in Lebanon and Taiwan was to get the hell in and get the hell out," Aderholt pointed out. "They damned sure didn't teach us to fight other people's wars or to fight all wars the same way . . . with a sledgehammer."[7]

The Army implemented an unconventional warfare option, secretly deploying teams of special-forces advisers led by Lieutenant Colonel Arthur "Bull" Simons, one of the Army's seasoned experts in unconventional warfare, to

Laos. The Army tried to have it both ways, however. After having the foresight to deploy special forces, who wore civilian clothing and carried civilian identification to mask their presence in Laos, the Army instructed the teams to provide the Laotians "basic military training on an infantry battalion level in a conventional military environment."[8] "I'm not surprised," Aderholt said, pointing out that Air Force brass, after reluctantly fielding retreaded special air warfare capabilities in the early 1960s, had shown a similar predilection for misusing them throughout the Vietnam War.[9]

Introducing the Helio Courier over Laos

When he first went to Takhli, Major Aderholt found a sleepy, windswept base in the middle of nowhere. Sprawling across a grassy plain 130 miles north of Bangkok, Takhli's three barnlike hangars and obtrusive concrete runway could be seen for miles against the dusty rural landscape. The only activity was his detachment's covert operations and the occasional buzz of a T-6 Texan bearing markings of the Royal Thai Air Force squadron stationed on the far side of the flight line. Constructed with U.S. funds, Takhli served as one of several SAC recovery bases in the event of general war. A succession of regional crises in the early 1960s brought swarms of U.S. warplanes to Thailand and assured that more U.S. construction funds would be made available for base upgrades. Meanwhile, Major Aderholt and his troops kept their secluded part of the base humming with undercover activity.[10]

When operating out of Takhli, they wore civilian clothing, carried civilian identification, and did not address each other by name or rank. Aderholt's cover name was Sakaffie. Larry Ropka described the change of pace at Takhli after Aderholt took charge and got involved in Laos. "Heinie damned near killed us when we first started going to the jungle," he recalled. "We would get the airplane loaded with food and gear at Kadena, fly all night, get to Takhli, work all day and night setting up the mission, and the next day he's still going strong." This inspired the younger officers. "I'm ten years younger than him, and I am dying," Ropka said, "but there was no way we were going to let this old bastard outwork us." He attributed Aderholt's "incredible energy and staying power" in part to the fact that he did not sleep the way normal people do, noting that "he could drop off instantly, anywhere, and did not have to go to bed like the rest of us." He recalled one summer day when the hangar was cooking in the noonday sun, he "went out looking for the boss and found him sitting in an old piece of chair, in a shrunken patch of shade, propped against a tree, sleeping like a baby."[11]

Aderholt reemphasized that having dedicated, resourceful people like those he had at Takhli was essential to running successful unconventional operations. For instance, he said Ropka, who was a navigator, could fix anything. He cited the example of his detachment having to rely on the Thai hosts at Takhli for refueling service. One of their trucks had rolled into a klong (Thai canal), and they could not get it out. The other truck was broken down. Ropka went over to the Thai compound and worked all night changing a transmission in the broken truck. Because there was no hoist available, two Thais were going to lie down under the engine and catch it with their feet. Ropka rigged a hoist over the engine instead and found material to make gaskets. Aderholt said he asked how long the repairs were going to last, and Ropka said he guaranteed the work for thirty days. "That son of a bitch lasted as long as I was over there," Aderholt said with a laugh.[12]

The troops were fully occupied with the mission while at Takhli, but normally rotated back to Okinawa on a monthly schedule so they could spend time with their families. "Heinie always took care of his people," Bob White said, "but the troops knew that the mission came first and must not be compromised. Heinie put up with no nonsense where the mission was concerned." No liquor was allowed, except for a couple of shots for the crews coming back off missions over Tibet. Later Aderholt let the men have beer, but nothing stronger. Everyone was briefed that the town outside Takhli was off-limits, and that no breach of curfew would be tolerated. A few had to learn the hard way. One was a senior master sergeant who slipped off base for a night on the town. Aderholt had him picked up and sent back to Okinawa for court-martial.[13]

In mid February, after completing his first Tibetan airlift cycle, Aderholt went to Bangkok and caught a ride on an Air America C-46 making a daily courier flight into Wattay Airport outside Vientiane, Laos. Sitting across the Mekong River north of Udorn Royal Thai Air Force Base, Vientiane was the seat of government in Laos. The royal palace was located to the north at Luang Prabang. Gordon L. Jorgensen, the CIA chief of station, met the plane and drove Aderholt back to his office next to the American embassy. Aderholt spoke highly of Jorgensen, who was aggressive, straightforward, and glad to have someone with Aderholt's experience advising on air matters. He filled Aderholt in on what the CIA was doing in Laos, and Aderholt explained that he was there to find out why Air America was not flying the Helio Courier and to prove it was capable of operating out of the remote airstrips in up-country Laos.[14]

The helio that Aderholt sent to Okinawa when he was in Washington had been sitting idle for months on the ramp at Wattay. Heretofore, light planes had not been able to operate on the crude airstrips in Laos. The L-20 and the British

Lysander had not survived. The Helio Courier had been sent to Okinawa for pilot checkout, but the pilots were unfamiliar with the plane and did not want to
experiment with it. Heinie also learned the pilots were reluctant to fly a single-
engine plane because of what might happen if the engine died and they went
down in the jungle. The agency had no air control center at Vientiane, and there
were no survival kits or search and rescue capabilities available to go to the assistance of downed aircrews. If they lost an engine in the durable C-46s and
C-47s, which they regularly flew into the few established bases in Laos, they
could still limp back home. The problem with the large transports was they
could not go into the makeshift airstrips up-country. The CIA planned to expand the number of dirt strips to support the special forces and other users at
remote sites, making it imperative that Air America pilots flying agency missions in Laos learn to operate the helio.[15]

Before leaving Washington, Aderholt had arranged for four additional helios
to be shipped to him in Thailand. Because Air America would soon have the
four new ones, he flew the helio that had been on the ramp at Wattay back to
Takhli to serve as a courier for the detachment. Over the next two months, he
personally logged one hundred hours in the helio instructing other pilots and
flying missions into Laos. When he got the new helios into Wattay, the Air
America pilots put them to good use making flights into outlying areas in connection with national elections held on 24 April. The right-wing government
controlled by General Phoumi retained power in elections, but the Red Prince
and other imprisoned Pathet Lao leaders escaped from Phone Kheng before
Phoumi could bring them to trial for treason. The escape spelled trouble for
government forces because it put heart back into the Pathet Lao insurgency in
up-country provinces.[16]

When Aderholt found that many of the Air America pilots were still reluctant to fly the helio into the most difficult landing sites, he went to Vientiane in
late April determined to prove once and for all that the plane was capable of
operating anywhere in Laos. In the rugged up-country areas of northern Laos,
there were only a few scarred patches left over from French colonial days that
could be used to land people and supplies. One had been carved out at Padong,
a mountain refuge for Vang Pao and his Hmong tribesmen overlooking the
Plaine des Jarres. Another was still under construction at Phongsaly hidden in
the mountains northwest of Dienbienphu near the Chinese border. Aderholt figured the best way to prove his point to the Air America pilots was to demonstrate that the helio could land on and take off from the toughest dirt strip. So
he approached Air America's chief pilot, Eddie Sims, and asked:

"What's the worst goddamn field up here?"

"Phongsaly," Sims answered without hesitation. "It's closed down and no-body can go in there. We tried a couple of times with poor results."

"You and I are taking the helio up there," Aderholt said. "In the morning at first light, we take off for Phongsaly. Throw an extra ten gallons, two jerry cans, in the back of the plane, and whatever else you want to take."

"First light," he reminded Sims before they called it a night. "By God, we're going up to Phongsaly and land on that damn field."

Aderholt, Sims, and a USAID representative named Jack Kennedy took off from Wattay at daybreak, arriving over Phongsaly while the morning air was still stable. They knew that trying to land in the heat of the day when convective instability had built up around the mountains meant trouble. The mountainside was a karst cliff jutting from the dark-green valley below up to over six thousand feet above sea level. There was only one way to land—over an escarpment and onto a runway that went two hundred feet one way and broke twenty degrees another way for two hundred more feet. Aderholt noted that it was about a twenty-degree turn, and you had to land *in* and take off *out*. "That son of a bitch was a killer," he said. "But we went up there, set the helio down and turned around, took off, landed four or five times . . . very smooth, no problem." When they parked to let Kennedy conduct USAID business at Phongsaly, however, armed rebels at the airstrip would not let them leave.[17]

Fortunately, Kennedy spoke Lao and was able to converse with the rebels. He learned that the villagers were suspicious about the purpose of their visit because the Red Prince and other Pathet Lao leaders had just broken out of prison at Phone Kheng. Kennedy convinced the rebels their mission was friendly and had nothing to do with the prison break. The rebels held them overnight, allowing them to leave the next morning with a warning not to come back. That was Aderholt's first and last visit to Phongsaly, which was under Pathet Lao control much of the time thereafter. When they returned to Vientiane, word got around fast about the helio's performance at Phongsaly. Over the next two days he checked out two men who were both great pilots, Eddie Sims and Robert "Dutch" Brongersma, chief pilot for Bird & Son. Although few were able to use Phongsaly, the pilots learned to fly the helio. Aderholt noted that Ron Sutphin was "the best STOL pilot ever." Others like Ed Deerborn and Joe Huzen later became legends in STOL operations.[18]

At Aderholt's request the CIA sent Major Robert Weaver, USAF expert in survival, escape, and evasion, on temporary duty to Takhli to train the Air America pilots who were flying the Tibetan airlift and missions into Laos. He established procedures and obtained equipment to help them survive in a hostile environment. Admiral Harry D. Felt's joint command in Hawaii sent a team to Vientiane to set up a rudimentary air control center, and Aderholt sent officers from Takhli (including Baginski, whom he borrowed from the 21st TCSq) to assist Jorgensen in planning and directing air operations in Laos and to develop an effective system for controlling Air America's airlift missions. Ropka explained that Air America ran a loose operation supporting a variety of customers (USAID, CIA, and other agencies) in Laos. It was not unusual for three or four planes to take off from Wattay early in the morning and all fly to the same destination because there had been no prior coordination. "Heinie really went to war with Air America over their inefficiencies," Ropka said. "This did not sit well with company bosses, but paid big dividends for increased airlift support in Laos."[19]

In his drive to get things done, Aderholt never let hurdles like regulations or protocol stand in his way. Once, when Admiral Felt's headquarters asked how it could be of assistance, Aderholt said he needed help in developing STOL sites. He failed to mention that the sites were in Laos. CINCPAC deployed a Seabee detachment to Takhli, thinking it was to be used in Thailand. As soon as the Seabees arrived, Aderholt flew them to Laos to extend the landing strip at Sam Thong (Lima Site 20), without obtaining embassy approval or documentation. After construction had been under way at Sam Thong for several days, Admiral Felt was amazed to learn that the detachment was in Laos without authorization. He sent a message pulling them out.[20]

On another occasion, after he had been at Takhli for a few months, Marshal Sarit Thanarat, military strongman of Thailand, asked to be briefed on the Tibetan airlift and clandestine operations in Laos. During the briefing Sarit expressed concern that the cover might be blown, and the whole world would know. If it was blown, it would be by the Americans, never by the Thais, he said. If the press found out and came to the Thai government, it would deny, deny, deny, he said, but he was not sure about the U.S. authorities. Sarit had two sons, both of whom were military officers. When the briefing was over, he asked Aderholt if he would take the oldest son, who was a lieutenant colonel in the army, and train him to be a tough commander. The son went back with Aderholt to Takhli and started flying with him into the rugged backwater landing sites in Laos. Things were going smoothly until the embassy in Vientiane found out. "The ambassador ordered me to the embassy and chewed my ass royally," Aderholt recalled. "He raised holy hell that I was flying the top Thai official's son into the insecure areas of Laos. I had to take him back to Thailand."[21]

Superpower Airlifts Raise the Stakes

The right-wing government in Laos was heading toward another crisis, one that would place even greater demands on operations at Takhli. The facade of political stability emerging from the spring elections crumbled in August when a military coup led by Captain Kong Le, an aggressive twenty-six-year-old paratroop commander of mixed Laotian and tribal parentage, overthrew the Phoumi government and installed neutralist Prince Souvanna Phouma as prime minister. General Phoumi fled Vientiane, retreating south along the Mekong to the right-wing stronghold at Savannakhet. After consulting with his uncle, Premier Sarit Thanarat of Thailand, Phoumi announced a counterrevolution. Many officers of the Force Armee Royale remained loyal to Phoumi; others joined Kong Le's self-styled Forces Armees Neutralistes. Initially, both newly arrived U.S. ambassador Winthrop Brown and the Communists stood on the sidelines watching developments with a wary eye, but this abruptly changed.[22]

After negotiations broke down and fighting escalated between the two armies in September, Souvanna Phouma formed an alliance with the Pathet Lao and turned to the Soviet Union for assistance. On the other side, the Thai government openly supported General Phoumi, while the CIA secretly assisted Phoumi's forces and armed the Hmong tribesmen under Vang Pao. By December 1960 the Land of a Million Elephants and the White Parasol was in a state of anarchy. When General Phoumi's army threatened Vientiane in early December, Soviet Il-14 transports flew more than thirty missions into Wattay Airport, delivering arms and supplies to besieged coalition forces. Despite the reinforcements, the city fell to Phoumi's army in mid December, sending Souvanna Phouma in exile to Cambodia, and Kong Le's forces withdrawing toward Xieng Khouang province in the northeast. Aided by a massive Soviet airlift and support from North Vietnam, the Pathet Lao forces poured onto the strategic Plaine des Jarres to take up positions alongside Kong Le's regrouping columns.[23]

Sightings of Soviet Ilyushin aircraft over the Plaine des Jarres and heavy truck traffic coming in from North Vietnam continued well into January, as Kong Le's forces and the Pathet Lao consolidated their positions. While stepping up support for the warring factions, the United States and the Soviet Union resorted to verbal attacks at the diplomatic level, each accusing the other of violating the Geneva Accords by bringing arms and ammunition into Laos. Unlike the covert initiatives taken by the United States, the Soviet Union made no attempt to conceal its airlift of military weapons and equipment to Kong Le and the Pathet Lao. Rather, Soviet leaders flaunted the airlift, boasting that it was the USSR's highest-priority supply operation since World War II.[24]

At home President Eisenhower kept president-elect John F. Kennedy informed on the Laos situation, warning that it was the gravest foreign policy crisis the incoming administration faced. Before his administration's Southeast Asia focus was blurred by troubling developments in South Vietnam, the new president approved a number of initiatives that were designed to bring about a favorable resolution to the Laos crisis. In addition to increased military aid to Phoumi's army and a token increase in U.S. military advisers in Laos, the president approved an expanded program of CIA responses to the crisis, including a covert project that was under way to arm, equip, and train the Hmong tribesmen under Vang Pao.[25]

The fighting in Laos continued to escalate into the spring of 1961. Reinforced by units of the People's Army of Vietnam, the Pathet Lao had a firm hold on the Plaine des Jarres and had made strategic gains along Route 13 toward Vientiane in early May when the two sides agreed to a cease-fire. When a new Geneva peace conference convened on 12 May to begin the lengthy process of negotiating terms for a permanent truce, International Control Commission representatives returned to Laos to observe compliance and report any violations. The fighting was far from over, but the lull was a respite for the dedicated crews in Aderholt's detachment and others who had been committed to around-the-clock support against a Communist takeover of Laos.[26]

Mill Pond: Poised to Strike the Plaine des Jarres

Throughout the months of crisis in Laos, Aderholt's detachment at Takhli had grown steadily as it got more involved in the CIA's support for General Phoumi's army and Vang Pao's guerrillas. Early in the crisis, the detachment's planes and other transports were hauling massive loads of arms and rice into Takhli for distribution to friendly forces in Laos. The runways at Takhli came alive with seemingly endless roars of engines as C-124s and C-118s hauled in tons of palletized supplies, and a steady stream of unmarked C-46s lifted off and headed across the Mekong River. While Air America C-46s airdropped the bulk of arms and supplies to Phoumi's and Vang Pao's forces, the Helio Couriers flew into the few remote landing sites, ferrying people and supplies into isolated mountain outposts. The heightened activity placed a strain on the detachment's operations, but the troops pitched in and got the job done.[27]

While a joint task force steamed on alert in the South China Sea, the Pentagon and the CIA acted jointly to beef up Air America and General Phoumi's newly created Royal Laotian Air Force with an odd assortment of planes in addition to the airlift capabilities that had already been increased at Takhli. The

Thai government provided the RLAF with T-6s, which went into action piloted by Thai volunteers and Lao pilots trained in Thailand. The U.S. Marines transferred four H-34 helicopters to Air America at Udorn in January, with the promise of additional helicopters later in the year. In early 1961 a rotational unit of F-100 Super Sabre jets from Cannon AFB, New Mexico, screamed into Takhli as a token USAF show of force. They parked on the far side of the flight line at some distance from Aderholt's undercover operations.[28]

Preparing for possible offensive strikes against the center of Pathet Lao support at Vang Vieng, the CIA secretly flew four black B-26s from Taiwan to Takhli in December and placed them under Major Aderholt's command. The detachment had the bombers ready to go, but the airstrikes were called off. After hostilities escalated in early 1961, the agency asked Aderholt to draw up requirements for a major airstrike against enemy concentrations on the Plaine des Jarres. Within twenty-four hours, the details had been worked out and were on their way to Washington. On 9 March, President Kennedy approved the planned airstrike as a deniable operation to be carried out by the CIA. The timetable for the operation, known as Mill Pond, gave Major Aderholt a little over a month to get all the planes and crews to Takhli and prepare them for the assault on the Plaine des Jarres. He was to have the bomber force ready to launch within hours of the Cuban invasion at the Bay of Pigs planned for 17 April.[29]

The small contingency force of four bombers at Takhli quadrupled in early April when twelve more B-26s and two RB-26Cs were flown in from Okinawa. Air America pilots were designated to fly the four B-26s that were already in place. The Air Force provided volunteer pilots and crews (wearing civilian clothes and carrying fake identification) to man the additional bombers and augmented the detachment's ground crews. Although crowded, the detachment was much better prepared to handle the augmentation than it had been when Major Aderholt arrived a year earlier. Navy Seabees had built a barracks with open bays and a small adjacent mess hall—facilities that occupants now dubbed the Ranch.[30]

Throughout the period Aderholt continued to send officers from the detachment to Vientiane to help direct air operations. One day when Larry Ropka and Ed Smith were pulling duty in Vientiane, Aderholt flew the Helio Courier over from Takhli, grabbed Smith by the arm, and told him, "You're coming with me to Saigon. There's a war starting down there." Swamped with air requirements in Laos, Ropka mildly objected. "But, boss, we've got a war right here," he said, and then waved to them as they departed for Saigon to meet with William Colby, the CIA station chief, on a top-secret project to airdrop South Vietnamese agents over North Vietnam.[31]

While civil war raged in Laos, the level of insurgency had risen steadily in South Vietnam as Viet Cong guerrillas sought to exploit growing dissent against the government of President Ngo Dinh Diem. Attempting to disrupt external support for the insurgency, the CIA began a program of inserting agents and saboteurs into North Vietnam. The sensitive nature of the missions precluded using American planes or pilots. William Colby turned to the 1st Vietnamese Transport Squadron, commanded by a dashing young Vietnamese air force officer named Nguyen Cao Ky, to fly the special missions over the north. Ky's daring and the fact that the VNAF chief of staff personally selected him for such a daunting mission might help explain the youthful officer's meteoric rise to power (first becoming VNAF chief of staff and then being elected president of South Vietnam) in the 1960s.[32]

Colby then went to Aderholt for help in setting up a training program for Ky and his pilots. That is when Aderholt took Ed Smith to Saigon, where they met with Colby, the VNAF chief of staff, and Ky and agreed to train Ky and other Vietnamese pilots in low-level night navigation and penetration—the same tactics Aderholt had employed during the Korean War and taught at the Farm in Williamsburg, Virginia. Leaving Smith in Saigon to organize and start the training program, Aderholt flew back to Takhli to take care of more pressing matters there. Smith stayed at Bien Hoa until the VNAF crews were trained, then returned to Takhli. While the airdrops were successful, the project was a dismal failure. Like so many other intelligence scenarios in Vietnam—where the allies ruled the skies but the enemy owned the countryside—the agents were compromised and all were captured or killed by the North Vietnamese.[33]

Aderholt sent Bob White to replace Smith in Laos. White was in Vientiane in March when a wild disturbance one night revealed a humorous side to the war that was unexpected. White said he and several other Americans were eating dinner at one of the three houses they occupied near Wattay Airport when shooting broke out all around Vientiane. An American came running over from next door, pulling on his bush jacket, and stuck his head in the door shouting, "Get those goddamn lights out!" The firing had picked up in intensity. Everyone thought another coup was taking place. Their only weapons were a few handguns and grenades, so White said they started laying plans either to swim the Mekong, or to race to the airport and fly out. He stumbled over a communicator on the floor who was broadcasting in the clear on his telegraph key telling the world they were under attack. Only later did they find out there was an eclipse that night and the natives were shooting at the serpent that was swallowing the moon.[34]

Back at Takhli, Aderholt received his promotion to lieutenant colonel while "up to his ass in alligators" with the Mill Pond operation. Of fifteen volunteer pilots the Air Force had sent to Takhli, only two had been in combat, and none had ever flown B-26s. Some were air transport pilots who had come from the Military Airlift Command; others had flown passenger aircraft or light aircraft like the L-20. The Air Force had rushed the pilots through transition training at Eglin and shipped them to Takhli. "Most had never dropped a bomb," Aderholt said, "so the first thing I had to do was build a bombing range in the Gulf of Siam, go down there, and teach them how to bomb."[35]

Most of the other augmentees came from PACAF units and were better suited to their assignments. Aderholt needed someone on his staff who was experienced in tactical reconnaissance, however, and neither the CIA nor PACAF had met that requirement. Knowing that his brother Warren, who was assigned as a fighter-reconnaissance adviser on Taiwan, would be perfect for the job, he sent a name request to HQ PACAF through the CIA chief of station in Honolulu. He signed the message using his pseudonym, Sakaffie. A message came back advising that it was not PACAF policy to honor name requests. "You state the requirement, and we will send you a qualified person," the message said. Aderholt fired a message back, with an information copy to the CIA, stating, "No thank you. I have been to the PACAF grab-bag before with disappointing results. I will go it alone." He then worked the request through back channels, and twenty-four hours later his brother Warren was on the ramp in Bangkok.[36]

As the date for the planned B-26 strikes drew nearer, Major Aderholt received word that PACAF's four-star commander, General Emmett "Rosie" O'Donnell, would be visiting Thailand and wanted a briefing on the Mill Pond operation. After O'Donnell's arrival at Takhli, one of the first questions the general asked was, "Who is this guy Sakaffie that sent that nasty message?" "He's gone," Major Aderholt answered. "He's no longer here." Then Captain Aderholt got up and gave the briefing. O'Donnell saw the family resemblance, walked over, looked at Warren's name tag, and turned back to his host. "You son of a bitch," he said.[37]

"Yes, General, that's my brother," Aderholt nodded, smiling sheepishly. "But your people would have sent me anything." He explained that the Air Force had sent fifteen nonstrike pilots to Takhli, and all but two had never been in combat. "We're in a war here," he said. "I want people who can shoot and drop bombs." General O'Donnell understood. An old warhorse who led the first B-29 raid on Tokyo in World War II and headed FEAF bomber command in the Korean War, O'Donnell had never been one to take no for an answer. That was the last heard about the incident.[38]

Warren Aderholt stayed at Takhli on temporary duty for four months before reporting back to his unit on Taiwan. For most of that period he served as both

At Takhli, Thailand, in 1961, RB-26C received battle damage on first Mill Pond reconnaissance mission in Laos.

intelligence and operations officer, briefing the aircrews, targeting missions, and scheduling them. While awaiting an execute order to conduct airstrikes, Mill Pond operations were limited to reconnaissance missions flying the RB-26Cs. Aderholt needed his brother there not only for his expertise as a reconnaissance officer, but because he was a known quality and had a wealth of combat experience. Ed Smith had served as the operations officer, but he was away for much of this period. Soon after Smith returned from training Ky's pilots at Bien Hoa, Aderholt had to send him with a team back to Washington to augment the Cuban task force. Leaving Warren to look after things at Takhli, Aderholt flew to Washington with them to coordinate on Mill Pond and the Cuban operation. While there, he went with officials from the Central American Division to negotiate with Nicaragua's president Anastasio Somoza for a departure base for the invasion force.[39]

Wearing civilian clothes, they flew at night to Managua for a two A.M. meeting with President Somoza. Representing themselves as businessmen from a front organization, United Fruit Company in New Orleans, they got Somoza's permission to use Puerto Cabezas, a remote airstrip on Nicaragua's eastern coast, as a departure base for the invasion. "I know who you are," Somoza said, adding prophetically, "I'm willing to support you, but be sure you get rid of that son of a bitch, or you are going to live with him the rest of your life." The next day Somoza's son, Anastasio Jr., flew with Aderholt in a C-47 to Puerto Cabezas for an inspection of the field. Aderholt made a sketch of the area for the agency to use in preparing for the invasion. Puerto Cabezas, known as "Happy Valley" to the pilots and crews, became the staging base for the invasion force.[40]

Reviewing the finalized air plan for the invasion while in Washington, Aderholt was surprised that the number of supporting aircraft was limited to fifteen B-26s. He argued for a larger strike force, which had been provided for in original planning, to make certain Castro's planes never got off the ground. His words fell on deaf ears, however, and he returned to Thailand with President Somoza's warning about Castro weighing heavily on his mind. He left Smith and the other officers behind in Washington to help with the Cuba operation. The CIA sent Smith to a secret base at Retalhuleu, Guatemala, where pilots from the Alabama Air National Guard were training Cuban exiles. While on a practice airdrop mission in the Highlands, he was instructor on a C-54 when the Cuban pilot became disoriented. One of the plane's wings clipped the mountainside, tearing off an engine. Smith took the controls and turned the crippled plane toward the coast. Limping back toward Retalhuleu, he pulled up to go over a fishing pier and couldn't make it. The C-54 plowed into the water. Training the Cubans was never dull, but Smith was ready to return to Takhli and the war in Laos when his time at Retalhuleu was up.[41]

When Aderholt got back to Takhli, he put the finishing touches to the Mill Pond operation, making certain the B-26s and crews were ready to execute the planned airstrikes against the Pathet Lao. On 16 April the B-26s were armed with bombs and rockets, and their guns loaded with ammunition. Plans to hang napalm canisters on the wings were dropped at the insistence of Ambassador Brown in Vientiane. At dusk Aderholt gathered the pilots and issued them blood chits, gold sovereigns, and fake papers identifying them as officers in the Royal Laotian Air Force.[42]

Warren Aderholt gave the pilots target folders and briefed them on the mission. They were to take off at dawn in four cells, with an Air America pilot leading each cell of four bombers, to make simultaneous strikes against key targets on the Plaine des Jarres. Two four-aircraft cells were targeted against the airfield at Xieng Khouang, with orders to crater the runway, destroy aircraft on the ground, and strike targets of opportunity. The targets for the remaining two cells were Pathet Lao concentrations in the Ban Ban valley and on the southern flank of the Plaine des Jarres. The pilots went to bed early, anticipating a dawn takeoff.[43]

In the predawn hours Major Aderholt woke the pilots to inform them that the mission was scrubbed. The White House, its confidence shaken by the debacle being played out at the Bay of Pigs, had called off the strikes at the last minute. The failed invasion caused President Kennedy to reassess the foreign policy initiatives he had approved relative to Laos in March. Charting a diplomatic course, as opposed to a course inviting greater confrontation, Kennedy lent U.S. support to a cease-fire in Laos and to reconvened peace talks in Geneva.[44]

The Bay of Pigs was a personal tragedy for Heinie and Warren Aderholt, whose Air National Guard friends had volunteered to fly B-26s in support of the invasion. Warren had served with the Alabama Guard after World War II, and Heinie had many friends, including the commander, Reed Doster, in the Air Guard unit. The CIA had recruited them as instructor pilots to train the Cuban exiles, not to fly combat missions. Things were going so badly for the invasion force, however, that Alabama Guard pilots flew B-26s into combat the second day in a desperate gamble to help pinned-down forces break out of the beachhead. By the third day it was all over. Four Alabama volunteers had given their lives in a losing battle for a free Cuba.[45]

Fidel Castro reportedly credited his victory at the Bay of Pigs to the lack of adequate air support for the invaders. The limited preinvasion strikes out of Happy Valley failed to eliminate Castro's small fighter force. Three Lockheed T-33 jets and five Hawker Sea Fury propeller-driven fighters survived the initial attack and were waiting for the bombers the next day. The fighters broke up the bomber attack, destroying two B-26s and driving the others away. The B-26 pilots were expecting fighter cover from the aircraft carrier *Essex,* but the mission had been canceled by higher authority. Without air support, the invasion collapsed the following day.[46] Had the larger invasion force recommended by initial air planners been approved and had fighter cover been provided, the outcome might have been different.

Back at Takhli, Aderholt's crews kept the Mill Pond B-26s in readiness for another three months. No air strikes were ever ordered, but the bombers continued to fly reconnaissance missions over Laos. To keep the aging fleet of B-26s airworthy, Aderholt had the services of a longtime friend, Roger Olds, who he claimed was "the best damn maintenance officer in the Air Force." He managed to get Olds to Takhli the same way he borrowed his brother Warren from the advisory group on Taiwan.[47]

Although none of the Mill Pond planes were lost over Laos, Warren Aderholt recalled that those flying reconnaissance missions were routinely exposed to ground fire and had become battle-scarred. He said that Roger Olds and his maintenance crews worked night and day keeping the planes patched up. One of the RB-26s was badly shot up on two successive missions, and Olds good-naturedly had his maintenance crews haul the plane into the hangar for major repairs on both occasions. After the plane was repaired the second time, one of the new pilots was supposed to make a high-speed taxi test but took off instead. Major Aderholt watched in disbelief as the RB-26 circled and came back in with its landing gears retracted. As he drove up, the pilot walked away from the plane, visibly shaken, and said, "Heinie, you're going to kill me. I forgot to put the gear down." Aderholt saw Roger Olds coming and grumbled, "I'm not going to kill you. You see that son of a bitch coming up in that jeep, he's going to kill you."[48]

The unmarked transport planes operating over Laos were also vulnerable to ground fire but normally steered clear of enemy-infested areas. The transports had no means of protecting themselves. At least one American transport had been shot down by the Pathet Lao, and a couple of U.S. Army advisers had been killed in combat. Although reopening peace talks in May created an atmosphere in which the two sides could agree to a cease-fire and ICC representatives could return to Laos, the prospects for a permanent truce were no better than they had been before Kong Le's military coup. The Pathet Lao forces used the break in fighting to tighten control over territories they had occupied with Soviet and North Vietnamese help for the past several months. The government forces used U.S. aid to strengthen their position, while the CIA concentrated more of its support on the Hmong tribesmen and their warrior leader, Vang Pao.

Arming Vang Pao: A Legend Begins

On a balmy evening in early January 1961 Major Aderholt received a message from CIA headquarters directing him to airdrop one thousand weapons to Vang Pao and the Hmong guerrillas the next morning at their mountain enclave at Padong. Pending approval of the airdrop, the agency had stored crates of rifles, grenades, and crew-served weapons packed in light Cosmoline at Takhli ready to load on unmarked C-46s. The planes were loaded overnight and lifted off after daybreak, heading across the Mekong to the drop zone at Padong. Carried out in full view of Pathet Lao forces encamped on the plains below, the C-46s dropped their cargo without incident.[49]

The CIA official responsible for arming and training Vang Pao and his tribesmen was James W. "Bill" Lair, a quiet Texan who had been in Thailand since 1951 and had married into a prominent Thai family. Aderholt had met Bill Lair briefly at the Farm in Williamsburg in the early 1950s, and they be-

Transport aircraft lands at remote Lima Site in Laos in early 1960s.

came good friends while working together in Thailand. In an arrangement mutually agreeable to the Thai and U.S. governments, Lair was both an undercover CIA operative and an officer on the Thai police force. As the architect of an elite commando force called the Police Aerial Resupply Unit, Lair was credited with cleaning up Thailand's lawless border regions during the 1950s. When the fighting escalated in Laos in 1960, he conceived the idea of expanding the PARU concept into the contested outlying regions across the Mekong. He gained CIA and Thai government approval to send PARU teams to organize and train the Hmong tribesmen under Vang Pao to carry out paramilitary operations against enemy forces in northern Laos.[50]

Vang Pao's military service started at the age of sixteen, when the French army returned to Indochina after World War II. He served with the French against the Vietminh and was given a commission commanding a Hmong unit in the Laotian army. In 1960, at the age of thirty-one, he was promoted to lieutenant colonel in the escalating war against the Pathet Lao. Major Aderholt had flown the helio into the Hmong enclaves on a number of occasions and met Vang Pao briefly at Padong. The two men became better acquainted in the months ahead as Operation Momentum (the project name for Hmong guerrilla activities in northern Laos) took root and grew.[51] Little did Aderholt know that his support for Vang Pao's people would lead to later sponsorship of their descendants thousands of miles from home. Nor could he foresee that the five-foot-five-inch Vang Pao would reach near-mythical heights in folklore handed down from a long and arduous Southeast Asia war.

President Kennedy had an affinity for unconventional military programs that outlasted his embarrassment over the Bay of Pigs. The president believed so strongly in counterinsurgency principles that he had considered appointing Edward Lansdale ambassador to the Republic of Vietnam, but opponents among regulars in the Pentagon and the State Department squelched the appointment. The development and use of unconventional forces to fight brushfire wars appeared justified by Soviet Premier Nikita Khrushchev's "wars of national liberation" speech in January. Considering the Soviet Union's massive supply of arms and equipment to the Pathet Lao, Bill Lair's initiative to develop the Hmong tribesmen into a trained guerrilla force fit neatly into the administration's strategic thinking. The president approved CIA plans to expand Operation Momentum incrementally over the coming months.[52]

Flying arms and supplies into the mountain strongholds became a routine occurrence for Air America pilots at Takhli as Vang Pao's army of guerrillas grew. During February and March, nearly four hundred additional PARU advisers along with a handful of CIA case officers were sent into Laos to expand the training program. The CIA case officers were people Aderholt had either known or worked with in the past, including Lloyd "Pat" Landry, Jack Shirley (who married a Thai princess and, like Lair, served on the Thai police force), Tom Fosmire, Joe Hudachek, William Young, and Anthony "Tony Poe" Poshepny. By June 1961 Vang Pao, with the CIA's help, had built an army that was more than five thousand strong and growing. Three outposts around the Plaine des Jarres, including Padong, had been overrun by the Pathet Lao, but the Hmong, undeterred, picked up their possessions and moved to other mountaintops nearby. During the months following the 1961 cease-fire, the PARU advisers returned to Thailand, but the CIA's support for the guerrillas continued in secret. In August, responding to a rash of cease-fire violations by the Pathet Lao, the Kennedy administration approved a plan to increase Vang Pao's armed strength to twelve thousand guerrillas over the next year. A year later, after Aderholt left Takhli, Vang Pao moved his headquarters into the valley of Long Tieng sitting several kilometers southwest of the Plaine des Jarres.[53]

Before and after the 1961 cease-fire, Aderholt worked tirelessly with CIA case officers and Air America pilots to develop a network of small landing strips in support of friendly forces throughout northern Laos. The Hmong villagers scratched out the dirt strips with picks and shovels that were airdropped to them. A simple but effective procedure was used to plan and develop the airstrips. Sutphin or other Air America pilots surveyed the proposed site from the air and had Vang Pao sketch a rough plan for the Hmong villagers. They put the plan in a canteen and flew over the village, dropping the canteen to the crowd below. "When they went back the next week, the Hmong would have the site cleared," Aderholt said. "They went in and landed on it. The villagers were paid if they had to move the huts and stuff."[54]

When Aderholt left Takhli in the summer of 1962, there were approximately forty of these small strips in northern Laos. Later, during the Vietnam War, they were called Lima Sites and were used for supporting special warfare operations and as forward staging bases for "Jolly Green" helicopters conducting rescue and recovery operations in Laos and North Vietnam. Flying into some of the newer strips was about as hazardous as landing at Phongsaly. Aderholt described one bare strip that was scraped off two ridges at fifty-two hundred feet above sea level. It was six hundred feet long and only thirty to forty feet wide. The Hmong had built the strip by filling the middle with dirt they had dug off the tops of the ridges. Pilots who landed at the dreaded strip, which sloped downward with a sheer drop off at the end, called it Agony.[55]

Initially, the Helio Couriers were the only aircraft available that could fly in and out of the small strips. That changed with the arrival of H-34 helicopters in early 1961, and the later appearance of STOL aircraft like the PC-6 Pilatus Porter. The bulk of supplies still had to be airdropped, however, and the daily demands for airlift support in Laos had begun to stretch the capabilities of Air America's C-46s and other transports. Aderholt got five Air Force C-123 Providers at Takhli to augment the C-46s and requested a DHC-4 Caribou STOL transport be brought from Vietnam to Thailand for testing. Air America pilot Fred Walker evaluated the Caribou's performance. On his initial flight into Padong, with Aderholt in the right seat, they landed short and skidded to the end of the runway. "We almost pranged the airplane," Aderholt said. "In the evaluation, the agency advised the Army that the Caribou should be equipped with reversible props, which made it a great aircraft."[56]

Two small contract airlines were started up to supplement Air America's operations, but only one survived. A fly-by-night outfit operating out of Vientiane with Taiwanese aircrews folded after one of its two planes was shot down near Padong. The other fledgling airline, started by William Bird, the head of a construction firm out of California, complemented Air America's operations as the U.S. military presence in Southeast Asia continued to build. Nearly fifteen years later, in 1975, Brigadier General Heinie Aderholt would call on Birdair to fly military supplies into the besieged Cambodian capital of Phnom Penh.

Both the general and the airline had blazed the Southeast Asia skies many times over to reach that juncture—the eve of America's abandoning the Vietnam War.[57]

In August 1961, when President Kennedy approved an increase in the number of Hmong being supported to twelve thousand, he also authorized increasing the U.S. military strength in Laos to include more special forces advisers. When renewed fighting broke out between government forces and the Pathet Lao in May 1962, the president ordered the deployment of approximately three thousand U.S. troops to Thailand as a show of force. The hostilities subsided, and the following month the warring factions in Laos formed a coalition government. On 23 July the delegates in Geneva signed new agreements proclaiming the neutrality of Laos. Although the 1962 agreements reduced the number of U.S. forces that had built up over the previous year, there was no letup in support for Vang Pao's guerrillas.[58] Aderholt's detachment continued to work with Air America in resupplying the Hmong until he left Thailand for another assignment in August.

Jungle Jim: Revival of the Air Commandos

Months before Aderholt's departure, the Kennedy administration's focus in Southeast Asia had shifted to the Republic of Vietnam, where the Viet Cong had stepped up its insurgency against the foundering government of Ngo Dinh Diem. In addition to more U.S. advisers, the Army's Green Berets and other special forces had begun deploying to Vietnam in greater numbers. In the autumn of 1961, the agency asked Aderholt to give an orientation to a colonel who had just brought a unit from Eglin AFB, Florida, to Bien Hoa AB, Vietnam, to train and advise the VNAF in special air warfare operations. The colonel was Ben King, who had met Aderholt briefly in the mess hall at Itazuka Air Base, Japan, that cold early morning in 1950 after he made an emergency landing with a planeload of Korean female agents. Colonel King had been told to go to Thailand and meet this fellow, Sakaffie, who would fill him in on CIA missions in Laos. "Lo and behold, it was Heinie Aderholt," King said. He recognized Aderholt immediately and thought to himself that maybe that wild tale he listened to that morning ten years ago was true.[59]

That the two men hit it off so well might have been overlooked by others on the ramp because of the contrast in styles. Aderholt was wearing sandals, shorts, and a T-shirt. King wore the distinctive air commando uniform General LeMay had authorized for the men of the 4400th Combat Crew Training Squadron (code-named Jungle Jim), which had been activated at Eglin in April to jump-start the Air Force's special air warfare program. The Thais were accustomed to seeing Americans wearing an odd assortment of military and civilian dress, but Colonel King's Australian-style bush hat, fatigues, blue scarf, and combat boots were new to them. Aderholt quickly learned that King was commander of the newly formed air commando squadron and had brought a special detachment to Vietnam under the code name Farm Gate.[60]

King explained that Jungle Jim responded to a directive from President Kennedy in February that the armed services increase their counterinsurgency or low-intensity war-fighting capabilities. The president made it clear that the mission was to train indigenous forces in counterinsurgency operations, not to fight their wars for them. Unfortunately, U.S. forces had not only neglected their own special war-fighting capabilities over the past decade, but had armed and trained smaller allied nations to fight conventional wars rather than the insurgent threats that had become prevalent in Third World countries. The Pentagon—ignoring warnings "that Southeast Asia countries were building conventional army forces when the major threat was by internal subversive groups with covert external support"—continued to respond as if external aggression were the main threat.[61] It was a mind- set that controlled America's approach to the escalating hostilities in Vietnam, leading inevitably to massive intervention and Americanization of the war. The two men discussed these and other problems at length during King's visit to Takhli, and while working together over the next few months.

Both men sensed there was utter confusion (centered in the Pentagon but prevalent throughout the armed forces) surrounding counterinsurgency warfare doctrine and capabilities, and the role they should play in the overall armed forces posture. The White House seemed to be COIN warfare's only true champion at the highest levels. Whereas President Kennedy had taken the gist of his strategy of flexible response from Maxwell Taylor's book, *The Uncertain Trumpet,* the former Army chief of staff was an advocate of limited war capabilities in the conventional sense. He was never a proponent of COIN warfare. Taylor reported after the Bay of Pigs fiasco that the CIA should relinquish responsibility for major paramilitary operations to the defense department. Ironically, state department planners in 1953 suggested the Army had missed an opportunity to slow the dominant trend toward nuclear weapons when it argued for a larger conventional army instead of tailoring its forces to meet brushfire wars. "Then, in 1961, the services started off complying with the spirit of the president's directive," Aderholt said, "but in reality they were only giving lip service to what many perceived as a bad idea or a passing fad of the Kennedy administration."[62]

Lieutenant Colonel Aderholt in civilian clothes following crash of helio at Lima Site 20, Sam Thong, Laos in June 1962.

Colonel Robert Gleason, who took over the Farm Gate detachment when Colonel King returned to Eglin, visited Aderholt in Thailand the following March. An Air America pilot met the colonel in Bangkok and flew him to Takhli. As he had done earlier with Ben King, Aderholt gave Gleason an orientation flight in the Helio Courier to some of the Hmong sites and arranged for him to fly as copilot on C-46 and C-123 airdrop missions. Gleason said he was unprepared "for what was about to happen" in the Helio Courier. Aderholt taxied out to the taxi strip at the end of the runway and received takeoff permission. They were parked perpendicular to the active runway. Gleason expected Aderholt to line up on the active runway, as was normally done, and take off. "Instead he applied full power from our parked position, released the brakes, and started his takeoff roll perpendicular to the takeoff heading," Gleason recalled. "Using only the width of the runway, he hauled back on the yoke, and to my amazement we were airborne."[63]

Bob White described a similar reaction to the helio during Colonel King's visit to Takhli. He had driven Aderholt and King down to the ramp where the helio was parked. A C-118 sat at the other end of the ramp, approximately 150 yards from the helio. They got in and Aderholt started the engine, cranked the flaps down, and headed toward the C-118. "Just before he was going to smack into the C-118, Heinie lifted off, clearing it with ease, and they were off and running," White said. "I kind of chuckled to myself and went back up to operations to hang around the radio." About an hour later Aderholt called on the radio and asked White to meet them. When they landed, and King stepped out of the plane, White asked how he liked the ride. "Jesus Christ, airplanes won't do what that airplane did," King exclaimed. White asked what happened. "He actually dove the plane to get it up to sixty miles an hour," King said. "This thing has to be like a marionette. Somebody with strings had to be controlling that airplane, because airplanes can't do what he made it do." They both looked at Aderholt. He grinned. "Goddamn right," he said.[64]

Aderholt loved flying the helio but soon after Gleason's visit cracked up the plane he had retrieved from Wattay Airport on his first visit to Vientiane in 1960. On his final flight out of Laos, the helio crashed on takeoff into the jungle at Sam Thong (Lima Site 20). He walked away from the accident but wounded his pride. White was duty officer the day a plane picked up his boss at Hong Kong and brought him back to Kadena. When Aderholt started down the steps from the plane, White said, "Well, there's Heinie Aderholt, ace helio pilot." "Goddamn you, Robert, don't start on me," Aderholt said. White replied, "Colonel, I'm just glad to see you walking down those steps instead of being carried down in a box." He noted, as an afterthought, that the crash did not seem to bother Aderholt much, because he never slowed down.[65]

During Gleason's visit, Aderholt spent many hours discussing counterinsurgency concepts with him, as he had done earlier with King. The Farm Gate detachment had been sent to Vietnam primarily to train the VNAF in special air operations and to support the Green Berets, but Aderholt noted that even then there was a tendency to Americanize the war. "Either because the 2nd Advanced Echelon [later the 2d Air Division] in Saigon didn't understand or didn't give a damn, the Farm Gate boys started flying close air support for the Vietnamese army," he said. "That should have been a job for the VNAF and its A-1s, not the Americans." The Farm Gate detachment flew psywar and resupply missions, but the combat role had primacy. Extremely critical of this fact, Aderholt argued that the U.S. counterinsurgency role should be concentrated on supplying local forces with arms and supplies, and training them in counterinsurgency tactics and techniques.[66]

When asked if Farm Gate was piecemeal — "a nickel when we should have gone in for a dollar" — Aderholt answered firmly, "No, we should never have gone in for the dollar." He was adamant that the air commandos had gone to Vietnam as a training cadre, and it should have stayed that way. He blamed Brigadier General Rollen H. Anthis, who had no COIN experience, and his 2d ADVON staff for misusing the air commandos. He described Anthis as "a raving madman" who "didn't know shit from Shinola about COIN warfare." Ironically, Anthis became known within the Air Force as "Mr. COIN Air," and the Pentagon assigned him to the Joint Chiefs of Staff as special assistant for counterinsurgency and special activities when he left Vietnam in February 1964.[67]

Aderholt insisted that the combat missions could and should have been left to the VNAF. "Hell, they were great pilots," he said. "We should never have had our regular Air Force and Army units over there. It should have been dealt with as an insurgency, and it should have been the Vietnamese's fight and not ours." This was a point that Colonel Gleason said all air commandos were in agreement on.[68] Their voices, unfortunately, were drowned out by the rolling thunder of U.S. intervention in the months and years ahead.

Aderholt soon had an opportunity to influence directly the development of air commando concepts and doctrine. During early summer he heard from his old friend and sponsor, Major General Cecil Childre, who had just made two stars as the head of plans and programs in Air Force headquarters. Slated to take over the USAF personnel function, General Childre controlled Air Force assignments and notified Aderholt that he was to report to Eglin in August as special assistant to the commander of the new USAF Special Air Warfare Center. The center had been activated in April, with Brigadier General Gilbert L. Pritchard as commander. Aderholt said he fought the assignment to Eglin. "I had the best damn job in the world," he stated, when interviewed after the Vietnam War. "The war was heating up. I was a lieutenant colonel and had more authority than I ever had as a general in the Air Force." General Childre explained that he had no choice. It was a mandatory assignment. General Pritchard needed his expertise at Eglin, and that was that. Aderholt saluted smartly and packed his bags. In August he and the family relocated to Eglin.[69]

6. THE AIR COMMANDOS: A BREED APART

After clearing CIA headquarters, Lieutenant Colonel Aderholt met General Pritchard and John R. Alison (of WWII air commando fame) at nearby Andrews AFB, where they departed aboard the SAWC commander's plane. Sweltering August heat bathed the tarmac as they taxied away from the terminal, roared down the runway, and rose into the maw of the setting sun—the rhythm of the engines low and resonant as they turned due south across the Potomac. For Aderholt the three-hour flight—taken up by a frank and kindred exchange of views about special operations with the SAWC commander and the man who had pioneered air commando operations in Burma during World War II—passed quickly. It was a pleasant introduction to his new assignment at Eglin AFB.[1]

He knew about Alison's reputation in special operations but had never met him. Twenty years earlier, as a lieutenant colonel during World War II, Alison had teamed up with Lieutenant Colonel Philip G. Cochran to create the Army Air Forces' original air commando unit in support of Brigadier General Orde C. Wingate's British "Chindit" jungle fighters in Burma. A self-contained, composite force of fighters, bombers, transports, gliders, helicopters, and light planes, the 1st Air Commando Group's success in Burma convinced General Henry H. "Hap" Arnold to activate two additional groups near the end of World War II. The groups were disbanded during the postwar rush to demobilize the armed forces. Alison returned to civilian life after the war but continued his affiliation as a reserve officer. The Air Force, upon activating the Special Air Warfare Center at Eglin, called him in as a consultant on the air commando experience in World War II.[2]

From this first meeting General Pritchard impressed Aderholt as the ideal commander for the special air warfare mission. At the age of forty-seven, Pritchard was an intelligent, energetic senior officer who had an open mind and readily grasped new ideas. In early 1962, when the general learned he would command the Special Air Warfare Center, he became airborne qualified by completing the Army's parachutist training school at Fort Benning, Georgia. Throwing the full weight of his experience behind the center's mission placed Pritchard in the direct line of fire with higher headquarters at Langley, where Tactical Air Command's senior staff kept a wary eye on the air commandos' flamboyant and independent pattern of operations. Pritchard fought for special air warfare concepts and capabilities even in the aftermath of President Kennedy's assassination in November 1963, when the gloss on the armed services' support for special forces quickly faded. This toughness endeared the commander to Colonel Aderholt, whose admiration for Pritchard grew during their three-year association at the Eglin-Hurlburt complex.[3]

When Aderholt arrived at Eglin, he was assigned as assistant director for operations instead of Pritchard's special adviser, as his orders had indicated. Glad to be in a position to influence the formative stages of special air warfare concepts and operations, he ran with the assignment and made the most of it. The director of operations, Colonel Earl J. Livesay, had special operations experience and fully supported Aderholt's initiatives to develop special air warfare doctrine, tactics, and equipment in support of global operations. General Pritchard called Aderholt "the best in the SAWC business." Promoted to colonel in January 1964, he moved to Hurlburt, where he served until August 1965 as commander and vice commander of the famed 1st Air Commando Wing.[4]

Centralized Control: A Doctrinal "Catch-22"

This period in Aderholt's career was a pivotal one for special air warfare and the air commandos and was a crossroads for U.S. involvement in the burgeoning war in Vietnam. In January 1963 Secretary of the Air Force Eugene M. Zuckert announced a major expansion program for special air warfare forces worldwide. The expansion tripled the strength of the air commandos, raising force levels from one thousand to three thousand men, and widened deployments of training detachments and mobile training teams overseas. The group at Hurlburt was redesignated the 1st Air Commando Wing in June, and the number of flying squadrons increased from two to six.[5]

The air commandos carried their training and advisory roles to Africa, Europe, and seven South and Central American countries in 1963, but their main focus was on Vietnam, where the war against the Viet Cong was going badly and casualty rates were rising. Ostensibly not engaged in combat, nine air commandos lost their lives to Viet Cong fire while carrying out the mission in Southeast Asia in 1963. Still, General Pritchard emphasized that he considered civic action to be one of the most important aspects of the mission. "If we can train allied air forces to use tactical air power as a nation building or civic action vehicle, we may never have to train them to drop bombs or fire rockets or machine guns," he stated. Civic actions were intended to stop Communist subversion before it reached the shooting stage. Painfully obvious to military advisers in Vietnam, however, the shooting there had already begun.[6]

The fiction that U.S. forces were engaged solely in an advisory role in Vietnam became harder to swallow in mid-1963 when operational control of the Farm Gate detachment at Bien Hoa passed to General Anthis's headquarters at Tan Son Nhut. Aderholt saw this change and the 2d Air Division's earlier assumption of command over USAF tactical units deploying to Southeast Asia as a part of JTF-116 as ominous signs of a more pervasive U.S. military presence in Vietnam. Concurrently, SAWC was tasked to provide counterinsurgency tactics and techniques training for Air Force personnel being assigned PCS to the war zone. The defense department still treated the war as a counterinsurgency, but General William W. Momyer stated that most senior commanders he talked to in 1963 believed it was rapidly expanding into a conventional conflict.[7]

Unfortunately, the assimilation of Farm Gate into 2d Air Division's centralized system of control made it impossible for the detachment to operate as a self-contained air commando unit. Aderholt pointed out that Farm Gate deployed initially "with a minimum number of people to fly a maximum number of sorties and go for 179 days," reminiscent of the original air commando units deployed in World War II. "It was a lean, mean, hardworking outfit—very successful, high morale, high-spirited," he said. A highly mobile, austere, and totally mission-oriented group, the commandos lived in tents, did their own maintenance, and left the administrative frills behind at Hurlburt. "They were flying a maximum number of sorties, five or six sorties a day per aircraft," Aderholt said, "but then they got organized under the Air Force system in 2d Air Division." He described the result: "They sent in a combat support group from Japan for the maintenance. They took over all the hangar space. Soon, instead of flying five missions a day, they were down to one or two, but they had gained a great number of people, and that became an irritant. They brought in so many people on top of them that it made it hard to stand in line and get your food."[8]

He compared the buildup in Vietnam against a drawdown during the Korean War when K-14 at Seoul was about to be overrun. "They evacuated everybody that didn't have anything to do with flying airplanes and dropping bombs," he said. "Lo and behold, the sortie rate went up because we didn't have so damn many people to support who weren't doing anything." He deplored what happened when units started deploying PCS to Vietnam. "We had to have shelters, air-conditioning, base exchanges, commissaries, chapels, and all the things that are nice to have but not absolutely essential," he explained. He believed that if the armed forces learned nothing else from their mistakes in Vietnam, they needed to get back to the bare essentials in waging low-intensity warfare.[9]

It was becoming increasingly evident that Vietnam had become a "catch-22" for air commando operations. The key to the problem was Air Force basic doctrine; the lock was service roles and missions. The former seemed impervious to change; the latter was jammed by the transition from massive retaliation to flexible response. When the Army and the Air Force responded to the call to develop counterinsurgency capabilities in 1961, they brought more than a decade of roles and missions imperfections into the process. Unresolved questions concerning the Air Force's support for ground forces during and after the Korean War had encouraged a buildup in Army organic aviation. This led to an overlap in the development of aviation capabilities for counterinsurgency warfare. General Childre had become concerned about the harmful effects of interservice rivalry on special air warfare forces in mid-1962 when he first discussed the Eglin assignment with Aderholt. He cautioned the Air Staff that the DOD policy of using Vietnam as a field laboratory lent encouragement to the Army and Navy to expand their air capability in the counterinsurgency field. Pointing out the inadequacy of the Air Force's equipment to do the job, he warned that if the Air Force did not strengthen and expand its air capability, the other services would move into the void.[10]

Since becoming a separate service in 1947, the Air Force had opposed ground commanders having organic air support, arguing that it duplicated USAF capabilities and violated core Air Force doctrine emerging out of the North Africa campaign in World War II that theater air power, to be effective, must be centrally controlled. The Air Force used these same arguments to oppose the Army's development of duplicative aviation capabilities for limited or counterinsurgency warfare. Unfortunately, the Air Force's intractability on the principle of centralized control versus dedicated air support precluded the air commandos from operating as a self-contained force, separately and distinctly from conventional air power, which Aderholt and others contended was sine qua non to special operations. The Air Force could not allow the commandos to operate as an entity outside the doctrine of centralized control (even if so inclined) because it might give the Army the rationale it needed to gain dedicated air support.[11]

The Air Force not only assimilated the air commandos into the centralized command and control structure in Vietnam but introduced extraneous missions and capabilities into special air warfare operations at Eglin and Hurlburt. An example was transferring a troop carrier squadron of C-123s from Pope AFB, North Carolina, to Hurlburt and converting it to an air commando squadron. The men now joining the air commando organization were not all volunteers, and probably not as carefully screened as those in the original Jungle Jim outfit. By the end of 1963 it was obvious that both the Air Staff and Tactical Air Command looked upon special air warfare forces as part of the conventional arsenal and were determined to keep a tight rein on their operations.[12]

An inane side to the drama was TAC's resentment of the air commando uniform. The air commandos' presence in Vietnam had made their distinctive uniform featuring the Australian-style bush hat better known at home but more unpopular at TAC headquarters. Consisting of the bush hat, jump boots, bloused green fatigues, and blue scarf, the uniform had become a sore subject at Langley, where TAC's senior staff contended that the air commandos were no different from the rest of the Air Force. General LeMay, in the presence of the TAC commander, General Walter C. Sweeney Jr., had given Colonel King permission in 1962 to wear the hat, but formal approval was not forthcoming until March of the following year. Then, in January 1964, TAC headquarters abruptly withdrew authorization to wear the hat, without giving a reason. General Pritchard successfully appealed the decision on the basis of the hat's operational value and boost to morale, but General Sweeney was not an avid supporter. Aderholt recalled briefing the four-star commander, with Pritchard present, when Sweeney interrupted him, snapping, "I want to tell you one thing. You people are no different from anybody else in the Air Force, with that silly hat and all." Aderholt said he was caught off guard by the outburst and responded with a remark to the effect that the air commandos were "a hell of a lot better" than the average person he'd seen in the Air Force. The general was not amused.[13]

Aderholt's stormy run-ins with TAC headquarters reminded him that more was at stake than a distinctive uniform in any resentment shown the air commandos. Part of it had to do with funding. Tactical Air Command's combat capabilities had yet to recover from a decade dominated by SAC's nuclear budgets. Funds now spent on what many senior commanders perceived to be outmoded aircraft and equipment, and an aberrant military concept revolving around civic action, meant that less was available for modernizing the tactical air forces. Budgetary concerns and the ruckus over using Vietnam as a laboratory for counterinsurgency warfare had restricted the development of new aircraft for the COIN mission. This meant that modernizing the air commando forces could be accomplished only through procuring and modifying existing aircraft.[14] How superfluous and how costly the so-called field laboratory would become when TAC's high-performance fighters took over the air war under the Johnson administration.

Among planes evaluated in Vietnam for the air commando mission during 1963 were the U-10 (USAF version of Helio Courier) and the YC-123 transport. At home SAWC also took an active role in evaluating the gunship, testing both the side-firing AC-130 and AC-47 aircraft on Eglin's gunnery ranges. The Navy agreed to release a number of A-1E aircraft to the Air Force, enough to equip two of the new air commando squadrons activated in mid-1963. Soon after joining the headquarters, Aderholt made several trips to Washington with General Pritchard seeking to speed up delivery of the A-1Es as replacement aircraft, because the wings were falling off the T-28s and B-26s. The Air Force had no suitable replacement aircraft available.[15]

Getting Special Air Warfare off the Ground

Aderholt's reputation as a patriarch of special operations in Southeast Asia had preceded him at Eglin and Hurlburt. Any number of Heinie Aderholt stories spread through the air commando community after Ben King, Bob Gleason, and the Farm Gate aircrews returned from deployments to Bien Hoa. Aderholt thought highly of both King and Gleason and worked closely with King during his first year at Eglin. Gleason had taken an air commando detachment to Panama under a project known as Bold Venture before Aderholt arrived, so they did not work together at Eglin. Gleason recalled, however, relying heavily on their earlier discussions in Thailand while operating in Panama. He said Aderholt's arguments gave him a different perspective on counterinsurgency operations that helped develop "the most extensive and effective civic action training program the USAF had undertaken up to that time." Working with the World Medical Relief Agency in Detroit, the detachment was able to "funnel millions of dollars of supplies into many countries of South and Central America."[16]

Colonel King, after returning from the initial Farm Gate deployment to Bien Hoa, had been reassigned as commander of the 1st Combat Applications Group (responsible to SAWC for research and development) at Eglin. He held this position until October 1963, later attaining the rank of brigadier general while serving as vice commander of Fourth Air Force at Hamilton AFB, California. Aderholt called Ben King "a great fighter pilot" and "a great great leader," whom everybody loved and respected. He said King's troops knew him as "Uncle Ben" and "would follow him to hell."[17]

King praised Aderholt's contributions at Eglin, crediting him with getting the air commandos and special air warfare moving in the right direction. "Nobody knew what in the hell we were supposed to do or how we were supposed to do it even though we had been at it for a couple of years," King recalled. "But Heinie knew, and if it hadn't been for Heinie and his guidance, we never would have gotten special air warfare off the ground." He said there were several full colonels and a general involved in special operations at Eglin and Hurlburt, but Aderholt was "the only one who had any concept of what we should be doing." He credited Aderholt's knowledge of special operations and his unique ability to coordinate and work with the Army's special forces and ranger battalions with helping to develop special air warfare doctrine and procedures throughout the defense department. "Heinie was certainly one of the first and most informed people in the special operations area then and now as far as I am concerned," King said.[18]

Aderholt's expertise in special operations and his positive "can do" approach to the mission not only inspired fellow air commandos, but won the respect of the Army's special forces. Giving the special forces what they needed in the way of effective air support was not only a vital part of the mission, but could go a long way toward healing past roles and missions rifts between the two services. The air commandos participated in joint exercises with their Army counterparts on a regular basis. Aderholt's approach to the exercises was no different from his approach to real combat—you were there to give it your all and to win!

To him there was no middle ground where it concerned the air commandos and special operations. He fought tirelessly for the mission. He fought tirelessly for the right people, planes, and equipment to carry the mission out. In 1997 a fellow air commando, Colonel William C. Thomas, said his first impression of Heinie Aderholt—that he was "a bulldog of a man, extremely intelligent in military operational matters, courageous (would back down to no one), and loved the military with every ounce of his being"—had not changed in the thirty-four years they had known each other. They met as lieutenant colonels in January 1963 when General Pritchard sent them to the Pentagon to represent the center at classified briefings on a forthcoming overseas deployment. They became acquainted on the flight to Washington. Thomas asked where Aderholt went to college. "Hell, Bill," Aderholt replied. "The only time I ever went to college was to see a football game."[19]

Thomas remembered feeling out of place at the briefings because he and Aderholt were the lowest-ranking officers there. A top DOD civilian chaired the meeting, with a roomful of general officers and high-ranking civilians in attendance. "After all the high-powered civilians and military had spoken, the chairman asked if anyone else had an input," Thomas said. To his surprise Aderholt stood up and stole the show with an impromptu presentation on the air commandos' capabilities. He made a strong case for putting the air commandos in charge of the deployment, claiming they could handle all communications, air and ground, with their TSC-15 van and mobility equipment. Thomas said the room broke into applause, and the chairman complimented Aderholt on his remarks. As they walked out, he reminded Aderholt that the TSC-15 van was out of commission because of rough treatment received during Swift Strike II air-ground maneuvers in August. "My job was to get this mission for General Pritchard," Aderholt explained. "We'll worry about the goddamn van later."[20]

Aderholt had worked closely with the Army's special forces in Southeast Asia and knew the problems they had in getting air support. He was also aware of the roles and missions brouhaha surrounding the board studying Army aviation requirements, which was headed by General Hamilton H. Howze. Just before leaving Okinawa, he had discussed the Army's aviation requirements with a member of the Howze board, Major General William B. Rossen, who was on a fact-finding tour to Southeast Asia. Accompanying Rossen was the head of the Army's John F. Kennedy Special Warfare Center at Fort Bragg, North Carolina, Lieutenant Colonel William B. Yarbrough. Aderholt demonstrated his detachment's capabilities for them by having a plane from Takhli airdrop prepackaged supplies to a special forces team at Site 20 in Laos. He said they were so impressed by the demonstration that Rossen wanted him to transfer to the Army.[21]

One of the first issues Aderholt raised with General Pritchard was the need to develop a workable close air support concept for counterinsurgency warfare. When the USAF Air Ground Operations School (AGOS) moved to Hurlburt in December 1962, neither the instruction nor the equipment was oriented toward the unique operating conditions in Southeast Asia. After the Korean War the Air Force, yielding to "a general feeling in the military—both Air Force and Army—that nonnuclear limited wars could not occur without immediate escalation," abandoned the airborne forward air controller (FAC) concept, which had been so successful in World War II and Korea. Peacetime joint training included no airborne FACs, and the Army manned the air control teams.[22]

When U.S. Strike Command was formed at MacDill AFB, Florida, in 1961, it assumed responsibility for air-ground operating doctrine. Close air support was still controlled by ground teams, now known as tactical air control parties, using expensive jeeps loaded with communications equipment. Although the use of airborne FACs was permitted when other means of control were not available, no steps had been taken to develop the capabilities that were needed in rugged areas where there were no roads or modern conveniences. With Pritchard's backing Aderholt followed through with a vigorous program to develop practical, low-cost alternatives for controlling air strikes in support of special forces camps in the wilds of Vietnam and Laos. His efforts, which included training enlisted forward air guides and obtaining compatible FM radios for use in the air and on the ground, continued well after he became commander of the 1st Air Commando Wing in early 1964.[23]

Commanding the 1st Air Commando Wing

Aderholt felt more at home at Hurlburt, where he could feel the heartbeat of air commando operations. His projects at Eglin directly involved the wing, and, having spent five months at Hurlburt while the headquarters building was being renovated, he had bonded with the troops. The air commandos were highly motivated volunteers, whose mental and physical toughness uniquely qualified them for the counterinsurgency mission. Aderholt saw qualities in some junior officers that he believed put them in line as leaders of tomorrow's Air Force. One was Captain James H. Ahmann, a U.S. Military Academy graduate who would rise to three-star rank in 1981 as director of the Defense Security Assistance Agency. There was no doubt in Aderholt's mind that Jim Ahmann would have made four stars and been Air Force chief of staff had he not become incurably ill and forced into early retirement. "He was that good," Aderholt stated.[24]

He had taken an interest in Ahmann after reading an end-of-tour report the captain wrote about his observations and experience in Vietnam. Ahmann had just returned from flying 115 combat missions with the Farm Gate detachment at Bien Hoa. "Boy, this guy really knows what the hell is going on," Aderholt thought, so he called Ahmann over to Eglin and told him that he was being transferred to SAWC headquarters for an indefinite period to recommend ways for improving the Vietnam operation. "Now look, Colonel, I'm not going to be a goddamn staff officer," Ahmann protested. "I went to West Point to learn to soldier, not to sit on my ass at headquarters." "No, you look," Aderholt said.

"With your brains and background, the Air Force is not going to let you bust your ass just flying airplanes. You might as well get that in your head right now." Ahmann came to work for Aderholt, and they became lifelong friends.[25]

Another rising star at the wing was Captain Richard V. Secord, who was also a hot fighter pilot and good friends with Jim Ahmann. They were one year apart at West Point. Aderholt and Dick Secord were destined to become great friends, but their relationship began on a sour note. "Not all was sweetness and light in my dealings with the wing," Aderholt admitted. Secord worked for the wing director of operations. There was bad blood between Aderholt and Secord's boss going back to their service together in the Korean War. "They truly disliked each other," Secord said. He saw it as just another feud between senior officers at the time, but had the feeling that Aderholt associated him with his boss, ergo he was the enemy.[26]

Aderholt said his first impression was that Captain Secord should enroll in charm school. He had clashed with the captain over the telephone before ever meeting him. "While I was still at Eglin, I called the wing and Dick got on the phone," Aderholt said. "He was an arrogant, insulting little bastard." Before slamming down the phone, Aderholt growled, "Captain, I want you to remember two things. One is I don't like your attitude. Two is one of these days I just might be your commander." What he did not say was that General Pritchard had promised him the wing commander's job as soon as he pinned on his eagles.[27]

When Aderholt replaced Colonel Gerald J. Dix as commander in March 1964, the 1st Air Commando Wing was a model of military pride and commitment. "You could feel the difference as soon as you entered the gate," he recalled. "When you came on Hurlburt, the air police were so goddamn sharp, you knew you were someplace special." With an authorized strength of 427 officers and 1,354 airmen, the wing maintained an inventory of 105 propeller-driven aircraft—including 58 fighters and bombers, and an array of transports and other supporting aircraft. "The men loved to fly, and their love for the mission was absolutely fantastic," Aderholt said. "It made me proud to be their commander." General Pritchard tried to convince HQ TAC in April that the wing commander's grade should be elevated to brigadier general but was unsuccessful. He later wrote that Aderholt was the most "can do" officer he had ever encountered. "He enjoys the adoration of his troops on a scale which I have witnessed only once in my career," Pritchard stated. "They would follow him any place, any time."[28]

After a rousing welcome at his first muster, the wing stood down for the day while the squadrons held orientations for their new commander. "That was my first exposure to the men as a group," Aderholt said. "They were a great bunch

Colonel Aderholt, Commander of the 1st Air Commando Wing, in 1964.

of people, and it became a real love affair over the years." The squadron commanders were exceptional. One of the fighter squadrons was commanded by Major Leroy W. Svendsen Jr., "a great fighter pilot and Steve Canyon look-alike," who became a two-star general after the Vietnam War. Aderholt thought so highly of Svendsen, he put him in command of the 6th Fighter Squadron when other officers who outranked him were competing for the job. Svendsen noted that Aderholt had a unique ability to recognize and reward "the doers" in the organization, and hence "was surrounded by a hard core of professional warriors."[29]

Captain Secord left in January on a temporary assignment to Iran. While Secord was away, the new director of operations, Lieutenant Colonel Sid Marshall, prepared an OER on him and sent it to the front office for Aderholt's endorsement. Marshall was not satisfied with the captain's attitude or performance, and this was reflected in the OER. Aderholt knew that a bad OER could wreck an officer's career, however, and his instincts told him there was more to Captain Secord than met the eye. He had been a boxer at West Point, which might account for his intensity and brusqueness. Behind that gruff exterior was an exceptionally bright military officer and a deep thinker. Aderholt could tell he had potential.[30]

He called Sid Marshall into his office and asked him to rewrite the OER, saying that he thought it was not fair and would ruin a promising young officer's career. Marshall refused to change the rating, on principle, but reminded Colonel Aderholt that he had the prerogative of rewriting the OER and sending it to General Pritchard for endorsement. "Colonel, if you don't like the OER, then you write it," Marshall said. Aderholt replied, "I will." So he rewrote the OER and got General Pritchard's endorsement. Sid Marshall later remarked that, despite their heated disagreement over the OER, Aderholt's friendliness toward him never changed.[31]

When Captain Secord returned from Iran in May, he reported to the command section late in the day and requested permission to see Colonel Aderholt. He strode into the office with a copy of the OER and laid it on the desk. "Colonel, I don't get this," he said. "I thought you hated my guts." Aderholt had given him the highest marks possible and commented that with a change in attitude he could be Air Force chief of staff someday. "Captain, your attitude stinks," he said. "But it doesn't matter what I think about you. I rated you on your ability and your performance. You got what you deserve. So, let's go have a drink." They went to the club and had several drinks. "We've been close friends ever since," Aderholt said. In his book, *Honored and Betrayed,* published in 1992, Major General Secord wrote that he owed much of his career and much of what he had learned about leadership to Brigadier General Heinie Aderholt.[32]

Aderholt emphasized that the NCO and officers' clubs played extremely important roles in esprit de corps and camaraderie among the air commandos at Hurlburt. "The enthusiasm with which they flew was the enthusiasm with which they drank," he said. "You could go in the club during happy hour, and every man who wasn't in the air or out of town was at the bar." He also noted that the pilots never let drinking interfere with their flying, or the other way around. An example he gave was Major Svendsen telling his squadron, "I don't care how much you drink, and I don't care if you sleep on the wing of the airplane if you can't make it home, but you will be there on time in the morning."[33]

Aderholt scoffed at the post-Vietnam syndrome within the Air Force to devalue club activities in the public relations war against alcohol abuse. He believed senior officers had an obligation to support the club and to go there with their people. While at Hurlburt, he relieved a squadron commander who disagreed. The commander belonged to the club but never came there with his men after work. When he did drop by the bar, he stayed to himself. Colonel Aderholt called him to the front office one day and asked why he never came to happy hour. "I have to work with the people out here, but I don't have to associate with them," the officer said. "When my day is over, I go downtown." "You asshole, you're relieved," Aderholt responded. "Where you get your pay is where you get your entertainment." Looking back on the incident, he laughed, recalling that he later replaced that officer in Thailand. "The son of a bitch made colonel," he said, "but not off the OER I gave him."[34]

At least one night a week Colonel Aderholt dropped by the NCO club to have a drink with the troops. "Of course, I didn't want to overstay my welcome," he said. "It might cramp their style, and they might think I was spying on them. A commander's got to be visible, though. He has to care about his people and show a genuine interest in their well-being. He can't fake it, because they will know it if he does." He also said he learned a lot from the troops, and listening to them helped keep his finger on the pulse of the wing's problems and solutions. "Your troops will tell you things at a squadron party they would never tell you at the office," he said. "You might take their comments with a grain of salt, but you do well to listen and to weigh what they say."[35]

Chief Master Sergeant Roland H. "Hap" Lutz, who served seven tours as a combat medic in Southeast Asia during the war, proudly recalled "the complete trust and authority" that Colonel Aderholt placed in him as medical superintendent in the 1st Air Commando Wing. Lutz recalled that all of Colonel Aderholt's top noncommissioned officers spoke overwhelmingly of his stature and leadership qualities. He described Aderholt as "a natural leader" who seemed to be omnipresent. "He would be out on the flight line at five o'clock in the morning, and he would be there at seven or eight o'clock at night," Lutz said. "You never knew where he might show up. He was everywhere."[36]

Chief Lutz noted that Colonel Aderholt was softhearted and caring when it came to the welfare of his troops and their families. He hastened to add, however, that the colonel was all business when it came to the mission, and his toughness and resilience were legendary. The chief recalled an occasion when they jumped together out of a U-10, and the colonel came down on a sharp stick protruding out of the ground. Lutz ran his parachute down and took his medical bag over to the colonel who was "bleeding like hell." It was a nasty cut. "I'm going to put a battle dressing on it," he said. Aderholt responded, "I don't want the goddamned thing. I've got a staff meeting." They got in the U-10 and returned to base. "I don't know if he ever got that wound treated," Lutz said, "but he wouldn't let me near it."[37]

Colonel Jimmy A. Ifland, an expert in photo reconnaissance, was a captain at Hurlburt when Aderholt took over the wing. Ifland described him as "a gruff, no-nonsense" commander who took an intense interest in photo reconnaissance and its role in special air warfare operations. Having been to Panama and to Vietnam twice with Farm Gate, Ifland and his combat cameramen had broken new ground in reconfiguring aerial cameras for use in the air commando planes. "Taking a ragtag air force and putting reconnaissance into it was a unique achievement," Ifland said in a 1997 interview, but added, "Looking back, I don't know what we accomplished, because there are no photo systems then or today that could penetrate the double and triple jungle canopies in Vietnam. In such dense growth you just have to find other ways to find the enemy." However, he had put together a briefing with thousands of photos and mock-ups showing how reconnaissance could support the special air warfare mission, and Colonel Aderholt had shown a keen interest in this aspect of Ifland's work.[38]

Soon after taking command, Aderholt called a meeting in the wing conference room and asked Ifland to give a presentation on aerial reconnaissance in Vietnam and Panama. The building was not air-conditioned, and the heat and humidity were unbearable. Ifland said everyone was fidgeting, and a major in the back of the room fell asleep. Colonel Aderholt stopped the briefing, woke the major, and pounded on the table. "He chewed butt like you wouldn't believe," Ifland recalled. "He told the men their attitude about intelligence and reconnaissance would change as of that moment. Everybody's eyes were big as saucers. I could have briefed for the next five hours and nobody would have blinked."[39]

What really impressed Ifland that day was an awakening by every person in that room to the fact "there was a lot more to the counterinsurgency business than dropping bombs or shooting bullets." He said Aderholt left no doubt in anyone's mind that reconnaissance was a vital means of collecting intelligence, and intelligence was the key to performing their mission effectively. As a result, Iflan received enthusiastic cooperation from the squadrons and was able to establish a solid training program on photo reconnaissance for the pilots and crews.[40]

On 10 July, after just over three months at Hurlburt, Colonel Aderholt was replaced as wing commander by Colonel Gordon F. Bradburn, who transferred in from Sewart AFB, Tennessee. General Pritchard said he had fought to keep Aderholt in the assignment but had lost the battle to HQ TAC, who insisted he did not have enough time in grade. Aderholt suspected there were other reasons. He was still an outsider to TAC regulars and had angered some senior officers by fighting too hard for special operations. Nevertheless, he had accomplished a great deal in the short time he commanded the wing and would do even more over the next year as vice commander. He had General Pritchard's full support, and there was unfinished business at Hurlburt.[41]

Water Pump: Training Laotian Aircrews

Before leaving Takhli in 1962, Aderholt laid the groundwork for deploying an air commando detachment to Thailand. He proposed such a deployment to Bill Lair before departing and raised the matter with the Air Branch when he cleared CIA headquarters in Washington. He envisioned the detachment complementing what the CIA's paramilitary activities and the Army's special forces were doing with counterinsurgency operations in Laos. "If the Pathet Lao broke the cease-fire, Vang Pao's guerrillas were vastly outnumbered without air support," he explained. "We needed to improve the Laotian air capabilities, and have sheep-dipped forces there to fly support missions if required." He also wanted the deployment to provide a foot in the door for Air Force civic actions and related missions in Thailand and Laos. After reporting to Eglin, he discussed the training project with General Pritchard and others at SAWC headquarters, and corresponded with Bill Lair about the subject.[42]

The need for improved air support became more urgent after the cease-fire between warring factions in Laos broke down in the winter of 1962–63. By early spring, reports of sporadic gunfire in northern Laos were a constant reminder that the Geneva agreements were not working. On and around the long-contested Plaine des Jarres, armed clashes occurred almost daily. The Communist violations were apparently aimed at gaining a strategic advantage by disrupting Vang Pao's guerrilla operations and expanding the areas under Pathet Lao control. The North Vietnamese seemed more intent on using the Laotian corridors to infiltrate men and equipment into South Vietnam.[43]

At the same time, the Diem government was losing the war against the Viet Cong. The insurgencies in Laos and Vietnam had their own distinctive characteristics and arguably were regarded as separate fields of battle by both sides. Enemy actions in northern Laos predictably ebbed and flowed with the monsoon seasons, while the Viet Cong's freedom of movement throughout South Vietnam, aided by sanctuaries and stoked by the infiltration of arms and men, transformed the insurgency there into a countrywide war of advantage and attrition. Because the two wars sprang from the same source, however, their strategies and their fates were inseparably linked. Despite massive U.S. military aid, the war in South Vietnam was becoming a disaster for government forces, who were outmaneuvered in battle and demoralized by the political strife and corruption plaguing the Diem regime. The tide of events toppling the government and leading to Diem's assassination on 2 November left a stain on the war that another decade of bloodshed could not wash away. Twenty days later the tragic loss of President Kennedy to a sniper's bullet in Dallas set the stage for all-out U.S. intervention in the war.[44]

Earlier, in June 1963, President Kennedy reassessed his Laos policy in light of the repeated cease-fire violations. After reviewing a program recommended by Ambassador Leonard Unger in Vientiane, he approved modest increases in military assistance. The deployment of an air commando training detachment, which had been included in Ambassador Unger's proposal, was deferred. In December the deployment came up again when Pacific Command headquarters in Hawaii asked the Joint Chiefs of Staff to send a training detachment of thirty-eight air commandos and four T-28s to Udorn, Thailand, to train Laotian aircrews in counterinsurgency tactics and aircraft maintenance. As a secondary mission, the detachment would be a ready force for contingency operations as directed by the unified commander.[45]

The Air Force confirmed the deployment, nicknamed Water Pump, on 9 March 1964. Four days later the detachment, commanded by Major Drexel B. Cochran, departed Hurlburt. After 179 days Cochran and his group were replaced by a second contingent headed by Lieutenant Colonel Bill Thomas. The detachment was augmented by three C-47 aircraft and twenty-one personnel. Colonel Aderholt had selected both Cochran and Thomas because they were proven combat leaders who got things done. Cochran said Aderholt had alerted him beforehand about a possible deployment, with instructions that he was to pick top instructor pilots and enlisted technicians for the mission but was not to reveal the destination. He recalled that so many air commandos volunteered for the mission that his most difficult task was narrowing the list to thirty-eight people. Aderholt and his former maintenance officer at Takhli, Major Olds, now stationed at Eglin, prepared the team for what they could expect upon arrival at Udorn and how they would interface with the CIA and other agencies in Thailand and Laos.[46]

At that time there were still only a few Americans in the Udorn area. Bill Lair's office, which had moved into an abandoned civil aviation building at Udorn, was the rear support headquarters for paramilitary operations in Laos. Other activities included Air America's helicopters, a small MAAG contingent consisting of three Army officers, and a relay station located a few miles east of town. There was also a USAF adviser attached to a Thai flying squadron at Udorn. The austerely manned and equipped Water Pump detachment, after it arrived, was the largest American contingent there. It also became one of the most successful and most durable U.S.military operations in Southeast Asia. Later made part of Project 404, which was created in 1966 as an administrative umbrella for U.S. personnel augmenting the attaché staffs in Laos, Water Pump was among the last U.S. remnants to leave when the war was abandoned a decade later.[47]

Although Water Pump personnel received a warm welcome at Udorn in 1964, living and working conditions were extremely austere. Reminiscent of Aderholt's orientation to Takhli four years earlier, Cochran and his men were without ground transportation. They resolved the problem by salvaging an old fire truck and a three-quarter-ton Army truck from the Air America refuse dump. The detachment's aircraft mechanics soon had the broken-down vehicles in working order. Cochran said soon thereafter they were visited by a brigadier general from PACAF headquarters, who observed the flight surgeon hauling water to their off-base quarters in a borrowed vehicle pulling an old Army water cart. There were seven troops hanging on the vehicle. "By god, you do need vehicles, don't you," the general said to Cochran. Not long afterward C-130 transports landed at Udorn and off-loaded new trucks for the detachment.[48]

Cochran recalled Aderholt telling them before leaving Hurlburt that they were to be responsive to the requirements of Ambassador Unger and would take their orders from Colonel Robert Tyrrell, the air attaché in Vientiane. "Colonel Aderholt said that no matter who thought they were in charge of us in Thailand, to let them think so, but to remember that we were taking orders from Colonel Tyrrell," Cochran said. He received the same guidance from Lieutenant General Joseph H. Moore, who replaced General Anthis in Vietnam. Cochran said he received "absolutely fantastic" support from General Moore, who told him to do whatever was necessary to help the ambassador in Laos, "but don't get in trouble." During the summer of 1964 when Laotian forces were heavily engaged in Operation Triangle in northern Laos, General Moore visited Udorn to see how things were going. Cochran said the general asked him how much the detachment was involved in Operation Triangle, but before Cochran could answer, Moore said, "Don't tell me. I'd probably have to stop you."[49]

Two weeks after Water Pump personnel arrived at Udorn, the shaky coalition government in Laos was rocked by another coup attempt. A major Pathet Lao offensive ensued, sweeping across the Plaine des Jarres and threatening Royalist forces to the east. In preparation for a counteroffensive known as Operation Triangle, the Water Pump detachment opened a forward operating location at Wattay airport and began training Air America and Thai pilots as well as Laotian aircrews to fly T-28 combat missions. Additional T-28s were flown to Udorn from South Vietnam to augment the detachment's combat capabilities. Some of Water Pump's sheep-dipped pilots flew combat missions in support of government forces and Vang Pao's guerrillas. The 1st Air Commando Wing's efforts at Hurlburt to train airmen and nonflying officers as forward air guides proved useful in controlling airstrikes in Laos. Using the "Butterfly" call sign, trained Water Pump personnel flew as combat controllers with Air America pilots over Laos to direct airstrikes in support of friendly forces.[50]

The detachment's special activities were not all concerned with combat operations. Soon after their arrival at Udorn, the flight surgeon started a fledgling medical civic action program in surrounding Thai villages. Using the rehabilitated fire truck for transportation, medical teams visited villages that were badly in need of their services. They took one of the minor Thai officials from Udorn Thani to interpret for them and to impress upon the villagers that the Thai government had provided for their needs, not the United States Air Force. This was the nation-building principle behind Air Force civic actions as taught at Hurlburt. Medics from the detachment also visited needy villages in Laos.[51]

When the original Water Pump volunteers returned to Hurlburt in late August, they left a small, but well-established civic action program behind at Udorn. Hap Lutz was one of the medics who deployed to Udorn with the second Water Pump group. The second group, which brought a larger team of medical personnel and supplies, was able to expand the civic action program. "We went out and stayed one or two weeks in different villages," Lutz stated. "We had skin clinics, internal medicine, dental clinics, surgical . . . you name it. We were field combat medics, and our training allowed us to handle all situations." This was Lutz's first venture into Laos. He was sent to replace another medic at Savannakhet (Site 39), where an Air America helicopter transported him to outlying sites when medical assistance was needed. Lutz said he did not stay long at Savannakhet, but this began a love affair with the Laotian people that brought him back for six more tours.[52]

A little-known aspect of the civic action programs was that the air commandos had arranged with the World Medical Relief of Detroit, Michigan, to obtain medicine and medical supplies at no cost to the U.S. or host governments. The Water Pump detachment received an initial shipment of five thousand pounds of free medical supplies with arrangements for resupply on a bimonthly basis as required. The close association between the air commandos and World Medical Relief, which had started during deployments to Latin American countries in 1962, continued long after the armed forces pulled out of Southeast Asia.[53]

After returning to Hurlburt, Cochran became Aderholt's director of plans.

He made several trips to the Pentagon to brief the Air Staff and DOD officials on the T-28 operation in Laos. On one of these occasions he received a rare compliment from General LeMay. "You gents done good," LeMay said. Cochran vividly recalled an encounter that reflected the expanding USAF role in Southeast Asia. In mid August, Ambassador Unger approved the first strikes in Laos by F-105 jet fighters. Cochran said he flew into Korat to brief the F-105 pilots for the mission, but their commander was not interested. "Tactics for F-105s are different from those used by 'Maytag Messerschmitts,' " he said. The following morning Cochran observed "the attack of the first F-105s ever committed to combat," while flying nearby in a U-10 Helio Courier. "They looked like they were on the dive bombing range at Nellis," he said. Two of the jets took major battle damage.[54]

Air Force RF-101s based at Tan Son Nhut and Navy RF-8As from the carrier *Kitty Hawk* had flown reconnaissance missions over Laos since May 1964. The following month newly arrived F-100 Super Sabres flew their first combat mission after one of the Navy jets was downed by antiaircraft fire near Xieng Khouang. On 5 August, in response to an attack on a U.S. destroyer in the Gulf of Tonkin, U.S. Navy fighters flew the first strike of the war against North Vietnam. During the ensuing maelstrom of 1964 and 1965, the two air commando squadrons of A-1Es in South Vietnam and the small Water Pump contingent of T-28s at Udorn were soon dwarfed by the first increments of a massive buildup in American air power.[55]

By the time Colonel Aderholt left Hurlburt in August 1965, the Americanization of the Vietnam War was already spiraling out of control. The Gulf of Tonkin incident a year earlier was a compass for changing the direction of the war. When tit-for-tat airstrikes failed to get results, President Lyndon Baines Johnson approved the on-again, off-again air campaign known as Rolling Thunder. The concurrent U.S. military strength in Vietnam had surged from 23,000 personnel in 1964 to 184,000 in 1965. The strength figures in Thailand were less dramatic but had more than doubled, going from 6,500 to 14,000. This was only the start. They redoubled the following year and by 1968 had spiraled to 536,000 military personnel in Vietnam and 47,600 in Thailand. There was no turning back. What began as a small counterinsurgency advisory effort had become a major American war.

Ground-Looping Bird Dogs, Training Butterflies

Throughout his first tour at SAWC headquarters and the 1st Air Commando Wing, Colonel Aderholt worked diligently to make close air support operations more effective, concentrating on improving air-ground communications and finding more practical ways of marking targets, and controlling or guiding strike aircraft over the target areas. Before the Air Ground Operations School moved to Eglin in December 1962, the Air Force had let its field equipment and know-how lapse. The resources that were available were more suited to a highly technical, sophisticated battle environment, while the air commandos operated in a low-budget counterinsurgency medium, demanding more expedient and less costly means of getting things done.[56]

When the air commandos found that forward air control vehicles could not be used effectively in Vietnam, the Army gave them O-ls to use as airborne FACs. When word got back to Hurlburt, Aderholt got approval to start an O-1 school. He sent Major Jerry Rheim and two other pilots to Fort Benning, Georgia, to bring in the first O-ls. The O-1 was a light single-engine observation plane, but TAC headquarters ruled that the FAC pilots had to be jet-qualified because they might be required to control strikes by high-performance jet fighters. This created problems at Hurlburt when trainees who had never flown a light plane with a tail wheel started ground-looping the O-1s. "Sweeney was furious," Aderholt said, noting that the TAC commander came down hard on General Pritchard to solve the problem.[57]

Pritchard had Bevo Howard, a famous stunt pilot who helped start civilian pilot training programs during World War II, come to Hurlburt and talk to the O-1 pilots. Aderholt recalled that Bevo Howard walked into the briefing room with a football. After Aderholt introduced him, he tossed the football into the air. The ball fell to the floor, bounced, and rolled under a table. "Think of that football as an O-1," he said. "If you fly the O-1, you are going to ground-loop once in a while." Aderholt said the pilots understood that, but "Sweeney sure as hell didn't." General Sweeney threatened to ground the pilots and transfer them if there were more accidents. "That scared the hell out of me," Aderholt said, "because we had some good guys flying the airplanes, and I was afraid they were going to get screwed."[58]

Aderholt called Brigadier General Delk M. Oden, the head of Army aviation at Fort Rucker, Alabama, whom he had met in 1962 when the Caribou STOL transport was introduced into Southeast Asia, and asked if he had any scrapped O-1s he could spare. "Hell, yes, come on up and take what you need," Oden said. Aderholt had his maintenance people drive to Fort Rucker and bring back four or five O-1s. "We rebuilt them and hid them over in a hangar," he said. "Whenever a guy would ground-loop an O-1, we would run in another one and not report it." He knew "his ass was grass" if General Sweeney found out but was willing to take the risk to save the careers of younger pilots.[59]

On another occasion one of the air commandos cracked up a U-10 at an auxiliary field tenanted by a small CIA outfit. The plane had struck some photographic equipment a camera crew inadvertently left on the grass runway. Fortunately, the CIA outfit at the auxiliary field also operated U-10s, and the commander was Aderholt's friend. To save the pilot from being grounded and shipped out, Aderholt called the commander and arranged to borrow a U-10 until the maintenance shop got his fixed. He and his maintenance chief went to the auxiliary field, swapped the numbers on the two U-10s, and flew the serviceable one back to Hurlburt. He then called Lynn Bollinger, owner of the Helio Corporation, who sent his chief engineer to Hurlburt to repair the damaged plane. As a favor to Aderholt, the plane was repaired without charge.[60]

A couple of months later Aderholt was at the office early in the evening when the inspector general from TAC headquarters walked in and said, "You won't like this, but I am down here to count your airplanes." He showed Aderholt a copy of an anonymous letter General LeMay had received alleging that the air commandos at Hurlburt were covering up a major accident. Colonel Aderholt went to the officers' club, while the inspection team went to the flight line to inventory the aircraft. About two hours later the IG came to the club and reported that something was wrong, the wing was missing two planes. Aderholt assured him that he must be mistaken, talked him into having a drink, and agreed to go back and recount the planes in the morning. Then Aderholt went to the lobby and called his maintenance officer, explained what had happened, and told him to pull some of the O-1s out of the hangar at Field Three. "Just make damn sure we have the right number," he said. The inspectors returned to the flight line the following morning and recounted the planes. The IG came to Aderholt's office and said, "You are not going to believe this." "What's that?" Aderholt asked. "You have two planes too many," the IG said. "He gave up and went back to TAC headquarters," Aderholt explained.[61]

Aderholt fought a bruising battle against the concept that only jet-qualified fighter pilots could be airborne forward air controllers. "Hell, it made no sense to use up the Air Force's jet pilot resources when we could train sergeants to be FACs," he stated. Much later, after the buildup in Southeast Asia, the Air Force did run low on fighter strength partly because so many pilots were spending their combat tours flying FAC aircraft. Soon after arriving at Eglin, Aderholt recommended that all nonflying air commandos be trained to control air strikes, either from the ground or while airborne flying in planes piloted by Air America or other pilots. General Pritchard finally got General LeMay's approval for the concept that air commandos would be trained to FAC themselves. Aderholt established a forward air guide school to train enlisted air commandos, combat controllers, and special forces people to call in air strikes and to guide aircraft onto their targets. Personnel who had come back from a tour with the air commandos in Vietnam developed a handbook that was used in training the other forward air guides.[62]

The enlisted and nonrated officer FACs in Laos were known by their call sign, Butterfly. The Butterfly controllers belonged to the Water Pump detachment but flew in the right seat of planes piloted by Air America pilots. They initially spotted targets for the T-28s operating over Laos but later directed air strikes by jet aircraft that were diverted from North Vietnam to hit targets in Laos. They did a remarkable job until General Momyer found out in early 1967 that enlisted men were guiding jet fighters onto their targets. He had them replaced with rated officers flying O-1s, who became known by their call sign as Raven FACs.[63]

Gold Fire I: "Can We Control Heinie?"

Concurrent with the massive buildup of air power in Southeast Asia, Major General Charles R. Bond Jr. became deputy commander of Seventh/Thirteenth Air Force headquarrters at Udorn. A soft-spoken, no-nonsense Texan, General Bond had been a maverick of sorts in his early years, leaving military service for a brief period in 1941 to serve as a volunteer with General Claire Chennault's Flying Tigers in China. His steady hand was appropriate for a headquarters serving two masters—General Momyer in Vietnam (who exercised operational control over Thai-based USAF tactical units) and Lieutenant General James W. Wilson in the Philippines (who had command jurisdiction over the units in Thailand). Bond had been at Udorn nearly a year when he learned in late 1966 that Colonel Aderholt was to take command of the 56th Air Commando Wing at Nakhon Phanom. He turned to a major on his staff and asked, half in jest, "Do you think we can control Heinie?"[64]

That major was Larry Ropka, who had transferred to Hurlburt when his CIA tour was up in July 1964 and then deployed to Thailand with the 606th Air Commando Squadron when Aderholt was reassigned to the Philippines. Aderholt and Ropka met General Bond two years earlier when he was deputy commander of Tactical Air Command's Ninth Air Force at Shaw AFB. They had worked together during Gold Fire I, a Strike Command joint test and evaluation exercise conducted in the vicinity of Fort Leonard Wood, Missouri, from 29 October through 13 November 1964.[65]

Initially, Strike Command had excluded counterinsurgency forces from Gold Fire I and denied a request from General Pritchard that the air commandos be given an opportunity to demonstrate their capability to contain or negate guerrilla activity in the exercise. Three weeks before the start of the exercise, however, higher headquarters alerted the SAWC commander that revised plans for Gold Fire I included a counterinsurgency phase and that special air warfare forces would participate. Pritchard picked Colonel Aderholt to command the small composite force of six U-10s, five B-26Ks, three C-47s, and an O-1 spotter plane. Their mission was to conduct special operations—including tactical airlift, reconnaissance, psychological warfare, and simulated strikes—against guerrilla forces operating in the exercise area.[66]

Gold Fire I was the largest air-land training exercise that Strike Command had conducted to date. Ropka recalled that participating forces had rented entire farms in the exercise area and built landing fields to accommodate C-130s and larger transports. The revised scenario for the maneuvers called for a large-scale invasion, preceded by a counterinsurgency phase lasting approximately a week. According to Ropka, Aderholt's experience during earlier maneuvers had convinced him that the Army guerrillas in Gold Fire I would cheat. "The guerrilla forces had become notorious for breaking the rules," Ropka stated. "They had large sums of money and used underhanded tactics such as paying local farmers to hide military vehicles, equipment, and soldiers in their barns. They had made it difficult, if not impossible, to conduct successful counterinsurgency operations against them." He said the air commandos were stymied, knowing the Army players had cheated on the rules, but unable to prove it. Colonel Aderholt was determined not to let it happen again.[67]

After briefing his suspicions to General Pritchard, he got permission to send Ropka and four other commandos to Missouri in advance to scout the area and to gather intelligence on guerrilla movements. A captain in the group owned an agriculture spraying operation, so they drove his truck with the company logo to Missouri as cover. Posing as a farm equipment salesman, Ropka checked into a motel where he served as the focal point, while the others were out spying on the "enemy." The brother-in-law of Sergeant Joe Monty, an NCO on the team, was a longtime member of the state highway patrol and, according to Ropka, "knew everybody and everything that went on around the Fort Leonard Wood area." With the brother-in-law's help, they were able to figure out the Army players' pattern of operations, and to trace their movements. "We learned where they were renting their cars, knew the cars they were driving and their license numbers," Ropka explained. "The guys were tracking them and calling me. I collated all the information on a daily basis and called it back to Hurlburt."[68]

About ten days into the undercover operation, Ropka got a call from Colonel Aderholt to close it down and return to Hurlburt immediately. General

Air commandos flew strike missions and trained Thai and Lao pilots for combat in the AT-28.

Pritchard learned that TAC headquarters had an inkling of what they were doing and had been nosing around, so he got nervous and called off the operation. When Ropka and the others got back, they reviewed their findings with Colonel Aderholt. Ropka said he was so excited about the success of their operation that he rushed back to Pritchard's office and pleaded with the general to keep the five men assigned to him until the counterinsurgency phase of the exercise was over. Pritchard finally relented but told Aderholt that he would lead the parade at his court-martial if they got caught.[69]

When the team returned to the Fort Leonard Wood area, the captain who owned the spraying company saw a Piper Cub for sale, purchased it, and introduced a spy plane into the undercover operation. Ropka said that by the time the exercise opened, the team knew where the guerrillas were, what they were going to do, and how they were going to do it. Armed with precise intelligence, Aderholt formed a special three-aircraft team consisting of a B-26K, a C-47, and an O-1E Bird Dog, which "played havoc with the guerrilla forces." The B-26 flew simulated strikes against guerrillas ferreted out by the low, slow-flying Bird Dogs. The C-47 served as the communications bridge between the spotter and strike aircraft and was the relay point between the aircraft and ground stations. Operating from a base in Malden, Missouri, the air commandos were burning up fuel faster than the civilian contractor could supply it.[70]

"We killed every guerrilla twice," Ropka said, laughing. "They changed umpires. They thought we were in collusion with some of the umpires, so they doubled them. They just could not believe we were capturing these guys coming out of barns or whatever on film." Not satisfied with just wiping out the guerrillas, Aderholt sent Ropka and Secord to General Bond's exercise headquarters in the backwoods of Missouri with a plan to defeat the entire invading force. "It became so obvious that we knew what was going on, they threw us out of the exercise," Ropka stated. "Dick and I were working with General Bond to end the war, and they told us to go home. They threw us out, not for being bad, but for being too good."[71]

General Bond praised the special air warfare unit's unique ability to provide effective air strikes on guerrilla targets as well as timely and valuable intelligence around the clock, which he said had enhanced the overall air capability. He also noted the exemplary way in which Aderholt and his forces had integrated into the overall tactical air command and control system. "I should be happy to have your forces in any command that I might have in the future," Bond declared. Aderholt shrugged. "We were good," he said, but added emphatically, "The credit must go to the wrench benders who kept those aircraft in commission and the pilots who flew the seven- to ten-hour missions." Not to mention the undercover spy operations, which nobody did.[72]

Chief Master Sergeant Hap Lutz recalled an earlier Strike Command exercise, Swift Strike III, held in the summer of 1963 before Colonel Aderholt became wing commander. During Swift Strike III, Lutz was a member of the counterinsurgency forces Blue team headed by the wing director of operations, Aderholt's alleged archenemy. Aderholt commanded the Red team. "We got our pants beat off. The Red team really mopped us up," Lutz said. For his role in Swift Strike III, Aderholt was awarded Strike Command's newly authorized Joint Services Commendation Medal. The command cited his "contagious enthusiasm and dedication to duty," crediting him "for the outstanding performance and tremendous success" of both conventional and unconventional warfare operations. Lutz added a commonly made observation about Colonel Aderholt: "He puts everything he has into everything he does. He doesn't like to lose."[73]

The colonel's enthusiasm extended to the monthly aerial exercises that the air commandos hosted to demonstrate their unique operations and capabilities to other government agencies and the public. The program consisted of a presentation by the SAWC briefing team, a static display, a daylight exercise conducted at Hurlburt Field, and a night ordnance delivery exercise conducted at one of the gunnery ranges. The daylight exercise, which consisted of various methods of aerial resupply, short field takeoffs and landings by STOL aircraft, personnel paradrops, and so on, did not demand the interest that audiences showed for the more spectacular weapons demonstrations that lit up the night.[74] When attendance at the daylight exercises dropped off, Aderholt (who was vice commander at the time) decided that the wing had to make the airlift events more interesting.

Larry Ropka had been at Hurlburt only a few weeks when Colonel Aderholt called him and another officer, Major Joseph Kittinger, to his office to discuss a scheme he had for putting more life into the daylight exercises. The two officers were assigned to the B-26 squadron but were on loan to the combat applications group specifically for the purpose of putting the day show together. Joe Kittinger, who had just returned from a combat tour flying B-26s in Vietnam, was a celebrated officer in his own right. Before joining the air commandos in June 1963, he served ten years in Air Force Systems Command, where he parachuted from 102,800 feet, the highest altitude ever jumped. Larry Ropka had been involved in developing aerial delivery techniques while serving with the CIA in Washington.[75]

"We have to jazz up the afternoon air show," Aderholt told the two majors. "I want you guys to put together an event to show these people how we drop live animals to guerrillas and natives out in the boondocks. Obviously, we don't have any water buffalos or cows, so you will have to substitute some pigs and chickens."

"Colonel, have you ever heard a pig squeal?" Kittinger asked.

"Of course I know how a pig squeals," Aderholt answered. "What does that have to do with anything? We have dropped pigs in combat and all over the place."

"I know, Colonel, but all these little old ladies that come out here . . . and the bunny huggers," Kittinger protested. "Don't you think it's going to scare the hell out of them and leave a bad impression about what we do?"

"We need to show people exactly what we do," Aderholt told them. "Just go ahead and do it."

They asked, "Where do we get a pig?"

"Get Monty to do it," Aderholt said. "He hunts pigs."

So the two majors left to carry out the colonel's orders. They had the detachment in Panama send them some bamboo crates to use for airdropping chickens and asked Sergeant Monty to help them find a pig. "Eglin's plumb full of pigs," replied Monty, who was an avid hunter. "I'll go get you one." So Monty went out near the garbage dump and trapped a wild pig. Kittinger described the animal as an "honest-to-god Russian boar hog" and said Monty kept it in a pen down by the hangar until the day of the air show. Ropka said the pig weighed about eighty pounds and was loud and mean. On the morning of the air show, they were still nervous about dropping the pig and returned to the vice commander's office to try to change his mind.[76]

"Colonel, I would really like to have you reconsider this," Kittinger said. "This pig drop is going to be counterproductive, and I don't think we should do it."

"No sweat," Aderholt replied. "I want you to go ahead and do it."

About that time the wing commander, Colonel Bradburn, walked in, and Aderholt said to him, "Joe and Larry don't want to drop that pig this afternoon."

Bradburn stopped and asked, "What pig?"

"We are going to drop this pig and some chickens to show these folks how we drop them all over Southeast Asia," Aderholt said. "Joe and Larry don't think we should do it, but I told them to go ahead and do it."

Kittinger recalled that the wing commander had a funny look on his face, "like maybe he didn't think too much about the idea either," but said that he just turned and walked out because "he kind of let Heinie do what Heinie wanted to do anyway." The two majors left to get the air show ready. The base veterinarian gave the pig a shot of phenobarbital, but one of the maintenance officers still had to wrestle the pig to the ground to get it into a harness and load it aboard the aircraft. The harness was padded with foam rubber that was nearly two feet thick to protect the pig when it landed. "We were in more danger of being hurt by the pig than he was from being dropped out of the plane," Ropka said, laughing.[77]

The aircraft participating in the air show took off approximately two hours before the guests were seated in the reviewing stands and orbited until it was time to make their runs from the initial points (IPs) to their prescheduled events in front of the spectators. The one carrying the pig also had four crates of chickens on board. "We had a timer on the crates, so they would pop open seconds after leaving the plane," Kittinger said, "and the chickens would fly out over the countryside." The pig was attached to a parachute, and a combat controller was standing by on the ground, ready to grab the pig and take him away from the landing zone. Aderholt and Bradburn were standing together near the microphone where Kittinger and Ropka were announcing the events. The stands were filled to capacity, with approximately three thousand spectators watching the show. The aircraft approached, flying at about 250 feet, and the loudspeakers announced that the aircrew was going to demonstrate how they dropped animals to indigenous people around the world. A murmur went through the crowd. Kittinger described what happened next: "You could hear that damned pig squealing over the roar of those engines even as they approached. They dropped him out along with the chickens. The chute opened perfectly, and that pig squealed all the way to the ground. You could have heard that damned pig from five miles away. He wasn't hurt. A pig will squeal from you just looking at him. But those little old ladies and bunny huggers didn't know that, and they were saying, 'Oh, my god. Oh, just listen. Oh, isn't that terrible.' That combat controller grabbed that pig and got him out of there. You could still hear that son of a bitch squealing half an hour later. Bradburn was livid. It was all Heinie could do to keep a straight face."[78]

Afterward Aderholt and Dick Secord were in his office laughing about the demonstration when Bradburn came in. "That was a *fine* demonstration," he said sarcastically. "We're glad you liked it," Aderholt said. Bradburn glared. "As long as I'm commander, it won't happen again," he said. Aderholt laughed. "I'm glad you told me because I was planning on dropping a cow next time," he said.[79]

Proponents of a Lesser War

Whatever activity the air commandos were involved in at Hurlburt during 1964–65, the war in Vietnam was never far from their thoughts. Nearly everyone agreed that South Vietnam was losing the war, but there were heated disagreements over what to do about it. The voices for helping the South Vietnamese develop a winning counterinsurgency strategy were unfortunately drowned out by the growing fervor for an American solution to the war. All the maverick warriors from Eglin and Hurlburt could do was watch with rising frustration as escalation of the war repudiated ten years of national military strategy guided by the principle that U.S. forces would not fight other nations' wars.

General David M. Shoup, who retired in December 1963 after four years as commandant of the U.S. Marine Corps, later wrote that the chiefs of the armed services before 1964 had "deemed it unnecessary and unwise for U.S. forces to become involved in any ground war in Southeast Asia." Shoup, who was awarded the Medal of Honor for heroism in the Battle of Tarawa in 1943, held strong opinions against the involvement of U.S. forces in the war. He blamed the escalation in part on the race among the four services to build up combat strength in Southeast Asia and on "the same old interservice rivalry to demonstrate respective importance and combat effectiveness."[80]

Once the force buildup began, few senior military officers dared challenge it. One who did so in discussions with higher officials was Air Force general Jacob E. Smart, who replaced Rosie O'Donnell as commander in chief, Pacific Air Forces, in August 1963. At one time Smart was seen as a candidate to succeed Admiral Harry Felt as commander in chief in the Pacific, a post traditionally held by the Navy. It was no surprise when Secretary of Defense McNamara appointed another admiral instead. General Smart's many admirers were disappointed, however, when he was reassigned to the European Command as deputy commander in chief after only one year at the PACAF helm. General Hunter Harris succeeded Smart in the top Air Force post in the Pacific on 1 August 1964. Smart later revealed that he had been relieved as PACAF commander for expressing views that were counter to the Pentagon's Vietnam policy. He maintained that Vietnam was a counterinsurgency war and the massive use of U.S. military power was the wrong way to fight it.[81]

Colonel Aderholt was one of the Air Force's most outspoken critics of the U.S. buildup in Southeast Asia. He advocated minimal U.S. involvement in the war and far greater emphasis on counterinsurgency operations by indigenous forces. He believed the war would be a long, drawn-out campaign that had to be won or lost by the Vietnamese. If the United States could not accept that, then it would be far better to back off now than to bog down U.S. forces in a quagmire from which it would be far more difficult to extricate them. Within these parameters Aderholt devoted much thought and study to more effective ways to apply the limited Vietnamese Air Force (VNAF) resources in combating the Viet Cong and the North Vietnamese infiltrators. Two officers Aderholt relied on extensively in these study efforts were Captains Ahmann and Secord.[82]

One of their concepts, the Joint Attack Force (JAF), was the later focus of a RAND Corporation paper entitled "SIAT: The Single Integrated Attack Team. A Concept for Offensive Military Operations in South Vietnam." "We felt so strongly about the concept that we got in terrible fights while we were working on it," Aderholt said. One thing they agreed on was that the concept had to make maximum use of indigenous forces if it was going to work. They envisioned using closely knit air-ground teams, comprising both visual reconnaissance and attack aircraft, in an attempt to aggressively isolate specific geographic areas. If the team succeeded in isolating one sector, the concept called for additional team efforts to keep spreading out through Vietnam like an oil slick. "Well, it didn't work because the U.S. military was moving in full scale and not even considering a small effort in a long, slow war," Aderholt said grimly. "We were going in there and kick the shit out of them and get out tomorrow. You just don't do that."[83]

Secord described the JAF as a simple concept of operations, but an anathema to Air Force planners because "it called for a lot of decentralization." He explained that it required dedicated visual reconnaissance sector by sector, with supporting strike assets dedicated over a wider area. The aircrews and the forces on the ground would become so familiar with a sector that they would be on top of the enemy "like a swarm of hornets" every time they moved. "You can't do that kind of an operation sitting in Saigon sending out automated frag orders," he said. While he and Ahmann worked on the concept, Secord said Aderholt was the driving force behind it. "If you read that study, you can put Aderholt's name on it," he said. He recalled that defending such concepts while criticizing others, such as the buildup and use of tactical fighters to peck away at targets over North Vietnam, kept them in constant hot water with the TAC generals.[84]

Colonel John A. Doonan, a retired Air Force chaplain, was a captain at Hurlburt from July 1963 to June 1965. "In sixteen months I personally buried thirty-three airmen," he said. "Many of them died in Vietnam. Others died on Range #52 at Eglin, desperately testing ways to bring more effective close-in support to our people under fire in jungles, rice paddies, and on rivers." He recalled that Colonel Aderholt was always the one to break the sad news to the families, and to make certain that everything possible was done to take care of them. Doonan described Aderholt as "father, protector, comforter, and pastor" to the families of those brave men who had been killed. He said the colonel's philosophy was, "To hell with the rules. They are still our people and part of this wing. It's the least we will do for those who died for their country—to look after their wives and families."[85]

Chaplain Doonan described Colonel Aderholt's attitude, determination, and dedication in the cockpit or in the office as "electrifying" and said the crews at Hurlburt would follow him anywhere and go wherever he sent them. He said the colonel was "truly considered one of the boys," but no one ever crossed over the threshold of military courtesy in the free moments of socializing. First and foremost he took care of his people with no thought to his own career. "In the process of taking care of his troops and their families, he ran afoul of a system or people with the system, who sought to squelch both his enthusiasm and his career," Doonan said. "He should have become a general officer years before his time."[86]

Jimmy Ifland recalled that Aderholt had really inspired the younger officers and had brought the kind of experience that was essential in explaining why things had to be done. He noted, however, that not all of SAWC's senior staff agreed with Aderholt's philosophy "that we had to let these people fight their own wars." He also said there were a number of senior officers at Eglin and Hurlburt who "stayed at arm's length from Aderholt because his approach to getting things done was certainly not the generally accepted way in the Air Force."[87]

"You could say the same for the wing commander, who didn't know anything about special air warfare," Aderholt said. "He wanted to get rid of me because I had the loyalty of the troops, but he hadn't figured out how to do it."[88]

Aderholt said he finally came to Bradburn's rescue by checking out in the A-1 aircraft and volunteering to command the 3rd Tactical Fighter Wing, which was deploying from England AFB, Louisiana, to Bien Hoa AB, Vietnam, in November 1965. To relieve overcrowded airfield space and facilities at Hurlburt, the 1st Air Commando Wing was scheduled to move to England AFB the following January. "I sure as hell didn't want to go to England AFB. It was time to move on," Aderholt said. "The genius who said coming in second was like kissing your sister must have been a vice commander." Unfortunately, however, General Childre was no longer on the Air Staff, and word came back from the Pentagon that Colonel Aderholt could not command the 3rd TFWg because he was not a jet pilot. The wing had both A-1 and F-100 aircraft.[89]

Colonel Aderholt called the officers' personnel section in Washington and was told his assignment had been changed to Clark Field in the Philippines. "I tore this guy's ass up," he said. An hour or so later the phone rang and General Pritchard was on the line. "That guy said you called him up and cussed him out," Pritchard said. Aderholt was still fuming. "You're goddamn right, General, they are screwing around with my assignment. I volunteer for combat in Vietnam and thought I was going to get the 3rd Wing. I go out and get combat ready in the A-1, and now they tell me that I can't command the wing. They are sending me to Clark Field." Pritchard said he was told it was an Air Staff–directed assignment. He calmed Aderholt down and told him to go on to Clark and try to get to Vietnam from there. Aderholt gave in.[90]

Pritchard thought the world of Aderholt, and it was obvious from a letter the general wrote the following spring that he was familiar with the myriad Heinie Aderholt stories. In the letter he said that he corresponded with Aderholt frequently. "What a guy," he wrote, "whether the problem is gluing an O-1 back together or finding a hundred cases of San Miguel beer for spook camps."[91] The feeling was mutual. Aderholt said it was tragic that Pritchard, who had made two stars while at Eglin, was not sent to Southeast Asia to take over the air war in South Vietnam. He described Pritchard as a "dynamic, hard-charging" commander who "would back you to hell and back." "He was a drinker and a hell-raiser, but he was a brilliant man, and he was a great leader," Aderholt said. "Gil Pritchard would have been the best commander that could have been sent to Southeast Asia at that time to fight the war in the south."[92]

7. FACES OF A MISBEGOTTEN WAR

General Harris seemed genuinely glad to see Colonel Aderholt when he dropped by the four-star commander's office on Hickam AFB en route to the Philippines in August 1965. The two men had been introduced four years earlier by Robert "Red" Jantzen, the CIA station chief in Bangkok, during the period that Aderholt ran covert air operations out of Takhli. Hunter Harris was not a particularly strong commander but was known throughout the Air Force as a gregarious, hands-on general who believed in taking care of his people. A military man through and through, Harris was born in 1909 while his father, an Army major, was stationed at Fort Sam Houston in San Antonio, Texas. After graduating from the U.S. Military Academy in 1932, he was detailed to the Army Air Corps and became a rated pilot in October 1933. Through the years he had flown almost every aircraft in the Air Force's inventory. He was vice commander in chief of SAC before succeeding General Smart as PACAF commander in chief just before the Tonkin Gulf incident in 1964.[1]

The last word Colonel Aderholt had about his assignment before leaving Hurlburt was that he would be the deputy inspector general at Thirteenth Air Force headquarters. The IG at the Thirteenth was Colonel Robert Gates, who previously served as General Pritchard's deputy at Eglin. Accompanied by Jessie and the children, Aderholt stopped at Hickam, where he was supposed to attend a five-day orientation course. He went to see General Harris on the first day to try to get the assignment changed. He knew from his tour in Germany that he wanted nothing more to do with the IG function. "I'm a combat soldier, not an IG," he said to General Harris. "I know as much about fighting the war in Vietnam as anybody, and that's where I ought to be." The general said in an

The Aderholt family at
Fort Walton Beach,
Fla., in 1964. (Left to
right) Jessie, George,
Janet, and Colonel
Aderholt.

understanding voice, "Heinie, you and the family enjoy the beach for a few
days and go on down to Clark. I'll see if we can't drum up something different
for you when you get there."[2]

When they arrived at Clark, Colonel Gates and his wife, Jenny, welcomed
them with traditional island leis and drove them to the guest quarters. "Bob,
don't take it personal, but I'm not going to be your deputy," Aderholt said on
the way over. "I'm just not cut out to be an IG." Gates did not discuss the matter, but the next morning Aderholt was standing in front of Lieutenant General
James W. "Whip" Wilson, who had one of the meanest reputations in the Air
Force. Like Harris, General Wilson took care of his people but had fired commanders on the spot when they failed to meet his standards. Unsmiling, Wilson
said, "I understand we have a little rebellion here." Aderholt replied, "Yes, sir.
That's true." He cited the same reasons he had given to General Harris, that he
was "a combat soldier" who knew special operations like the back of his hand.

"I would be no good to you sitting behind a desk or writing up IG reports," he said.[3]

"General Harris called me," Wilson said. "He said you were a big, bad air commando. I don't have anything for you in my headquarters, but they need a colonel in the materiel wing to run plans and operations. That's the best I can do." Aderholt left and went to the 6200th Materiel Wing headquarters where he met the commander, Colonel Harry L. Waesche, an officer he later described as a "fantastic" person and one of the finest men he had ever known. The deputy commander was Colonel Peter R. DeLonga, who became a good friend and rose to two-star rank during the waning years of the Vietnam War. Although Aderholt was with the wing less than a year, it proved to be a fast-paced, rewarding assignment with "a great group of people."[4]

Kicking the Tires and Lighting the Fires

Although units from Clark were not directly involved in combat in Vietnam, the base was the U.S. military logistics hub for Southeast Asia operations. To support the buildup of air power in Vietnam and Thailand, the base population doubled to sixty thousand people between 1963 and 1967, making Clark the second-most-populous USAF installation. A 350-bed hospital was completed in 1964 to serve as a medical center for the war's sick and wounded. The materiel wing was deeply involved in supporting the combat units, and the USAF units and bases in Thailand were General Wilson's responsibility as Thirteenth Air Force commander, although the Seventh Air Force commander in Vietnam exercised control over their operations. The mission at Clark was critical to the overall war effort, and the support operations sustained a high level of readiness throughout the protracted conflict.[5]

During Colonel Aderholt's orientation briefings, he learned that one of the greatest threats to the mission was the rising crime rate on Clark, particularly the theft of government property. Afterward he was present at the Thirteenth Air Force commander's weekly staff meeting when the combat support group commander reported on recent thefts at the base. During the discussion that followed, General Wilson mentioned an earlier incident when one of the base's fire trucks had been stolen. Aderholt's look of amusement caused the general to glare at him and ask, "What is so goddamn funny, Colonel?" Aderholt replied, "Sir, I'm no expert, since nobody steals from the air commandos, but how can anybody drive off in something as big as a fire truck without the firemen and guards at the gate knowing what is going on?" Wilson snapped back, "Answer your own question—you're the big bad-ass air commando. I'm putting you in charge of cleaning up Clark. I want you to stop the natives from stealing us blind."

"Yes, sir, you support me, and I will give it my best shot," Aderholt replied.

"You'll do better than that," Wilson said. "I will back you to the hilt, but if you don't get the job done, I'll run your ass off."[6]

Aderholt thrived on challenges. With General Wilson's approval, he inaugurated a vigorous antitheft program under the supervision of the air police squadron at Clark. The squadron moved many of its personnel out from behind desks and into operations to strengthen the new program but still lacked the resources needed to secure the base. Wilson authorized Aderholt to make up the difference by addressing the troops in every unit on base and rounding up volunteers to serve as air police augmentees. "We've got a problem, men, and need your help," he told them. "I have drawn three hundred softball bats from supply and ordered seven hundred more. We are going to walk this goddamn base, and we are going to stop the theft on this base. The men who volunteer for five hundred hours, I will see that [they get] a commendation medal." The response was overwhelming. By the end of 1965 the air police squadron's operations had been augmented by more than one thousand volunteers.[7]

Major Arthur E. "Gene" Overton, who was a pilot on Clark at the time, recalled that the sprawling installation was protected by twenty-seven miles of perimeter fence. There were hundreds of acres of open area known as the "pea patch" between the fence and the base complex. There were large gaps in the fence where thieves had either broken through or had stolen the metal fencing. The pea patch, which was covered with buffalo grass eight feet high and laced with miles of tunnellike trails, protected the thieves more than it did the base. Colonel Aderholt had the buffalo grass cut down and the fences repaired but realized that the air police needed more than augmentees if they were going to stop thieves. They needed all the speed and mobility they could get to cover the entire base and the pea patch as well.[8]

He went to General Wilson to get funding for motorcycles. "General, these guys are willing to pay for their wheels if we will finance them," he explained. "I will fly up to Japan and get the motorcycles." Wilson approved the funds. Aderholt and Overton flew a DC-6 to Japan to purchase the motorcycles (forty for the security police and thirty-five for other personnel) and bring them back to Clark. "The air police ran motorcycle patrols, while we had an L-20 in the air nearly every night droning around, dropping a flare every now and then," Aderholt said. Then one of the men suggested that horses would be better for patrolling the perimeter fences because the motorcycles made too much noise. Aderholt said to Wilson, "Why don't we get some horses?" The general agreed, and Aderholt and the troops flew down to Australia and bought twenty horses for the riding academy at Clark. Fifteen of the horses were reassigned to the air police squadron. In December the squadron reported that it had added mounted police to its force.[9]

When Aderholt learned that gangs were not only breaking through the fences but actually stealing them, he called on his old friend from Korean War and CIA days, Bob Brewer, to find out how to sabotage the posts. They were stealing the cyclone fencing, knocking the concrete poles down, and taking the reinforcement bar that was inside. Brewer, who was in Manila training the Filipino special forces, suggested putting an explosive substance known as composition 4 in the concrete poles. "We got some composition 4 and tried it," Aderholt said. "One night a guy ran out and hit a fence post with his sledgehammer, and it blew up. No more breaking down the fences after that."[10]

On another occasion he got a call at home around midnight that a gang of thieves had stolen M-16 rifles and were leaving the base going back over a hill at the rifle range. He gave orders to have everyone assemble at the firing range, then called the head of the Philippine constabulary and had them put a blocking force on the other side of the hill. Using helicopters and firing M-16 rifles, Aderholt and his men drove the thieves over the hill and into the arms of the constabulary waiting on the other side. They recovered all of the stolen rifles. The next morning at the staff meeting, Aderholt reported the operation to General Wilson, adding, "You know, General, I told you that nobody steals from the air commandos."[11]

General Wilson had reason to be pleased with the antitheft program. By the end of June 1966 serious crimes and incidents, that is, major thefts, housebreaking, and armed robberies, during the previous six months had decreased by almost two-thirds, from sixty-six to twenty-six. The monetary value of property reported lost or stolen during the six-month period totaled $78,412, compared to $343,222 during the last six months of 1965, a decrease of $264,810. At the same time, the recovery rate for lost property had doubled, from 15 to 29 percent. Aderholt was first to admit there was a price to pay for cleaning up the base, however. He recalled that the first night they brought the horses in from Australia, a C-141 suffered major damage when it struck a loose horse on the runway. Not long afterward he and Gene Overton accidentally dropped a flare from the L-20 on the hospital and set it afire. On yet another night he got an urgent call that one of the augmentees had killed an intruder. He hurried to the scene and found that a black airmen he had posted on a culvert leading from off-base had struck an intruder with a baseball bat and killed him. When asked by the air police what they were to do with the body, Aderholt told them, "Back your truck up to the fence and throw his ass back where he came from." The colonel had his life threatened by gangs outside the base, but the threats were never carried out.[12]

The Manila newspapers were already up in arms over false reports of Filipinos being executed on base. Aderholt had the augmentees, who usually reported after the theater let out at nine P.M. to begin their rounds, hold mock burials at the fence line to discourage would-be thieves. One night he had them stage a mock killing, with augmentees yelling loudly as they chased a lone individual sprinting toward the fence. A large group of Filipinos, attracted by the shouts, had gathered on the other side to see what all the noise was about. As the make-believe thief hit the fence and tried to climb over, he was bathed in light when an L-20 flew over and dropped a flare. The men chasing him opened up with machine guns, firing blanks. He fell backward onto the base. The armed men gathered around him to shield the body from the crowd across the fence. A military ambulance, its siren screaming, pulled up, and the medics got out, threw the body into the ambulance, got back in, and roared off. "We thought we were really onto something because things sure were quiet for a few nights," Aderholt said. "But the Manila papers started raising hell about us mowing people down with machine guns, and that was the end of that."[13]

When he addressed the units at Clark about security, Aderholt had warned them against becoming involved with the criminal element on the outside. "These crooks have people on the inside who are requisitioning supplies and driving them out the front gate, taking them down to Manila, and shipping them out to Indonesia," he told the troops. "If anyone approaches you with a proposition or you see any suspicious activity, I want you to report to me." Several days later a sergeant reported seeing a civilian in the NCO club giving large sums of money to other people and overhearing their conversation about stealing an entire shipment of reconnaissance film. An undercover operation disclosed where and when they were going to steal the film, and how they were going to do it. Aderholt had their vehicle marked with a luminous substance and followed it the night of the theft in an L-20. When the thieves got to Manila, the Filipino FBI was waiting for them. The arrest led to breaking up a ring that had infiltrated the base and had been working hand-in-hand with employees in base supply and the motor pool.[14]

By all accounts the thefts at Clark were symptomatic of the greater problem of crime and corruption that plagued Filipino society. During the 1965 elections presidential candidate Ferdinand Marcos won a landslide victory at the polls by declaring war on Filipino smuggling, murder, and government corruption. Although he would be driven into exile years later for the same crimes,

President Marcos got off to an impressive start in early 1966 by using marines, paratroopers, and naval gunboats to crack down on Luzon's notorious gangs of smugglers. Part of the strategy that Marcos adopted was an air plan that was proposed to him by Thirteenth Air Force to reduce and ultimately prevent smuggling into the Philippine Islands. General Wilson and Colonel Waesche gave Colonel Aderholt credit for developing the plan.[15]

Among other accomplishments while he was at Clark, Aderholt organized and established an airlift system utilizing organizational aircraft to fly combat troops on rest and recuperation leave from Vietnam to Bangkok and Manila. Colonel Waesche noted in mid-1966 that the airlift had not missed a single schedule while transporting over four thousand personnel per month.[16] Although Aderholt was swamped with mission responsibilities at Clark, his thoughts were never far from the air commandos and the escalating war in Vietnam and Laos. The commandos knew they could count on him, whenever the time, wherever the place.

One day an airmen at wing headquarters answered the telephone, and the caller, in a crackling voice distorted by static, identified himself as Doc Lutz calling from Texas. He asked to speak to Colonel Aderholt, pleading frantically that it was an emergency call only the colonel would understand. After what seemed like an eternity to the caller, Colonel Aderholt finally came on the line. "Happy, what in the hell is going on?" he asked. He knew Hap Lutz was back in Laos for a second tour and that his call sign at Savannakhet was "Texas 7." Chief Lutz had reached him on a field phone from Laos and feared that he might lose the connection at any moment. To protect his location and the mission, he quickly explained the reason for his call in a code that he knew the colonel would understand.[17]

Lutz urgently needed medical supplies to help the people of Attopeu, the home of General Thao Ma, chief of the Royal Laotian air force. Because General Ma's T-28s were bombing and strafing their positions daily, the Pathet Lao had targeted Attopeu in retaliation. The general had called Chief Lutz to his office and sought his help in getting medical supplies. He stated that the Pathet Lao were burning and pillaging the town, killing, raping, and maiming the inhabitants. The medical staff was completely out of supplies and equipment as a result of the onslaught. Lutz's own supplies at Savannakhet and those back at the Water Pump detachment in Thailand were nearly depleted. Hap said he turned to the one person he knew who could break through the bureaucratic logjam to get the needed supplies. He called Colonel Heinie Aderholt.[18]

Lutz provided a shopping list of urgently needed items, leaving it up to the colonel to get the quantities he could. He never asked how Colonel Aderholt got the supplies or where they came from, but was notified two days later that an aircraft had landed at Udorn with a full load of cargo addressed to him. Hap recalled the event: "I flew to Udorn in a Lao C-47 scrambled for the occasion to get our precious cargo. Once we loaded the aircraft—and I mean fully loaded, to the extent there was barely room for me and the crew—we took off utilizing the entire runway. We stopped briefly in Savannakhet to refuel for the flight to Attopeu. With an escort of four T-28s, with General Ma in the lead aircraft, we headed for Attopeu. We landed without incident and downloaded the lifesaving medical supplies and equipment."[19]

Former Water Pump commander Colonel Bill Thomas told a story about asking Aderholt's help in getting a half-dozen cases of San Miguel beer for his Army special forces friends at Da Nang, Vietnam, in the spring of 1966. Soon after Aderholt left Hurlburt, Thomas had volunteered to go back to Southeast Asia, where he became the senior operations adviser for the 41st VNAF Combat Wing at Da Nang. He became friends with Lieutenant Colonel Ray Call, who was in charge of the nearby special forces outfit. Ray had done favors for Thomas and the Vietnamese airmen, so Bill asked if there was anything he could do for Call and his troops in return. "We could sure put away a few cases of San Miguel beer," Call said, thinking it was out of the question. Thomas thought immediately of Heinie Aderholt, who was already helping him get surplus furniture from Clark for the VNAF wing. His fighter squadron adviser, Major Les Hewitt, had flown to Clark to bring the furniture back to Da Nang. He called Aderholt, who asked how many cases of San Miguel the special forces wanted. Because the plane would be loaded with furniture coming back, Thomas asked him to squeeze in as many cases as they could.[20]

Thomas said the next day he was notified that a DC-6 was in the landing pattern, and the pilot wanted to talk with him. "Yes, it was Heinie Aderholt flying the DC-6 from Clark, and on board was furniture for the VNAF and one hundred cases of San Miguel beer," Thomas said. "Heinie signed a chit for it. Ray paid in full on delivery." He noted that Aderholt had never met Ray Call before then, but had made a friend for life. It was another example that Aderholt was always there for the men in combat and always had a helping hand for those who needed it.[21]

When Colonel Aderholt got back to Clark, General Wilson informed him that General Harris had called and wanted him on the next flight to Hawaii. Wilson understood that PACAF had a special assignment earmarked for Aderholt in Saigon. Earlier, Barney Cochran (now assigned to the Pentagon) had alerted Aderholt that the Air Force had an urgent requirement to set up a recovery operation for downed pilots in Southeast Asia. During discussions with

A-1 of the 602d ACSq
delivers ordnance in
Laos, 1967.

General Harris, Cochran had mentioned Aderholt as the ideal person to develop and head the recovery operation. Harris agreed and called Aderholt in to
PACAF headquarters to talk it over.[22]

When Aderholt met with General Harris, he was told that the Air Force, as
executive agent for escape and evasion, was going to establish an organization
in Saigon to recover downed pilots and U.S. personnel who were missing in
action. Later named the Joint Personnel Recovery Center (JPRC), the new organization would be part of the top-secret Studies and Observations Group, a
clandestine outfit activated in January 1964 and formerly named the Special
Operations Group. Harris told him that he would be put on TDY orders so his
family could remain in base housing at Clark while he was gone. "You are not
bound by any preconceptions and can write your own ticket," Harris said. "Just
go out there and put together something that will work." Aderholt reminded
Harris how badly he wanted a combat wing and that the Air Force had reneged
on making him a wing commander in Vietnam because he was not jet-quali-

fied. The general promised him a combat wing after going to Saigon and getting the JPRC up and running.[23]

General Harris suggested that he meet with his intelligence director, Colonel Ernest F. John, before returning to the Philippines. It turned out that John had gone through flight training with Aderholt in World War II, and they had received their wings and commissions in the same graduating class in May 1943. He told John that his concept for the JPRC was to set up dedicated recovery teams using Army rangers or special forces backed up by close air support. John argued that the teams should be all blue-suiters because it was an Air Force mission. "The Army has forces trained for this type of mission, and we don't," Aderholt reasoned. John persisted. "We can train our own forces," he said. Aderholt exploded. "Like hell we can," he said. "We don't have time. I will use the Army forces already trained to do the job." He said he knew the officer in charge of training the Army rangers and would ask for their help. If they did not come through with the resources, he would use the special forces in theater. "I'm not going to sit here quibbling with you," he said. "We have a hot mission, and I am going to get on with it." The meeting was over.[24]

Like other military officers who were opposed to escalating the war in Southeast Asia, Aderholt not only wanted to be personally involved in the conflict but felt duty bound to be there. He knew Jessie and the children would be well cared for at Clark. General Wilson was as tough as they come but was more than fair and took care of his people. He became Aderholt's champion at Clark, and Aderholt liked and respected him. Air Force OERs don't come any higher than the one Colonel Waesche wrote on Aderholt. Stating that he was an "outstanding air leader" and "definitely General Officer material," Waesche recommended his promotion to brigadier general. General Wilson concurred.[25]

Bright Light: Setting up the JPRC

For a time, until he could get the JPRC operational, Colonel Aderholt commuted between the Philippines and Saigon taking care of business at both ends. When he left Hickam after his talks with General Harris and Colonel John, Aderholt flew to Saigon to discuss the project with Seventh Air Force and SOG. He met first with Brigadier General George B. Simler, the Seventh Air Force director of operations, at Tan Son Nhut. Simler, who would pin on a second star in October, had been base commander at Kadena when Aderholt commanded the CIA detachment there. They had become friends, and Aderholt trusted Simler's judgment on setting up the JPRC and establishing a working relationship with General William C. Westmoreland's headquarters at MACV. General Simler agreed that the JPRC should be collocated with SOG and should make maximum use of the Army's special forces capabilities.[26]

Colonel Donald Blackburn, who was on his way out as SOG commander, also agreed with Aderholt's concept of operations for the JPRC. In April, Blackburn was replaced at SOG by another Army colonel, John K. Singlaub, who was an equally strong supporter of the JPRC concept. On the way to Blackburn's office, located in one of several commercial buildings that MACV headquarters occupied downtown, Aderholt's uniformed driver got caught in rush-hour traffic. As they drove slowly down Cong Ly, the four-lane boulevard leading from Tan Son Nhut into the city, the passing scene became a diorama of the changes since Aderholt was last there. The spreading shade trees, the pastel villas and walled gardens, the delicate bougainvillea and hibiscus that had once given Cong Ly a special charm and aura were choking to death on dust and exhaust fumes. The onrush of military and civilian vehicles—the roaring engines, the blaring horns, the squealing tires—was at war with a nation's culture and the environment.[27]

An ungodly roar of engines was heard coming from the other direction. Suddenly a grotesque string of riders straight out of a Hell's Angels movie appeared on the opposite side of the boulevard and roared past them on full-size motorcycles, barreling down Cong Ly toward Tan Son Nhut. "What in the hell is that?" Aderholt asked. "Those are construction workers with RMK-BRJ," the driver answered. "They are everywhere, building air bases, new buildings, a MACV headquarters near Tan Son Nhut—you name it, they're building it." "It looks like they cleaned out the streets back home to get laborers," Aderholt growled. "Those bastards will kill whatever relations we have left with the Vietnamese people." The Viet Cong don't need a psywar program, he thought, because we are doing it for them.[28]

The closer they got to the center of town, the more snarled the traffic. Every intersection became an angry choke point, every driver a kamikaze. Ahead of them, an impatient taxi squeezed around other cars and raced down the sidewalk before darting back in ahead of a straggler. Americans were everywhere, their oversize vehicles plowing through a sea of bicycles, motor scooters, small taxis, and rickshas. That evening when Aderholt stayed with friends who had rented a villa in town, he looked out from the balcony and inhaled the pungent odors of Vietnamese food and *nuoc mam* sauce wafting up from street vendors, restaurants, and neighboring residences. When darkness fell over the city, Tu Do and its side streets came alive with the revelry, the vibrant sounds, and the luminescent lights of Saigon's nightlife. In contrast, the armed guards, the sandbags, and the concertina wire around government buildings and residences gave the appearance of a city under siege.[29]

Off in the distance toward Tan Son Nhut an occasional orange flare glowed brightly, faded, and went out. The blades of a curious helicopter passed overhead stirring the night air, while a pair of VNAF A-1Es circled on the horizon. An exchange of gunfire sounded miles away in the vicinity of Cholon, a predominantly Chinese section of Saigon, then fell silent. Somewhere a string of firecrackers went off—or was it a machine gun? Well before the cathedral bells sounded curfew, all was quiet, and except for an eerie noise now and then, the shadowy, melancholy streets enjoyed a few hours' relief. What a goddamn crazy way to fight a war, Aderholt thought. We have come over here, taken all their housing, taken over their streets, taken over their war, and will surely lose the Vietnamese people even if we win the war. "The Americans in Saigon were living better than they would have at home," he would say later, adding ruefully: "If we had fought that war right and not dumped all those Americans over there, we wouldn't have needed that shameful commissary and BX system, all those air conditioners and refrigerators. We wouldn't have tactical fighters pissing away bombs all over North Vietnam, or the B-52s carpet-bombing the South, which we were supposed to be defending. We wouldn't have lost all those brave pilots and million-dollar aircraft. We wouldn't have needed a Joint Personnel Recovery Center."[30]

Colonel Aderholt ran into more interservice red tape in getting the JPRC approved, organized, and under way than he had anticipated. First, he hit a snag when the Army refused his request for rangers. Aderholt pushed for a dedicated force—arguing that he should not have to ask for resources every time he planned a mission—but officials up the chain of command disagreed. He went ahead and wrote an embryonic plan for the JPRC that relied on in-theater resources, but implementation was delayed while the Air Force and the Army worked out their differences over single-manager responsibilities for the organization. In late April the services agreed on a compromise that made the JPRC an element of MACV SOG under General Westmoreland, with terms of reference that preserved the Air Force's primary interest in search and rescue.[31]

While Aderholt waited impatiently, the JPRC's activation was delayed further when MACV J-3 (Operations) recommended activating the JPRC separately from SOG, and the Air Force tried unsuccessfully to regain control of the function by putting Seventh Air Force in charge. Finally, after months of delay, the JPRC was activated on 17 September 1966 as a separate staff division within the Studies and Observations Group. Colonel Aderholt was in charge of the JPRC, which was given the code name Bright Light. His small staff consisted of an Air Force officer (Major Lester Hansen), an Army officer (Major Charles Boatwright), and three Army enlisted men. Upon activation the JPRC acted as the focal point for all intelligence information relating to detained or missing personnel in Southeast Asia. The information was used to plan and conduct recovery operations for downed airmen in evadee or escapee status and U.S. or allied prisoners of war.[32]

Aderholt had no part in the roles and missions squabble over who would control the JPRC. Seventh Air Force did not inform him that it had reversed its position on the matter. A change of commanders in July might have influenced the about-face. Lieutenant General William W. "Spike" Momyer, who replaced Lieutenant General Joseph H. Moore in July, was a doctrinal scholar who had strong opinions about Air Force roles and missions. He had a dual role as Westmoreland's deputy commander for air operations, which, according to the Air Force's reading of joint doctrine, made him the single manager for air operations in the MACV commander's area of responsibility. Unyielding in his quest for centralized control of air operations, Momyer rejected out of hand any special arrangements for air support that compartmentalized or fragmented the use of Seventh Air Force resources.[33]

Momyer, who was an authority on tactical air power, barely tolerated the air commando forces under his command. He expressed disdain for the "nickel and dime forces" used in "so-called wars of liberation," stating that he did not believe the Air Force should be involved with "so-called" low-performance aircraft delivering firepower. In Vietnam, Momyer's bias showed in his lack of appreciation for what the air commandos could do with their retrofitted WWII aircraft and hybrid gunships. He frowned on the nonconformity and near cult following that the air commandos had attracted since they were reestablished in 1961. Soon after taking charge of Seventh Air Force, Momyer banned the Australian-style bush hats worn by the air commandos, along with baseball hats, unit insignias, and other special devices sometimes worn on field uniforms. The air commandos were authorized to wear the bush hats in the United States and elsewhere but had to lay them aside when they came to Vietnam for combat. "This irks them no end," a reporter wrote. Momyer maintained that the special uniforms should not have been authorized in the first place.[34]

Years later the former commander of the 14th Air Commando Wing at Nha Trang, Colonel Gordon Bradburn (who had also replaced Aderholt as wing commander at Hurlburt), recalled briefing General Momyer soon after the new Seventh Air Force commander arrived. Bradburn said that Momyer curtly informed him that he was going to "educate you guys back into the Air Force."

During his thirteen-month tour, Bradburn felt that Momyer barely tolerated the wing. When he met with the Seventh Air Force commander privately before leaving Vietnam for his next assignment as chief of the special air warfare office at USAF headquarters, Momyer cautioned him not to defend or promote air commando capability unduly, "since to do so would obviously conflict with his concept of an all-jet Air Force."[35]

Aderholt was disappointed by Momyer's decision to ban the air commando hat, but not surprised. For some time there had been a move afoot to bring the air commandos into line with the rest of the Air Force. General Momyer became the right commander at the right time to suppress their image in Vietnam. Momyer, who previously headed Air Training Command, was known as a strict disciplinarian and a stickler for regulations. To admirers he was a brilliant staff officer, scholar, and air tactician. Detractors found him cold, arrogant, and aloof. Combat commanders in Southeast Asia respected Momyer's knowledge of air power and his tactical skills. Despite his distinguished combat record as a fighter ace in World War II, however, he did not come across to the combat crews in Vietnam as an inspiring leader. To those who believed the war demanded vision, inspiration, and audacity from top commanders, the general appeared to be the wrong man at the wrong time.[36]

Lieutenant General John P. Flynn was a colonel serving as vice commander of the 388th Tactical Fighter Wing at Korat Air Base, Thailand, during the Momyer years. A highly decorated pilot who had flown fighter combat in World War II and Korea, Flynn was captured by the North Vietnamese when his F-105 Thunderchief was shot down over Hanoi in 1967, and was a prisoner of war for more than five years. He described Momyer as "a charming man" and "a highly experienced officer" whom he "respected very much," but recalled that during a visit to Korat the top airman failed to say anything that would inspire the pilots. Instead, he told them to be careful when they went into Route Package 6—the Hanoi and Haiphong sectors, which were the most heavily defended targets in North Vietnam—because no target there was worth one F-105. Flynn said that really shocked him because every day he and the wing commander, Colonel Edward B. Burdett, impressed on the pilots how important it was to go in and take out a target so they would not have to go back and hit it the next day, and here was the four-star commander telling them not to stick their necks out.[37]

Flynn saw the apparent dichotomy as evidence of a serious communications gap between the top echelon and the combat force. He pointed out that General Momyer and his senior staff did not come around often, which was probably a good thing because they were out of touch with the combat force and with hard-charging commanders like Ed Burdett, Robin Olds, and John Giraudo. "The force had a tiger combat attitude which they could not communicate to the headquarters," Flynn said, "and I think that was one of the most distressing parts of the war because we had men dying for what they considered to be an important, noble effort. They understood the politics of the situation, and they were willing to do it." Flynn said the gap bothered him then and still bothered him when the war was over.[38]

Considering General Flynn's insights and those of other airmen who were deeply involved in the war, a clash between General Momyer and Colonel Aderholt over combat air operations seems to have been inevitable. The stage was set for their first encounter when Momyer became Westmoreland's air deputy and the JPRC was activated with Aderholt as commander. The first time something went wrong with a JPRC mission, Aderholt would not only have to answer to Colonel Singlaub at SOG and General Westmoreland at MACV, but would have to explain to General Momyer in his office at Tan Son Nhut. "I agree with everything Flynn had to say about Momyer," Aderholt would comment later, "except that I personally did not find him all that charming."[39]

The JPRC Becomes Operational

Colonel Aderholt actually commanded the JPRC less than three months, from its activation on 17 September through 4 December, but Major Hansen said it seemed much longer because they got so many things done. Hansen recalled that he and other members of the small JPRC staff worked "ungodly hours," constantly encountering problems without precedents they could turn to for answers. There was no griping or goldbricking because the men believed what they were doing was too important. Hansen noted that Colonel Aderholt had the uncanny ability of getting people involved to the extent they were eager to get back on the job even when they were exhausted. "He convinced you that you could make things happen," Hansen said. "I am not sure exactly how he did this, but I know that he did."[40]

The JPRC had become semioperational on 29 August and was ready to go into action when it was activated on 17 September. A first priority had been to establish specific operating procedures for the new organization. Aderholt arranged meetings with all agencies involved with escape and evasion in Southeast Asia to solicit their ideas. When formal operating procedures were approved, the next step was informing the combat units about the JPRC and its mission. "Boatwright and I were in the field constantly briefing aircrews and intelligence officers," Hansen said. "We went everywhere, to Army and Air

Force bases throughout Vietnam and Thailand, and to Navy carriers en route to duties on Yankee Station." Aderholt, meanwhile, was engaged in getting the JPRC's initial recovery efforts under way.[41]

Although the JPRC did not have resources dedicated to its recovery operations, which Aderholt believed was a tragic mistake, SOG's covert unit of Chinese Nung mercenaries led by Green Berets provided a ready source of trained and motivated troops for the Bright Light teams. The Nungs were fierce fighters who were known as the special operations Ghurkas of Southeast Asia. They had emigrated to Vietnam from China's Kwangsi Province and settled in the Cholon district of Saigon. The Army helicopters that were used to infiltrate and exfiltrate SOG's special reconnaissance teams were also available to support the Bright Light teams, but the JPRC had to rely on Seventh Air Force's centralized airlift system for large troop movements. The JPRC also had to clear close air support requirements through Seventh Air Force even though Aderholt planned to use Vietnamese Air Force A-1Es, which in low-threat areas had advantages in loiter time and maneuverability over jet fighters. The A-1Es could work beneath the overcast that often sheltered enemy targets in Southeast Asia from effective strikes by jet aircraft.[42]

The JPRC got involved in its first recovery mission after a weak beeper signal was heard on 23 September by aircraft operating in northern Laos near the border with North Vietnam. The signal came from the general area of where an F-4 aircraft piloted by Captain Robert Waggoner had gone down eleven days earlier. The next day CINCPAC authorized a recovery operation, contingent upon approval from the American embassies in Bangkok and Vientiane. The JPRC obtained approval from Bangkok, but a message came back from Ambassador William Sullivan in Vientiane that he had resources in Laos better suited to the task. When a ten-man team moved into the area on 26 September, airborne searches were withdrawn to avoid attracting enemy forces. An extensive search of the area and interrogation of villagers failed to produce any sign of the downed pilot or his plane. Military officers in Saigon typically blamed Ambassador Sullivan for the team's lack of success, attributing the failure to his tight control over U.S. military activity in Laos and the three-day delay in getting the recovery operation under way.[43] The problems with delays and response times in the Vietnam War were not unique to Laos, however, but were prevalent throughout the combat zone.

The JPRC's next recovery operation got better results. After receiving a report late on 29 September that an F-4C was down in Laos, Search and Rescue forces launched a recovery operation at first light the next morning and recovered one of the pilots. The rescue crew could not locate the other pilot but sighted his parachute in the trees. Because the ruggedness of the terrain precluded further rescue efforts, the Joint Search and Rescue Center called on the JPRC for assistance. The JPRC obtained the necessary approvals and launched a Bright Light team the following morning. Infiltrating in a CH3 helicopter, the team recovered the body of Major Saul Waxman (USAF), who was apparently killed when he released himself from the parachute harness and fell one hundred feet to the ground.[44]

The third Bright Light recovery operation was undertaken after a Navy A-1H, call sign Canasta 572, went down in North Vietnam on 12 October. The pilot, Lieutenant Robert Woods, made voice contact with another Navy plane after ejecting safely and becoming lost in the jungle. Search and rescue efforts were unsuccessful, however, because North Vietnamese soldiers were closing in on the downed pilot, and dense tree cover prevented lowering a sling to him. Receiving a call for assistance on 14 October, the JPRC readied a Bright Light team and sent it to the carrier USS *Intrepid* at midnight for a launch at first light the next morning. Inclement weather kept the recovery team from launching until 16 October, when it was helilifted into North Vietnam, landing approximately eight hundred meters from Lieutenant Woods's last known position. Sweeping toward the target in skirmish formation, the team engaged a North Vietnamese armed patrol, killing all four members. Their mission compromised, the team leader requested exfiltration. One helicopter was hit by ground fire at the exfiltration point and again on the way out. After several days of futile electronic and visual searches from the air, the operation was suspended. Lieutenant Woods, who lived to tell his story, had been captured by North Vietnamese soldiers.[45]

Planning for a much larger Bright Light operation—the raid of a prisoner of war camp in the Mekong Delta—had been under way before the JPRC's activation on 17 September. The Vietnamese Army's interrogation of a seventeen-year-old former Viet Cong seeking amnesty under the government's *chieu hoi* (open arms) program revealed that on 25 August he observed an American being held prisoner in the delta. He gave a detailed description of the American prisoner and the location of the prison site. The description fit that of Edward R. Johnson, a black sergeant who had been captured in 1964 while serving as an adviser to the South Vietnamese Army. Johnson reportedly had suffered brutal treatment at the hands of his captors. Intelligence officials also thought the POW in the delta might be another black American, James E. Jackson, who had only recently been captured by the Viet Cong. Colonel Aderholt and the JPRC were less intent on identifying the American prisoner than they were on getting him safely back.[46]

An Operation Called "Crimson Tide"

The JPRC experienced inordinate delays in its efforts to verify the defector's story and to attempt recovery of the American prisoner. For nearly two weeks RF-4s from the 460th Tactical Reconnaissance Wing at Tan Son Nhut tried to obtain aerial photography of the alleged prison site, but the results were inconclusive. The RF-4 crews not only had problems with the cloud cover that nearly always hung over the Viet Cong–infested Mekong Delta below Saigon, but apparently had photographed the wrong area. When the Army reinterrogated the defector, Pham Teu, on 28–29 September, he could not locate the prison site in the photographs. To make sure the job was done right, Major Hansen flew over the area in an O-1 aircraft with a combat cameraman on board to obtain low-level, oblique photographs of the site. Trying not to compromise the mission, they did not circle the target but made a single pass on the way down to Soc Trang, an old French airfield now used by Americans, where they stopped for lunch. They made another pass over the target on the return to Bien Hoa. The defector was able to identify the prison site on the photographs and agreed to take a polygraph test, which was administered on 11 October. The results indicated that he probably was telling the truth, and the JPRC was told to go ahead with final arrangements for the raid.[47]

Aderholt said he could not have wanted better support than he got from Jack Singlaub and SOG, but he was disgusted with the lack of urgency shown by the senior staff at MACV and Seventh Air Force headquarters toward the recovery mission. He had Chuck Boatwright and Les Hansen rush to complete a plan for the raid on the POW camp, which he named "Crimson Tide" for Alabama's great football teams and personally coordinated with MACV and Seventh Air Force offices having an interest in the operation. At MACV headquarters he was furious when General Westmoreland's chief of military intelligence, Major General Joseph D. McChristian, would not take time to see him. He had to leave the plan with a clerk and did not receive McChristian's coordination until several days later, after the plan was finalized.[48]

After briefing Seventh Air Force on the Crimson Tide mission, Aderholt left Tan Son Nhut with an uneasy feeling that the operation was becoming unduly complicated by needless delays and the involvement of too many different staff elements. Knowing the A-1s could work under the fifteen-hundred-foot overcast forecast for the delta during this time of year, he wanted a VNAF squadron from Bien Hoa to deploy planes to Can Tho, where they would be close to the target area but had to staff the requirement through Seventh Air Force rather than going directly to the VNAF. Major John L. Plaster, a former SOG officer with three tours in Vietnam, wrote that the recovery operation was "overwhelmed by bureaucracy," involving "everyone from the IV Corps senior adviser to the Seventh Air Force commander and eight different sections of the MACV staff."[49]

The Crimson Tide plan called for a surprise raid on the Viet Cong camp by a company-size force of Nung mercenaries on 18 October. Aderholt arranged with Seventh Air Force to airlift the recovery force from SOG's forward operating base at Kontum in the Central Highlands to Can Tho, an Army aviation battalion headquarters in the delta, early on the morning of the eighteenth. After being fed and briefed on the mission, the raiders would be flown aboard Army helicopters to Soc Trang, where they would reassemble and launch the mission. Three days before the raid Captain Frank Jaks, a seasoned special forces officer stationed at Kontum, was chosen to lead the raiding party. The only other Americans among the raiders were volunteers whom Jaks picked to be platoon leaders.[50]

On the morning of the raid there were things about the mission that still bothered Colonel Aderholt. There had been too many delays. It had been nearly three weeks since Les Hansen photographed the prison site, and more than six weeks since the informant had defected. The target might have been compromised, or it could be a trap. He knew that Viet Cong forces in the delta were reportedly using prisoners to call in airstrikes against fellow Americans operating in the area but had been unable to substantiate the reports. He was concerned that too damned many people were involved, and there were too many things that could go wrong. He would have sworn even louder had he known that the airlift support had been thrown off schedule at the last minute to drop off supplies at another base en route or that Seventh Air Force headquarters had arbitrarily canceled his request for VNAF A-ls to support the mission and laid on F-100 jet fighters instead.[51]

Captain Jaks and his force of more than one hundred men were left waiting at Kontum airfield for nearly three hours wondering when the Air Force C-130 would come for them. To obtain air transport for the mission, the JPRC had to go through Tan Son Nhut's airlift request net, which, like the tactical air control system, was centralized for efficiency and economy of operation. The centralized system let airlifters make maximum use of transport aircraft that were already scheduled, rather than tying up aircraft by dedicating them to special missions. Aderholt made certain that the Crimson Tide request was assigned the highest priority, but the schedulers at Tan Son Nhut still laid on another stop for the C-130 to off-load general cargo en route to Kontum. A delay in off-loading the cargo made the plane three hours late picking up Jaks and his men.

For an operation whose success depended on precision planning, timing, and execution, Crimson Tide was off to a bad start.[52]

The recovery team's delay in departing Kontum threw the entire schedule off. Arriving late at Can Tho, the men ate lunch hurriedly and received a rushed briefing on the mission and the target. They were flown to Soc Trang, where 12 UH-l "Huey" helicopters were waiting to lift them into battle. By then they were four hours late. Back in Saigon, Colonel Aderholt cursed Seventh Air Force's centralized control system, which he blamed "for screwing things up." Not only had delayed airlift support put the entire operation at risk, but the VNAF A-1s had not shown up at Can Tho. The worst was yet to come. The raiders were briefed according to MACV intelligence information to expect no opposition forces within ten miles of the landing zone. They landed on top of the famed U-Minh 10 battalion, the only fully mobile Viet Cong battalion in the delta transported by sampans.[53]

As word trickled back on how the raid was going and the fate of the raiding party, Aderholt's anger rose. Crimson Tide was turning into a disaster. The weather had deteriorated badly by the time the helicopters descended on the landing zone, causing one formation of four Hueys to become disoriented. Two formations came down on the primary landing zone, while the third set down across a small canal at the edge of the camp. The defector, Pham Teu, had joined the raiding party to point out fortifications and areas that were booby-trapped, but he was of little help. As soon as the Hueys were on the ground at the landing zone, heavy machine-gun fire opened up all around them. The third formation was hit coming in. One Huey was shot down and the American platoon leader killed. Then all hell broke loose. The raiding party unwittingly had landed in the middle of the rest area for the heavily armed Viet Cong.[54]

Pinned down by a superior force nearly one thousand strong, Captain Jaks called for air support. The entire third Nung platoon was separated from the main force and taking heavy fire. Jaks wondered what happened to the VNAF A-1 cover they were promised. Then he heard the scream of jet fighters but could not see them through the overcast. The fighters, which were F-100s flying preplanned sorties out of Bien Hoa, had been diverted to the target area by the Tactical Air Control Center at Tan Son Nhut. Bombing through the low cloud cover, the F-100s scattered the Viet Cong but inadvertently hit the third Nung platoon, destroying a helicopter and causing more casualties than were lost at the hands of enemy forces that day. An Army observer noted wryly that the results were worse than having no air support at all.[55]

Night descended on the recovery force before helicopters could be brought in to lift them out of the target area. Aided by a flareship, the survivors staved

General William W. Momyer (left), Seventh Air Force commander, arrives at Nakhon Phanom in late 1966.

off probing attacks until dawn came and they could be rescued. The Viet Cong had slipped away under the cover of darkness. They left behind two of their own, who were taken captive but refused to give any information regarding U.S. prisoners. Friendly casualties included two Americans and eleven Nungs killed in action, and seventeen Nungs missing in action. The heavy losses were a wrenching experience for the newly formed JPRC and were the basis for much soul-searching in the days ahead. Although the Viet Cong released both Johnson and Jackson a year later, it was never known whether either man was the prisoner that Captain Jaks's force had tried to rescue.[56]

Although SOG and the JPRC bore ultimate responsibility for the failed mission, there was plenty of blame to go around. Flawed intelligence and bureaucratic delays, which were perennial problems in the Vietnam War, had doomed the mission before it ever started. The enemy's strategic initiative and grassroots intelligence were invariably one step ahead of MACV's technological wizardry. The tons of regurgitating data in the combined center for intelligence with its sophisticated photographic and computer equipment, which General Westmoreland said had evolved into "a thoroughly professional agency" under

McChristian's guidance,[57] was no match for the mother lode of information available to the enemy or his freedom of movement and unencumbered action. The situation was not helped by the too-brief tours that most Americans served in the combat zone.

Seventh Air Force shouldered no blame for the fiasco. Criticisms about the lengthy delay in airlifting the recovery force on the morning of the raid could not prevent it from happening again. Without dedicated assets the JPRC had no choice but to factor such problems into future recovery operations. The accidental airstrikes on friendly troops resulting from the use of F-100s rather than the A-1s that the JPRC requested were the fortunes of war and were certain to happen again. Called "short rounds" in the military vernacular, inadvertent bombings of friendly troops and civilians, although endemic in warfare, occurred more frequently in Vietnam than in most wars because there were no clear battle lines, and enemy forces often mingled with civilians or maneuvered close to friendly forces to thwart air attacks. Aderholt was told in no uncertain terms by General Momyer that as a user rather than a provider of air support, the JPRC had no authority over which aircraft or air munitions were employed to support its missions. That was Seventh Air Force's responsibility.[58]

The Seventh Air Force commander sent for Colonel Aderholt after General Westmoreland complained to him about the ineffective air support for Crimson Tide. Singlaub had briefed Westmoreland the morning after the operation. The scene in General Momyer's office was tense. Aderholt tried to explain, but Momyer interrupted him. "You people never listen," he snapped. "If you had turned the request over to us instead of coming out here meddling and stating that you wanted the VNAF and the A-1s, this would not have happened." Aderholt objected, pointing out that the raid was four hours late getting started because the C-130 did not get to Kontum on time. The weather deteriorated. He had asked for VNAF A-1s because they could work under the overcast. Seventh Air Force sent F-100s instead. They did not have a FAC and could not see the target. The men on the ground called them in, and they hit the wrong target. "They had to bomb through the overcast," Aderholt said. "The A-1s wouldn't have that problem." Momyer bristled. "Colonel, you aren't listening," he said. "From now on you do things our way. You state your requirement to Seventh Air Force, and we will determine what you need." Aderholt was dismissed.[59]

Aderholt did not realize at the time that he had made a mortal enemy. General Momyer had come to Seventh Air Force on a mission to centralize all participating combat air forces under his control as Westmoreland's deputy for air operations. It was an impossible quest, considering the array of military aircraft employed in Southeast Asia, the diverse operating doctrines of the parent services, and their intense parochial interests. The Army had its own air control system in Vietnam and never consented to integrating its helicopters into the USAF system. The Marine air arm operating in the northernmost corps area of Vietnam, although pooled with Seventh Air Force resources during the Tet Offensive of 1968, primarily supported its own ground forces and never accepted Momyer's contention that they were under his centralized control. The Navy compartmentalized its airstrikes against North Vietnam, coordinating operations but not submitting to Seventh Air Force control. The Air Force, which allowed SAC's B-52 bombers to operate independently of Seventh Air Force, did not obey its own doctrine. Westmoreland's successor, General Creighton W. Abrams, praised centralized air power by pointing to the faucet of tremendous firepower that could be turned on or off throughout the war zone, but Momyer was frustrated in his quest for unconditional control of air forces in Southeast Asia. It never happened.[60]

In *Air Power in Three Wars,* published in 1978, General Momyer stated, "Airmen know the centralized control of air power in a theater of war can best serve armies and navies; to fragment air power is to court defeat. In North Africa, Europe, Korea, and Vietnam this principle has been proven time and again."[61] There was indisputable evidence that centrally controlled air power was effective in Vietnam. In 1968 Seventh Air Force turned on a Niagara of tremendous, flexible firepower to help crush the nationwide Tet Offensive and lift the siege at Khe Sanh. But there had been exceptions in the other wars that Momyer cited. In World War II the air commandos were a dedicated force for Wingate's raiders. In Korea, Aderholt's small detachment had been dedicated to special missions and was semiautonomous in carrying them out. In Vietnam, where the daily grind retained basic characteristics of counterinsurgency warfare, there was ample room for more exceptions. Many engagements were skirmishes where a trickle of air support could do the job as long as it was timely and accurate. The single-manager system had the power to divert preplanned sorties to assist troops in contact, but aircraft were often far from the scene of battle, unfamiliar with the ground situation, and not always carrying the right ordnance for the situation.

Aderholt believed there needed to be exceptions to centralized control, and that the JPRC was one of those exceptions. He had argued for dedicated resources from the outset, and lost. They had accomplished a lot in a short period of time, including building extensive files on American POWs/MIAs and developing new recognition signals for downed airmen. The smaller recovery operations had gone according to plan, although the evading pilots had not been recovered. The constipated bureaucracy they had run up against in Crimson

Tide, however, was counter to Aderholt's nature and, as far as he was concerned, kept the JPRC from being all that it could be. The run-in with Momyer convinced him things would not change, and he was more eager than ever to command the wing that he had been promised. At the first opportunity, he flew to Hawaii to see General Harris.[62]

The timing of his visit was right. General Harris said the Air Staff had deployed an air commando squadron (the 606th) to Nakhon Phanom, Thailand, a small base on the border with Laos, and wanted to make it a full-time wing. Harris wanted him to go to Nakhon Phanom in December to activate the wing and serve as its first commander. Aderholt, of course, readily agreed. Excited about the assignment, he caught the next flight back to Saigon and got Colonel Singlaub and the MACV chief of staff to release him. There was an anxious moment, however, when General Momyer's office called and left a message that the general wanted to see him. Aderholt was uneasy as he drove out to Tan Son Nhut. He knew that Momyer controlled air operations out of Thailand even though the units belonged to General Wilson at Thirteenth Air Force. He entered Momyer's office expecting the worst.[63]

Momyer came right to the point. General Harris had called him about the wing commander's job, but Momyer thought Aderholt should reconsider. Although Momyer argued that it was too soon after activating the JPRC for Aderholt to leave, it could have been that the general had someone else in mind for the Nakhon Phanom assignment. Aderholt explained that the only reason he agreed to come to Saigon and set up the JPRC was because General Harris had promised him the wing commander's job. Furthermore, MACV agreed to release him and he had already accepted the assignment. He could tell that General Momyer was not pleased with the decision, but he thought no more about it. He would be reporting to General Wilson even though Momyer had operational control of the wings in Thailand. In view of later actions, it is reasonable to assume that Momyer challenged the assignment with General Harris, who had made a personal commitment to Aderholt, and lost. In early December, Colonel Aderholt took over at Nakhon Phanom.[64]

According to Brigadier General Charles E. "Chuck" Yeager, General Momyer insisted on picking his own wing commanders. General Yeager wrote in his biography that Momyer refused to accept him as commander of the 35th Tactical Fighter Wing after he had been recommended for the assignment by Air Force headquarters. At the time, Yeager was a colonel commanding the 405th Fighter Wing assigned to Thirteenth Air Force at Clark. He had never met Momyer but heard that he was "a brilliant tactician" and was looking forward to serving under him. General John D. Ryan, who replaced Harris as

PACAF commander in February 1967, intervened, but Momyer stood his ground. Momyer had formed strong opinions about the famous test pilot without ever having met him. A year later Yeager was the wing commander at Seymour Johnson in North Carolina when Momyer came back from Vietnam to head Tactical Air Command. Yeager said they spent two hours together during the TAC commander's orientation visit to Seymour Johnson, and Momyer never spoke a word to him.[65]

Had Colonel Aderholt known how strongly opinionated Momyer was, or how the four-star commander's prejudices would affect his career, he would still have taken the wing commander's job at Nakhon Phanom because he believed so strongly in the air commando mission and because it was not in his nature to back down from a fight. At SOG Colonel Singlaub had given Aderholt a glowing evaluation, which was backed up by Major General John N. Ewbank and Lieutenant General John A. Heintges, the MACV deputy commander. Ewbank called Aderholt "one of the most thoroughly professional officers known to me in the field of counterinsurgency warfare." All three men considered him to be general officer material and recommended his promotion to brigadier general.[66] How incredibly different the Seventh Air Force commander's reaction would be to Colonel Aderholt's brand of leadership while commanding the 56th Air Commando Wing at Nakhon Phanom, Thailand.

8. THE TIGERS OF NAKHON PHANOM

Colonel Aderholt took command of the 606th Air Commando Squadron at Nakhon Phanom in December 1966 and began molding it into a wing with control and supervision over Thailand-based special air warfare operations. When the squadron (nicknamed "Lucky Tiger") was activated in March, its small force of T-28s and special air warfare personnel had augmented capabilities of the Water Pump detachment that Colonel Aderholt sent to Udorn from Hurlburt in 1964. Another squadron, the 602d Tactical Fighter Squadron, flew A-1 Skyraiders out of Nakhon Phanom in support of search and rescue missions in Laos. In June the base received a detachment of A-26s under Project "Big Eagle" for combat evaluation as a night interdiction weapons system over Laos. Activation of the 56th Air Commando Wing in April 1967 consolidated the myriad special air warfare activities in Thailand under Colonel Aderholt's command.[1]

Stepping off the plane onto the pierced steel planking (PSP) that carpeted the ramp, the six-thousand-foot runway, and the two taxiways at Nakhon Phanom, Aderholt was reminded of the makeshift landing fields U.S. forces had carved out of the jungles during World War II. Adding to the aura of wars past, rows of propeller-driven fighters and bombers, many of them armed and ready for the night's missions, baked in the midday sun. Colonel Lee Volet, an experienced F-105 pilot who became deputy wing commander near the end of Aderholt's tour, said the base had the biggest collection of propeller aircraft he had seen since World War II. The men were readily identifiable as air commandos because they were unaffected by General Momyer's uniform ban and wore their distinctive jungle hats.[2]

Aderholt's spirits soared at the welcome sight of the air commandos and their vintage warplanes, which he believed were the most effective weapons for the jungle war in Laos, but he was shocked by conditions at the remote base that Navy Seabees had built in 1963. The installation had taken a mud bath during the rainy season, there was no mess hall, and other facilities were extremely limited. His first priorities were to improve living conditions for the men and to get everyone at Nakhon Phanom (fondly called "Naked Fanny" by the troops) involved with the mission. He had to make do with the resources that were available, however, because General Harris had told him not to ask for additional personnel to form the new wing. Consequently, he managed the complex organization from a headquarters that would have been thin even for a squadron.[3]

Aderholt loved the challenge, and he loved the troops, many of whom had served with the 1st Air Commando Wing at Hurlburt when he was there. He was as much energized by his mission responsibilities at Nakhon Phanom as the men were inspired by his dynamic and fearless leadership. Picking up where he left off at Takhli four years earlier, Aderholt believed the men and the mission of the 56th Air Commando Wing could make a real difference in the way the war was being fought. He felt at home, having formed close ties with senior Thai and Laotian military officers (including Air Vice Marshal Boon Choo Chandrubeksa, commander of the Royal Thai Air Force, and legendary Hmong leader General Vang Pao in Laos) and had served with top CIA officials in Thailand and Laos. Major Secord was at Udorn serving as the CIA's air adviser for operations in Laos. After leaving Hurlburt, Secord had attended the Air Command and Staff College at Maxwell, then served briefly with the CIA office in Saigon while Aderholt was there with SOG. He relocated to Udorn in August 1966 when his duties in Vietnam became too mundane. At the American embassy in Vientiane, Colonel Paul "Pappy" Pettigrew had come from Eglin to serve as air attaché and special adviser to Ambassador William Sullivan, a strong proponent of special air warfare who had worked behind the scenes to have the air commando forces deployed to Nakhon Phanom.[4]

Colonel Aderholt's brother Warren worked for Pappy Pettigrew in Vientiane. He had been assigned to Seventh Air Force headquarters on a project codenamed Phyllis Ann, which involved radio direction finding operations in specially equipped C-47s. Warren hated the headquarters assignment, so his older brother got him a position with the Water Pump detachment working under the air attaché's office in Vientiane. Seventh Air Force did not want to release him, but Warren cited a DOD regulation prohibiting brothers from serving at the same time in Vietnam unless both were volunteers. Both Aderholts were in

Saigon at the time, so Seventh Air Force had to honor Warren's request for transfer. He later developed an inner-ear infection and had to be air-evacuated back to the United States.[5]

The stage was set for a combat tour that was made to order for Colonel Aderholt and promised to be a capstone to his career in special operations. His troubles with General Momyer, however, which were exacerbated by the cumbersome command arrangements in Thailand, often overshadowed his highly innovative and effective command of the 56th Air Commando Wing. Major General Bond, the Seventh/Thirteenth Air Force commander at Udorn, was favorably impressed by his past contacts with Aderholt at TAC and by what Major Ropka (who had come over with the 606th Air Commando Squadron) and others had told him about the legendary colonel. Unfortunately, however, Bond's divided loyalties to General Wilson in the Philippines and General Momyer in Vietnam complicated his relationship with Aderholt and his air commandos. While Wilson actively supported Aderholt's dynamic leadership at Nakhon Phanom, Momyer's autocratic control of the wing's combat operations not only showed disdain for the men and the mission, but manifested intense dislike for their strong-willed, hell-for-leather commander.[6]

"Lead, Follow, or Get Out of the Way"

Colonel Aderholt's command of the 56th Air Commando Wing gave new meaning to the slogan "Lead, follow, or get out of the way." A fellow air commando Colonel Bill Keeler stated that Aderholt's superior leadership inspired everyone in his command to accomplish feats "even they themselves thought impossible." He was able to do this because his people knew that he cared about the mission, cared about them, and cared about their families. At the same time, Keeler noted, Aderholt flaunted "a shameless disregard for his own career by attacking incorrect principles and actions taken by his senior officers."[7] Major General James A. "Cotton" Hildreth, who was a lieutenant colonel commanding the 1st Air Commando Squadron at Pleiku in South Vietnam when he first met Aderholt in 1967, echoed these sentiments. Hildreth expressed "tremendous admiration and respect" for Aderholt's "combat leadership" at Nakhon Phanom. He pointed out that the jet fighter wings and even the B-52 bombing missions received more publicity and were more highly decorated, whereas the combat losses for the A-1s were exceeded only by the F-105. "You might expect under these circumstances to find the 56th a unit with low morale, but to the contrary, there was not a more gung-ho outfit in any service in Southeast Asia," Hildreth said.[8]

Colonel Volet recalled that when he became Aderholt's deputy in October 1967, the morale in the wing surpassed all that he had witnessed in twenty-five years as a fighter pilot. "They believed they were capable of doing anything," Volet said. He attributed this to Colonel Aderholt's remarkable leadership. "In all my years in the military, Heinie was one of the very few commanders of men that I had met," he declared, observing that the troops would have done anything the commander asked of them because they knew it was "for the good of the Air Force and our country." He noted that Aderholt was unpolitical to a fault and was concerned "only for the welfare of his men, the accomplishment of the missions assigned to the wing, special air operations, and helping the Thais that lived around the base."[9]

The morale at Nakhon Phanom was at rock bottom when Aderholt first took over. "They had first-rate people, but leadership at the top stunk," Aderholt said. He recalled that General Bond was totally dissatisfied with the Lucky Tiger squadron commander, who had broken the rules by having his wife in Thailand. Aderholt was unforgiving in his criticism of the former commander. "We were at war and the goddamn commander has his wife in town," he growled. "How in the hell can you control the rest of the men if you have your spouse sitting off-base and you're going home at night?" He said there was no discipline, the men had women in the barracks, and little was getting done. He immediately imposed a midnight curfew and set a vigorous pace to keep the men busy, out of trouble, and totally mission oriented.[10]

Major Kittinger had deployed to Nakhon Phanom in June 1966 with the detachment of A-26s. "We had an average colonel commanding us until Heinie Aderholt showed up," he said. "Heinie came in with guns blazing and got involved with everything like he always did since I had known him. It was just like night and day." Kittinger noted that within a few weeks the whole tenor and spirit of the organization had changed because Heinie Aderholt was commander. He did not ask aircrews to fly missions that he would not fly himself. The flying time more than doubled under his command. There were five thousand people at Nakhon Phanom. Colonel Aderholt knew everyone by name, and all knew him.[11]

As he had done at Hurlburt, Aderholt made a point of visiting the NCO club, the airmen's club, and the officers' club at least one night a week. He got little sleep. "We had a twenty-four-hour operation," he said. "We flew night and day." When he was not flying, he went to his trailer, slept for an hour, woke up, and made a sweep around the flight line where the night crews were working. He repeated this procedure throughout the night. The men swore that he never slept. There was some grumbling when he put staff offices on the same twelve-hour, seven-day-a-week shifts that the mechanics and pilots worked, but this soon turned to pride in the knowledge they were vital to the mission. He held weekly musters at the theater to keep everyone informed about mission performance. "We had people who were totally dedicated," Aderholt said. "They were there to fight and win a war."[12]

Although the wing was authorized no additional people, the headquarters was flooded with paperwork after it was activated. Aderholt had never understood why the armed forces could not leave the mountains of unessential paper work at home when they went into combat, and told his people to ignore every scrap of paper coming into the wing that had nothing to do with fighting the war. "I told them to throw the useless documents in the waste basket and to do nothing unless we got another query," Aderholt said. "We eliminated 80 percent of the crap that came in there and had nothing to do with the war." He could not believe the unrealistic requirements coming down from the Pentagon. For instance, the Air Force had a master plan to build brick chapels at all its bases. In Thailand this meant replacing "perfectly good wooden chapels" with permanent brick structures. Aderholt challenged the requirement, noting that the building being used as a chapel at Nakhon Phanom had been air-conditioned by his people and would hold two hundred worshipers, but never more than twenty were in attendance. "Can you imagine?" he stated. "We were over there to fight a war but acted like we planned to be there forever." There were other basic needs requiring more immediate attention.[13]

One morning as he was driving across the ramp, Colonel Aderholt met a chief master sergeant running from the flight line toward the barracks. He slammed on the brakes and asked, "Hey, chief, what's the big hurry?" The sergeant stopped and walked over to the truck. "Sir, I'm not in a hurry now," he said sheepishly. "I just shit my pants." The colonel asked, "Where is the closest bathroom?" "Up at the barracks," the sergeant replied. The colonel's eyes narrowed. "You mean you don't have a crapper on the flight line?" "No, sir," he answered. "You stand there," Aderholt said, while he got on the radio and ordered the base commander to report to the ramp. When the base commander arrived, Aderholt told him to drive the sergeant to the barracks, wait for him while he showered and changed clothes, and bring him back. Upon their return, Aderholt told the base commander that he had until sundown to build an outdoor toilet with two seats for the men on the flight line, or he was fired. "We had a ceremony that afternoon dedicating the little brown shithouse on the flight line," Aderholt said, laughing. The story quickly spread throughout the base. The base commander, a SAC type, departed soon thereafter.[14]

Cotton Hildreth, a strong leader in his own right, had flown 285 combat missions in the A-1E while he was at Pleiku. He recalled that Aderholt kept the officers' club at Nakhon Phanom open twenty-four hours a day because most of his wing's missions were at night, and the club was busiest during the early-morning hours. "From the bar talk, one might think there was more danger and excitement in the club than a mission over Tchepone," Hildreth said. The rowdy welcome that Aderholt had given the new base commander, also from SAC, was one of the stories overheard at the bar. The wing executive officer met the colonel on arrival, helped him get settled in, and took him to the club to meet Colonel Aderholt, who had just come off a mission. It was a hot night, made for cold beer and laughter. The new colonel, who was built like a lumberjack, towered over Aderholt. He stuck out his hand, and said, "Hi, I'm your new base commander."

"Not yet, you aren't." Aderholt said. "You haven't been tested."

"What do you mean?"

"First, we have arm wrestling," Aderholt said. The brawny colonel proceeded to beat everyone at the bar at arm wrestling. The bartender set up beers all around.

"Now we have Indian leg wrestling," Aderholt said. The colonel defeated everyone again, and Aderholt ordered beers all around.

Several beers later he said, "To be base commander, you have to ram your head through the club wall."

"I'll do it if you will," the colonel replied. "You go first." The walls were constructed of thin plywood, and Aderholt knew where the studs were. He backed up, rammed his head through the wall between the studs, and staggered back with his face scratched and bleeding.

"It's your turn," he said, taking out a grease pencil and drawing a circle over the stud. The colonel lowered his head, hit the stud, and bounced back. Aderholt marked it again, and the colonel gave it another try. The stud won, and they put the colonel to bed. The next morning he reported to the command section, looking terrible. Colonel Aderholt asked, "How do you feel?"

"Not too good," he replied. "I think my neck's broken."

"Good. *Now* you're the base commander," Aderholt said. He later mentioned that the colonel was "the best damned base commander" he had ever seen.[15]

A rousing GI party that was thrown one Sunday morning to clear out loose rocks that had worked up through the pierced steel planking runway was not untypical. When the A-26s and A-1s started tearing up their propellers from the rocks during takeoff, Aderholt called the base commander around eight A.M. and told him to muster everyone on base. "I want ten six-by trucks, and I want one of them filled full of ice-cold beer," he said. There were four thousand people on the flight line. Aderholt addressed them with a bullhorn, explaining that the rocks on the runway had been nicking propellers and endangering the planes and crews. "So we are going to walk the runway and pick up every damned rock bigger than a quarter," he stated. "These trucks are going to follow, and we are going to drink beer. When we finish, we are going to drink all the beer that's left in the clubs and the base exchange." Aderholt said the men thought it was great because every colonel and lieutenant colonel was out in front picking up rocks. The empty beer cans were loaded in the A-26 bombay and dropped over the Ho Chi Minh Trail by Joe Kittinger and the Nimrods.[16]

Colonel Aderholt showed intense interest in every aspect of the mission. This included a dynamic civic action program complete with doctors, dentists, veterinarians, and engineers. The counterinsurgency training and support for the Thai air force were critical in helping the Thai armed forces defeat Communist insurgents in the northeast provinces. Although Communist activity in Thailand was small compared to neighboring countries, it had become a serious problem by 1966. There had been a marked rise in terrorist activity, including the assassination of government officials, in the border regions. With U.S. assistance the Thais won the war against the insurgents "hands down." Meanwhile, Aderholt had turned up the voltage on the wing's combat missions in Laos, particularly the interdiction of enemy forces moving down the Ho Chi Minh Trail.[17]

The Momyer-Sullivan Wars

Resting on the Thailand side of the Mekong River across from the Laotian town of Thakhet, the base at Nakhon Phanom was ideally situated for air operations against the Ho Chi Minh Trail. It was near the central panhandle of Laos, where the trail's two most prominent choke points, Nape Pass and Mu Gia Pass, lay a short distance to the northeast on the border with North Vietnam. Efforts to interdict the trail evolved into a political struggle between Seventh Air Force and the American embassy in Vientiane when Ambassador Sullivan began to question both the weight of effort applied against the trail and its failure to stem the flow of enemy traffic. Before leaving Washington for Vientiane in late 1964, the ambassador was invited by Secretary of Defense McNamara to communicate directly with him on military matters in Laos. The ambassador said that he never intended to accept the offer because he knew of no better way to ruin his relations with the military commanders than to go over their heads to a civilian boss.[18]

After being in Laos for a while, however, Sullivan decided to use his influence with McNamara to obtain a dedicated force of propeller-driven attack aircraft to counter the enormous increase in North Vietnam's truck traffic on the Ho Chi Minh Trail. The ambassador lost patience with the military's persistence in sending high-performance jet aircraft against the trail only during daylight hours. "When that obviously didn't work, they then informed policy makers in Washington that the only alternative was to expand the ground war into Laos, and asked for a couple of hundred thousand troops to take care of the problem," Sullivan said. Although this might have worked, he knew that President Johnson had no intention to invade Laos and no desire to commit two hundred thousand more troops to Southeast Asia. He finally decided to write McNamara: "I said that, although I was no expert in air warfare, I could not accept the military's contention that high-speed, high-performance jets were the best instruments to attack slow-moving trucks which traveled only at night under a thick jungle canopy. I asked whether the Air Force still had any propeller-driven attack aircraft that could operate at night and could use machine guns and rockets as well as bombs. If so, I wondered if some could be deployed to Thailand to cover the trail in Laos."[19]

The ambassador noted that, unfortunately, when McNamara acted on the request, he coupled it with a high-tech scheme called "Igloo White" for creating an electronic barrier across Laos. Sullivan complained that the ill-conceived barrier concept, which relied on movement sensors and antipersonnel cluster bombs, had negligible results "except to create a lot of three-legged monkeys in Southern Laos." He was elated, however, that McNamara did move deliberately to establish an air wing at Nakhon Phanom with a collection of vintage fighters and bombers to carry out the sort of air interdiction mission that he had in mind. "In due course, Heinie arrived to command that operation," Sullivan stated. "He and his small group were enormously inventive in developing new tactics and weapons systems."[20]

The ambassador noted that under Aderholt's command, the wing's kill rate per sortie as well as the numerical kill rate overall "far exceeded the rather feckless efforts of the all-jet Seventh Air Force in Saigon." To his dismay, however, Seventh Air Force chose not "to accept the lessons of this experience, but rather to smart under its consequences." A personal war ensued between Sullivan and Momyer, whom the ambassador accused of reaching "the fatuous conclusions that jets could do anything—including jungle interdiction—better than propeller-driven aircraft," with Aderholt and his undaunted wing hanging in the balance.[21] Christopher Robbins wrote in his book, *The Ravens,* that the two men "conducted a long duel through numerous jovial telegrams (Sullivan signing his 'Sopwith Camel Company,' Momyer signing his '20th Century Avionics') which masked a more serious difference of opinion."[22]

Some of the more lively jousting scenes in the Momyer-Sullivan wars occurred at the Southeast Asia coordinating committee (SEACOORD) sessions, where key U.S. military commanders and the U.S. ambassadors to Laos, Thai-

Colonel Aderholt
welcomes Ambassador
William Sullivan to
Nakhon Phanom in
1967.

land, and Vietnam met to discuss topics of mutual concern. Sullivan hosted the first meeting in Vientiane in 1964, at the request of Maxwell Taylor while he was the ambassador in Saigon. Subsequent gatherings were held in various places, primarily at Saigon or Udorn. "A great deal of our discussions in SEACOORD had to do with operations against the Ho Chi Minh Trail," Sullivan recalled in a 1970 interview, noting that these dealt with both ground and air operational proposals. The meetings were also a place to address the allocation of air resources for the Laos operation, and to thrash out some of the problems resulting from the complex command arrangements in Southeast Asia.[23]

Ambassador Sullivan felt partly responsible for the "bastardized" Seventh/Thirteenth structure because he pressed Admiral Ulysses S. Grant Sharp, the Pacific theater commander, to have air operations being conducted in North Laos, in support of the Lao ground forces, operationally controlled from Udorn. Sullivan argued that having the CIA and other Thai-based covert support for North Laos centered at Udorn, and the intelligence and command lines from North Laos flowing into there, made it much simpler to have Udorn control the air support. "As far as the panhandle—the Ho Chi Minh Trail area—that was obviously an integral part of, and an extension of, the war in South Vietnam, and it seemed to me very sensible to have that focused at Saigon," Sullivan said. Another concern was the political sensitivity associated with Thailand's active involvement, and that of the U.S. embassy in Vientiane, in military operations in Laos. Sullivan said that the headquarters structure at Udorn, in its original conception, was supposed to have some operational control and functions, but by the time it got "mauled over" in the Air Force bureaucracy had ended up more subordinate to Seventh Air Force than originally intended. From his vantage point, having the operational control of all Air Force assets vested in Saigon made his job more difficult and air support in North Laos less effective.[24]

The ambassador knew that Seventh Air Force resented what was perceived to be his interference in air operations in Laos, and that he was mockingly referred to as Field Marshal Sullivan by the military hierarchy in Saigon. His detractors did not take into account the ambassador's exceptional background in Southeast Asia affairs, his knowledge of counterinsurgency warfare, or the wealth of advice available to him via his air attaché, Colonel Pettigrew, and other military advisers in Vientiane. Pappy Pettigrew was a seasoned air intelligence officer, with extensive Southeast Asia experience. Sullivan stated that the requirement for dedicated air resources to support North Laos was misunderstood by Seventh Air Force, who thought he wanted to control them or to have his own private air force, which was not the case at all. "While I'm sure that I never fully appreciated all the problems that Seventh Air Force had in Saigon," he said, "I feel equally sure that they didn't appreciate the problems we had up there."[25]

A large part of Sullivan's complaint was that air support for North Laos consisted mostly of residual sorties from the Rolling Thunder air campaign against North Vietnam. Aircraft that could not complete their missions over North Vietnam because of weather or other reasons were diverted to targets in Laos. This prevented ground forces in Laos from planning for a specific allocation of sorties flown by pilots who were familiar with the target area or by aircraft that were loaded with the right ordnance for the situation. The ambassador believed that a special force dedicated to operations in Laos was the only reasonable means of correcting the problem.[26] The 56th Air Commando Wing under Colonel Aderholt was the closest thing to dedicated air support that Sullivan would have during his four years in Vientiane.

The initial force of eight A-26As (known by their call sign as "Nimrods") had proved their effectiveness in night interdiction during the few months before Colonel Aderholt arrived on 9 December. The night armed reconnaissance and loiter capabilities of the A-26 made it a formidable weapon system in the Laotian environment. General Bond's headquarters reported in September that the A-26 was "doing a good job in its interdiction role" and had been able to operate at night with relative impunity. Thus far, only one A-26 had been shot down, and this occurred on a daylight mission. Seventh Air Force was still not convinced that propeller-driven aircraft could survive over the Ho Chi Minh Trail, however, and had already challenged a proposed deployment of eight AC-47s to Nakhon Phanom. Four AC-47s provided from resources in South Vietnam had already been lost at night over Laos. Ambassador Sullivan, meanwhile, had become enthusiastic about the results achieved by the A-26s, reporting that they had conducted night interdiction in Laos with an "excellent degree of success." In October he asked Admiral Sharp to support a request for eight additional A-26s in lieu of the disputed gunships.[27]

Seventh Air Force opposed the ambassador's request, contending that the A-26 evaluation was incomplete because it had been conducted during the monsoon season when there was little enemy movement and vehicular activity. There remained doubts within Seventh Air Force headquarters whether any propeller-driven combat aircraft could survive strikes against heavily defended targets in Laos. The ambassador pointed out that the coming dry season with its lucrative targets during the hours of darkness was precisely why additional A-26s were needed. Admiral Sharp and General Harris supported the ambassador's position and agreed to his request for an additional eight A-26s at Nakhon Phanom. At this juncture General Harris had selected Colonel Aderholt to go to Nakhon Phanom as the new commander. He arrived on the scene in December unaware that the Seventh Air Force commander and staff were still smarting from the "end run" by their nemesis in Vientiane.[28]

The differences between Momyer and Sullivan carried over into Aderholt's already strained relations with the Seventh Air Force commander. Because both he and the array of vintage aircraft were sent to Nakhon Phanom over Momyer's objections, Aderholt was treated differently from other wing commanders. This was conspicuous to all when Momyer barred Aderholt from attending Seventh Air Force commanders' conferences. Actions the wing took to justify the ambassador's confidence seemed to make matters worse. Sullivan believed Aderholt and the wing could do no wrong; Momyer believed they could do no right.[29]

Every time their paths crossed, the doctrinal gulf between Momyer and Aderholt revealed itself in an adversarial way. For instance, their opposing views on forward air controllers spoiled their only meeting at Nakhon Phanom.

When Aderholt first got there, the Butterfly FACs that his air commandos had trained at Hurlburt were still active in northern Laos as part of the Water Pump operation. They normally flew in the backseat of liaison aircraft flown by Air America pilots and controlled strikes by jet fighters diverted from North Vietnam. During a rare visit to Nakhon Phanom, Momyer exploded upon learning that for the past three years his jet fighters had been directed on targets in Laos by enlisted personnel and nonrated officers. "I told Momyer that enlisted FACs were flying with Air America pilots and were doing a terrific job," Aderholt said. "I had no idea he did not know who was controlling Seventh Air Force strikes in northern Laos. He was fit to be tied." On returning to his headquarters, Momyer had a FAC training school created at Bien Hoa and subsequently replaced the Butterflys with Raven FACs, who were rated Air Force officers having at least six months' experience in Vietnam.[30]

Aderholt thought this was foolish. "It was a gross waste of resources," he said. "The Momyer crowd talked about economy of force. Hell, they didn't know what economy of force was." He pointed out that the rules became so rigid, nobody could FAC Air Force jet fighters but other jet pilots. The Air Force transitioned SAC pilots and transport pilots through single-engine jet training so they could qualify to FAC jet aircraft before attending the school at Hurlburt. These pilots were designated as "A" FACs, whereas those in Southeast Asia who had not flown jets were classified as "B" FACs. The "B" FACs could control airstrikes by VNAF and other piston-engined planes but could not FAC jet aircraft unless it was an emergency.[31]

This rigidity carried over into the postwar Air Force. Aderholt still thought it was wrong thirty years later. "The handpicked sergeants we had were as good as any FACs out there," he said, "and were just as good as what they have today." Some were better than others, but that is true of any group. Aderholt swore that the Butterfly FACs were well trained, knew what they were doing, and could be depended on to do the right thing at the right time. "The job got done, and it was done well," Aderholt said. "There was never a 'bad bullet' or bad airstrike while combat controllers served as FACs." He added philosophically, "They believed they could do just about anything, and when you believe like that, you often can."[32]

Truck-Busting on the Ho Chi Minh Trail

Colonel Aderholt's first month as commander was a turkey shoot for the A-26s. While logging a small fraction of the sorties flown against the Ho Chi Minh Trail, the Nimrods scored a disproportionate share of the truck kills. Seventh

Air Force flew more than 3,000 sorties against the trail in December and destroyed or damaged 194 trucks. Although the A-26s flew only 195 of the total sorties, they tallied an incredible 126 of the 194 confirmed truck kills. This meant that the A-26s killed roughly 64 percent of the trucks while flying fewer than 7 percent of the sorties, no mean achievement by Seventh Air Force standards or anyone else's. The Nimrods suffered some battle damage, but only one had gone down. Two months into the dry season, the Nakhon Phanom truck-busters had aced the criteria Seventh Air Force laid down when it sought to extend the Big Eagle evaluation.[33]

Colonel Aderholt had been at Nakhon Phanom only a few days when the Nimrod squadron commander was shot down. Aderholt had flown out to the Bolovens Plateau (at the lower end of the Laotian panhandle) in a helicopter to cut Christmas trees for the troops. As they were returning with three Christmas trees protruding from the helicopter, Joe Kittinger came on the radio to report that Nimrod 31 had gone down near the trail with the squadron commander and another crew member on board. Kittinger was piloting another A-26 nearby, heard the beeper, and spotted the downed aircraft. It was dusk and would soon be dark. Aderholt asked if they had the rescue forces coming out. He knew from his experience with the JPRC that the rescue forces would not launch at night. Kittinger said that a flareship had arrived and the Jolly Greens were coming back from up north, would make a pass in the area of the downed crew, and pick them up if they could.[34]

Aderholt reached General Bond on the radio and got approval to launch his Huey helicopter from Nakhon Phanom if the Search and Rescue forces at Udorn would not respond. "If SAR decides they can't go in at night, I'm going in to get my people," Aderholt said. General Bond told him to go ahead, and for him to be backup. The returning Jolly Greens picked up two men, but when Aderholt's helicopter arrived overhead, a third person said, "Hey, what about me?" "Thinking the enemy might be laying an ambush, we checked to see if there had been a third guy down," Aderholt said, "and sure enough there had been a navigator on board for his first orientation ride. The commando helicopter picked him up and brought him back."[35]

Instead of a pat on the back, Aderholt said he got a nasty message from higher headquarters directing him to take all rescue gear off his aircraft and to attempt no future rescues. He had installed winches and other rescue gear in some of the helicopters in case they were needed. These were taken off and stored. A few months later General Bond called and asked for help in rescuing a Navy pilot who had gone down in Laos. He was responding to a personal call from the Seventh Fleet Commander. The Search and Rescue force was not available for a night mission because of their late return from Site 36. "The pilot was close in with the enemy, and they didn't think he would be there the next morning," Aderholt said. "General Bond called me and asked if I could put a helicopter up."[36]

Unfortunately, when the winch was retrieved from storage and reinstalled, it was hooked up improperly. The men were not trained to install the equipment, were pressed for time, and had not checked their work. They arrived at the scene to attempt the rescue, but as they were pulling the pilot up from the jungle floor, he hung on a tree, causing the aircraft to swerve and shear the cable. The arm of the winch broke, dropping the pilot. "Obviously we had killed him," Aderholt said. "I was furious with my people for hooking it up wrong, but even more so with the bureaucrats who made us take the equipment out of the aircraft." Later, a friendly guerrilla patrol came upon the pilot's cadaver and confirmed what happened. "That one has worried me for a long time," Aderholt said. "I killed that guy, but I wouldn't have if they had not been so goddamned parochial and taken our capability away."[37]

A composite force structure and Aderholt's command of the tactical unit operations center at Nakhon Phanom contributed to the success of the Nimrods. The aircrews had become familiar with the terrain and road systems and made maximum use of the real-time intelligence developed daily by the collocated Cricket FACs. Aided by Nakhon Phanom's proximity to the trail, the A-26s could loiter over the target area twice as long as jet aircraft. Their low airspeed and side-by-side seating permitted easier target acquisition. Close coordination with Meo or Thai ground observers in northern Laos further enhanced their effectiveness. The A-26 had a limited flare capability but had to call for flareships to assist with more lucrative targets. Unlike other Seventh Air Force aircraft, most of which were diverted to Laos from their original targets, the A-26s were armed for their assigned mission.[38]

Aderholt immediately began exploring ways to exploit more fully the unique capabilities of the A-26s. Initially, the planes had been limited to the Steel Tiger sector, an area extending southward through the Laotian panhandle past Tchepone to the Tiger Hound sector adjacent to South Vietnam. In November they began flying missions in the more heavily defended Barrel Roll sector, the Pathet Lao stronghold to the northeast. The impressive results racked up in December not only proved the A-26s could operate effectively against the trail, but supported Aderholt's contention they were the best weapon for the job. His biggest worry was that their limited availability made it impossible to keep the entire operational area covered. As an interim measure, he got approval in early January to augment operations in Steel Tiger with

T-28s (call sign, Zorro) that were not being used in the Thai training program. After a week of daylight familiarization missions over the trail, the Zorros phased into the night interdiction program on the eighteenth of January. Over the ensuing months the A-26s, T-28s, and A-1s (after the wing was activated) teamed up over the Ho Chi Minh Trail to write a new chapter in air interdiction history.[39]

An experience he had when introducing the T-28s into the interdiction effort nurtured his distrust of centralized control by Seventh Air Force. When he asked for approval to commit the T-28s to night interdiction, Aderholt advised that under no circumstances should these aircraft be fragged against heavily defended targets in daylight. They could not survive. No sooner had the T-28s entered the fray when Seventh Air Force fragged them for a daylight rescue mission. Four T-28s were launched to assist an O-1 pilot who had gone down in a heavily defended area. The first T-28 that rolled in on the target was shot down, killing the pilot and destroying the plane. "Seventh Air Force, in its infinite wisdom, sent us a message stating that's one, don't let it happen again," Aderholt said. "I, of course, went right back with a message reminding them to please not frag us for daylight strike missions on the trail."[40]

Aderholt and his people worked diligently at improving tactics and techniques, and by February had put a hunter-killer team concept into action over the trail at night. Captain Tom Deacon, a T-28 pilot, suggested using a hand-held starlight scope in the O-1s to detect trucks on the trail at night. Aderholt got one of the night-vision devices from the CIA through Major Secord at Udorn. The scope was used in both O-1 and C-123 aircraft to zero in on the trucks at night, and the A-26s and T-28s went in for the kill. General Momyer later wrote, "The most important innovation of this period was to install a starlight scope in a C-123." The scope was mounted in a C-123 by sticking the device through a hatch in the belly of the aircraft and securing it with a bungee cord inside the plane. An operator stretched out on a mattress and scanned the road through the scope. The compatible cruise speeds of the aircraft added to their effectiveness. The strike force, experimenting with a variety of ordnance loads, found that guns, cluster bomb units, and napalm were consistently the most effective munitions against trucks and truck parks.[41]

By the spring of 1967, the A-26s and T-28s—operating in the Steel Tiger and Barrel Roll areas of Laos, and to a limited degree in North Vietnam—had erased any doubts about their effectiveness in interdicting the truck traffic at night. The strike force, which still had not received all of the additional A-26s that were promised to Ambassador Sullivan during the fall, had ten A-26s and

Colonel Aderholt (center) with General John Ryan (left), CINCPACAF, and Lieutenant General James W. Wilson (right), Thirteenth Air Force commander, on flight line at Nakhon Phanom in 1967.

ten T-28s in operation. The A-26s had destroyed 275 trucks and damaged that many more. The T-28s, which were late getting into the fray, had destroyed 42 trucks and damaged 68. To expel any doubts, the Lucky Tiger forces did not claim truck kills unless they exploded or burned. The combined force had struck a variety of other targets such as truck parks, gun emplacements, road cuts, and so on, with spectacular results. The A-26s, for example, had attacked over twelve hundred truck parks, resulting in more than one thousand secondary explosions. Many of the attack aircraft had returned with battle damage, but only three A-26s and one T-28 had been shot down.[42]

In the three months that Aderholt had been at Nakhon Phanom, he had instilled confidence in his troops that, short of positioning ground forces across the waist of Laos, the composite force at Nakhon Phanom had the best chance of stopping traffic on the Ho Chi Minh Trail. The only thing holding them back was a lack of resources and a very short leash at Seventh Air Force headquarters. Instead of winning praise for their extraordinary achievements, however, their unbridled enthusiasm and absolute dedication to the mission had incurred the wrath of the Seventh Air Force commander.[43]

Aderholt got off to a bad start with General Momyer during his first two weeks at Nakhon Phanom. When General Harris decided to retire at the end of January 1967, he sent a message to wing commanders in Thailand asking for their ideas on improving the air war. Aderholt called Major Secord, who flew over from Udorn, and they spent the evening working on a proposal that all A-26 assets (twenty-nine total in USAF) be transferred to Southeast Asia with a replacement training unit set up at Clark. Aderholt forwarded the proposal through Thirteenth Air Force to General Harris, with an information copy to Seventh Air Force. "I also recommended they give us another squadron of A-1s," Aderholt said, "and told them let's go get those trucks."[44]

A day or so later Aderholt answered the telephone, and Momyer's deputy commander, Major General Gordon M. Graham, was on the line. "Heinie, you are in trouble," he said. Aderholt asked, "What do you mean?" Graham explained, "It's that message you sent to Hunter Harris. Momyer is furious." Aderholt said, "But I just responded to a request from General Harris." Graham said, "It wasn't coordinated with this headquarters, and it affects us." Aderholt replied, "You know he's not in my administrative chain of command. I info'd him." Graham said, "Look, I'm just giving you a heads up." A terse letter from Momyer followed, reminding Aderholt who was running the air war and directing him to coordinate all operational matters with Seventh Air Force. Aderholt swore he was not trying to "pull Momyer's chain" when he fired off another message through Thirteenth Air Force proposing to double the T-28s at Nakhon Phanom and use them in the night interdiction program.[45]

Aderholt's experience with Seventh Air Force over the coming weeks reinforced the impression he had at the JPRC that rigid centralized control as it was practiced in the Vietnam War worked to the enemy's advantage rather than ours. Seventh Air Force persisted in fragging the wing's aircraft with the wrong ordnance for their missions, despite Aderholt's complaints. They routinely either fragged the aircraft with bombs and rockets, which were worthless for night interdiction, or endangered the aircrews with a perilous mix of bombs and napalm. Aderholt explained that his planes had poor lighting, and a pilot could blow himself up if he went down to napalm a truck and hit the wrong switch. Napalm and cluster bomb units had proved to be the most effective munitions against the trail. Aderholt advised Seventh Air Force of the problem and asked that the wing be allowed to determine its own ordnance loads. Seventh Air Force said no, so he changed the ordnance loads anyway. "I wasn't going to risk my people with munitions we knew weren't worth a damn or would get them killed," he said. "So they came up and inspected us. We had bombs and rockets running out of our ass, and were short on the others." They would not accept his explanation and wrote him up for violating regulations. "We will tell you what you will put on those airplanes, and you will adhere to it," he was told. So he had Air America come get the rockets, which "weren't worth a damn," and take them up to Tony Poe, who was with Vang Pao's guerrillas, and he launched them off the ground.[46]

Finding Seventh Air Force unresponsive, Aderholt rarely bothered to ask for their approval when making improvements to the wing's operations. During the winter months the abort rate for the O-1s at Nakhon Phanom rose dramatically because the prevailing winds were strong and gusty out of the northwest, normally exceeding the maximum crosswind component of the lightweight aircraft. To solve the problem, Aderholt had the civil engineers scrape a small airstrip out of the rice paddies going across the end of the runway. One of the first things General Bond asked when he came to visit was how they had stopped the aborts. Aderholt proudly showed him the new airstrip. Bond asked, "Did you get permission for that?" Aderholt admitted that he had not. "Close it down," Bond said. The next day there were high winds, and the O-1s were aborting again.[47]

On the same visit General Bond discovered that the wing had unauthorized radio links with the CIA at Udorn, the embassy in Vientiane, and Vang Pao's guerrillas. Bond asked what they were used for, and Aderholt replied, "Aw, not much, General, we get intelligence from them, and they can tell us if the weather is bad in the target area." He explained that a few of the A-26 missions were fragged into northern Laos in Vang Pao's area. Sometimes they would arrive in the target area and the weather had turned bad. The radio contact gave them the weather before launching, so they would fly the missions in Tiger Hound. They could not simply abort the missions, or Seventh Air Force would want to know where they got the weather report. Bond asked, "If you hit targets in Tiger Hound, what do you do?" Aderholt said, "We just report them as being in northern Laos." Bond ordered him to close down the unauthorized radios.[48]

Aderholt got around the problem by asking Major Secord to call him every night at six P.M. and tell him whether it was clear to go north or not. "They have taken my radios away from me," he explained. "Our guys don't appreciate flying a four-hour flight up there and hauling their bombload back." Secord said, "I'll do it." He had radio communications with the outposts in northern Laos and relayed the up-to-date information to Aderholt. "That was asinine to have to work that way," Aderholt said later, adding that General Bond was a "good guy and had just been covering his ass."[49]

Ambushed at Udorn

Not long after Colonel Aderholt had been reprimanded by General Momyer for communicating directly with General Harris about the air war, Ambassador Sullivan brought Senator Stuart Symington to Nakhon Phanom for briefings on air operations in Laos. The Missouri senator, who was an influential member of the Senate Armed Services Committee and a former secretary of the Air Force, was in Southeast Asia on a fact-finding tour. Symington was hawkish early in the war but by 1967 had begun to waver in his support for U.S. intervention. His trip to the war zone was a prelude to Senate hearings on the air war to be convened during the month of August. Major Secord had accompanied the senator on his Laotian tour, including a trip to Lima Site 36.[50]

While at Nakhon Phanom, Symington was being briefed by Major Kittinger on A-26 operations when he turned to Aderholt and asked, "Are you trying to tell me this A-26 is better than the F-4s we are building in St Louis?" Aderholt said, "Senator Symington, I'm not trying to tell you anything. We are just briefing the facts." Symington said, "What you are telling me is that your airplane is better." "No, sir, those are your words. All we are doing is comparing the record on operations in Laos," Aderholt insisted. He admitted afterward, "None of us knew they manufactured the F-4 in Symington's district. Anyhow, we weren't trying to put down the F-4. It saved our ass up north."[51]

Despite Ambassador Sullivan's enthusiastic support for Aderholt's operations in Laos, Seventh Air Force was adamant in its opposition to beefing up the air commando forces at Nakhon Phanom. Shortly after the 56th Air Commando Wing was activated in the spring, their differences came to a head at a tension-filled meeting of the SEACOORD committee held at Udorn. Sullivan invited Aderholt to brief the committee on the proposal he had made to General Harris for improving interdiction in Laos and informed General Momyer that he wanted Aderholt at the next meeting. On the day before the meeting, Sullivan called to remind Aderholt about the briefing and said he would see him at Udorn the following morning. "Sir, I can't attend without orders from General Momyer," Aderholt said, "and I have heard nothing from him." Sullivan said, "Well, I will take care of that."[52]

Later that day General Graham called. "Heinie, the boss is really pissed off at you and Sullivan," he said. Aderholt asked, "Why is that?" Graham said, "Because Sullivan sent down a hot message about how you and the Sopwith Camels were winning the war. General Momyer told me to tell you that you will be at Udorn tomorrow, but you are not to open your mouth." A message followed advising that Colonel Aderholt was to meet General Momyer's aircraft on arrival at Udorn the following morning. He went out with General Bond to meet the plane. He was standing on the ramp in his air commando uniform when Momyer came off the plane, walked by him, spun around, came back, and said, "I want to see you in Bond's office."[53]

"I've had my share of ass-chewings, but this one took the cake," Aderholt recalled. "Momyer was enraged, ranting and raving. He accused me of being a traitor, of being disloyal to the Air Force." Aderholt tried to explain that he had not asked to be invited to the meeting, but the general wouldn't listen. "We are going in this meeting, and you are not going to say one word," Momyer ordered. "I have to have you in there because the ambassador made an issue of it, but you will not say a word." Aderholt said, "Fine."[54]

After Ambassador Graham Martin called the meeting to order, Momyer's faithful intelligence officer, Brigadier General Jammie Philpott, briefed the committee on a plan that would increase the number of B-52 sorties against the Tchepone area of the Ho Chi Minh Trail. The approval of both Ambassadors Martin and Sullivan was required because the sorties would be flown in Laos from Sattahip Air Base in southern Thailand. General Momyer had not been a proponent of augmented B-52 operations until overridden by General Westmoreland and the Air Staff. In August 1966 he had opposed the buildup at Sattahip, stating that the B-52s had been "relatively ineffective." Sullivan, who had abrasive discussions with Westmoreland on the subject, doubted whether the political fallout—including a rash of civilian casualties in Laos—would justify the lack of defining results. When Philpott finished his briefing, Sullivan turned to Momyer and said, "I'll tell you what, Spike. I'll go along with you on the B-52s if you will take those four stars and give them to Aderholt for fifteen minutes and let him tell us how interdiction against the Ho Chi Minh Trail ought to be run."[55]

"The colonel is not familiar with all Air Force requirements," Momyer said. "The A-26s he asked for are deployed to Southern Command in Panama."

Sullivan smiled. "Well, Spike, I didn't know they had a war in Panama," he said.

Momyer glared at Aderholt and told him, "Give your briefing."

Aderholt stood up and presented the shortest briefing he had ever made in his life—summarizing the A-26 proposal he had made to General Harris earlier—and sat down.[56]

Momyer was infuriated. Ambassador Sullivan said the general "decided he would cut Heinie down to size," and that he embarrassed everyone at the meeting with "a sophomoric performance"—putting Aderholt in a brace and lecturing him about his status "as an underling of the Seventh Air Force." "Martin and I knew better than to interfere in Air Force campfire rituals, and West-moreland seemed a bit abashed by the whole show," Sullivan said. "Heinie didn't blink an eye."[57]

Aderholt was churning inside, however. As he was leaving the meeting, Pappy Pettigrew asked where he was going. "I'm getting out of here before I have to knock a four-star general on his ass," Aderholt told him. Later, in General Bond's office, he was asked, "What are you going to do?" Aderholt was so angry, he said he felt like resigning. Bond bit off a plug of tobacco and drawled, "Heinie, you are not going to let him run you off, are you?" Aderholt said the more he thought about it on the way back to Nakhon Phanom, the more he decided "to fight that son of a bitch to the very end."[58]

A week or so later Colonel Walter B. Forbes arrived from Seventh Air Force headquarters to take over the tactical unit operations center and to exercise operational control of operations at Nakhon Phanom. Colonel Forbes's duties at Tan Son Nhut had included briefing General Momyer twice a day on air operations in Vietnam. One Sunday in June, Momyer called him in and gave him three days to pull people together to set up an organization at Nakhon Phanom known as the Steel Tiger Task Force. Forbes said he honestly did not know whether Momyer "fired me or promoted me when he sent me to Nakhon Phanom." His operation grew into Task Force Alpha, which was responsible for the infiltration surveillance center at Nakhon Phanom, but initially he was there to monitor Aderholt's wing operations for Seventh Air Force. Forbes noted, however, that he and Aderholt became great friends and the so-called "operational control" he exercised was in name only.[59]

Sid Marshall, who had worked for Colonel Aderholt at Hurlburt, arrived at Nakhon Phanom during the late summer of 1967. He was in the office one day when Ambassador Sullivan called. The ambassador told Aderholt that he was going back to Washington on a trip and would be conferring with President Johnson. He did not want Aderholt's career ruined and asked permission to raise the issue of his difficulties with General Momyer and Seventh Air Force. Marshall said Aderholt asked the ambassador not to bring up the matter, because he did not want to embarrass the Air Force or to give the appearance of using political influence.[60]

When the Going Gets Tough

The upbraiding Aderholt had taken at Udorn and the humiliation of having another colonel brought in over him at Nakhon Phanom might have broken a lesser man. Aderholt was hurt and angry, but his fighting spirit was pumped up.

He bristled when a message came in unduly restricting operations against targets in Laos. The message stated that the Seventh Air Force commander did not believe there was a target in Laos worth losing a pilot or an aircraft. Aderholt mustered the pilots and read them the message. "I don't agree with the commander of Seventh Air Force," he said. "We are out here to fight a goddamned war, and we are not going to be intimidated by the enemy." He told them that the pilots who pressed when they had a valid target would be put in for the highest Air Force medal authorized. "I will be out there with you, but the North Vietnamese won't intimidate the 56th Wing," he said.[61]

Marshall said that when he arrived three months before Aderholt's departure, the colonel met him at the flight line in his staff car but did not have time to talk because he was due for a mission briefing in a few minutes. He told Sid to take the car and see him back at his office at five thirty P.M. Marshall later learned that Aderholt flew interdiction missions against the trail "three, four, or five times a week." He noted for a commander at Aderholt's level that many missions a month would have been well above average. "Needless to say, his troops would follow him anywhere," Marshall said. "They were devoted to him."[62]

In his final evaluation of Aderholt before rotating in June, General Bond called him "a real combat leader" who flew "in all his aircraft as pilot and on any type mission—many of them the toughest." He said Aderholt was, without doubt, the most knowledgeable officer he had ever known in the field of special air warfare and had proved this "time and again" since taking over command of the wing at Nakhon Phanom. "He is a master in the field of operations and tactics involving air commando type aircraft and helicopters," Bond wrote. "The operational accomplishments of his T-28, A-26 and C-123 aircraft . . . have set records of which the Air Force can be proud." Bringing to mind his earlier conversation with Major Ropka about whether they could control Heinie, Bond stated that Aderholt never needed supervision, but "had to be 'held back' at times because of his 'can do' attitude and enthusiastic approach to any problem." General Wilson endorsed the evaluation, recommending Aderholt's immediate promotion to brigadier general.[63]

Major General William C. Lindley Jr., who replaced Bond at Udorn, found it hard to believe that Colonel Aderholt was excluded from Seventh Air Force wing commanders' conferences. He called Aderholt and said that he was to accompany him to a forthcoming commanders' conference at Tan Son Nhut. "Sir, I'm not invited," Aderholt said. Lindley insisted. "That must be an oversight," he said. Aderholt assured him that it was not an oversight, that he was not invited. "Nonsense," the general said. "You heard me. You are going." So they flew down in the Seventh/Thirteenth commander's C-54.[64]

Aderholt stated that he purposefully was the last person to deplane because he did not want the others to be embarrassed for him when he was turned away. General Momyer's protocol officer, who was an old acquaintance, met the plane. He spotted Aderholt and asked, "Heinie, what the hell are you doing here?" Aderholt said, "Ask General Lindley. I told him I wasn't supposed to come." Lindley huddled with the protocol officer, then told Aderholt to take a staff car, have a night on the town, and meet them back at the plane the next day. The other commanders, especially Colonel Robin Olds and Colonel Edward Burdett (who was later killed over North Vietnam) were furious that he had been shunned, but Aderholt saw it as just another display of pettiness toward himself and the 56th Wing.[65]

Soon thereafter Aderholt's lingering difficulties with the Seventh Air Force commander paled in comparison to those facing another fearless warrior, Colonel Jack Broughton, deputy commander of the 355th Tactical Fighter Wing at Takhli. Colonel Broughton had charges brought against him by the Air Force for allegedly covering up for two of his pilots who hit a Russian ship, the *Turkestan,* in North Vietnam, and then lying to investigators about it. The *Turkestan,* which was off-loading cargo at the port of Cam Pha, was hit when the pilots attacked guns that had fired on them from the harbor. To protect the pilots, Colonel Broughton had destroyed the film from their gun cameras. At the time of the incident he was acting wing commander in the absence of his boss, Colonel Robert L. Scott Jr. Aderholt was ordered to Clark Air Base to sit on the board at Broughton's court-martial, which was presided over by Colonel Chuck Yeager.[66]

During the court-martial proceedings, the story came out that Broughton had stripped the gun camera film from its canister and exposed it after the pilots returned from the mission in question. He was at the officers' club that evening when the unexposed film was brought to him for a decision on what to do with it. During the Air Force's investigation of the *Turkestan* incident, Colonel Broughton had foiled investigators by giving evasive answers to poorly phrased questions. The wing kept the wraps on what happened until a visiting two-star general from higher headquarters asked Broughton during an informal chat how the morale stayed so high when the pilots were "getting their ass shot off up north." The colonel said it was because the men had camaraderie and took care of each other. He then confided off the record that he had protected his pilots when Air Force investigators grilled him about the *Turkestan* affair, explaining that they had asked the wrong questions. The general excused himself, located a telephone, and reported the conversation to his headquarters.[67]

As the senior commander in Thailand, Major General Lindley at Udorn had court-martial jurisdiction and was the one who brought charges. Before pressing charges, General Lindley reportedly went to Takhli, gave Broughton and his people a pat on the back, and said, "Come on, you can tell me everything." "They told him everything, and then he turned around and charged them," Aderholt said. The court-martial board reduced the charges, finding Broughton guilty of destroying government property and ordering him to pay damages in the amount of the destroyed film. Nevertheless, the court-martial ruined Colonel Broughton's career, and he retired from the Air Force soon afterward. Aderholt returned to the wing, mustered his pilots, and told them: "I've just come from the most disgusting episode of my life. I have seen a great injustice done. If you go out and hit the wrong target and mess up badly and come back here, don't you tell anybody. If I come up and pat you on the back and start asking questions, just say, 'Screw you, Colonel.' Because when the time comes that I have to raise my hand and swear, I'll have to appear against you as a witness."[68]

Just before the Broughton affair, Colonel Aderholt had protected one of his own officers from taking the blame for a Seventh Air Force mistake. When a FAC aircraft from Nakhon Phanom was shot down over North Vietnam, Seventh Air Force had opened an investigation into the incident because the O-1s were prohibited from flying over the north. An investigating officer from Seventh Air Force headquarters wanted Aderholt to bring charges against the operations officer who had been on duty when the mission was fragged. Aderholt had already conducted his own investigation and learned that the FAC had spotted trucks across the border and checked in with the C-130 airborne command and control center, which belonged to Seventh Air Force, to bring in fighters. The C-130 called in fighters, and the O-1 was shot down during the ensuing operation. "If you want to charge somebody, charge General Dunham [Brigadier General William Dunham headed Seventh Air Force operations], that's his command post," Aderholt told the investigating officer. "My command post didn't send him over there. Your command post did. Go back and tell your boss I have court-martial jurisdiction. If they want to press charges, they can charge me or General Dunham. His people approved their going into North Vietnam." The matter was dropped.[69]

On another occasion one of the wing's light planes was en route to Bangkok with a passenger when the engine quit. The two men had parachutes, but by the time the pilot tried to restart the engine, they were too low to bail out. When the pilot brought the plane in, the landing gear hung on a ledge and they slid to a stop against a mountain. The wing sent a helicopter out and brought them back to Nakhon Phanom. Because all accidents (not combat losses) were critiqued to the Thirteenth Air Force commander once a month, Aderholt flew to Clark with the other wing commanders to meet with General Wilson. One of the commanders said his wing's accident was not the pilot's fault, that he had been unlucky. When Wilson got to Aderholt, he growled, "Well, I guess you are going to tell me your goddamn pilot was unlucky." "No, General, I'm telling you he was one lucky son of a bitch," Aderholt answered. "He was unlucky that his engine quit, but he was damned lucky that he put it down where he did and survived. He did a damned good job." Wilson said, "Well, ground him and get rid of him. I don't like unlucky people." Rather than ground the man, when Aderholt got back to Nakhon Phanom, he called Vientiane and asked Colonel Pettigrew if he needed a pilot. "I'm sending you one," Aderholt said.[70]

Aderholt's friends in Thailand and Laos helped the wing out of a number of scrapes. One time an A-1 returning from a combat mission landed too close to an Air America plane and chopped the vertical stabilizer off. The A-1 was undamaged. Instead of reporting the accident and going through a lengthy investigation, Aderholt asked Major Secord to get in touch with Air America and see if they would take care of their aircraft without reporting it. "They said sure, they would handle it, and that was the end of the problem," Aderholt said.[71]

When a U-10 hit a post while landing at a village with no runway, it was reported to Colonel Aderholt as a major accident. "We don't have major accidents," Aderholt said, and sent his maintenance people out with a flatbed truck to bring the U-10 back to the base and repair it. A grizzled sergeant was working on the wrecked U-10 in the hangar area when Brigadier General Frank Everest, the Air Force director of safety, came through on an inspection visit. The general approached the sergeant and asked how long he had been working on the wrecked plane. "Oh, about a month," the sergeant replied. Everest said, "Pretty major accident, wasn't it?" The sergeant answered, "No, sir. Colonel Aderholt don't have accidents." The general's brow raised. He asked, "What do you call this?" The sergeant scratched his head. "I don't know, General. All I do is work on them," he said. The next morning Colonel Aderholt had his safety officer write up an accident report and backdate it.[72]

. . . The Tough Get Going

Colonel Aderholt's men say that he left Nakhon Phanom the way he had come in, blocks up and props churning. General Momyer was still wielding the tyranny of centralized control in Saigon and ruling Seventh Air Force with an iron hand when Aderholt left, but he had outlasted his old boss at Thirteenth Air Force, General Wilson, by three months. Wilson's replacement, the distinguished Tuskegee Airman, Lieutenant General Benjamin O. Davis, endorsed Aderholt's OER with the observation that if he was given more equipment and a green light, "he would try to win the war himself."[73] General Momyer could attest to that.

Major Richard Secord at Nakhon Phanom in 1967.

During Aderholt's final weeks as commander, the 56th Air Commando Wing's combat record was unexcelled. From 21 October to 19 November, the wing was credited with 254 confirmed truck kills in the Steel Tiger sector, accounting for roughly 70 percent of all trucks that were destroyed. Altogether, Seventh Air Force aircraft had destroyed a total of 350 trucks. The wing's strike aircraft damaged an additional 69 trucks and probably destroyed or damaged 59 others. What bothered Aderholt the most was that 3,514 truck sightings had been made (3,131 with the starlight scope), but only 1,834 trucks had been struck. Nearly that many had not been attacked, partly because there were not enough strike aircraft available. To Aderholt this proved his point that the wing could have made a substantially larger impact on interdicting the Ho Chi Minh Trail had he been given the resources requested a year ago.[74]

The interdiction results during these four weeks were exceptional when compared to the first five months of 1967. Over that five-month period, Aderholt's A-26s and T-28s had destroyed 351 vehicles and damaged or destroyed 412. Aderholt pointed out that these statistics showed that the aerial interdiction program against the Laotian panhandle lines of communication had not been satisfactory during the 1966–67 dry-season campaign. Enemy truck traffic moved in great numbers during that period and had not been effectively interdicted. After May the southwest monsoon washed out the Ho Chi Minh Trail and halted vehicular movement in the area. The rainfall was less than expected but did not end until 30 September. As the dry season got under way, there was a predictable rush of enemy activity, but it came much earlier in the season. Unknown at that time, the enemy was moving south in massive numbers to launch the siege at Khe Sanh and the countrywide Tet Offensive of 1968. Westmoreland's intelligence gurus knew something was up, but were not sure what.[75]

The CIA's Thai and Hmong road watch teams continued to play an important role in reporting enemy movement in Laos, but the wing's innovative use of the starlight scope and continuous overflight of the area by pilots familiar with the terrain had become more reliable sources for truck sightings. At the start of the dry season, the road watch teams were out along the trail, and the CIA office at Udorn was supposed to advise the wing when the first trucks came through and at what choke point. Aderholt's friends, Bill Lair and Pat Landry, ran the operation. Major Secord was their operations officer. On the night of 21 October one of Aderholt's T-28 pilots was out on the trail and spotted the season's first large-scale truck movement. There was a long line of trucks, lights on, heading south. The T-28 took out two of the trucks and called in the A-26s. A total of eight trucks were destroyed that night.[76]

At first light the next morning, an O-1 pilot flew over with a handheld camera and took pictures of the burned-out trucks. When the film was developed, Aderholt called Secord and asked him if they still had road watch teams out on the trail. "Oh, yes, we've got them out there," he replied. Aderholt said, "Dick, inform Pat Landry that we just destroyed eight trucks last night heading south at Delta." He heard Landry in the background say, "Tell Heinie he's full of shit." Aderholt got in his T-28, flew to Udorn, and threw the photographs on the table. "Full of shit, huh," he said. Apparently, the teams had been sitting too far off the trail to keep from being seen and had missed the trucks when they passed through.[77]

A Seventh Air Force directive changing the wing's reporting procedures appeared deliberately designed to suppress the 56th Wing's outstanding results against enemy trucks in Laos. Previously, the wing forwarded its operations reports (Oprep 4s) to Seventh Air Force, CINCPAC, JCS, and the embassies in Bangkok, Vientiane, and Saigon. Seventh Air Force directed the wing to send its report only to Seventh Air Force, where it would be consolidated with those of the other wings. When the reports were consolidated and forwarded to Air Force headquarters, the wing's truck kills were lumped with those of the other wings and were credited to their jet aircraft. The kills were reported as having occurred in North Vietnam rather than Laos. The same information was released to the press, leaving the false impression that jet aircraft had accounted for all of the destroyed trucks.[78]

The change in reporting procedures was doubly suspicious, coming at a time when the Pentagon was debating whether jet aircraft or prop aircraft were more effective in the war. At this stage in the conflict, it was evident that both jets and props were needed—if for no other reason, because the props could not go north and could not survive over heavily defended targets unless jets were there to suppress the enemy guns. Colonel Aderholt believed that a healthy mix of both was needed, and that more, not fewer, prop aircraft were required to do the job right. He emphasized this in his end-of-tour report, which was forwarded through PACAF headquarters to the Air Staff.[79]

Before Aderholt left Nakhon Phanom, the base had started preparing for the activation of Secretary McNamara's sensor-oriented antiinfiltration system known as Igloo White—another high-tech scheme in an extremely low-tech war. A joint team from the Pentagon came out and gave a briefing on the system, which required Navy crews to fly out over the trail in daylight and put in sensors. Aderholt asked, "You mean to tell me you are going to fly straight and level up the Ho Chi Minh Trail at five hundred feet in broad daylight and put the sensors out?" A Navy commander said simply, "That's our mission." Aderholt took him out over the trail at five thousand feet and said, "Let me show you something." He started down, and the guns opened up before they could level off.[80]

When Aderholt mentioned this to the PACAF commander, who had flown in to check on the progress of the new system, he was told, "Don't dramatize this, Aderholt. If we have any trouble, we will put the B-52s in to clean out the flak." The Navy squadron assigned to Nakhon Phanom to plant the sensors was VO-67, a specialized unit of highly trained pilots and crews. The squadron lost three OP-2E aircraft to enemy fire in a very short period and was abruptly withdrawn in June 1968 after losing 25 percent of its aircraft over the Ho Chi Minh Trail. The A-1 Skyraiders were also withdrawn from the daylight seeding missions and were replaced by F-4 Phantoms. Aderholt disagreed that massive B-52 strikes were an effective weapon against the trail. They rained bombs on the trail and the surrounding jungle floor, but either the trucks bypassed the craters, or coolie battalions had the roads repaired before the huge bombers got back to home base.[81]

Aderholt knew that General Ryan's attitude toward him was influenced by what he had heard from Seventh Air Force. On one of the general's visits to Nakhon Phanom, he had mentioned that Ambassador Sullivan was a big problem for Seventh Air Force and that Aderholt was responsible for feeding him information. "Sir, I have nothing to do with this," Aderholt protested. Ryan asked, "Then how does he get his information?" Aderholt shrugged. "The same way we do, I guess," he replied. "His air attaché is on distribution for the frag orders and other Seventh Air Force messages. He gets the same information we get." General Ryan thought for a moment and said with finality, "Aderholt, regardless of what you or Sullivan come up with, we are not assigning a designated A-1 squadron or anything else to Laos." That was the extent of their conversation.[82]

Aderholt's end-of-tour report criticized Seventh Air Force's interdiction program for paying more attention to road cuts than to primary targets such as trucks and gun positions. He listed what he considered to be the most significant shortcomings in the Tiger Hound and Steel Tiger areas. The routes in those areas were not kept under twenty-four-hour surveillance, because Seventh Air Force refused to concentrate enough resources on the problem. The practice of diverting sorties from targets in North Vietnam satisfied the requirements of centralized control but consistently put F-4s and other high-performance jets over the trail carrying ordnance that was wrong for the target. Aderholt was big on innovations but believed costly, harebrain schemes such as Igloo White hindered the interdiction effort rather than helped it, and were better left in the laboratory.[83]

The end-of-tour report contained a proposal for an aggressive, around-the-clock interdiction campaign—carefully planned, effectively integrated, and aggressively pursued—for reducing the flow of Communist supplies through the Laotian panhandle. The beauty of the proposal was that it could be put into action immediately with existing Air Force resources and within the current political constraints and rules of engagement. He proposed an interdiction force made up of propeller and jet-powered aircraft (especially B-57 Canberras, which he believed were best for the job)—the props for FAC and strike in permissive defense environments, and the jets for flak suppression and strikes in more heavily defended areas—operating continuously along the road network in Laos, giving the enemy no safe time of day or night in which to repair the roads or move his vehicles. The proposal outlined the aircraft, ordnance, and tactics that were required for the interdiction effort to be effective.[84]

Colonel Aderholt also addressed the accomplishments of the wing's mobile training teams and civic action programs, which had no apparent interest to the Seventh Air Force and PACAF commanders, but had made a major contribution to counterinsurgency operations and nation building among the Thais and Laotians. Composed of eighty-four officers and men, most of whom were doctors and medical technicians, with a scattering of other highly diversified skills, the wing's civic action program had expanded the work begun by the Water

Pump detachment in 1964. This included the introduction of a floating medical center on the Mekong River to help the tens of thousands of people who were completely isolated during the rainy season. A major goal was to counter the insurgent cells that had been in place along the Mekong for years.[85]

He took a backhanded swipe at centralized control in his report, noting that the 56th Wing was capable of producing considerably more combat sorties than it was flying. The wing was permitted to fly missions only that were planned and directed by higher headquarters, which were consistently less than it was prepared to launch. Under the Seventh Air Force system, the wing could not take advantage of the additional combat capability that was being generated but not used. Aderholt noted that the wing commander could employ the added sorties effectively but did not have that prerogative. He recommended, therefore, that wing commanders be given discretionary authority to dispatch sorties over and above those directed by higher headquarters. "In fact, it may even be time to recognize that wars are not won by adherence to policies and directives formulated for the administration of peacetime activities," he concluded.[86]

Regulations required that Colonel Aderholt debrief the PACAF commander before proceeding to his next assignment. He looked forward to debriefing the commander and discussing the end-of-tour report he had submitted earlier. He was proud of the men in the 56th Air Commando Wing and all that they had accomplished together over the past year. Despite the misunderstandings with Seventh Air Force, which would follow him to his next assignment, he would not have missed being their commander for anything in the world. Ambassador Sullivan had written to the Air Force chief of staff praising the wing and Aderholt's leadership. "The morale of his unit was outstanding and they prided themselves in responding to the most difficult and most hazardous tasks," Sullivan wrote. "As Colonel Aderholt's principal customer, I can assure you that his performance has made a believer out of me."[87]

Aderholt had always thought of Hickam as a laid-back military installation, but found its vintage tile-roofed stucco buildings—the headquarters complex still bearing the scars of the Japanese attack on Pearl Harbor twenty-five years earlier—and its palm-lined drives uniquely appealing. The command section was larger than his entire wing headquarters had been at Nakhon Phanom. He had risen early, completed his morning run, and arrived at seven o'clock sharp for the appointment with the PACAF commander. When he arrived, the general was not in. The deputy commander, Lieutenant General James V. Edmundson, said it might be best if he did not wait for the commander, that it might not be productive. As Aderholt started to leave, the PACAF commander walked in, did not speak, nodded, and went into his office. Edmundson followed him in, came back out, and told Aderholt he could go in.[88]

When Aderholt entered, the general had his back toward him, did not greet him, and did not acknowledge his presence. "Colonel Aderholt reporting as ordered, sir," he said. There was no answer. Aderholt waited a respectable time for a response, and when there was none, he excused himself and left. The PACAF commander never turned to address him or look in his direction. "I could take the personal hostility," Aderholt said later, "but not the implied insult to the men of the 56th Wing." The general obviously had read the end-of-tour report and did not concur with what it said. General Edmunson was clearly embarrassed that Aderholt had been kept waiting. Three decades later he wrote Aderholt to tell him what "a magnificent job" he had done at Nakhon Phanom and to acknowledge that he "didn't get the recognition and support that should have been coming."[89]

Aderholt felt betrayed that morning at Hickam, knowing that the commander's mind and others' were closed to his proposals for improving air operations in the war and that his report would go forward to Washington with PACAF's rebuttal. He left the building and strode angrily back to the guest quarters where the family was waiting. They had joined up at Clark and had flown to Hawaii after clearing Jessie and the children out of the off-base quarters they had moved into when Colonel Aderholt went to Nakhon Phanom. At least they could look forward to the next assignment. Major General Thomas G. Corbin, who had replaced General Pritchard at Eglin, had visited Nakhon Phanom and asked Aderholt to come back to Eglin and be his director of operations. They were going home, but he was melancholy that night. He told Jessie, "Today confirmed what Dick and I have said all along. We are losing the war, and we don't even know it."[90]

9. WEATHERING THE STORM

The auditorium filled rapidly, settling into rows of sky-blue uniforms trimmed in silver braid. From the podium Colonel Aderholt looked down on the array of burnished stars seated up front. After debriefing the TAC commander and senior officers at Langley, he had gone to the Pentagon to report to the Air Staff about his tour in Southeast Asia. Major General Corbin asked to approve his remarks beforehand, but Aderholt refused. He offered to provide a summary, but not the report in its entirety. "I told the general that it was my end-of-tour report, and nobody was going to make me change it," Aderholt said. "That did not sit well with him, and we didn't get along too well after that." General Gabriel P. Disosway had commented favorably on Aderholt's debriefing at TAC headquarters, but the colonel's blunt critique of Seventh Air Force's interdiction of the Ho Chi Minh Trail touched a raw nerve at the Pentagon.[1]

He opened his remarks by condemning the practice of consolidating all strike results in the out-country war into a single format, both in official reports and in public releases, because it gave the false impression that the targets were all struck in North Vietnam by jet aircraft. "I can condone the United States Air Force lying to the American people . . . if it protects the force and helps us win," he said. "I can't condone the United States Air Force lying to itself until it believes its own lies." He proceeded to explain that the 56th Air Commando Wing's vintage force of propeller aircraft had been the predominant truck killer on the Ho Chi Minh Trail although it had flown only a small fraction of the Seventh Air Force sorties against the trail. The wing had received no recognition from Seventh Air Force for its accomplishments. He then briefed the proposals he had made for effectively interdicting the enemy's lines of communication.[2]

Using matting laid by coolie battalions, North Vietnamese trucks continue to roll down the bombed-out Ho Chi Minh Trail.

"They really took me apart when the briefing was over," Aderholt said with a laugh. An indignant three-star general stood and said, "I resent your comment about the Air Force lying to itself. Can you be more specific? What do you mean by making such a statement?" Aderholt answered, "Very simple, General. The facts speak for themselves. The last six months of my tour at Nakhon Phanom, every truck we killed, every target we destroyed, was credited to jet fighters. All you have to do is look at the Oprep 4s. For instance, on 3 December the Nimrods destroyed fourteen trucks at Mu Gia Pass, but the Oprep 4 doesn't show that. So if you lie about your weapon system, you will surely end up with second-rate weaponry." He also pointed out that he had asked that the cluster bomb unit, which had proved to be the best truck killer in Vietnam, be put back into production, but had never received an answer.[3]

Lieutenant General John R. Murphy, who had preceded General Bond at Udorn and served for a few months as Bond's deputy, came to Aderholt's defense. He had been reassigned to the Pentagon with the Office of the Secretary of the Air Force upon completing his Southeast Asia tour in the summer of

1966. Aderholt recalled, "Just when it looked the darkest that day, General Murphy jumped on my side and said, 'Aderholt is right.' That was rewarding, to have a guy who is a great combat pilot say that." He flew back to Eglin that afternoon knowing his report had struck few chords within the Air Staff, yet glad that he "told it like he saw it" anyway.[4] A less than rousing welcome for a returning warrior, the experience left him with a premonition that life back in the shadow of Tactical Air Command might get worse before it got better.

The Calm before the Storm

Colonel Aderholt's first months as the Special Air Warfare Center's director of operations were routine—training personnel for combat in Southeast Asia, testing new equipment, planning and conducting exercises, deploying teams to assist emerging nations, and so on. While he was away, the special air warfare activities had become even more assimilated into Tactical Air Command's force structure and operational doctrine. The command seemed more interested in a new forward air controller aircraft, the OV-10 Bronco, which came off the production line in early 1968, than it was in special mission aircraft for the air commando forces. An exception was the advanced gunship program, particularly the AC-130 Spectre, a protoype model of which had been sent to Vietnam in September 1967 to undergo combat evaluation. The tests, which were conducted from September to December, demonstrated that the AC-130 (which had night-vision equipment and heavier armament) was far superior to the AC-47 Spooky gunships and to Seventh Air Force fighters in the close air support and interdiction roles. In attacks on enemy lines of communication, the test aircraft had destroyed 38 trucks of the 94 that were sighted.[5]

General Westmoreland and the Army were greatly impressed with the advanced gunship's performance. After undergoing an all-out refurbishment of its sensors and other equipment in the United States, the prototype AC-130 returned to Southeast Asia in February and flew combat missions out of Thailand and Vietnam through November 1968. The results were impressive. On night interdiction missions, the AC-130 destroyed 228 trucks and damaged 133. It supported troops in contact on 28 of 151 missions and accounted for 240 enemy killed. The strain of combat had taken its toll on the lone prototype, however, and in late November it was ferried back to Wright-Patterson AFB, Ohio, because of critical equipment malfunctions.[6]

While a debate ensued over whether to develop a mixed gunship force or to concentrate solely on developing the AC-130, Colonel Aderholt became convinced that TAC generals were lukewarm in their support for the gunship program. High-level interest on the Air Staff and the Air Force secretary's office, fanned by the Army's enthusiasm for the weapons system, kept the program alive. Work on the gunship was centered at Wright-Patterson AFB, Ohio, where Colonel Ronald W. Terry headed a small office of dedicated officers and civilians within the Aeronautical Systems Division. Colonel Terry conducted the AC-130 test in Vietnam. He had been involved with gunship development since the summer of 1964, when, as a captain, he put his fighter pilot experience to work on the concept at Wright-Patterson. The gunship concept had started at Eglin during Aderholt's first tour there but had received little support from TAC headquarters at the time.[7]

The prototype AC-130's initial combat tests were being conducted when Colonel Aderholt left Nakhon Phanom. He retained an intense interest in the advanced gunship's progress when reports of its success started coming back from Southeast Asia. Secretary of the Air Force Harold Brown selected the AC-119 as the primary gunship to augment the AC-47s, but approved a small force of AC-130s to allow the program to go forward. The secretary had expressed concerns that modifying C-130s into gunships would adversely affect critical airlift resources. General Momyer believed the impact on the airlift fleet would be minimal, a view that he reversed after leaving Saigon as Seventh Air Force commander. Before the end of 1968, there were four AC-130 gunships in Thailand flying combat.[8] Testing and demonstrating the gunship's capabilities was a function of Colonel Aderholt's office at Eglin.

One of Aderholt's first priorities when he got back from Southeast Asia was to reassemble as many members of his experienced team of air commandos as he could, but this took time. In August 1968 Major Ropka returned from a six-month combat tour in Thailand to oversee worldwide counterinsurgency exercises and operations. Major Secord came back in September as Aderholt's deputy. Secord had seriously considered resigning from the Air Force over the debacle in Vietnam, but Aderholt talked him out of it. By year's end he got Major Ifland reassigned to the headquarters when his tour in Vietnam was up. Others followed. Some, like Jim Ahmann and Joe Kittinger, had moved into other fast-track assignments and were not available.[9]

Major General Corbin left Eglin in June 1968 and was replaced by Brigadier General Robert L. Cardenas, who had previously commanded the 18th Tactical Fighter Wing at Kadena, Okinawa. On 8 July the Air Force redesignated the Special Air Warfare Center as the Special Operations Force. The 1st Air Commando Wing became the 1st Special Operations Wing, and its squadrons were renamed accordingly. To some the redesignations and the reduced rank of the center commander were ominous signs of downgrading the air commandos on the part of higher headquarters. Were air commandos, once again, to be disbanded and relegated to Air Force history? they wondered. The suspense mounted in August when General Momyer returned from Southeast Asia to take over Tactical Air Command.[10]

The War Had Followed Him Home

Colonel Aderholt had a feeling that the war had followed him home when General Momyer came back to Langley. That same month General Ryan reported to the Pentagon to be Air Force vice chief of staff. A year later Ryan replaced General McConnell as chief. Aderholt knew that he would not be asked for his recommendations on the war in Southeast Asia anytime soon. The Air Force considered Momyer to be its leading authority on tactical air power during the Vietnam era, and his direction of air operations in Southeast Asia went unchallenged even after we lost the war. That Momyer was chosen by the steering committee to oversee the final report for Project Corona Harvest, a self-evaluation of USAF operations in Southeast Asia, was an indication that the Air Force did not want an objective analysis of its role in the war.[11]

The former Seventh Air Force commander fell into the same trap as many of his contemporaries: a natural tendency to blame everyone but himself for the way the war was prosecuted in Vietnam. His end-of-tour report begins with an apology that the war was "probably the most difficult we have ever fought," then blames the "many restraints, limited objectives, lack of mobilization, failure to declare a state of war and the divided home front" for adversely influencing "the prosecution of the conflict and the results the military could produce."[12] The general bitterly resented Ambassador Sullivan's control over military operations in Laos. In a letter from his Corona Harvest files, Momyer wrote that "Sullivan was magnificent in frustrating our desires . . . to use the B-52s in Laos." Referring to Laos at one point as "that miserable little country," he suggested that the ambassador's motives were to preserve "his own private war by limiting the scale of our effort."[13]

The frustrations of the war were painfully obvious in official correspondence between his return from Southeast Asia in 1968 and his retirement in1973. In January 1969 Momyer sent General Westmoreland (who was now the Army chief of staff) a copy of a report the Seventh Air Force staff had put together on air operations during his command. The tone of the letter was exuberant. He said there was no doubt that Westmoreland's strategy in Vietnam had been the right one for the circumstances and that the enemy was beaten when he relinquished command to General Creighton Abrams. He called the Tet Offensive "a tremendous defeat for the enemy" and stated, "Abe is now exploiting that defeat by reducing the enemy to a point of military impotency."[14] Less effusive when he sent the report to General Ryan, however, Momyer wrote, "In hindsight we could have done some things differently, but we did the best we could with the prevailing conditions."[15]

A year later Momyer was still optimistic, but less sanguine, about the war. After returning from a trip to Southeast Asia at the end of 1969, he reported to General Ryan that the lines of communication in Laos were "alive again with major truck movements and the enemy shows no indication of slowing down the fighting." He noted there was the same pattern of movement as previous years, adding euphemistically that "we should see and kill more trucks this season than in any other previous year." Taking a page from Aderholt's end-of-tour report, he said, "We may be on the verge of a morale problem if we don't get to flying the pilots at a higher rate and working the maintenance people longer hours. I am even more convinced after this trip we need to reduce the number of units and work their tail off."[16]

In October 1970 a letter that Momyer wrote to a student at the National War College was more recriminatory. He returned to the theme that the political objectives had so limited the application of our military forces that they could not produce the decisive effects required to achieve a negotiated settlement. He drew the conclusion that a more valid evaluation of the political objectives in Vietnam would have revealed that the military forces could not produce the conditions dictated by the objectives. "Thus, there would have been a change in the political objectives or a decision not to commit forces with a consequent loss of the country," he wrote. "It seems to me we didn't face up to the realities of these circumstances."[17] Nearly a year later, he wrote that sometimes he thought the Joint Chiefs of Staff should have resigned as a body to drive home the folly of the civilian strategy for fighting the war. "I look back on the war with much regret that we were not permitted to take the action that would have won the war and saved many precious lives," he stated. "We the military must share some of the blame since I don't think we resisted to the degree the severity of the decision demanded."[18] He did not concede that the war's escalation was flawed or that decision makers might have been misled by the military high command in Saigon.

In December 1972 General Momyer came close to conceding the fallacy of U.S. military intervention in Vietnam in a letter to General Disosway, who was now senior vice president of LTV Aerospace Corporation. He expressed a belief that the South Vietnamese might be able to weather the storm if they could "muster the leadership and guts to fight," pointing out that they had been given "enough equipment to whip the North Vietnamese no matter how severe the attack." Speaking of leadership, he admitted, "The North Vietnamese have had it while the South Vietnamese haven't. We saw this on our first visit to Vietnam in 1961. The problem really hasn't changed."[19] Again, the former top air commander in Saigon did not lay blame for South Vietnam's military inadequacies at the door of Americanization of the war, where many military experts thought it belonged.

Aside from the political constraints, General Momyer's greatest concern about how air power was employed in the Vietnam War had to do with his lack of centralized control (the so-called "single-manager concept") over the B-52s and aircraft of the other services. Not that changing this would have affected the outcome of the conflict, but the issue had repercussions for future wars. Neither General Momyer nor his contemporaries ever conceded that the Vietnam War was different, or that it should have been fought differently, from other wars. To the contrary, in his Corona Harvest report of 18 July 1974, Momyer drew a lesson from "the bitter experience" of the Vietnam War that the Air Force "should not waste scarce time and money developing specialized aircraft for counterinsurgency." He took an unequivocal position left over from the nuclear fifties: "There is sufficient capability in the airlift forces to handle the most unsophisticated requirements of a developing nation with the exception of organized firepower. If situations provoke this level of violence, the issue probably demands an organized military effort comparable to a limited war. Hence the employment of general purpose forces is more appropriate to the conflict."[20]

Brigadier General Cardenas recalled that when General Momyer came to Eglin the first time, they met privately to discuss issues the TAC commander was concerned about. When they were alone, Momyer asked Cardenas, "How long have you known Colonel Aderholt?" The SOF commander explained that he first met Aderholt while heading up special plans for Strike Command in 1963. He told Momyer that Aderholt was the most knowledgeable person he knew in the field of special operations. "You know he is going to get you and SOF in trouble," Momyer said. Cardenas answered as tactfully as he could that Aderholt's record since he had been in command indicated otherwise. Momyer dropped the matter but warned Cardenas, "If he screws up, you are both gone." Cardenas later recalled, "So Heinie stayed and we had arguments with TAC but no problems. And we did many wonderful things for TAC that made their name renowned throughout Central and South America. Heinie was behind most of those."[21]

A year later Cardenas was gone. In July 1969 he transferred to Spain as vice commander of Sixteenth Air Force. Before leaving, however, the SOF commander had taken steps to eliminate the air commando uniform. Not long after General Momyer's visit to Eglin, Cardenas wrote the TAC commander proposing that the air commando uniform be eliminated. He stated that the distinctive hat had always been controversial and, in his opinion, had been a source of derision. "I believe that the jungle hat is as outmoded as is the concept that SOF units must be equipped with all the old cast-off airframes possessed by other countries," he wrote.[22] Momyer, of course, agreed. He recalled standing up to the adverse publicity when he banned the special uniform in Seventh Air Force, and that General Westmoreland had commended Seventh Air Force troops for being the most military in appearance of all forces in Vietnam. "The sooner we can clean up the appearance of the commando units the better," he wrote Cardenas. "These special uniforms should not have been authorized in the first place."[23]

When Cardenas left in July, Momyer's assistant deputy for operations at TAC headquarters, Brigadier General Joseph G. Wilson, came to Eglin as the new Special Operations Force commander. Wilson had served in Southeast Asia as commander of the 8th Tactical Fighter Wing at Ubon, Thailand, from December 1965 to September 1966. Aderholt had known him since 1961, when they met at Takhli during an Air Boonshoo Exercise. He thought they were on friendly terms, but this perception changed when the general called Aderholt into his office one day and asked him, "Why don't you turn in your papers and retire from the Air Force?" Aderholt replied, "I'm not about to get out. I will put my record up against anybody's. I intend to hang in until the end." Wilson did not pursue the matter.[24]

Then, out of the blue, Aderholt was told that he was to be transferred to TUSLOG, the U.S. logistics command in Turkey. He went to see Wilson and asked, "Why? I'm the most experienced officer in Southeast Asia operations that you have. I'm training people, running programs. Why?" Wilson was noncommittal. Aderholt successfully fought the assignment but knew his days at SOF headquarters were numbered. "My antenna was up," he said, "and I got the message that the TAC Mafia didn't want me around." He suspected that General Momyer's opposition to the AC-130 gunship program, which Aderholt enthusiastically supported, was behind the sudden rush to get rid of him.[25]

The AC-130 Gunship Demonstration

There was no doubt in Colonel Aderholt's mind that Cardenas was shipped out because the general had defended him to the TAC commander. He now believed that Wilson had come to Eglin with an agenda that included getting rid of SOF's strong-willed director of operations. Word had reached Aderholt that the TAC commander had branded him as a troublemaker with close ties to the CIA. "Momyer told them that I worked for the CIA," Aderholt said. "He really thought I was a CIA agent, that they had infiltrated the Air Force." Aderholt had made no enemies on the TAC staff, as far as he knew. His office had worked with the TAC operations staff on a number of projects, and they had no major differences of opinion. Aderholt got the impression that TAC was more interested in developing aircraft for tomorrow's wars than for fighting in Vietnam, but had not voiced this opinion to the TAC staff. He had strongly supported the development of gunships for use in Southeast Asia, however, which apparently had run afoul of the TAC commander's policy.[26]

By the end of the 1960s the armed forces had returned their focus to the high-threat environment of Central Europe, if indeed it had ever left. General Momyer had the pivotal role in developing the next generation of first-line tactical aircraft, and he still believed the Vietnam War had proved that modern, high-performance fighters and other jet aircraft were adaptable to any level of conflict. He stated that other threats in other areas would be a reflection of the principal threat in Europe, only on a smaller scale. When there were increased demands for gunships in Vietnam, Momyer took a position directly opposite the one he stated as Seventh Air Force commander. He opposed any further diversion of airlift resources to gunships or other roles and did not want to expend time and effort on increasing the survivability of AC-130s. He called the AC-130 an exceptional weapon system in a semipermissive defense environment but said that "it had to give way or become extinct when the enemy brought the full weight of his best defensive weapons against it."[27]

Aderholt agreed with the need to be able to react with regular forces but did not believe that the force was "properly balanced to meet the range of threats now facing us." "We need all the bright ideas we can get," he stated. "Dogmatic preconceptions can only lead to catastrophe in the military profession." Faithful to that belief, he fought tirelessly for the gunships and other innovations that would enhance air support in Vietnam. "We were not fighting a war in Europe," he said. "As long as we were fighting one in Southeast Asia, which was an entirely different environment, we had to do everything in our power to protect American troops on the ground." He later stated, "The AC-130 was without question the finest close air support system employed in Southeast Asia." Noting that no unit in Vietnam was ever overrun when a gunship was on station, he believed that had the Air Force gotten the advanced gunships "sooner and made more of them," it might have changed the outcome of the war.[28]

Aderholt and his staff were even more impressed with the advanced gunship's capabilities after the AC-130A was modified to give it better standoff range to improve survivability, better night targeting equipment, and better fire control systems. The reconfiguration (known as Surprise Package) armed the advanced gunship with forty-millimeter Bofars antiaircraft-type guns from the Navy and twenty-millimeter Gatling guns, giving it tremendous firepower. Colonel Terry came to Eglin from Wright-Patterson to coordinate with SOF on flight testing the Surprise Package gunship before deploying it to Southeast Asia. The test flights were conducted from 28 October to 15 November 1969 at Eglin, and the reconfigured gunship left for combat evaluation in Southeast Asia on 25 November.[29]

The advanced gunship quickly made believers of military commanders in Vietnam. General George S. Brown, who replaced Momyer at Seventh Air Force, asked for faster action on Surprise Package modifications to the other AC-130As in combat and for support in replacing the aging AC-130As with newer "E" models. Secretary of the Air Force Robert Seamans, who took office in February 1969, endorsed General Brown's position. Tactical Air Command, however, expressed strong opposition to the proposal. The command considered AC-130 gunships suitable only for special warfare forces in low-order conflicts and lightly defended areas. It did not want to deplete the tactical airlift capabilities for a weapon system it regarded as survivable only if the enemy chose not to use all his weapons. General Ryan also opposed expanding the gunship fleet.[30]

Colonel Aderholt and his troops helped stir the debate earlier with a breathtaking demonstration of the advanced gunship's capabilities at Eglin. Headquarters USAF, at the Army's request, had directed TAC to put on a live gunship demonstration at Eglin for senior Army commanders. While Aderholt's office was getting ready for the event, Headquarters TAC sent a message instructing SOF to play down the gunship's capabilities to keep from jeopardizing more important Air Force programs. According to Secord, the TAC message infuriated everybody in SOF operations. Discussing the message with the SOF commander, Colonel Aderholt stated that he was not going to put on a "half-assed" show deemphasizing the capabilities of the gunship. "I am not going to ask my people to be party to a lie," Aderholt said. "If TAC insists on it, they can have somebody else do the demonstration." When the SOF commander did not say anything, Aderholt went back to his office and told Secord and Ropka to put on a show their audience would not soon forget.[31]

The demonstration was held at night on range 52, with more than two hundred Army generals and colonels observing from the stands. The scenario involved a succession of gunships (AC-47s, AC-119s, and AC-130s) coming in with increasing capability and laying down fire support for a make-believe hamlet. There was polite applause from the stands when the AC-47s and

AC-119s made their firing passes at the targets, and then it was the AC-130's turn. Ropka recalled that it was a hushed night, without a breeze stirring, and a large cloud of gun smoke still hung over the target area as the AC-130 made its final approach from over the bay. The pilot, who was talking to Ropka and Secord on the ground, asked, "What are we going to do?" Secord told the pilot to start firing as soon as he got into the safety arc and to keep firing until he emptied the guns. The results were spectacular. Ropka described the scene: "This AC-130 comes up, we can't see him of course, he's up at 6,000 feet or so, and suddenly turns on all of his guns. He started shooting and went all the way around shooting, until he runs out of ammunition, which must have lasted thirty seconds. My mouth is hanging open, and I said, 'My God, have you ever seen anything like that!' The Army generals in the stands were getting out flashlights to write orders for gunships."[32]

Colonel Aderholt knew the impressive display of firepower would send higher headquarters into orbit but was not one to do things halfway or to misrepresent weapons that would save American lives in Vietnam. The AC-130E's lethality in combat proved him right. Although General Momyer was "quite skeptical about the advertised capability" of the advanced gunship at the time, he later admitted that "the AC-130 became the best truck-killing weapon in the war."[33] The official history of the People's Army of Vietnam reported that the number of trucks lost to American aircraft during the 1970–71 dry season rose to 4,000, of which 2,432 (60.8 percent of the total number of trucks lost) were destroyed by AC-130Es. Admitting that the AC-130Es "established control over and successfully suppressed, to a certain extent, our night-time supply operations," the history noted that truck drivers feared the gunships, and some abandoned their vehicles when they heard the gunships flying overhead.[34]

When General Wilson left abruptly in February 1970 to take command of Nineteenth Air Force at Seymour Johnson AFB, North Carolina, Aderholt figured it was only a matter of time before the TAC commander came at him from another direction. It would not be through the new SOF commander, Brigadier General LeRoy J. Manor, who previously commanded the 835th Air Division at McConnell AFB, Kansas. General Manor had completed 275 combat missions while commanding the 37th Tactical Fighter Wing in Vietnam, and quickly earned the admiration and respect of the tough, battle-hardened air commandos. From 8 August to 21 November 1970, General Manor wore a second hat as commander of the famed raid on the prison camp at Son Tay, North Vietnam, to attempt the rescue of American prisoners of war. In May 1970 Aderholt was told about the planned raid while in Washington on other business. Larry Ropka, who was reassigned to the Pentagon to help plan the raid, recalled Aderholt's terse advice: "You can get away with anything—once."[35] Dick Secord called this the first cardinal rule of covert operations, one he had learned from Heinie Aderholt.[36]

Colonel Aderholt chose not to bother General Manor about his problems with General Momyer and TAC headquarters, although he respected the new SOF commander and enjoyed working for him. Late one night at home, he got a call from a friend in the Pentagon warning him, "Heinie, they are out to get you. Don't call me at the office, call me at home. You had better get out of there." Not wanting to put General Manor in the middle, Aderholt went to the office early the next morning and called Major General Peter R. DeLonga, whom he had known in the Philippines and was now in logistics planning with the office of the secretary of defense.

"Pete, I'm in real trouble," Aderholt said. "I've got to get a job and get out from under Momyer at TAC. I would like to go back to Thailand. Do you know the commander over there?"

"Yes, I know Ted Seith," DeLonga said. "As a matter of fact, they need a commander over there in the Air Force Advisory Group." Major General Louis T. Seith commanded the Joint U.S. Military Advisory Group in Thailand. Aderholt got the assignment with General Seith and returned to Thailand in June 1970 for a two-year tour as chief of the Air Force Advisory Group in Bangkok. Aderholt never told General Manor why he left so abruptly but was glad that he would have future opportunities to serve with Manor, who rose to three-star rank in 1976. Meanwhile, Aderholt looked forward to returning to Southeast Asia. He left behind a fledgling fraternal organization that he and Dick Secord had taken the lead in founding. In 1969 they had joined with others to form the Air Commando Association, a brotherhood of warriors who were dedicated to seeing that the spirit and tradition of the air commandos lived on.[37]

Colonel Bill Thomas recalled a special tribute that was paid to "Heinie and Jessie at a big going-away party" that was held for them at the Hurlburt officers' club. Thomas and nine other parachutists (air commandos and Army rangers) made static line jumps, landing in the water directly in front of the club. "I jumped first with Lieutenant Colonel Tucker, the ranger camp commander, who insisted on jumping in honor of his very close and dear friend, Heinie Aderholt," Thomas said. Noting that General Manor was out of town, Thomas said he "caught more than a little polite *hell* when the general got back." Thomas said he could not locate the commander for permission before the party, but added, "I really think he would have given approval." He knew there was mutual respect between the two officers. Years later, when asked about Heinie Aderholt's service, General Manor summed it up in a sentence: "This country needs more men like him."[38]

With the Advisory Group in Bangkok

Colonel Aderholt described his two years as chief of the Air Force Advisory Group in Bangkok "as really a very uneventful tour except that we moved the Thai Air Force along." He enjoyed working for General Seith, a superb officer who later rose to four-star rank as chief of staff, Supreme Headquarters Allied Powers Europe, and he had already developed close relations with the Thai air force leaders during his previous tours. A report by a Tactical Air Command liaison officer in October 1970 noted that Colonel Aderholt had shaped up the advisory staff and had established strong rapport with the Thai air force. The Thais respected Aderholt because he was tough, sincere, and got things done.[39]

Aderholt knew the Thai pilots were good because the 56th Air Commando Wing trained them. All their aircraft were assigned to the Tactical Air Command under Air Chief Marshal Suwait.The two men hit it off from the start, and if there was any way Aderholt could help the Thais build a first-class air force, he was determined to do it. Bringing the same drive and initiative into the advisory role that he had always shown as commander, he started new programs and broke through the administrative red tape to get Suwait's forces what they needed in the way of supplies and equipment to sharpen combat efficiency.[40]

On the trip out he stopped at Clark Air Base to see if there were salvaged items that would be useful to the Thai forces. While there, he ran into one of his former commandos, who was in charge of the ordnance depot at Clark. When Aderholt asked if there was anything in surplus the Thais could use, he found out they were getting ready to destroy 16 million rounds of fifty-caliber machine gun ammunition that was outdated. He talked them into holding up destruction until after he got to his new assignment and found a way to have the ammunition shipped to Thailand. As soon as he got to Bangkok, he arranged to pay the transportation charges out of the military assistance program and to have the 16 million rounds shipped from the Philippines to Bangkok. "Years later the Thai Air Force was still firing that perfectly good ammo that we were going to throw out," Aderholt said.[41]

General DeLonga transferred from the Pentagon to Seventh Air Force as the deputy for materiel about the same time Aderholt reported to Bangkok. When Aderholt inquired about surplus ammunition in Vietnam, he was told they rou-

(Left to right) Richard Secord, Larry Ropka, Heinie Aderholt, Robby Robeson, and Erich von Marbod at Fort Walton Beach, Fla., when Aderholt was recalled to active duty in 1973.

tinely sank unused ordnance in the ocean to get rid of it. Regulations required that broken lots or canisters with unfired munitions left in them following a mission be turned in for destruction. DeLonga and Aderholt set up an arrangement whereby the advisory group sent a plane to Saigon monthly and brought the ammunition that was to be destroyed back to Thailand. The Thais relinked the ammunition and used it.[42]

Things were going exceedingly well until the summer of 1971 when General Seith's tour ended, and he returned to Washington for an assignment on the joint staff. Seith's successor was Major General Andrew Evans, whose first words to Aderholt were: "I don't want you and wish you would get the hell out of here, but General Ryan won't agree to that." His reasons were that Aderholt could not get along with Momyer and could not get along with Tactical Air Command. Aderholt thought it might also be because his dog had chased Evans's mother-in-law into the water at the beach one day and wouldn't let her out. That was during his first tour at Eglin. "You never know," he said. Once Evans saw how well Aderholt got along with the Thai high command, however, their relationship improved.[43]

Aderholt's friendship with Thai commanders and his knowledge of Thai customs helped break down barriers. Once when Evans was planning a reception for General Lucius D. Clay Jr., who ran Seventh Air Force before becoming PACAF commander in August 1971, the general had sent invitations to the Thai commanders and senior staff, but no one responded. He called Aderholt in and wanted to know why there was no response from the Thai Air Force. "I told him the way I always handled it was to invite Air Marshal Boonchoo and tell him the following members of your staff are invited and anyone you want to add," Aderholt said. "If Boonchoo comes, everybody comes. Do that for the other services, and you have a full house." He said Evans did it that way, and the place was overflowing. He almost regretted helping out with the reception when Evans told Clay and a bevy of PACAF generals that Aderholt thought Vang Pao was the only real general in Southeast Asia. "I had to explain that I was talking about combat generals, not higher command," Aderholt said. "It was a tense moment, but that broke the ice."[44]

General Evans gave Aderholt high ratings on his evaluations, emphasizing that he enjoyed a position of confidence with Thai air force leaders that would be difficult to replace when he left. Soon after arrival, Aderholt had convinced them to shift their basic combat posture from air defense to close air support and counterinsurgency, based on a more solid analysis of the basic threat. According to Evans's deputy, Army Major General James J. Gibbons, this reorientation plus Aderholt's efforts to build a tactical air control system in Thailand resulted in the most effective close air support operation the Thai air force had ever conducted. He advised the Thais on developing required operational capabilities for A-37 aircraft and prepared them to transition into their first squadron of the new fighters. In addition to the funds he saved by obtaining excess munitions for the Thais, he arranged for them to get thirteen excess OH-13 helicopters for training, thus releasing their H-34 helicopters for operational duty. He introduced other cost-saving initiatives that made the Thai air force a far more efficient and effective force than it had been previously.[45]

He had been back in Thailand only six months when Major General Wilson, his former boss at Eglin, was reassigned to Vietnam as the deputy for operations. Aderholt said he held no grudge against Wilson and dropped in to see him whenever he went to Tan Son Nhut. On one visit Wilson said, "We finally got it done!" Aderholt thought he was going to say we had won the war. He asked, "What's that?" The general said, "We've finally computerized the frag."

For Aderholt, that pretty much said it all. "That's why we are losing the war," he thought afterward. "We worry more about computerizing the goddamn frag than we do winning the war. We've hung all our roles and missions baggage, our doctrinal hang-ups, our computers, our gadgets, and our centralized control wizardry on the South Vietnamese, and they can't win either."[46]

In June 1971 Ambassador Sullivan ran into Colonel Aderholt during a visit to Bangkok and was surprised to find that he had not been promoted to general officer rank. When he left Laos in the spring of 1969, Sullivan had gone back to his old job in Washington as deputy assistant secretary for East Asian and Pacific affairs at the State Department. Sullivan wrote to the Air Force about Aderholt when he returned from the Bangkok visit. Sullivan stated that during his years as ambassador to Laos, it had been a privilege to have worked very closely with a great number of Air Force officers who performed remarkable feats under extremely complicated conditions both in the military and political sense. He explained: "The air war in Laos, fought as it was for many years in a semi-clandestine mode of operation, under unorthodox command and control relationships, tested the ingenuity, the discipline, and the professional skills of the United States Air Force to a remarkable degree. As a very close observer of these events it has been my judgment that the Air Force responded magnificently to this challenge."[47]

Sullivan went on to say that of all the officers he had known during that period, none were more outstanding than Heinie Aderholt. He described Aderholt as "a splendid leader of men" whose wing at Nakhon had the finest morale of any Air Force unit he ever visited. "His flair for improvising tactics, equipment, command arrangements, made him invaluable during those years," Sullivan wrote. "I fear, however, that some of the very resourcefulness which made him so uniquely qualified to perform in the context of Laos may not have been congenial to some of his superiors who viewed Air Force operations in a more orthodox perspective."[48] The letter was filed away.

Friends noted that Aderholt never seemed to lose "his spunk or his spirit" during the twilight of his career, because he knew he was right about the war and right about the air commandos. He loved the Air Force and he loved special operations. There was no reason why the two had to be incompatible. Stalwarts like Joe Kittinger understood this. Since leaving Nakhon Phanom in early 1967, Kittinger had not seen much of Aderholt until 1972, when he was back at Udorn flying F-4s. He recalled that Aderholt threw a big party at a hotel in Bangkok for all of his friends in the air commandos and special operations. Kittinger said it was a wonderful party. Halfway through the evening, everybody threw Heinie Aderholt into the pool, and he almost drowned a couple of guys he didn't know could not swim. Less than a month later Kittinger was shot down in an F-4 and became a prisoner of war in North Vietnam. As he sat in a POW camp, Kittinger said he thought many times about that wonderful party and what real leaders like Heinie Aderholt meant to the United States Air Force.[49]

As he and Jessie prepared to leave Bangkok in the summer of 1972, Aderholt wrote a letter home predicting that it was only a matter of time before we would be chased out of Vietnam without any friends left to protect us. So-called Vietnamization would not work because we had taught them the wrong things, made them overreliant on American leadership, and set an example they would be unable to follow. Cambodia was now embroiled directly in the war, with the U.S.-backed government under Major General Lon Nol striving to defeat Pol Pot's Communist Khmer Rouge. Aderholt was more confident about Thailand's security, however. We bought time for them if the war accomplished nothing else, he thought. With our help they were building a vibrant economy and strong armed forces and had dealt effectively with the internal Communist threat. All the blood and treasure that we had poured into the rest of Southeast Asia was, still, a heavy price to pay.

Isolated at Eglin

When the time came for reassignment, Colonel Aderholt asked that he be returned to the Special Operations Force at Eglin to write a history of what had been accomplished in the low-intensity warfare field and in special operations in Vietnam. He believed it would be useful to the school there to have a record of special operations over the past decade. Orders arrived assigning him as adviser to the air defense commander at Tyndall AFB in Panama City instead. He protested the assignment, pointing out that he had asked for SOF or Eglin because his experience would be useful there and it was his retirement home. He had only six months before retirement, and sending him to Eglin would save the government the cost of a second move. If sent to Tyndall, he would make an issue of it on those grounds. A message came back changing the assignment to Eglin as adviser to the commander of the 48th Air Rescue Group.[50]

When Aderholt reported for duty at Eglin, the group commander, Colonel John C. Gordon, asked him to write a special study on a project he had worked on while heading SOF operations. While visiting SOF to see if his earlier papers were still there, he ran into the SOF commander, Major General James A. Knight Jr., whom he had met in Southeast Asia. They spoke, and Aderholt went into operations to ask about the papers. A few days later Gordon told Aderholt there had been a complaint about him. Aderholt said, "What do you mean?" Gordon said that General Knight had told him to keep Aderholt out of the SOF, that he had been over there creating problems. Aderholt assumed that word had come down from Momyer, to keep him away. He never went into SOF again.[51]

There was nothing for him to do at Eglin, so he jumped at the opportunity when Larry Ropka and Dick Secord asked him to come to Washington for a few days to assist with special Southeast Asia projects, including plans to improve Cambodia's small air force. Secord had just completed the Naval War College and was assigned to the Pentagon as desk officer for Laos, Thailand, and Vietnam under the assistant secretary of defense for international security affairs. Ropka was special assistant to the principal deputy assistant secretary (comptroller), who was the focal point for DOD resources in Southeast Asia. His boss was Erich F. von Marbod, who Rokpa said was the only person he knew who had more bureaucratic courage than Heinie Aderholt. Because they were working on sensitive issues, Aderholt made several trips to Washington on invitational orders without signing out or informing anyone at the rescue group where he was going.[52]

When he returned from one trip, Colonel Gordon called him in and said, "I understand you have been AWOL." Aderholt replied, "If you are talking about my not coming in for duty, that's right. I have not been coming in for duty." Gordon said, "You know it is a very serious matter." Aderholt said, "I don't know why. You didn't have a job for me, Colonel. You and I know that I was just put down here because I was going to protest if they assigned me to Tyndall. My career has been with the commandos from start to finish, and I was denied that. Tactical Air Command didn't want any part of me." Gordon frowned, saying, "Well, I don't know what we are going to do about it." Aderholt fished the invitational orders from his pocket. "Here, how about taking a look at these orders from the secretary of defense," he said. "That is where I have been." The matter ended there.[53]

Colonel Aderholt retired from the Air Force on 1 January 1973 and went to work for Northrop Aircraft Incorporated as a consultant. One of the projects he handled for Northrup was looking into the possibility of buying out Air America and letting Northrop operate it. This fell through, however. The war was winding down, and the CIA's sponsorship of Air America had been exposed. The agency was ready to get rid of the clandestine airline altogether.[54]

While he was on a business trip to California, Aderholt received a call from home that Lieutenant General John Roberts, head of Air Force personnel, was trying to reach him. General Roberts said it was urgent for Aderholt to call him back. Aderholt knew what the call was about and had been expecting it. Erich von Marbod had already revealed that plans were under way to have him recalled to active duty, sent back to Bangkok as deputy of the U.S. Military Assistance Command and Joint U.S. Military Advisory Group in Thailand, then promoted to brigadier general. He was urgently needed back in Thailand to coordinate on Thai-based military assistance for Cambodia and the withdrawal of men and equipment from the war zone. "We are going to recall you to active duty," General Roberts said when Aderholt got back to him. Aderholt asked, "Do I have a choice in the matter?" Roberts said, "Not really, if you pass the physical." Aderholt said, "Fine. When do you want me?"[55]

Recalled to Active Duty

Nothing about Heinie Aderholt's Air Force career was ever ordinary, and his recall to active duty on 8 October 1973 was no exception. He was sworn in at his home in Fort Walton Beach by Colonel Dick Secord. Erich von Marbod was there, but it took a commissioned officer to do the honors. The Aderholts had thrown an all-night party for close friends, and Secord swore Aderholt in at his bar. Larry Ropka and many others were there to celebrate the occasion. Before reading the orders, Secord stated that as the senior officer present, he would administer the oath. Immediately after the ceremony, Aderholt announced that Secord was no longer the senior officer present. As dawn broke over the bay, Erich said, "We've got to get back to Washington pronto. Let's get this show on the road." He turned to Aderholt. "Where's your uniform? Make sure you wear all your medals." They had to scramble to find a uniform because Aderholt did not have one. His friends helped him piece together a uniform with a chestful of the right ribbons, and a few hours later they touched down at Andrews Air Force Base.[56]

Aderholt was supposed to have been briefed thoroughly at the Pentagon before leaving for Thailand, but he departed earlier than expected because student riots had sparked a political firestorm in Bangkok. Year-long protests and demonstrations against the military government of Thanom Kittakachorn led to an explosion of rage and violence against heavily armed soldiers and police on 14 October, a day that became known as Black Sunday. The Thanom government was overthrown the day after. Erich decided that Aderholt "had better go now!" "I didn't go through PACAF or CINCPAC," Aderholt said. "I arrived in Thailand and reported to a very irate Army major general." One of the first things he had to do was have uniforms made. He had given the borrowed uniform back and had to report in civilian clothes.[57]

The irate Army major general was Thomas W. Mellen, who had succeeded Aderholt's former boss, Major General Evans, four months earlier. "Well, Colonel, I didn't ask for you," Mellen said to Aderholt. "I don't need you, and

I don't want you, but I can't do a damn thing about it because I've been told you are here to stay. In fact, I don't know what I'm going to do with you." Aderholt replied, "Sir, if you read the orders from the secretary of defense, it says that I'm going to be your deputy." The problem was that Mellen did not know what he was going to do with the deputy he already had, Air Force Colonel D. A. Curto, who worked for Aderholt during a previous tour at Hurlburt. Secord and von Marbod wanted to avoid complications by having Curto transferred out, but Aderholt said, "No, he used to work for me. He's a good guy. He's got a daughter in school, and I don't want to disrupt them. I'll get along with him, leave him there." He recalled Secord and von Marbod telling him that he was making a mistake, and they were right. After a month or so of trying to get along, Aderholt said that he had to pick up the phone and ask that the colonel be found another job.[58]

Although Aderholt got his marching orders directly from the Pentagon, he tried not to alienate General Mellen. He said, as a result, that he and Mellen "got along famously as we went along" and got a lot of things done. One of Aderholt's undercover assignments was to run interference for a special team, the Thailand Liaison Detachment, that was set up under von Marbod's office to coordinate on the war in Cambodia without the knowledge or hindrance of headquarters bureaucrats up the chain of command. Planning to set up the detachment, headed by Colonel E. E. "Johnny" Johnson, had been ongoing since Aderholt's visits to the Pentagon during his last six months at Eglin. The detachment was set up under General Mellen, but reported directly to von Marbod. Among other actions, they took the Water Pump detachment out from under the 56th Air Commando Wing at Nakhon Phanom and put it under Mellen's command to help train the Cambodian air force.[59]

Although Aderholt enjoyed a special relationship with the Thais, there was a short-lived protest from a student faction, possibly triggered by an article written by Jack Foisie of the *Los Angeles Times*. In the article, which carried a Bangkok dateline, Foisie found Aderholt's appointment "unusual" and suggested that it might have something to do with his past activities in Thailand and the fact that he was an "officer famed for his direction of unpublicized operations in Laos." He also intimated that since the United States was no longer directly involved in Vietnam or Cambodia, there was new interest in assisting the Thais with their insurgency problem. Foisie's article reflected the media cynicism that had dogged U.S. actions since the beginning of America's troubled involvement with the war in Southeast Asia.[60]

As these developments unfolded, Aderholt's promotion to brigadier general was held up for seven months while the Air Force conducted an extensive background investigation, which included contacting former commanders and associates such as his nemesis, General Momyer. Although Momyer had retired in September 1973, the month before Aderholt came back on active duty, he still carried a lot of weight in the Air Force. General Ryan had also retired and was succeeded on 1 August as Air Force chief of staff by General George Brown. When Aderholt heard that Momyer strenuously objected to his being recalled and promoted to star rank, he flew to Washington to meet with General Brown. He felt vindicated when General Brown said, "Heinie, I wouldn't worry about Spike if I were you. Hell, he's retired. He's off active duty and you're on." "I guess you're right, General Brown," Aderholt said.[61] He reported the chief's reassurances to von Marbod and flew back to Thailand. The sun was setting on U.S. military presence in Southeast Asia, and he had a lot to do.

10. MISSION ACCOMPLISHED

When Colonel Aderholt returned to Bangkok in October 1973, the military situation and the status of U.S. forces in Southeast Asia had changed radically since his departure the year before. The Linebacker II air campaign against North Vietnam, launched the previous December, led to a cease-fire agreement, effective 28 January 1973, providing for the release of American and allied prisoners of war in exchange for U.S. withdrawal of combat forces from South Vietnam. Subsequently, President Nixon signed Public Law 93-52, cutting off funds for direct or indirect combat activities by U.S. military forces in, over, or off the shores of South Vietnam, Cambodia, or Laos, effective 15 August 1973. Although fighting in Laos officially ended in February, the Air Force continued to fly sorties over the Ho Chi Minh Trail and other lines of communication through Laos into April. Remnants of the Seventh Air Force headquarters at Tan Son Nhut relocated to Nakhon Phanom, Thailand, in February 1973, and the last U.S. combat troops left South Vietnam by the end of March. U.S. strike operations over Cambodia halted in August. The U.S. combat role in Southeast Asia was over, but the military asssistance and advisory roles were not.[1]

The withdrawal of major U.S. elements from Thailand began in 1973. The remaining USAF units in Thailand were still assigned to Thirteenth Air Force in the Philippines. In May 1973 Cotton Hildreth, now a brigadier general, took command of the Thirteenth Air Force advanced echelon at Udorn. He represented the Thirteenth Air Force commander on operational, logistics, and administrative matters in Thailand and exercised command supervision over all Thailand units assigned to the Thirteenth. In October, the same month Aderholt returned to Thailand, his former boss at Eglin, Lieutenant General LeRoy Manor, arrived in the Philippines as Thirteenth Air Force commander.[2] In Cambodia, a low-profile U.S. military presence had been in place since the activation of a military equipment delivery team in Phnom Penh in 1971 after Lon Nol rose to power. An Army general headed this team and was responsible to both the commander in chief, Pacific, in Hawaii, and the U.S. ambassador to Cambodia.[3]

Aderholt's interaction with these other military functions was largely peripheral—providing liaison between U.S. forces and the Thai government—except when running interference for von Marbod's special task force or carrying out other missions for higher headquarters. General Mellen commanded the Bangkok garrison until July 1974, when Robert C. Hixon, another Army major general, replaced him. By this time Aderholt was a brigadier general, having been promoted two months earlier. Less than a year later, on 30 April 1975, Aderholt replaced Hixon as commander, USMACTHAI, and chief, JUSMAGTHAI. In this capacity he answered jointly to the U.S. ambassador to Thailand, Charles Whitehouse, and CINCPAC, Admiral Noel Gaylor. Behind the scenes he still responded directly to the JCS chairman, General George Brown, and to Erich von Marbod in the Pentagon, however.[4] The command relations throughout Southeast Asia in the twilight of U.S. military presence in the region were skewed, but no more so than during the protracted Vietnam War.

Twilight of an American Odyssey

The *Los Angeles Times* article by Jack Foisie that stirred a mild student outcry in Bangkok against Aderholt's assignment also caused political ripples among congressional doves at home. Congresswoman Patricia Schroeder of Colorado sent Secretary of Defense James R. Schlesinger a copy of the article, which had appeared in the *Denver Post* on 5 December 1973, along with a letter expressing concern that Colonel Aderholt was being recalled at this time because much of his career was involved in counterinsurgency work, including secret raids in Laos. She sought assurances that the unusual assignment was not part of some hidden agenda to continue a military presence in Southeast Asia past the time for U.S. withdrawal.[5]

Assistant Secretary of Defense John O. Marsh Jr., responding for Secretary Schlesinger, advised Congresswoman Schroeder that Colonel Aderholt was recalled for the Bangkok post because no other officer was "so well able to fill the bill." Marsh explained that Aderholt was "a recognized expert on the problems of Thailand," who had "the respect, confidence and cooperation of the current Thai Leadership." He made the point that Aderholt, who had served in both combat and noncombat roles in the region, was well-known in Thailand for his efforts to promote donations of medical supplies and equipment from private U.S. sources for use with the many poverty-stricken natives of Thailand and Laos. Marsh reassured the congresswoman that the decision to recall Colonel Aderholt "was taken with due regard for the best interests of the United States, including those of helping to bring about stability and peace in Southeast Asia."[6]

In an initial assessment of the situation, Aderholt advised von Marbod that the new Thai government remained firmly under the influence of the military, which was pro-U.S. in orientation. Embassy officials had failed to exploit this advantage, however, because U.S. military advisers were excluded from all important negotiations with the Thai government. Aderholt intended to rectify this oversight. Experience had taught him that he could get faster and more favorable results by dealing directly with senior Thai military leaders, while following the ambassador's policy guidance and keeping him informed. He noted that the United States had pumped vast sums into Thailand during the past decade, but got little in return except for the use of Thai bases, which was in the Thai national interest anyway. He believed it was time to use U.S. military influence "to maximize Thai cooperation" and to "get more for our money."[7]

Aderholt cited Cambodia as a prime example of where greater Thai cooperation would be useful. The Khmer Rouge continued to gain strength in Cambodia while the United States simply poured in materiel and the Royal Thai government stood on the sidelines. Saving Cambodia was in the Thai national interest, and the government could and should be doing more to help. Although Cambodia presented an "enormous challenge," Aderholt believed that a concerted U.S.-Thai effort might offset the current imbalance favoring the North Vietnamese and their clients. "We have simply not designed an effective strategy to cope with Cambodia nor have we convinced Thais to seriously join in a concerted effort to help." The initiatives to create a Khmer air force training and support program at Udorn, and to start a Thai assistance effort within Cambodia, were steps in that direction.[8]

While emphasizing that USMACTHAI was "a key to effective U.S. influence in Thailand for the long haul," Aderholt concluded that the organization itself was grossly overstaffed and needed surgery. With the buildup of U.S. forces during the Vietnam War, the organization had grown into an unwieldy staff of over six hundred people. Aderholt described it as "a busy bureaucracy which spins along generating inertia but moving very little." Subsequently, following guidelines approved by the secretary of defense, Aderholt was able to effect sizable reductions in the advisory staff and yet achieve greater influence over Thai military policy.[9]

Two Air Force chiefs of staff (General Brown and his successor, General David C. Jones, both of whom moved up to become JCS chairman) and a host of commanders involved with the withdrawal of U.S. forces from Southeast Asia were convinced that the Pentagon made a wise decision in recalling Aderholt for the Bangkok post when it did. General Hildreth, for one, noted the marked improvement in his ability to get things done after Aderholt returned to Thailand in October 1973. As commander of the advanced echelon at Udorn, Hildreth was faced with the formidable task of reorganizing for peacetime readiness the training of Air Force units in Thailand when the war ended for U.S. combat forces in August. Practically every related task (for example, control of air traffic, construction of a bombing and gunnery range for keeping aircrews qualified, and proficient in weapons delivery) required highest-level Thai approval, and in some cases support. Hildreth's only avenue for approaching the approving authorities was through the joint advisory group or the embassy.[10]

Hildreth complained that before Aderholt arrived, he had repeatedly made his requirements and requests for assistance known at country team meetings without success. He attributed this to the fact that General Mellen had no previous experience in the political or military environment of Thailand and the ambassador, William Kintner, had no hands-on experience in foreign affairs. Hildreth's written communications had gone unanswered and were not acted upon. "I was reaching the end of my rope when Heinie was recalled to active duty and assigned as deputy commander of JUSMAG, Thailand," Hildreth said. "With his contacts in the Thai military/government he was able to cut through the bureaucratic red tape and enable us to do the job." With Aderholt running interference, U.S. forces had a gunnery and bombing range operational within a few months, and a Thai airways and approach control equipped, manned, and operational in even less time. "Heinie deserves all the credit for our success during this critical transition period, and I will be forever in his debt for it," Hildreth said.[11]

Hildreth called Aderholt and asked for his help on another occasion. Aderholt asked what was wrong. "These bastards are stealing me blind," Hildreth said. "Air conditioners, you name it, they are taking it right out the front gate. It's got to stop. Can you help?" Aderholt stated that he could but asked that Hildreth make the request through the Thirteenth Air Force commander, General Manor, because he controlled the bases. "We don't want him to think we are overstepping our bounds," Aderholt said. "Just have General Manor call me, and we will get the problem resolved." General Manor called, and Aderholt agreed to go to Air Marshal Suwait and get his help in eliminating organized thievery on bases occupied by USAF units.[12]

The Thais retained complete sovereignty over their bases. Each base used by the USAF had a Royal Thai air force commander who was responsible for installation security and who controlled everything coming on and going off. They controlled the gates. They controlled the Thai workers. They controlled the contractors. Anyone who opened a barbershop or any kind of business on base had to go through the Thai base commander. Everything a contractor did, including every load of dirt that came on base, was taxed. Aderholt knew there was no way that thievery on the scale described by Hildreth could be happening without the involvement or approval of the Thai base commanders. He went to Air Marshal Suwait and told him that his base commanders were running the biggest theft ring ever against USAF forces. Suwait assured General Aderholt that he would help however he could.[13]

Air Marshal Suwait ordered a three-star general who was in charge of the bases to accompany General Aderholt. They went to Korat Air Base, where they spent two nights staked out in the control tower observing the theft ring's operations through a starlight scope. On the first night they spotted Thai guards stealing air conditioners out of buildings occupied by Americans and taking them to the Thai base commander's house. The next night a truck pulled up to the base commander's house and moved the air conditioners to the flight line, where they were loaded aboard a Royal Thai air force cargo plane and flown away. General Aderholt and his Thai companion reported their findings to Air Marshal Suwait. "You multiply that by all the theft at the other bases, and we really have a problem," Aderholt said. "I understand that commanders are just supplementing their pay by taking from the rich Americans. All we want is to stop the thievery, so let's cut a deal."[14]

The air marshal agreed to replace the base commanders with officers who would put a stop to the thefts. In return, Aderholt arranged for the Thais to administer the various services handled by private contractors on base. This rewarded the Thai commanders for controlling crime on their bases and replaced the ill-gotten gains that were now lost to them. "Overnight all the Thai base commanders were relieved from their posts," Aderholt said. "What American commanders did not know is that they were all promoted to better jobs. Their replacements had direct orders from Air Marshal Suwait to stop the thefts. Everybody won. Everybody was happy."[15]

General Aderholt hastened to add that similar situations had existed on American bases throughout Asia. "The Thais were just masters of the game," he said, with feeling. "The Thais always loved the Americans," he said, pointing out that there was never a serious problem between the Americans and their Thai hosts even though the two governments had not negotiated a status of forces agreement. This meant that American servicemen who committed crimes in Thailand were tried in the Thai courts. On the eve of the U.S. withdrawal from Thailand, there were only five Americans serving jail sentences there. The king pardoned two of those after Aderholt submitted a request through the ambassador. This was a small number indeed, considering the thousands of Americans who served in Thailand during the Vietnam War. There were nearly fifty thousand U.S. military personnel assigned there at the height of the force buildup in Southeast Asia. "If the Thais had not liked us, if we had not been welcome, there is no way we could have withdrawn leaving that few people in jail," Aderholt stated.[16]

There would have been other personnel left behind if General Aderholt had not taken the initiative to ship nineteen servicemen accused of commiting minor crimes to Clark Air Base for custody before the Thai courts tried them. The servicemen, who came from units already withdrawn from Thailand, were being held under house arrest at the JUSMAG compound in Bangkok awaiting their appearance in court. Their trials had been delayed for months, and Aderholt could not get the embassy to take action. Finally, he went to the ambassador with a plan to relocate the detainees to the Philippines without prior Thai government agreement. "Whatever you do, I didn't approve it," the ambassador said. Aderholt went to see General Kriangsak Chamanan, supreme commander of the Thai armed forces. He explained that the Thai courts had been dragging their feet on trying the nineteen detainees and that U.S. forces could not withdraw and leave them behind. "Hey, we are trying to tell you something," Kriangsak said. "Get them out of here. Nobody is going to say anything." General Aderholt then set up a C-130 for a dawn evacuation of the nineteen servicemen without the permission of the U.S. embassy or the Thai government. General Kriangsak later remarked, "I told you it would be no problem."[17]

It was the twilight of an American military odyssey in Southeast Asia, one that divided the nation and left the American psyche scarred for years to come. General Aderholt had been at Takhli at the start of that odyssey, had been intensely involved in a variety of key roles throughout the protracted journey, and was uniquely qualified to be the senior officer in charge as the sun set on U.S. military presence in the region. His friend and comrade, Cotton Hildreth, left Thailand in January 1975 to serve as senior Air Force member of the Weapons Systems Evaluation Group with the Office of the Secretary of Defense. "I left during the early stages of our unit deactivation and military withdrawal," Hildreth said, "but with Heinie on scene I knew it would be the huge success it was."[18]

Supporting the Khmer Republic from Thailand

The Thailand Liaison Detachment's raison d'être was to make the Khmer air arm a better fighting force. It started with the ad hoc planning that Aderholt had participated in at the Pentagon before his retirement and a subsequent paper Dick Secord wrote recommending a program to save Cambodia. Before Aderholt's recall to active duty, Larry Ropka and Johnny Johnson had gone to Thailand and Cambodia. Bypassing the normal chain of command, they set up a safe house in Bangkok, where they drafted a plan for improving the Khmer air arm's war-fighting capabilities. The plan, which was approved by Secretary of Defense Schlesinger, was published in November 1973 under the title *Tactical Air Improvement Plan, Cambodia*. Aderholt had a key role in the plan's implementation after he reported to Bangkok.[19]

The detachment's urgent assignment in the fall of 1973 was to prepare the Khmer air force to play a more effective combat role, within existing resources, during the current dry season. The U.S. bombing halt on 15 August put the onus of air support in defense of the Khmer Republic squarely on the shoulders of its unready, fledgling air force. The air arm had made some progress with the help of the military assistance team in Phnom Penh but was no substitute for American air strikes. Although the liaison detachment could not make up for that loss, it hoped through more experienced training and logistics support to give the Khmer airmen a fighting edge against an insurgent offensive.[20]

Even with U.S. air support, the ability of the Khmer Republic to survive another dry season offensive was in doubt. Without it, Lon Nol's government was in grave danger of collapsing. The critical factor was the will of the people in the population centers, principally Phnom Penh, to continue supporting the government. Unfortunately, popular support had been undermined almost to the point of internal collapse by rampant inflation, corruption, and lack of security. There was hope that sustained U.S. airlift support and improved Khmer tactical air capabilities would at least give the Lon Nol government a fighting chance at survival.[21] The government's situation appeared so hopeless, however, that Lon Nol offered to negotiate with the insurgents "without prior conditions," but the offer was refused.[22]

Establishing a training program for the Khmer air force in Thailand was a first priority after Aderholt's arrival. The Water Pump detachment, which he

In April 1975 Hmong refugees are evacuated from Long Tieng secret air base in Laos in a C-130 arranged by General Aderholt.

arranged to have moved under General Mellen's command, was ideally suited to train the Khmer air arm. The backbone of the small strike force was the AT-28, which Water Pump crews had relied on for years to train Thai and Laotian pilots and maintenance personnel. The detachment was also skilled in flying and maintaining the Khmer air force's mixed bag of other aircraft, including a handful of AC-47 gunships, C-123Ks, O-1s, and AU-24 Helio Stallions. Aderholt got approval from Thai military leaders for the Khmer airmen to be trained at Udorn, and they brought Major Tom Deacon to Thailand to run the training program. Chief Master Sergeant Jim Cherry was recalled to rework the Cambodian helicopters and T-28s, which were in terrible condition.[23]

General Aderholt had a more pivotal role in orchestrating the airlift of weapons, munitions, fuel, and rice to Phnom Penh and besieged provincial enclaves in Cambodia. Insurgents kept the roads in Cambodia closed most of the time, leaving only the Mekong River and the airlift as lines of communications. Air Force C-130s had been flying both air-land and airdrop missions to Cambodia from U-Tapao airfield since before the U.S. bombing halt of August

1973. After the bombing halt, U.S. officials became concerned that USAF C-130s could be shot down, with a loss of U.S. armed forces personnel. General Aderholt got involved in the spring of 1974 when the Air Force chief of staff, General Brown, asked that an alternative to the USAF airlift be found as soon as possible, and the JCS concurred.[24]

One of the alternatives was to make the Khmer air force self-sufficient in airlift, by bolstering the small fleet of C-123s and providing additional training in Thailand, but this would take time. Once the program was started, a minimum of twelve months would be required for the Khmer air arm to reach self-sufficiency. The secretary of defense did not approve the plan for Khmer air force self-sufficiency until November 1974. General Aderholt earlier received approval from the Thai Supreme Command to establish a USAF C-123K mobile training team at Udorn. Meanwhile, however, other means had to be found for replacing the USAF aircrews.[25] This is where General Aderholt's unique experience commanding the Tibetan airlift and resupplying Vang Pao's Hmong guerrillas in Laos came to bear on the problem.

Contracting the Cambodian Airlift

Aderholt had raised the subject of contract airlift with General Brown in early 1974, when he went to Washington to refute unfounded allegations General Momyer and others had made against him. "General Brown, I'm not your problem," Aderholt said. "Your real worry is the Cambodian airlift." Brown asked, "What do you mean?" Aderholt said, "One of these days we are going to lose a C-130 crew, and there will be political repercussions." Brown asked, "What do you suggest we do?" Aderholt said, "Very simple. We use contract airlift." Brown asked, "Can you write me a plan?" He subsequently sent a JCS team to Thailand, and Colonel Ropka fed the plan to them.[26]

A meeting held in Bangkok on 16–21 May 1974 to address the airlift problem was a good example of why back channels to the Pentagon existed. General Brown specifically mentioned contract carriers as an alternative to USAF aircrews, and General Aderholt recommended at the May meeting that Birdair, a division of Bird and Sons, be offered the airlift contract. Air America was shutting down, and Aderholt considered Birdair to be the most reliable of the remaining contract carriers that had experience in the region. Bird and Sons, a West Coast contractor who had operated in Southeast Asia since the early 1960s, was reputable, financially solvent, and politically acceptable to the Thai government. Aderholt proposed that Birdair provide qualified aircrews to fly the USAF C-130s out of U-Tapao, which was similar to the way he had run the Tibetan airlift from Takhli twelve years earlier.[27]

There had been continuing Air Staff interest in the threat to USAF crews fly-ing the Cambodian airlift since General Brown first raised the issue at a staff meeting in December 1973. Despite this and the fact that General Brown had specifically flagged contract airlift as a proposed solution to the problem in April 1974, there was still opposition from some commands represented at the Bangkok meeting in May. The PACAF vice commander, a three-star general, had misgivings about contracting the airlift because there would be little reduction in the actual cost of the operation to the USAF and no significant reduction in USAF personnel. He did not believe the proposed contract would be in the best interest of the Air Force. The plan was finally approved by the JCS on 27 June 1974. Two days later General Brown (before moving up to become JCS chair-man on 1 July) directed that contract negotiations be expedited with Birdair.[28]

General Aderholt, meanwhile, conducted intensive negotiations with the Royal Thai government on the proposed contract, keeping General Brown, Ad-miral Gaylor, and Erich von Marbod informed on progress. The Thai prime minister approved the concept on 13 August, after being encouraged to do so by General Kriangsak, Air Marshal Dawee, and other top military leaders. A week later General Aderholt notified General Brown that he had reached "com-plete agreement" with General Kriangsak for the use of U-Tapao for contract airlift support of Cambodia. There was a provision that U.S. forces would award Thai Airways Company a state-run enterprise, a separate service contract for op-erational support of the airlift. Other stipulations were that only five C-130 se-rial numbers, registered in Cambodia, could be used, and the planes were to have no national markings. On 26 August, General Jones (the new Air Force chief of staff) authorized sole source contracts with both Thai Airways and Birdair. The primary flying contract with Birdair was signed on 28 August, and the support services contract with Thai Airways was signed on 4 September.[29]

Birdair promptly hired retired Air Force C-130 crewmen and reservists, who needed to be trained only in the new all-weather delivery system being used in the airlift. The contract required the carrier to provide five C-130 crews capa-ble of making five delivery sorties into Cambodia daily, or as many as ten if necessary. The Air Force provided the unmarked C-130s and full maintenance support. The Khmer air force was responsible for search and rescue if a plane went down. On 27 September General Aderholt advised General Brown that the first airdrop by a contract crew had been flown the previous day without in-cident. On the twenty-eighth General Brown thanked Aderholt for the progress toward freeing USAF aircrews from the Cambodian airlift operations. The JCS chairman stated that he looked forward to mid October "when we will be free from worry over domestic political concern and difficulty should we suffer a loss of an Air Force crew in Cambodian support operations." By 8 October the remaining USAF aircrews in the Cambodian airlift were replaced by Birdair employees.[30]

While working the contract airlift problem, General Aderholt remained involved in the plan for Khmer air force self-sufficiency. On 1 November Secretary of Defense Schlesinger approved providing additional C-123 transports and training to the Cambodians, but wanted all DOD and contract airlift support terminated by the end of June 1975. Military leaders convinced Secretary Schlesinger to keep the contract option open, arguing that surge requirements or an increased enemy antiaircraft threat might require missions in the high-flying C-130s beyond mid-1975. The argument would be for naught, however, because plans for contract continuance and Khmer air force self-sufficiency both were soon overtaken by an avalanche of Communist victories throughout Southeast Asia.[31]

General Aderholt recalled that in the autumn of 1974, "we could see the handwriting on the wall." He had Major Jerry Klingaman, a member of the Thailand Liaison Detachment, prepare evacuation plans to recover aircraft from Vietnam and Cambodia to keep them from falling into enemy hands. Aderholt explained that half the airplanes weren't flying, and he wanted to bring all of the hulks and broken planes to Thailand and rehabilitate them because the Air America facility was closing down. "As we fixed them, we would bring others back, so we were going to slowly withdraw a large number of aircraft out of Vietnam that were not flying anyway," he said. "We could send the planes back in flyable condition as they were needed." General Louis Wilson, the PACAF commander, came through Bangkok and read the plan. He liked it and took it to Saigon to Ambassador Martin, who scrapped the plan because he said it manifested a "defeatist attitude" and would lower Vietnamese morale.[32]

Word got back to Washington, and von Marbod called Aderholt. "Oh, he was irate," Aderholt recalled. Erich was upset that too many people were getting into the act. "Goddamn it, you get off the air," he stormed at Aderholt. "I gave you that star, and I will take it away from you." Aderholt stated, "That's your prerogative." Later, when "things started really going to hell," Aderholt said he got another call from Erich. He asked, "Heinie have you got that plan? Brush it off. I'm coming back out there to implement it."

"And he did," Aderholt said.[33]

Maximizing the Cambodian Airlift

The Year of the Cat opened with a roar in both Cambodia and Vietnam. A barrage of crushing defeats rocked South Vietnam, starting in January across the border from Cambodia when North Vietnamese troops captured the entire province of Phuoc Binh, just fifty miles from Saigon. President Gerald Ford urgently dispatched Air Force chief of staff, General Jones, to Saigon to reassure President Nguyen Van Thieu that the United States stood behind him. "You could smell defeat in the air," Jones recalled. "There was no confidence." The Air Force's top general said it came home to him that "we had made an awful lot of mistakes." One was that the Americans had never built any self-confidence into the Vietnamese forces. He recalled when he was there as deputy for operations and vice commander in 1969, MACV and Seventh Air Force never gave the Vietnamese any tough missions. "We took those on ourselves when we ought to have been doing just the opposite," he said.[34]

General Jones stopped over in Bangkok after meeting with President Thieu. The despair he had sensed in Saigon occupied his thoughts. He asked Aderholt, "What are we going to do about Vietnam? What is your impression? What would you do?" Aderholt said, first thing, he would kick all the U.S. civilians out. They lived like kings in expensive villas downtown and contributed nothing to fighting the war. Then he would send the military personnel home, bring in a small dedicated team of qualified people, set up a task force like the Thailand Liaison Detachment, and start all over again. General Jones asked, "How many people?" "Thirty or so," Aderholt said. "They would be out in the field. They would live with the Vietnamese and they would fly with them. They would go in bare-base and be supported out of Clark." General Jones asked him to write up a one-page concept on what needed to be done if he were put in charge there.[35]

The following afternoon Jones called and asked Aderholt to go with him to Nakhon Phanom early the next morning. En route, the general said he had read the concept paper and talked with Ambassador Kintner. "Kintner says you can go in June," he said. "I'm going to promote you and put you in charge over there. What do you need?" Aderholt said that he would have to be extended, because his recall was only for three years. He would have to pick his own people, the same way they had worked the Cambodia problem. "The third thing, I want them to take that asterisk off my name on the generals' list." The asterisk meant that his appointment had been political. "No problem," Jones said.[36]

Aderholt started planning for his departure in June. He met with General Manor and his staff at Clark. General Wilson came out for the meeting and brought members of his staff from Hickam. Aderholt said that nearly everybody in PACAF wanted to get on the special team he was forming. "I had to tell them that I already had my own people," he said. He was all set to go to Vietnam in June, but this too was overtaken by events when Saigon fell to

North Vietnamese and Viet Cong forces in April.[37] In the meantime, he had his hands full with the rapidly deteriorating military situation in Cambodia.

The Khmer Rouge had launched its largest dry season offensive ever on New Year's Day. On 14 January Lieutenant General John J. Burns at Nakhon Phanom advised General Brown and Admiral Gaylor that the Khmer Rouge had thrown ninety-six battalions against Phnom Penh and another thirty-three battalions against the lower Mekong. General William Palmer reported from Phnom Penh that the Cambodian army, Forces Armees Nationales Khmeres, had acquitted themselves outstandingly, utilizing their tactical mobility and their superior fire power, both air and ground, to great advantage. Thus far the enemy around Phnom Penh had been stopped well short of their objectives, while suffering heavy casualties. General Burns warned, however, that the enemy controlled the banks of the lower Mekong, and massive air resupply of the capital city might be required unless convoys could get through.[38]

By the end of January air lines of communication were the only way in or out of Phnom Penh and other population centers in Cambodia. The Khmer Rouge had closed all major highways and effectively interdicted the Mekong. U.S. communications channels were flooded with messages concerning increased airlift requirements since General Burns's grim assessment of the situation on the fourteenth. Birdair had already surged to ten missions a day, which was the limit of its contracted capability, but this would not sustain Khmer government defenses. The Air Force did not want to recommit USAF crews to the airlift but was prepared to do so if necessary. General Kriangsak, in negotiations with General Aderholt, helped to ease the problem by authorizing additional unmarked C-130s at U-Tapao, and agreeing to an expanded contract with Birdair. General Aderholt then turned to an old friend, Colonel "Bags" Baginski, for data on getting maximum payload capacity out of the C-130Es being used in the airlift.[39]

When the Cambodian situation worsened, Erich von Marbod called early one morning and said, "Heinie, it looks like the war is over. The Mekong is closed and the situation is critical. We are going into the tank tomorrow to see if there is anything we can do to save Phnom Penh." Aderholt asked, "How can I help?" "We have to beef up the airlift, but the Joint Chiefs and Congress have ruled out committing Air Force units or personnel," von Marbod replied. "Do you have any idea how we can increase tonnage of the existing operation as a stopgap measure?" Aderholt said, "I'll get back to you." "You have twelve hours," Erich said. "Its six P.M. here, and the Joint Chiefs are to meet first thing in the morning on a decision."[40]

General Aderholt called Major Klingaman and filled him in on the problem, so he could start putting together a revised airlift plan. He then contacted Ambassador Gunther Dean in Phnom Penh to determine revised airlift tonnage requirements. Aderholt's next call was to Colonel "Bags" Baginski, a protégé from his ramrod days at Takhli who now commanded the 374th Tactical Airlift Wing at Clark. Certain that the C-130Es in the Cambodian airlift were not carrying their maximum capacity, as had been the case when he took over the Tibetan airlift in 1960, Aderholt obtained data from Baginski that could be used to raise airlift tonnage out of U-Tapao to satisfy the increased requirements in Phnom Penh.[41]

Aderholt learned from Baginski that the USAF transports not only were operating well below the emergency wartime planning limit, but had been carrying half their capacity all through the Vietnam War. Baginski confirmed that the C-130E could safely carry a fifty-five-thousand payload, but had been limited to thirty thousand pounds or less because of peacetime restrictions. "That made me wonder how much tonnage and how many aircraft we wasted during years of combat flying less than a wartime military load," Aderholt said.[42]

Two hours before the deadline, General Aderholt wired von Marbod a detailed plan for meeting the tonnage requirements at Phnom Penh. He explained that the surge in airlift support for Phnom Penh could be met within present funding authority if waivers were granted for aircrew flying time and for aircraft operational limitations up to 175,000 pounds gross weight. The supplemental contract with Birdair made available twenty-seven sorties per day with fifteen aircrews if USAF flying time requirements were waived to permit 160 hours per month per aircrew. He justified the waiver on the basis that civilian aircrews were exempt from additional duties and responsibilities unique to military service. "Air America and Continental Air Service operated at comparable monthly flying rates for many years without degrading aircrew effectiveness or compromising safety," he advised.[43]

The U.S. team in Phnom Penh confirmed that the city's minimum daily requirement was 600 tons, comprising 15 tons general cargo, 45 tons fuel, and 540 tons of ammunition and rice. This requirement could be met using available aircraft and crews if authorized to operate up to a limit of 185,000 pounds maximum gross weight. This was 15,000 pounds under the emergency wartime planning limit, but still sufficient to airlift 25 tons of actual cargo per sortie. The 600-ton daily requirement for Phnom Penh could be satisfied by twenty-four sorties per day, which was within the twenty-seven sorties presently contracted for with Birdair. Since aircraft participating in the airlift had been carrying only 16.3 tons per sortie, the requested waivers would increase cargo tonnage by approximately 35 percent, with a corresponding percentage decrease in required sorties and aircrew exposure in the air and on the ground at Phnom Penh's Pochentong airport. Additional reductions would be realized in

Brigadier General
Aderholt and four
A-1Hs evacuated from
Vietnam to U-Tapao in
1975 and returned to
the United States.

total cost and aircraft handling operations at both the on-load and off-load points.[44]

General Aderholt proposed that airlift operations be extended over a twenty-four-hour period with the heaviest activity occurring during daylight. Night operations would permit maximum utilization of personnel and equipment. He had looked at other solutions, such as using Birdair and Continental Air Services aircraft, but had discounted them. Their combined assets of three DC-6s and three C-46s could transport only up to 115 tons per day. In addition to failing to satisfy the requirement, these aircraft were not cost effective and further complicated loading and off-loading operations. The introduction of civil aircraft also required having to reopen negotiations with the Royal Thai government.[45]

If this concept was approved, Aderholt strongly urged that Colonel Baginski, whom he called "the most knowledgeable airlifter in this theater," be designated as the on-scene Air Force commander at U-Tapao responsible only to the Air Force chief of staff to insure contractor compliance with the concept and safety of operation. He recommended that a full-time Air Force flight surgeon be provided at U-Tapao to observe the well-being of the contract aircrews, and that Colonel Baginski be given authority to grant on-the-spot waivers of USAF aircrew requirements based on the flight surgeon's advice. Also required was clear authority for direct coordination with the customer at Phnom Penh. "Neither Colonel Baginski nor myself envision this as a cowboy operation, but view it as the most acceptable alternative of those left to us," Aderholt stated. "This only requires that we depart from our peacetime restrictions and operate our aircraft midway between normal gross weights and wartime emergency gross weights."[46]

Aderholt got a call from von Marbod explaining what happened at the JCS meeting. When General Brown read Aderholt's message recommending that Baginski be put in charge of the Cambodian airlift, he turned to General Jones and said, "Who is your most knowledgeable airlift man?" Jones rang Major General Maurice Casey, a veteran troop carrier commander who was in charge of strategic mobility for the JCS, and asked, "Who is the best airlift man in the theater?" Casey said, "Bags Baginski." General Brown said, "Wrap it up." General Jones immediately directed that Colonel Baginski be put in charge of airlift operations at U-Tapao and be given authority to waive all Air Force restrictions on aircraft and aircrews, without compromising safety. The PACAF vice commander, Lieutenant General Winton W. Marshall, recalled that General Jones wanted Baginski "in place at U-Tapao and in charge at 0600 on the day he called." General Jones later called General Aderholt and said to let him know if anyone interfered with Colonel Baginski. General Kriangsak, meanwhile, approved the interim introduction of commercial carriers, and short-term contracts were signed with Airlift International of Miami and World Airways of Oakland for the supply of three DC-8s and crews to supplement Birdair for a period of twelve days.[47]

Colonel Baginski went immediately from Clark to U-Tapao and assumed command of the expanded operation. According to plan, he granted a waiver to increase maximum gross takeoff weight and stripped the aircraft of all extraneous equipment to raise the gross cargo loads to the required levels. After a short visit to U-Tapao on 14 February, General Wilson reported to General Jones that he had met with Colonel Baginski and Birdair pilots and was impressed by what he had seen. "I might add that I met Admiral Gaylor at U-Tapao on his return by C-130 from a visit to Phnom Penh," Wilson stated. "He seemed pleased with the professionalism of the entire operation, commented on the absolute criticality of its success to the survival of the Khmers, and indicated that Khmer morale was being shored up immeasurably by our increased efforts."[48] General Aderholt later said General Wilson asked if he knew why the airlift was pulled out from under PACAF and put directly under Colonel Baginski, and that he had denied knowing anything about it—a denial he regretted having to make because of their friendship and his high regard for Wilson.[49]

As the siege on Phnom Penh tightened in late February and March, the airlift was expanded further to include commercial DC-8s hauling rice on shuttles between Tan Son Nhut and Pochentong Airport. After his visit to Phnom Penh in mid February, Admiral Gaylor reported on the hopelessness of the military situation, stating that he believed a political settlement was urgent. The danger to aircrews from the rocketing and shelling of Pochentong airport grew worse by the day. General Marshall, vice CINCPACAF, visited U-Tapao on 17 March and reported that Colonel Baginski was "doing a magnificent job, particularly in working with the contract aircrews, keeping their spirits up and being sensitive to their worries." He noted that the contract aircrews were growing increasingly worried about the shelling and rocketing of Pochentong and might have quit if not for Baginski's superb leadership. The words of one crew member—"I am so goddamned scared"—summed it up for all.[50]

When President Lon Nol and his family left Cambodia on 1 April, it was too late for the peace talks that Ambassador Dean and other U.S. officials had hoped his departure might bring. With victory at hand, the Khmer Rouge had no incentive to negotiate a settlement. Within the Khmer armed forces, only the air arm retained an offensive capability, and it was fast eroding. By 6 April it was painfully obvious to the senior USAF officer on the scene that it "was simply a matter of time." He expected the Khmer air force to cease being an effective fighting force by 15 April. On the eleventh, Birdair C-130 air-land missions were suspended because Americans were being evacuated from Phnom Penh the following day. The evacuation of Khmer aircraft to Thailand continued until Phnom Penh fell on 17 April. The evacuation of Americans from Vietnam had started on 6 April and continued through the twenty-ninth, the day before the North Vietnamese occupied Saigon.[51]

The sustained airlift operations in support of the Khmer Republic were described as the largest since the Berlin airlift of 1948–49. From 11 April 1973 to 17 April 1975, USAF C-130s (including those crewed by Birdair) and contracted DC-8s flew 5,413 air-land missions, delivering more than 123,000 short tons of rice, ammo, fuel, and supplies. The C-130s flew more than 3,000 missions airdropping nearly 40,000 short tons of rice and ammo to Khmer enclaves. This was more than three times the tonnage delivered to Khe Sanh in 1968. While the huge airlift had been conducted under increasingly difficult and hostile conditions, it was completed with no losses of aircraft or American lives.[52]

The training and logistics support that Colonel Johnson's liaison detachment set up in Thailand helped make the Khmer air arm a viable force to the very end. The evacuation of Khmer aircraft had gone according to plan, although half of the force of nearly two hundred aircraft had been either destroyed or captured by the enemy. On 11 April there were 73 Khmer aircraft bedded down in Thailand. Twenty-four additional aircraft made it out of Cambodia to a safe haven in Thailand over the next week. Overall, 97 Khmer aircraft (including 50 T-28s, 7 AC-47s, and 10 C-123s) evaded capture by the enemy.[53] An additional 121 South Vietnamese aircraft (including 22 F-5Es, 27 A-37s, and 11 A-1s) recovered at U-Tapao during the final three days before Saigon fell.[54]

During the final days of the war, von Marbod brought his team out from Washington to oversee the evacuation of South Vietnamese aircraft and helicopters, including spare parts and equipment, and to keep as many as possible from falling into Communist hands. General Aderholt explained that the plan was to fly everything into Thailand, to salvage as much as they could for shipment back to the United States, then give the excess planes and equipment to the Thais. He noted that the Thais had their eye on the F-5E Freedom Fighters that came out of Vietnam, but he could not get authority to turn the planes over to them. The Thais did receive a number of excess aircraft, however, and were grateful for it.[55]

The von Marbod team arrived in Saigon four days before the city fell to the Communists, and traveled to the nearby base at Bien Hoa, where they recovered some valuable equipment while under artillery fire from the enemy. Returning to Saigon, von Marbod called on Ambassador Martin, who warned him against foolishly risking his life since the soon-expected truce would allow for evacuation of equipment as well as people. An official history noted that von Marbod apparently lacked Martin's confidence and returned to Bien Hoa, again under fire, to supervise the recovery of additional high-value equipment.[56]

Just hours before North Vietnamese troops overran Bien Hoa, Aderholt got a frantic call from von Marbod, who was penned down in a trailer, under fire. "Where is that goddamn airplane you were supposed to send me?" he yelled. Earlier, Aderholt had arranged for a Birdair flight to Bien Hoa to bring von Marbod and his team back to Thailand. The plane had not arrived. "There is something wrong," he told von Marbod. "I will send another plane." He called Major General Earl Archer, General Burns's chief of staff at Nakhon Phanom, and learned that Burns had ordered him to stop the plane because there was a surface-to-air missile threat. "There is one angry goddamn assistant secretary over there with a team," Aderholt told Archer. He called Baginski and said, "Whatever you've got, divert it into Bien Hoa now and pick up von Marbod!"[57]

Concurrent with the Communist victories in South Vietnam and Cambodia, the Pathet Lao moved to take over in Laos. After the Birdair contract was canceled, General Aderholt got an urgent call to evacuate Hmong tribesmen who were abandoned at Long Tieng. The caller said, "We have to get C-130s into Vang Pao's headquarters in Long Tieng or they are going to be slaughtered." Aderholt knew that Air America planes were still available at Udorn to assist the Hmong, but there was likely no evacuation plan. He called U-Tapao. Two C-130s had not been returned to Clark yet, but there were no crews left at U-Tapao to fly the planes into Laos. Aderholt heard that Matt Hoff, a Birdair pilot, was at Don Muang waiting to board a flight home. He then called the Thai air marshal who ran the airport and asked him to stop Hoff, even if they had to arrest him. "There was one agitated American when he got on the line to me because he missed his plane," Aderholt recalled.[58]

Aderholt hurriedly explained the situation to Hoff, who said, "Well, you've already messed everything up. How do we get paid?" Aderholt said he would pay them from the military assistance fund. Hoff said, "How much?" Aderholt said, "I don't give a damn! This is a matter of life and death! What about five thousand dollars a trip?" Hoff said, "Good!" Aderholt said, "We'll pay all the crew five thousand dollars a trip. But get your ass in gear, we don't have time to lose!" He then called the JCS chairman, General Brown, and got authority to divert the C-130. "General, do anything you want," Brown said. "Whatever you think you can put in there to help the Hmong, you do it. You have my support." Aderholt called U-Tapao and ordered them to launch the plane as soon as Hoff arrived. Aderholt said the last flight out of Long Tieng set a record, carrying three hundred refugees stacked in the C-130, even on the tailgate, to freedom at Udorn. The C-130 and the smaller Air America planes could not evacuate all the refugees, and thousands had to be left behind.[59]

Commanding the Joint Advisory Forces

Throughout the hectic opening months of 1975, General Aderholt was actively engaged in protecting U.S. interests in a rapidly deteriorating military environment, with little or no support from the advisory group commander, Major General Hixon. As far as Aderholt was concerned, Hixon had become more of a hindrance than a help since replacing Major General Mellen the previous July. He described Hixon as "a wild man" who had little interest in advising or aiding the Thai military forces, and who "spent all his time out in the field playing soldier and jumping out of helicopters." The general apparently had always envied the paratroopers and wanted to be one of them. "He declared he was going to get one thousand jumps and started jumping every day," Aderholt recalled. "He dedicated two helicopters, and he would jump four or five times a day." Hixon brought a female captain with him as his assistant, and every day they were out in the field instead of staying home and taking care of business.[60]

Making matters worse, the Army brought in "another wild man" from Korea to run the support group. "He and the troops in the support outfit were getting drunk and raising hell, and he was out playing combat football and rappelling out of helicopters," Aderholt said. He asked Hixon, "What are you going to do about this crazy son of a bitch?" Hixon said that he did not see anything wrong with what the colonel was doing. Finally, there were so many complaints, the Army sent the inspector general out to investigate. Aderholt told the IG that the colonel would not make "a good two-striper in the Air Force," but Hixon defended him. Nothing came of the investigation.[61]

General Hixon was relieved after only ten months as commander because he could not get along with Thai military leaders and threatened to suspend the military assistance program to the Thai armed forces. He had ignored a directive from Secretary Schlesinger's office and spent most of his time trying to get one thousand parachute jumps. General Aderholt replaced Hixon as commander on 30 April 1975, the day Saigon fell to the Communists. A crimson curtain had come down on the Vietnam War, but there was work yet to be done. General Aderholt's primary mission now was to tie up all loose ends in Thailand and see that the remaining U.S. forces there were withdrawn in an orderly fashion and without incident. "It was a piece of cake after the past four months," Aderholt said. He only wished that the concerted effort he and von Marbod's team had put forth to improve the Khmer air arm's fighting capabilities had not been too little, too late.[62]

General Aderholt continued to foster good relations between the U.S. forces and their Thai hosts. The strain on those relations resulting from the U.S. pullout in Southeast Asia was awkward for both sides. Aderholt reported that U.S. prestige had suffered a painful decline with the fall of South Vietnam, Cambodia, and Laos to the Communists. "The psychological impact upon U.S. and Thai policy makers, and most important the Thai people, was staggering and profound," he stated. Because the United States had not intervened during the crisis, the Thais sought rapprochement with their new Communist neighbors. Their efforts were unsuccessful, however, and by year's end they had begun to swing back to the U.S. side. "Unfortunately, our U.S. newspapers have painted the Thai 'anti-U.S.' campaign far more dismal than it really exists," Aderholt wrote in December 1975. "The Thais still love Americans and we go about our business without harassment."[63]

A failure to keep the Thai government advised during the *Mayaguez* incident in May 1975 added to an erosion of confidence between the two allies. After Cambodia seized the American vessel on 12 May, U.S. rescue efforts included an assault on Koh Tang Island by Marines inserted by helicopters from U-Tapao and supporting naval air strikes to suppress enemy fire. The U.S. forces launched the assault from Thai soil without informing the host government. "That sat very poorly," Aderholt recalled. Some Americans, on the other hand, believed their Thai hosts should have done more militarily to help the Khmer government in its war against insurgents. Although Thai military leaders allowed the USAF to train Khmer airmen at Udorn and authorized the sustained Cambodian airlift from U-Tapao, they refused to become militarily involved in the conflict. A Bangkok newspaper reported in late February, "It is well-known in diplomatic circles that the Thai Foreign Ministry has been steadfastly resisting recent American efforts to drag Thailand into the Cambodian war."[64]

A change of ambassadors in the middle of the 1975 crisis apparently did not help matters. Edward E. Masters was acting chief of mission between Ambassador Kintner's departure in March and the arrival of Kintner's successor, Charles Whitehouse, in May. Whitehouse transferred to Bangkok from Laos, where he had served as ambassador since August 1973. He was a WWII bomber pilot and a veteran foreign service officer with several years' experience in Southeast Asia, but still found a way to alienate both the U.S. military officers who worked for him and the Thai supreme command. General Aderholt later stated that Ambassador Whitehouse showed "prejudice" against the military in Thailand, and that "animosity" had developed between the Thai military and the U.S. embassy while Whitehouse was there.[65]

Although he resented the arrogance some embassy officials displayed in their dealings with Thai military leaders, General Aderholt did his best to nurture a good professional relationship with the ambassador and his staff. He had learned to live with arrogance, which unfortunately had been America's handmaiden in Southeast Asia since the start of the Vietnam War. One of Aderholt's favorites on the embassy staff was William D. Toomey, a former Marine Corps officer who was counselor for economic and commercial affairs, and from time to time served as acting deputy chief of mission. Toomey described Aderholt as "a firm and decisive leader" who "did not mince words," was "refreshingly candid," and "understood how to motivate the troops." Toomey noted, however, that General Aderholt had trouble with Ambassador Whitehouse and some "pompous" embassy officers.[66]

Aderholt's main concern was the ambassador's policies, which he believed were driving a wedge between the United States and its friends in the Thai government. His differences with the ambassador ran deep but had not affected their relationship when he received a performance evaluation from Whitehouse in November 1975. The ambassador sent the evaluation to Aderholt with a note, on which he had penned, "I don't know whether this will get you promoted, but it should at least get you into heaven!" Whitehouse recognized the outstanding job Aderholt had done as commander and strongly urged that he be promoted to major general.[67]

At the time, Aderholt had just officially closed a third major USAF base in Thailand, his former command at Nakhon Phanom. "For me, this was a very sad, memory-awakening occasion," he recalled. As the Stars and Stripes was lowered for the last time, many past events flashed through his mind: "the Nimrods and Zorros, first successful night truck killers and the great people who flew and maintained them, the Sandys and Jolly Greens and the impossible missions that somehow succeeded." But most of all he thought "of all those guys that flew away and did not return." General Aderholt sent the flag from Nakhon Phanom to the Air Commando Association "for safekeeping and as a reminder over Hurlburt Memorial Park of the tragic sacrifices which were made by so many brave men."[68]

The closing of Udorn and Korat had also been announced, and little remained of the mighty USAF force posture that had built up in Thailand during the Vietnam War. Aderholt wrote that over the past year, "We saw most of our old Air Commandos, USAF, and all of our Air America and Continental Air friends leave here for all parts of the world. With these departures ended an era that produced many heroes, men who will forever live in our memories. These men accomplished feats of courage and bravery beyond man's most extensive expectations—unfortunately, all for a losing cause."[69]

In early 1976 General Aderholt stopped at CINCPAC on the way back from Washington. Admiral Gayler's headquarters was particularly concerned about the status of residual U.S. forces. The JCS planned to keep up to four thousand troops in Thailand, but negotiations with the Thai government had stalled. The CINCPAC chief of staff, Lieutenant General William G. Moore Jr., commented to him, "Hey, we are not getting much reporting from your outfit out there." Aderholt said, "That's right, because I have been ordered that everything I send out has to be coordinated with the political-military officer. That son of a bitch won't let anything out." Moore said, "Why don't you go back out there, write it up, and send it through back-channel traffic, eyes only." When he got back to Bangkok, Aderholt had his staff prepare a message addressing ongoing negoti-

Colonel Aderholt with
traditional Thai dancer
at Nakhon Phanom in
1967.

ations with the Thai government, and the key issues pertaining to residual U.S. forces in Thailand. He sent the secret message through back channels to CINCPAC, for Admiral Gaylor's eyes only.[70]

The gist of the message, which was sent on 9 March, was that Thai military leaders completely supported a continued U.S. presence in Thailand, but that negotiations between the Ministry of Foreign Affairs and the U.S. embassy had been emotional and were going nowhere. "While we have, in the past months, justified to ourselves our requirements in Thailand, we have not seen fit to apprise Thai officials of the requirement until recently," General Aderholt stated. "They have listened to our words and observed our actions, and the disparity between the two may be one reason we are having difficulty reaching an accord at this time." He noted that, as a sovereign country surrounded by Communists, the Thais were obviously concerned about their future. In the past year they had watched South Vietnam, Cambodia, and Laos come under Communist domination without the United States going to their assistance. They had also observed continued reductions in their military assistance and foreign military sales programs. "Such actions cannot but raise serious doubts in their minds as to future U.S. intentions to support Thailand and therefore raise doubts as to their advisability in allowing a U.S. presence in their country," he cautioned.[71]

When General Aderholt sent the message, he emphasized that the embassy was privy to the information being reported but had not coordinated on the message itself. Two days later he arrived at the office, and there was a copy of the message on his desk, which CINCPAC had retransmitted to the Pentagon with an information copy to the U.S. embassy in Bangkok. "Oh, shit," he thought. In a few minutes the phone rang. The ambassador was on the line. "General, this is Charlie Whitehouse," he said. "I would like to see you in my office at once." When Aderholt walked in, Whitehouse was livid. "You have double-crossed me," he accused. "You have stabbed me in the back." Aderholt tried to explain that he wore two hats and had been asked by Admiral Gayler's headquarters to summarize the situation through back channels. Clearly stated in the message was the fact that it had not been coordinated with the embassy.[72]

"It doesn't matter," the ambassador said. "I have lost confidence. I have talked to Admiral Gayler, and we have decided to relieve you."

"Fine," Aderholt replied. "If you will let me use the telephone, I will call General Jones now and tell him, and I should be able to get out of here in twenty-four hours."

"That's a little hasty," Whitehouse said. "We need you for the withdrawal. We have decided the first of May would be a good date."

"That's fine with me," Aderholt said, and left. That night he told Jessie they would be leaving on 1 May.

A few days later the ambassador called and asked, "Could you play golf with me today?"

While on the links, Whitehouse said, "I have been thinking—since the withdrawal is going so well, you should stay on until August, if that is all right with you."

"Mr. Ambassador, it doesn't make any difference to me either way," Aderholt said. "I was recalled to come over here. I can stay or I can leave. But if you have lost confidence in me, I don't see how you can have me sticking around."

"Well, maybe it is not as bad as it seems," Whitehouse said.[73]

General Aderholt's warning that embassy negotiations with the Royal Thai government were leading nowhere had already come true. On 20 March the prime minister announced a decision that all U.S. forces would be asked to leave Thailand, with the exception of a 270-man military advisory group element in Bangkok. At this time the Thailand-wide strength of U.S. forces had been reduced from twenty thousand on 1 July 1975 to approximately thirty-eight hundred personnel. In making this decision, the civilian government had gone against the advice of its military leaders. On the first of March the supreme command had presented a written position paper to the prime minister clearly supporting a residual U.S. troop presence at several operating locations throughout Thailand. The paper had not delineated the numbers of troops but concluded that a residual U.S. presence benefited Thailand's security.[74]

The irony in this situation was that just two weeks later, in national elections held on the fourth of April, the Thai people, by an overwhelming majority, voted the present government out of office. Mostly pro-U.S. candidates were elected to office, and the leftist political parties were rejected. Aderholt had reported to the ambassador that the Thai supreme command predicted this would happen, with the new government taking a fresh look at the U.S. withdrawal issue. Unfortunately, embassy officials were unable to reverse their earlier blunders after the new government took over. The situation had not improved when General Aderholt retired as commander on the first of August.[75]

In a debriefing report at the time of his retirement, General Aderholt criticized the embassy for having completely alienated the Thai military. "During my sixteen-year association with Southeast Asia, I have never seen U.S. prestige so low nor have I seen such incompetency and indecision in our foreign service," he stated. To the general and his staff, it appeared that the embassy had followed a plan designed to eliminate the remaining U.S. military influence in Southeast Asia. "Whether by design or otherwise, we have now very clearly conveyed to the Communists that the U.S. has no intentions of resisting aggression in this area," he concluded.[76]

Farewell to an American Warrior

General Aderholt's last weeks as commander were consumed by the accelerated withdrawal of U.S. forces to meet a 20 July deadline and the closeout of Military Assistance Command functions. Over his objections the decision to retain only a small advisory group in Bangkok had resulted in downgrading the commander's position to colonel. He believed this "only confirmed to the Thai military and responsible people in the government the U.S. abandonment of Thailand and Southeast Asia." On 25 June MACTHAI held its last parade in Thailand. A month later General Aderholt departed Bangkok. He was the last American general to serve in Southeast Asia.[77]

Aderholt had asked General Wilson, the PACAF commander, to retire him. "He was a great guy. I admired him, and he wanted to do it," Aderholt said. Ad-

In 1972, at a Royal Thai Air Force gala honoring the Aderholts, Jessie returns a traditional greeting, known as a *wai*. To her left is Royal Tai Air Force commander Air Chief Marshal Kamol.

miral Gayler had put him in for the Distinguished Service Medal and sent a message to Bangkok that he wanted to retire him. Aderholt insisted on General Wilson retiring him at Hickam AFB, however, and Admiral Gayler came there for the ceremony. "I couldn't let you leave without being at the retirement, and I want to present your award," the admiral said. General Aderholt thanked him for the award, but said he would have felt much better if the admiral had protected him instead of being so quick to concur when Ambassador Whitehouse called. Gayler assured Aderholt that it had not been intentional.[78]

On the first of August, with Jessie by his side, General Aderholt retired from active service for the second and final time. After a visit home they returned to Bangkok, where a vice presidency awaited him with Air Siam. On 16 August the Soviet Communist party newspaper *Pravda* noted General Aderholt's return to Thailand. The newspaper announced that General Aderholt had been appointed vice president of the Thai airline, where he would be engaged in organizing tourist trips for U.S. military personnel. *Pravda* interpreted this to mean: "The Pentagon's propensity for organizing these trips by U.S. service-men to Asian countries is quite easily explained. The Americans have been forced to get out of Vietnam, Laos, Campuchea and Thailand. Nor does the population of Okinawa, South Korea and the Philippines like the U.S. troops very much. . . . Therefore, the Pentagon is having to think up masquerades in-volving a change of clothes for its military."

General Aderholt smiled wryly when asked about the *Pravda* dispatch. It was not the first time his methods or his motives had been misinterpreted, and it would not be the last. The mystery and misinformation surrounding his years with the CIA and covert operations had dogged his Air Force career and had now followed him into retirement. Colonel Michael E. Haas, air commando and historian, wrote that "General Aderholt's remarkable life as leader, fighter, and airman reads like an adventure novel spanning the entire cold war era."[79] Haas also wrote that there wasn't really anything or anyone else quite like him in the Air Force, and that he was "a mixed blessing according to many."[80] Ac-knowledging that maybe he was "somewhat of a maverick," General Aderholt believed that the Air Force had been good to him and that he had served the Air Force well. He added, however, "I think it is absolutely essential that the Air Force record the bad with the good, if we ever hope to eliminate the bad."[81]

Anyone who was around Heinie Aderholt for long knew that he was an un-equivocal and unabashed warrior and patriot. Although vehement in his criti-cism of the way we fought the Vietnam War, he was no apologist for America's involvement in the war. In a nostalgic letter following his visit to Nakhon Phanom with General Jones in January 1975, he wrote that many people asked if the results were worth the price. His answer was, "I say hell yes, because every U.S. generation had to pay its price to understand freedom and democracy never came cheap." In closing, he quoted the hottest fighter pilot of them all, Brigadier General Robin Olds, who said, "When the weeping and wailing of the candy asses is jaded and done—America will look back and know—that what she did and how her men performed—was right. And pride will slowly grow." Olds also promised that the self-pity and hypocrisy would quickly disappear whenever the nation found herself in trouble. "Mark my words," he said.[82]

After his retirement General Aderholt was invited to address the Interna-tional Lions Club at the Erawan Hotel in Bangkok. The group wanted him to talk about the American involvement in Southeast Asia and its aftermath, but Aderholt stated that he could not speak for the U.S. government. "I came here today to talk about the World Medical Relief organization and what we can do to alleviate suffering," he said. A Swedish woman in the group, who had spo-ken to him earlier about the war, asked anyway, "Can you just tell us why the

United States was meddling around in Southeast Asia?" Aderholt said he would answer that one question and then get back to his message about medical relief. His answer to the question got a standing ovation: "For your information, what we tried to do in South Vietnam, we did for your country in World War II. We went to Europe to liberate you from the goddamn Nazis. We came to Southeast Asia to try to make the North Vietnamese stop infiltrating the South and restore freedom of choice to the people there. We were successful in your country, and that is the reason you can come here today and ask stupid questions."[83]

In the final analysis, he was a warrior and leader in the best tradition of the United States Armed Forces—a line officer and field commander who drew strength from his own unique reservoir of individuality, integrity, compassion, and humility. Truly an airman for all seasons, he would have fit in well flying and fighting alongside the Air Force founding fathers—pacesetters who built an armada in the sky from shoestrings and dreams—not a tin soldier in their midst. If he had picked a role model, it might well have been Major General Claire L. Chennault, a fellow southerner who was a lion among the mavericks of yesterday's Army Air Corps. Larry Ropka said the parallels between the two men were so similar that Aderholt could have been a reincarnation of Chennault.[84] Humbled by this comparison to a man he called "one of history's greatest air generals," Aderholt unwittingly drew a parallel in December 1976 when he quoted Claire Chennault in a letter to *Air Force Magazine*: "Peculiarly, the officer who exercises initiative, dares to think differently and succeeds, no matter how brilliant his success may be, is often side-tracked in his career at the first opportunity. Neither his associates nor his superiors understand him, and lack of understanding leads to lack of confidence. But I believe that men who 'insist upon flexibility in all things' and who retain their individualism, are the ones who win battles, especially in the air. Fortunately, our nation has had enough of them when they were needed. I hope we always do."[85]

General Aderholt's leadership philosophy might have been best summed up in his own words. "My definition of leadership versus management," he said, "is that managers do things right, but leaders do the right thing, regardless."[86] The study of General Aderholt's military career clearly shows that he always tried to "do the right thing, regardless." That is the way he would want to be remembered.

EPILOGUE

The legend has grown since General Aderholt retired from active duty the second time in the summer of 1976. Approaching his eightieth birthday at the dawn of a new century, the general remains totally commited to the service of his nation, to his beloved air commandos, and to helping victims of war and oppression. He still thrives on getting involved and getting things done. His inspiring leadership, his compassion for people, and his dedication to military honor and integrity were saluted in recent years by General LeRoy Manor, whose words sustain the theme that Heinie Aderholt "is a legend regardless of one's interpretation of legendary."[1]

For three decades General Aderholt has been a driving force behind the Air Commando Association, which he cofounded at Hurlburt Field during the turbulent Vietnam War years. Most members of the two-thousand-strong association have served with or under him at one time or another, General Manor pointed out. "They all know Heinie, and he knows the majority of the members on a first-name basis," Manor said. "They all respect him highly and regard him as the number one Air Commando." He credited Aderholt with keeping the association actively involved in providing humanitarian assistance to widows and children of airmen who lost their lives in the service of their country, and to people around the world who suffered from the results of military action, economic hardships, diseases, or disasters. He invariably took the lead in organizing the association's relief efforts. General Manor said that "books could be written about Heinie's efforts to bring relief" to the Hmong in Laos and to destitute people in Guatemala and other Pan-American nations.[2]

General Aderholt has been an entrepreneur and respected businessman in the Fort Walton Beach community outside Hurlburt Field for the past twenty years.

When he agreed to be a consultant to Air Siam upon retiring in 1976, he also started the Southeast Asia Travel Agency with Richard Armitage, a Naval Academy graduate who had spent six years in Vietnam. Despite *Pravda*'s allegations, the travel agency was not a front for the CIA and was not connected directly or indirectly with the U.S. government. Aderholt's brief association with Air Siam ended when the company went out of business in 1977. They negotiated a charter service with a company in the Philippines, but the Thai government refused to grant the company a charter to operate out of Bangkok. The travel agency folded, and Armitage returned to Washington, D.C., where he worked on Senator Robert Dole's campaign for president, and later on George Bush's campaign.[3]

General Aderholt remained in Bangkok a while longer as a consultant with Bill Bird's airline. One lucrative contract they had was to transport one hundred thousand live goats and sheep from Bombay to the United Arab Emirates. The business was going well until the Indian government began raising the tariff on operations out of Bombay and on the import of aircraft parts. He then started a rattan factory in one of Bird's warehouses in Bangkok, and they exported rattan furniture to a company he had set up in Fort Walton Beach after his first retirement in December 1972. He returned to Fort Walton Beach in 1979 to run the furniture business, which he eventually named Far East Interiors, and now owns two stores, the original one at Fort Walton Beach and another a few miles farther down the beach. Other business interests include representing various Fortune 500 companies in Vietnam, and serving on the board of directors for Computerized Thermal Imagery.[4]

Another venture the general had become involved in before leaving Bangkok was to obtain user rights for an airfield on the island of Male in the southern Maldives that could serve as a contingency base en route to the Middle East in the event Diego Garcia closed down. He envisioned that the airfield, which had been used by the British during World War II as a refueling base for planes going to and from Singapore, could also be used as a refueling stop for military flights from the Philippines to Diego Garcia if they were denied access to Singapore. Aderholt flew to Dallas for a prearranged meeting with Ross Perot about financing the operation. Perot told Aderholt that he had "pulled Uncle Sam's chestnuts out of the fire" one time too many and did not intend to get involved with anything like that again. Aderholt admired Perot because of his unselfish support of a number of POW/MIA initiatives, most of which had not panned out. When Perot later ran for president, Aderholt—who was drawn to the candidate's U.S. trade policies and unquestionable patriotism—headed up his Northwest Florida campaign. "He was leading both Clinton and Bush when he decided to withdraw," Aderholt recalled.[5]

Aderholt had also continued his World Medical Relief work with various charities while in Thailand. After returning home, he and Hap Lutz got the Air Commando Association even more involved in relief efforts in Central America and other parts of the world. "We did this out of a sense of duty," the general explained, "as a way of saying 'we're sorry' for the way the United States reneged on its promises to those who fought and died in the name of freedom." They founded the nonprofit Threshold Foundation to supplement and expand the association's relief work. The name was later changed to the McCoskrie Threshold Foundation to honor Colonel Roland K. McCoskrie, who had followed Aderholt as commander of the 56th Air Commando Wing during the Vietnam War. Aid in the form of medical and food supplies was critically needed in strife-torn Central America, which had emerged in the 1980s as the last front of the Cold War.[6]

When the leftist Sandinista guerrillas overthrew the Somoza regime in Nicaragua in the summer of 1979, General Aderholt remembered the warning that the Nicaraguan president had made during their early-morning encounter in 1961 about the consequences of allowing Cuban dictator Fidel Castro to remain in power. In the aftermath of the Marxist takeover in Nicaragua, anti-Sandinista rebels known as Contras found refuge in neighboring Honduras but got little support from the United States until after Ronald Reagan became president in 1981. In addition to sending clothing, medical supplies, and other humanitarian assistance to refugee camps in Honduras, the Air Commando Association arranged for medical supplies to be shipped to El Salvador, and coordinated efforts to fly medical supplies and clothing to Guatemalans caught in the crossfire between government forces and leftist guerrillas.[7]

While the relief operations in Central America during the 1980s supported the Reagan administration's efforts to stop Communism from spreading in the region, the primary aim was to relieve the suffering of the people. Nevertheless, both the Air Commando Association and World Medical Relief were denounced by ultraliberal groups and their supporters in Congress. The news media erroneously linked both organizations to the CIA and incorrectly reported that General Aderholt and the Air Commando Association were engaged in clandestine support for the Contras. Aderholt adamantly denied that either he or the association were involved in any way with these operations. He referred to former servicemen who did covertly support the Contras as "patriots," however, and said he would have volunteered to resupply the freedom fighters but had not been asked. Although he stays in touch with old friends from the CIA, Aderholt insists that he has not worked directly or indirectly for the agency since the early 1960s.[8]

Brigadier General
Heinie Aderholt, 1975.

The Air Commando Association did not let the undeserved criticism evolving out of the so-called Iran-Contra affair hinder its worldwide humanitarian relief efforts. So there would be no misunderstanding, the McCoskrie Foundation advised World Medical Relief that it was a separate entity from the association. The relief effort continued through the Cold War period after Iran-Contra was resolved, and afterward. In 1987 the government of Guatemala selected the Air Commando Association to receive the "Order of the White Orchid," the highest award given for services demonstrating "the embodiment of brotherhood, friendship, and loyalty to the Republic of Guatemala." President Vinicio Cerezo presented the award to General Aderholt in behalf of the association at a special ceremony in June 1987.[9]

Actively involved in MIA/POW matters during the post–Vietnam War years, General Aderholt accepted an invitation along with Gary Best and several other people to visit Moscow in 1988 to talk with the Russian Peace Committee about missing Americans who had not been accounted for in Southeast Asia. The Peace Committee, which was headed by a former KGB agent known only as the professor, offered to assist in obtaining information from Vietnam on missing Americans. In return, Best was asked to use his relationship with Afghan prime minister Bulbuddin Hekmatyar to get Russian POWs back from Afghanistan. Best successfully negotiated for the return of two Russian prisoners but was unable to win the release of an additional eighty-five captives because the Afghans demanded $1 million a head for their return. Nothing came of the Peace Committee's pledge to track down missing Americans.[10]

Growing out of this visit, the group formed the MEGA Oil Company, with Gary Best as chief executive officer, and agreed to rework some of the derelict oil wells in the former Soviet republic of Azerbaijan. General Aderholt recalled that the MEGA group bought two rigs in Oklahoma City and flew them to Baku, the capital of Azerbaijan. The group got almost two dozen derelict wells back into production but had to go out of business when they could not get support from the Bush administration. Meanwhile, the Azerbaijan government wanted assistance in training five thousand Azeri troops for rapid deployment missions in their escalating war with the Armenians in Karabakh. Aderholt and Secord, who had retired in the rank of major general, made arrangements to establish a training program for the Azeris, but withdrew from the project when a government official stole $10 million that had been set aside for the training. "The whole thing was a disaster," Aderholt said, "and we were glad to get out when we did."[11]

At home General Aderholt and the brotherhood of air commandos were frustrated by what appeared to be a continued lack of emphasis on USAF special operations in the post-Vietnam era. At times it seemed that they were the only ones in the Air Force family who truly cared about preserving the legacy and tradition of special air operations. In April 1980 the abortive Iranian hostage rescue attempt sparked renewed interest in joint special forces plans and capabilities, but the Pentagon was slow to respond. The Air Force's belated response nearly three years later was to merge its special operations and air rescue forces under a numbered air force, newly activated by the Military Airlift Command at Scott AFB, Illinois. This realignment relieved TAC of the responsibility, but limited the mission and scope of special operations, and diminished the historic role of the Eglin-Hurlburt complex as the center of special air warfare activity. Four years later Hurlburt Field regained its status as the nerve center for special operations, but this resulted more from developments beyond the USAF's control than from increased interest on the Air Force's part.[12]

In 1987, against the opposition of the defense department, Congress obligated the services to support their elite forces when it enacted legislation creating the unified Special Operations Command under a four-star general. The

Army and the Navy established their service components as major commands, but the Air Force dragged its feet. Although returning the center of special operations activity to Hurlburt in August 1987, the Air Force did not establish the Air Force Special Operations Command at Hurlburt until nearly three years later, in May 1990. During the intervening period General Aderholt worked with Larry Ropka, who was a principal deputy assistant secretary of defense in the Pentagon during 1986–88, in an attempt to have the Air Force's special operations forces patterned after the original air commandos, but was unsuccessful.[13]

Another battle dear to the general's heart was fought and lost in 1993 when the Air Force redesignated the 1st Special Operations Wing (former 1st Air Commando Wing) as the 16th Special Operations Wing. During a massive restructuring of the Air Force, the USAF chief of staff, General Merrill A. McPeak, directed that the approximately one hundred active wings surviving the shake-up be redesignated to preserve the service's early lineage and history. When both a 1st Fighter Wing and a 1st Special Operations Wing emerged from the process, McPeak redesignated the special operations wing to keep from having two units with the same numerical designation. General Aderholt protested on behalf of the air commandos, but to no avail. Fearing that the combat history of the 1st Air Commando Wing would be lost in the shuffle, he did convince the Special Operations Command to sponsor the publication of two histories preserving the air commandos' legendary combat experiences in World War II, Korea, and Southeast Asia.[14]

Like all American veterans, General Aderholt was deeply offended in June 1998 by the spurious charges aired on the television premiere of *Newsstand* (produced by CNN and *Time*) that U.S. forces used deadly sarin nerve gas against American defectors in Laos in 1970 during Operation Tailwind. Knowing the charges were untrue, Aderholt, General Secord, and the Air Commando Association offered their services and support to the Special Forces and Special Operations Associations who brought suit against the show's producers. As a result of actions taken by the Special Forces and Special Operations Associations, CNN and *Time* broadcast a retraction, dismissed the show's two producers, and reprimanded correspondent Peter Arnett for his role in reporting the story. General Aderholt stated that all three associations would hold out until CNN terminated Arnett's employment and compensated those who had been harmed by his irresponsible reporting. One former SOG member had already sued for $100 million, and others were bringing suit.[15]

The general's priority mission in recent years has been to honor the Hmong for their tremendous sacrifice while supporting American objectives in the Vietnam War, and to aid the needy families who had resettled in the United

States and those who were left behind in Laos. He got involved in the project after being invited in July 1995 to speak at the first Hmong National Recognition Day sponsored by the American Legion and the VFW in Denver, Colorado. When accepting the invitation, General Aderholt recalled that day in the fall of 1960 when he first met General Vang Pao, who was a major at the time, at Padong, Laos. "We drank that powerful rice whiskey and, with Bill Lair, talked about the forthcoming air resupply of weapons and ammo for the Hmong guerrillas to assist them in the fight against the Communist forces in Laos," he recalled. He noted that the U.S. government was looking for allies to support its policies in Southeast Asia, and the Lao-Hmong were seeking to gain equal rights as free citizens of Laos. "Not only were they seeking freedom and equal rights, but they were willing to fight and die for it," he said.[16]

Vang Pao and Bill Lair, representing the U.S. government, reached agreement that day at Padong, Aderholt recalled, and Vang Pao led his people in a thirteen-year war against the Communists. "The Hmong believed they had a trustworthy ally, the United States of America, who would stand by them to the end, and never go back on the solemn promises that had been agreed to," he said. Thirteen years later they had suffered terrible losses—nearly 40,000 killed out of a population of about 250,000. When the Americans pulled out, Vang Pao and some of his people were allowed into the United States, but most were abandoned in Laos, where they were brutally punished for their wartime alliance. "They were doused with deadly chemicals from the air, forced from their homes and villages, and incarcerated," Aderholt said. "Many died being tortured or starved to death." Those who fled to Thailand were incarcerated in squalid refugee camps for years and now faced forced repatriation back to Laos. "This was their reward for years of tying down thousands of North Vietnam's best soldiers in Laos to help relieve the pressure on U.S. forces in South Vietnam," Aderholt said. "Had they not done so, those soldiers would have been available to fight in the south, drastically increasing our casualties there."[17]

General Aderholt had expected to see General Vang Pao at Denver, but the once powerful Hmong leader, who now lived in California, declined to attend the event unless he could run it. From all reports, the aging Hmong general lived more in the past than the present and had neither adapted well to American culture nor accepted the reality of a Laos that was different from the one he had known. Vang Pao allegedly kept a firm grip on the loyalty of the older Hmong by keeping hopes alive of eventually returning under arms to their homeland, a dream that was as blind as it was unrealistic. "It was not going to happen," Aderholt said. Many of the elders who migrated to the United States could not speak English and consequently never received their citizenship. They eventually were denied benefits, such as food stamps and social security. The younger Hmong had fared well in their new homeland. "Some ninety or more have received their Ph.D.'s, and hundreds their master's degrees," Aderholt stated. "Few, if any, are receiving any type of assistance. Some are officers in the U.S. military. One served on the POW/MIA Joint Task Force for two years in Bangkok."[18]

Following his Recognition Day address in 1995, General Aderholt agreed to serve as an adviser to the Lao-Hmong American Coalition. At their next annual gathering, which was held at St. Paul, Minnesota, he arranged for several distinguished military leaders, including General Manor and former Air Force chief of staff General Michael Dugan, to preside over ceremonies honoring two hundred uniformed Lao-Hmong elders who had fought in the Vietnam War. General Aderholt has met with congressmen representing districts where the Hmong elders have settled in the United States, to address the issue of welfare, food stamps, and other benefits.[19]

Since 1996 General Aderholt has turned his attention toward the plight of the Hmong left behind in Laos who have suffered from our withdrawal from Southeast Asia. In March 1998 he visited Laos with Bill Lair and met with Ambassador Wendy Jean Chamberlain, members of her country team, and nongovernmental agencies, to discuss helping the Hmong who remain in Laos. He found that the Laotian hill tribes and Laos as a whole were in serious economic trouble. Adding to the misery, live ordnance that was still on the Plaines des Jarres and the Ho Chi Minh Trail area took hundreds of lives each year, including many children's. Princess Diana's bomb disposal teams were engaged in exploding the ordnance, but much needed to be done in the way of humanitarian assistance. "We are punishing the innocent people of Laos by not providing more assistance," Aderholt said. Returning home, he reported that Ambassador Chamberlain, who came to Colorado to address the Lao-Hmong American Coalition, had offered full assistance of her country team in initiating a hill tribe humanitarian program. "Ambassador Chamberlain is a real professional and is doing a great job representing our country," he stated.[20]

Upon returning from Laos, General Aderholt got the air commandos and the McCoskrie Threshold Foundation fully involved in providing humanitarian assistance to the Hmong in Laos. "The embassy there will solve many of the problems," he said, "but there is much for us to do." The embassy agreed to sponsor the foundation as a nongovernment organization, allowing it to serve as the primary support organization for the Sam Neua Province Hospital, in an area populated by Hmong tribesmen, and to send in volunteer workers with badly needed medical and humanitarian supplies. The air commandos immediately started work, along with Harry Vickers (a missionary with the First Baptist Church of Oklahoma City), to get a forty-foot container ready for shipment to Laos. Aderholt's plan is to get all of the Hmong involved and to start a massive program of shipments through nongovernment agencies from countries doing humanitarian service in Laos. If the program is a success in Laos, he plans to expand it for the Montagnards in Vietnam. "My ambition is to institutionalize a program that will drastically alter the lifestyle of the Hmong in Laos and the Montagnards in Vietnam," Aderholt said. "We can take this program to really great heights and do a tremendous amount of good."[21]

General Aderholt describes the assistance to the Hmong as "my last major project in this lifetime." This brought a knowing smile from other air commandos, for as long as there are tomorrows, they know Heinie Aderholt will be up front encouraging them to do more. In a letter "humbly seeking support in settling this long overdue obligation" to the Hmong, Aderholt said that "abandoning these loyal allies, in 1975, without a real effort to evacuate them . . . and never looking back" was shameful. An air commando responding to the appeal wrote, "When Heinie *humbly* seeks I respond!!" The response was overwhelming.[22] Not only is compassion etched into the air commando creed, but the ghosts of the Vietnam War are never far away.

In June 1996 a weekly newspaper near Whiteman AFB, Missouri, printed a letter from a retired air commando, James A. Taylor, about a chance meeting with another veteran of the Vietnam War. Taylor and a man about fifteen years his senior had stepped outside of a building on base at the same time to have a smoke. They struck up a conversation, and the more they talked, the more it became obvious that their paths had crossed, or very nearly so, in the jungles of Southeast Asia some thirty years ago. The talk turned to the men they had served under during the war, and the more they spoke of one brigadier general, the more attentive the older man became. He knew the younger man had to be talking about Heinie Aderholt. "Sure enough, we both had served with and for Heinie," Taylor wrote. "The 'old man' stood more straight, more alert and said, 'I can't believe it' over and over. For about 20 minutes, two old air commandos shed 30-plus years and stood in the sweltering jungles once again, on real estate, in countries that we were never officially in."[23]

Taylor said that he and the old man had not even exchanged names but warmly shook hands and parted—one to the west and the other to the north, probably never to meet again. "But, for 20 minutes, we were in another place and another time and I will always cherish this chance meeting with that old man," Taylor said. He then recalled the pride with which he and the old man remembered their association with General Aderholt. "Heinie was the best commander I ever served with in nearly 25 years in the Air Force," Taylor stated emphatically. "He was the kind that did not make waves, he made hurricanes. If the plush officeholders in D.C. wanted something that couldn't be done, they called Heinie and his troops."[24] This is the legacy that Brigadier General Heinie Aderholt and the air commandos leave to the United States Air Force and the warriors who come after them.

ACRONYMS

AAF	Army Air Forces
AB	air base
ADC	Air Defense Command
ADF	automatic direction finder
AFB	Air Force Base
AGOS	Air-Ground Operations School
ARC	air rescue and communications
ARCS	Air Rescue and Communications Service
AWOL	absent without leave
CAT	Civil Air Transport
CHECO	Contemporary Historical Evaluation of Combat Operations
CIA	Central Intelligence Agency
CINCPAC	Commander in Chief, Pacific Command
CINCPACAF	Commander in Chief, Pacific Air Forces
CNN	Cable Network News
COIN	counterinsurgency
CONUS	Continental United States
CSAF	Chief of Staff, United States Air Force
DFC	Distinguished Flying Cross
DOD	Department of Defense
FAC	forward air controller
FEAF	Far East Air Forces
GHQ	General Headquarters
GI	government issue
HUMINT	human intelligence
ICC	International Control Commission

ID	identification
IG	Inspector General
IP	initial point
JAF	Joint Attack Force
JCS	Joint Chiefs of Staff
JPRC	Joint Personnel Recovery Center
JTF	Joint Task Force
JUSMAG	Joint United States Military Advisory Group
JUSMAGTHAI	Joint United States Military Advisory Group, Thailand
KGB	(Soviet) Committee of State Security
MAAG	Military Assistance Advisory Group
MACTHAI	Military Assistance Command, Thailand
MACV	Military Assistance Command, Vietnam
MAP	Military Assistance Program
MATS	Military Air Transport Service
MIA	missing in action
NATO	North Atlantic Treaty Organization
NCO	noncommissioned officer
OER	officer effectiveness report
ORI	operational readiness inspection
OSS	Office of Strategic Services
PACAF	Pacific Air Forces
PARU	Police Aerial Resupply Unit
PCS	permanent change of station
POW	prisoner of war
PSP	pierced steel planking
RAF	Royal Air Force
RCT	regimental combat team
RLAF	Royal Laotian Air Force
RMK-BRJ	Raymond International, Morrison-Knudsen, Brown and Root, and J.A. Jones
ROK	Republic of Korea
SAC	Strategic Air Command
SAWC	Special Air Warfare Center
SEACOORD	Southeast Asia Coordinating (Committee)
SEATO	Southeast Asia Treaty Organization
SOF	Special Operations Force
SOG	Studies and Observations Group
SOTFE	Special Operations Task Force, Europe
STOL	short takeoff and landing
TAC	Tactical Air Command
TCSq	troop carrier squadron

TDY	temporary duty
UN	United Nations
UNC	United Nations Command
U.S.	United States (of America)
USAF	United States Air Force
USAFE	United States Air Force in Europe
USAID	United States Agency for International Development
USMACTHAI	United States Military Assistance Command, Thailand
USO	United Service Organizations
USSR	Union of Soviet Socialist Republics
VFW	Veterans of Foreign Wars
VIP	very important person
VNAF	Vietnamese Air Force
WWII	World War II

NOTES

Prologue: The Man and the Mission

1. Brigadier General Harry C. Aderholt, interview by Hugh N. Ahmann, USAF Oral History Collection, Maxwell Air Force Base (hereafter AFB), Ala., Air Force Historical Research Agency (hereafter AFHRA) File K239.0512-1716, 12–15 August 1986, pp. 21, 25.
2. Ibid., 4, 12.
3. Lucile Dorroh Burton, recollections of Harry C. Aderholt, Aderholt Collection, AFHRA, Maxwell AFB, Ala., 1 July 1994.
4. Ibid.; "Will Hurl Leather in All-Star Classic," undated newspaper clipping, Aderholt Collection, AFHRA, Maxwell AFB, Ala.
5. Colonel Joseph W. Kittinger Jr., interview by Lieutenant Colonel Robert G. Zimmerman, USAF Oral History Collection, Maxwell AFB, Ala., AFHRA File K239.0512-807, 5 September 1974, p. 60.
6. Major General James R. Hildreth, recollections of Harry C. Aderholt, Aderholt Collection, AFHRA, Maxwell AFB, Ala., undated.
7. Lieutenant General LeRoy J. Manor, recollections of Harry C. Aderholt, Aderholt Collection, AFHRA, 22 March 1994.
8. Richard Secord, *Honored and Betrayed* (New York: John Wiley and Sons, 1992), 57.
9. Kittinger, interview by Zimmerman, 5 September 1974.
10. Richard H. Kohn and Joseph P. Harahan, ed., *Air Superiority in World War II and Korea* (Washington, D.C: Office of Air Force History, 1983), 70.
11. General William W. Momyer, *Air Power in Three Wars* (Washington, D.C.: HQ United States Air Force, 1978), 10, 81–101.
12. Ambassador William H. Sullivan, recollections of Harry C. Aderholt, Aderholt Collection, AFHRA, 17 April 1994.

13. Brigadier General Harry C. Aderholt, interview by Warren Trest, Aderholt Collection, AFHRA, 15 August 1995.

14. Ibid.; Colonel Michael E. Haas and Technical Sergeant Dale K. Robinson, *Air Commando! 1950–1975: Twenty-Five Years at the Tip of the Spear* (Fort Walton Beach, Fla.: n.p., n.d.), 11–15.

15. Aderholt, interview by Trest, 15 August 1995.

16. Ibid.; Haas and Robinson, *Air Commando!* 16–19.

17. Aderholt, interview by Trest, 15 August 1995.

18. Brigadier General Harry C. Aderholt, official USAF biography, Secretary of the Air Force Public Affairs, Aderholt Collection, AFHRA, 1 July 1975.

19. Aderholt, interview by Trest, 15 August 1995.

20. Ibid.; Haas and Robinson, *Air Commando!* 30; Philip D. Chinnery, *Any Time, Any Place: A History of USAF Air Commando and Special Operations Forces* (Annapolis: Naval Institute Press, 1994), 96.

21. Haas and Robinson, *Air Commando!* 32–37; Aderholt, interview by Trest, 15 August 1995; Timothy N. Castle, *At War in the Shadow of Vietnam* (New York: Columbia University Press, 1993), 34–36.

22. Momyer, *Air Power in Three Wars*, 10, 11.

23. Colonel Robert L. Gleason, recollections of Harry C. Aderholt, Aderholt Collection, AFHRA, 28 March 1994.

24. Aderholt, official biography; Aderholt, interview by Trest, 15 August 1995; Chinnery, *Any Time, Any Place*, 9.

25. Aderholt, interview by Trest, 15 August 1995; Haas and Robinson, *Air Commando!* 48–51; Chinnery, *Any Time, Any Place*, 94–96; Castle, *At War in the Shadow*, 66, 67.

26. Peter G. Tsouras, *Warriors' Words: A Dictionary of Military Quotations* (London: Arms and Armour Press, 1992), 468.

27. Aderholt, interview by Trest, 15 August 1995.

28. Ibid.

29. Ibid.

30. William H. Sullivan, Deputy Assistant Secretary for East Asian and Pacific Affairs, to Lieutenant General Robert J. Dixon, DCS/Personnel, HQ USAF, in Aderholt Collection, AFHRA, 1 July 1971.

31. Benjamin O. Davis Jr., *Benjamin O. Davis Jr., American: An Autobiography* (Washington, D.C.: Smithsonian Institution Press, 1991), 298.

32. Aderholt, interview by Trest, 15 August 1995; Haas and Robinson, *Air Commando!* 61, 62.

33. Aderholt, interview by Trest, 15 August 1995.

34. General David C. Jones, interview by Lieutenant Colonel Maurice Maryanow, USAF Oral History Collection, Maxwell AFB, Ala., AFHRA File K239.0512-1664, p. 179, 5 August and 15–17 October 1985; 20, 21 January and 13, 14 March 1986.

35. Aderholt, interview by Trest, 15 August 1995.

36. Ibid.

37. Brigadier General Robert L. Cardenas, recollections of Harry C. Aderholt, Aderholt Collection, AFHRA, 24 June 1994.

38. General William W. Momyer, *Corona Harvest Report*, 18 July 1974, chap. 3; General William W. Momyer to Major General R. H. Ellis, HQ USAF, Momyer Corona Harvest Collection, AFHRA File 168.7041, 22 July 1969.

39. Aderholt, interview by Trest, 15 August 1995.

40. Ibid.

41. Aderholt, official biography; Jack Foisie, "U.S. Air Force Retiree Recalled for Thai Post," *Los Angeles Times*, 4 December 1973; Aderholt, interview by Trest, 15 August 1995.

42. *A Brief History of U.S. Military Activities in Thailand* (Honolulu: Commander in Chief, Pacific Command History Branch, 1978), Maxwell AFB, Ala., AFHRA File K712.01, January 1978, p. 45.

1. The Call to Arms

1. Aderholt, interview by Ahmann, 12–15 August 1986, p. 27; Aderholt, interview by Trest, 15 August 1995, p. 2.

2. Aderholt, interview by Ahmann, 12–15 August 1986, p. 27; Aderholt, interview by Trest, 15 August 1995, p.2; Brigadier General Harry C. Aderholt, interview by Warren Trest, Aderholt Collection, AFHRA, 18 April 1996, p. 1.

3. Aderholt, interview by Ahmann, 12–15 August, p. 27; Aderholt, interview by Trest, 15 August 1995, p. 2; Aderholt, interview by Trest, 18 April 1996, p. 1.

4. Aderholt, interview by Ahmann, 12–15 August 1986, pp. 14, 15.

5. Ibid., 24, 25.

6. Ibid., 16; AGO Form WD66-B, in Master Personnel Record of Brigadier General Harry C. Aderholt, Aderholt Collection, AFHRA, 30 August 1955.

7. Aderholt, interview by Ahmann, 12–15 August 1986, pp. 15, 16, 25, 26.

8. Ibid., pp. 16, 26; Major General Edward F. Witsell, Adjutant General, to Captain Harry C. Aderholt, Master Personnel Record, Aderholt Collection, AFHRA, 10 October 1947.

9. Aderholt, interview by Ahmann, 12–15 August 1986, pp. 16, 17.

10. Ibid., 19; Alan L. Gropman, *The Air Force Integrates, 1945–1964* (Washington, D.C.: Office of Air Force History, 1978), 32.

11. Aderholt, interview by Ahmann, 12–15 August 1986, pp. 19, 20.

12. Ibid., 20.

13. Ibid., 18; Gropman, *Air Force Integrates*, 9, 10, 45, 46; Colonel Noel F. Parrish, "The Segregation of Negroes in the Army Air Forces," Air Command and Staff School, Maxwell AFB, Ala., AFHRA File 239.04347, May 1947.

14. Gropman, *Air Force Integrates*, 86–88; Aderholt, interview by Ahmann, 12–15 August 1986, p. 17.

15. Aderholt, interview by Ahmann, 12–15 August 1986, p. 20.

16. Ibid., 18, 22.

17. Lieutenant General Benjamin O. Davis Jr., official USAF biography, Secretary of the Air Force Public Affairs, 1 May 1969; Davis, *Autobiography*, 157–61.

18. Aderholt, interview by Ahmann, 12–15 August 1986, p. 22; Davis, *Autobiography*, 298; Gropman, *Air Force Integrates*, 12–14.

19. Captain Harry C. Aderholt, Efficiency Report, Master Personnel Record, Aderholt Collection, AFHRA, 28 January–31 March 1948.

20. Aderholt, interview by Trest, 18 April 1996, p. 3.

21. Ibid., 1.

22. Ibid.; Aderholt, interview by Trest, 15 August 1995, p. 2.

23. Aderholt, interview by Trest, 18 April 1996, pp. 1,2.

24. Ibid., 2.

25. History of 21st Troop Carrier Squadron, 1 July–1 October 1950, AFHRA File SQ-TR-CARR-21-HI, September 1950, pp. 1, 6; Robert F. Futrell, *The United States Air Force in Korea, 1950–1953* (Washington, D.C.: Office of Air Force History, 1983), 70.

26. James F. Schnabel, *United States Army in the Korean War. Policy and Direction: The First Year* (Washington, D.C.: Office, Chief of Military History, 1972), 125–34.

27. Aderholt , interview by Ahmann, 12–15 August 1986, pp. 28,29; Aderholt, interview by Trest, 18 April 1996, p. 2.

28. Aderholt, interview by Ahmann, 12–15 August 1986, pp. 28, 29; Aderholt, interview by Trest, 18 April 1996, p. 2.

29. History of 21st Troop Carrier Squadron, 1 July–1 October 1950, AFHRA File SQ-TR-CARR-21-HI, September 1950; 21st Troop Carrier Squadron to Commanding General 5th Air Force, Historical Summary of Tactical Operations, 15 October 1950, AFHRA File K-SQ-TR-CARR-21-HI, August 1950.

30. Aderholt, interview by Trest, 18 April 1996, pp. 6, 7.

31. History of 21st Troop Carrier Squadron, 1 July–1 October 1950, p. 2; Futrell, *United States Air Force in Korea*, 155, 156, 381; Aderholt, interview by Trest, 18 April 1996, p. 3.

32. Schnabel, *United States Army in the Korean War*, 173–77.

33. Aderholt, interview by Trest, 15 August 1995, pp. 2,3; Aderholt, interview by Trest, 18 April 1996, p. 3; Schnabel, *United States Army in the Korean War*, 169–71.

34. Aderholt, interview by Trest, 18 April 1996, p. 3; Aderholt, interview by Trest, 15 August 1995, p. 4.

35. Schnabel, *United States Army in the Korean War*, 216; Roy E. Appleman, *United States Army in the Korean War: South to the Naktong, North to the Yalu* (Washington, D.C.: Office, Chief of Military History, 1961), 654–58.

36. Appelman, *United States Army in the Korean War*, 658; Aderholt, interview by Trest, 15 August 1995, p. 3; Schnabel, *United States Army in the Korean War*, 233.

37. Aderholt, interview by Trest, 18 April 1996, p. 3; Colonel Robert Brewer et al., audiotape , Fort Walton Beach, Fla., Aderholt Collection, AFHRA, 23 April 1994, p. 3.

38. Brewer, audiotape, 2, 3.
39. Ibid., 3–5.
40. Ibid.; Aderholt, interview by Trest, 18 April 1996, p. 3.
41. Aderholt, interview by Trest, 18 April 1996, p. 3.
42. Haas and Robinson, *Air Commando!* 12, 13.
43. Brewer, audiotape, 4.
44. Ibid.
45. Haas and Robinson, *Air Commando!* 13, 15; Aderholt, interview by Ahmann, 12–15 August 1986, pp. 30, 31; Aderholt, interview by Trest, 18 April 1996, p. 7.
46. Statement by Brigadier General Harry C. Aderholt to Warren Trest, 6 February 1998.
47. Ibid.
48. Aderholt, interview by Trest, 18 April 1996, p. 3.
49. Brewer, audiotape, 1; Schnabel, *United States Army in the Korean War*, 274–78.
50. Appleman, *United States Army in the Korean War*, 721, 763–65; Schnabel, *United States Army in the Korean War*, 257–76.
51. Brewer, audiotape, 1.
52. Ibid., 2; Appelman, *United States Army in the Korean War*, 754, 755.
53. Schnabel, *United States Army in the Korean War*, 272; Appelman, *United States Army in the Korean War*, 685, 732, 744, 773.
54. Aderholt, interview by Trest, 18 April 1996, p. 4; Aderholt, interview by Trest, 15 August 1995, pp. 3, 4.
55. Aderholt, interview by Trest, 18 April 1996, p. 7.
56. Aderholt, interview by Trest, 15 August 1995, pp. 8, 9; Aderholt, interview by Trest, 18 April 1996, p. 4.
57. Aderholt, interview by Trest, 15 August 1995, pp. 8, 9; Aderholt, interview by Trest, 18 April 1996, p. 4; Schnabel, *United States Army in the Korean War*, 273–78.
58. Aderholt, interview by Trest, 15 August 1995, pp. 8, 9; Aderholt, interview by Trest, 18 April 1996, p. 4; Schnabel, *United States Army in the Korean War*, 273–78.
59. Futrell, *United States Air Force in Korea*, 258, 259; Aderholt, interview by Trest, 15 August 1995, p. 3.
60. Aderholt, interview by Trest, 15 August 1995, p. 4; Aderholt, interview by Trest, 18 April 96, p. 4.
61. Brewer, audiotape, 5.
62. Ibid.
63. Ibid., 6; Haas and Robinson, *Air Commando!* 14; Aderholt, interview by Trest, 15 August 1995, pp. 5, 6.
64. Brewer, audiotape, 6, 7.
65. Schnabel, *United States Army in the Korean War*, 305; Futrell, *United States Air Force in Korea*, 271; Appelman, *United States Army in the Korean War*, 417.
66. Schnabel, *United States Army in the Korean War*, 306–9.
67. Futrell, *United States Air Force in Korea*, 268; Aderholt, interview by Trest, 18 April 1996, p. 4.

68. Aderholt, interview by Trest, 18 April 1996, p. 4.
69. Brewer, audiotape, 19, 22; Haas and Robinson, *Air Commando!* 13; Aderholt, interview by Trest, 15 August 1995, p. 7; Aderholt, interview by Ahmann, 12–15 August 1986, p. 52.
70. Aderholt, interview by Trest, 18 April 1996, p. 6.
71. Aderholt, interview by Trest, 18 August 1995, pp. 3, 4.
72. Schnabel, *United States Army in the Korean War,* 326, 331, 351–55; 378–406.
73. Futrell, *United States Air Force in Korea,* 75, 384; Aderholt, interview by Ahmann, 12–15 August 1986, pp. 55, 56.
74. Futrell, *United States Air Force in Korea,* 75, 384; Aderholt, interview by Ahmann, 12–15 August 1986, pp. 55, 56.
75. Ibid.
76. Ibid.; Aderholt, interview by Trest, 18 April 1996, p. 8.
77. Brewer, audiotape, 19; Aderholt, interview by Trest, 15 August 1995, pp. 7, 8; Aderholt, interview by Trest, 18 April 1996, p. 6.
78. Brewer, audiotape, 19; Aderholt, interview by Trest, 15 August 1995, pp. 7, 8; Aderholt, interview by Trest, 18 April 1996, p. 6.
79. Brigadier General Benjamin H. King, audiotape, Carefree, Ariz., Aderholt Collection, AFHRA, undated.
80. Aderholt, interview by Trest, 15 August 1995, pp. 6, 7.
81. Ibid.
82. King, audiotape, 1; Brigadier General Benjamin H. King, official USAF biography, Secretary of the Air Force Public Affairs, 15 March 1969.
83. King, audiotape, 2, 3.
84. Ibid., 3, 4.
85. Aderholt, interview by Ahmann, 12–15 August 1986, p. 55.
86. Ibid., p. 39; Aderholt, interview by Trest, 15 August 1995, p. 6.
87. Aderholt, interview by Trest, 15 August 1995, p. 6; Schnabel, *United States Army in the Korean War,* 378–406.
88. Aderholt, interview by Trest, 15 August 1995, p. 5.
89. Aderholt, interview by Ahmann, 12–15 August 1986, pp. 39, 40.
90. Monthly histories of 21st Troop Carrier Squadron, Maxwell AFB, Ala., AFHRA File K-SQ-TR-CARR-21-H1, January-July 1951; Aderholt, interview by Trest, 18 April 1996.
91. Aderholt, interview by Trest, 18 April 1996.

2. On Assignment with the CIA

1. Brigadier General Harry C. Aderholt, notes, Aderholt Collection, AFHRA, December 1996, p. 1.
2. Ibid.
3. Ibid.; Aderholt, official biography, 1 July 1975.

4. Aderholt, notes, December 1996, p. 1.
5. Lieutenant Colonel C. W. Denning, Chief, Military Personnel Division, CIA, to Major Harry C. Aderholt, Aderholt Collection, AFHRA, 19 September 1951; Aderholt, interview by Trest, 18 April 1996, p. 14.
6. Aderholt, interview by Trest, 18 April 1996, p. 14.
7. Haas and Robinson, *Air Commando!* 16; Aderholt, statement to Trest, 6 February 1998.
8. Haas and Robinson, *Air Commando!* 18, 19.
9. Brigadier General Harry C. Aderholt, audiotape, Fort Walton Beach, Fla., Aderholt Collection, AFHRA, April 1997.
10. Ibid.; Aderholt, interview by Trest, 18 April 1996, p. 14.
11. Aderholt, notes, December 1996, p. 2; Aderholt, interview by Trest, 15 August 1995, p. 10.
12. Aderholt, notes, December 1996, p. 2; Aderholt, interview by Trest, 15 August 1995, p. 10.
13. Aderholt, notes, December 1996, p. 2; Aderholt, interview by Trest, 15 August 1995, p. 10.
14. Aderholt, notes, December 1996, p. 3.
15. Ibid.
16. Ibid.
17. Ibid., 3, 4.
18. Ibid., 4.
19. Ibid.
20. Ibid.
21. Aderholt, audiotape, 15 April 1997.
22. Ibid.
23. Ibid.; Aderholt, notes, December 1996, p. 5.
24. Aderholt, audiotape, 15 April 1997; Aderholt, notes, December 1996, p. 5.
25. Aderholt, interview by Trest, 18 April 1996, pp. 14, 15.
26. Aderholt, notes, December 1996, p. 7; Aderholt, audiotape, April 1997, p. 2.
27. Aderholt, interview by Trest, 15 August 1995, p. 12; Brewer, audiotape, 26; Aderholt, notes, 6, 7.
28. Brewer, audiotape, 26.
29. Aderholt, notes, pp. 6, 7.
30. Ibid., p. 7.
31. Aderholt, audiotape, April 1997, p. 2; Brigadier General Harry C. Aderholt, videotaped interview by Hugh Ahmann and Warren Trest, USAF Oral History Collection, AFHRA, June 1995.
32. Aderholt, audiotape, April 1997, p. 2; Aderholt, videotaped interview by Ahmann and Trest, June 1995; Aderholt, notes, p. 5.
33. Aderholt, audiotape, April 1997, p. 2; Aderholt, videotaped interview by Ahmann and Trest, June 1995; Aderholt, notes, p 5.

34. Aderholt, videotaped interview by Ahmann and Trest, June 1995.
35. Aderholt, audiotape, April 1997.
36. Ibid.
37. Ibid.
38. Ibid.

3. Cold War Rituals

1. Robert Frank Futrell, *Ideas, Concepts, Doctrine: Basic Thinking in the United States Air Force, 1907–1960*, vol. 1 (Maxwell AFB, Ala.: Air University Press, 1989), 419–32.
2. Alfred Goldberg, ed., *A History of the United States Air Force, 1907–1957* (Princeton, N.J.: D. Van Nostrand, 1957), 121–27, 158, 228, 229; Warren A. Trest, "View from the Gallery: Laying to Rest the Admirals' Revolt of 1949," *Air Power History* (Spring 1995): 17–29.
3. Goldberg, *History of the United States Air Force*, 115–19; Futrell, *Ideas, Concepts, Doctrine*, 449, 450.
4. Earl H. Tilford Jr., *SETUP: What the Air Force Did in Vietnam and Why* (Maxwell AFB, Ala.: Air University Press, 1991), 1–40; Aderholt, interview by Trest, 18 April 1996, pp. 17, 18.
5. Aderholt, interview by Trest, 18 April 1996, pp. 17, 18; History of the Eighteenth Air Force, January-June 1953, vol. 1, AFHRA File K470.01, p. 161.
6. Aderholt, interview by Trest, 18 April 1996, p. 17.
7. History of the Eighteenth Air Force, January-June 1953, vol.1, AFHRA File K470.01, pp. 2, 5.
8. History of the Eighteenth Air Force, January-June 1954, vol. 1, AFHRA File K470.01, pp. 157–62.
9. Aderholt, interview by Trest, 18 April 1996, p. 17.
10. History of the Eighteenth Air Force, January-June 1954, vol. 1, AFHRA File K470.01, p. 157.
11. Aderholt, interview by Trest, 18 April 1996, p. 17.
12. Ibid.
13. Ibid.; Aderholt, official biography, 1 July 1975.
14. Aderholt, interview by Trest, 18 April 1996, p. 17; Aderholt, official biography, 1 July 1975.
15. Martin E. James, *Historical Highlights: United States Air Forces in Europe, 1945–1980* (Ramstein AB, Germany: HQ USAFE Office of History, 1980), 25, 26, 28, 33; J. C. Hopkins, *The Development of Strategic Air Command, 1946–1981* (Offutt AFB, Neb.: HQ SAC Office of History, 1982), 33, 62.
16. James, *Historical Highlights*, 26; Aderholt, interview by Trest, 15 August 1995, p. 15.
17. Aderholt, interview by Ahmann, 12–15 August 1985, p. 55; Aderholt, interview by Trest, 18 April 96, p. 16; Haas and Robinson, *Air Commando!* 19.

18. Aderholt, interview by Trest, 15 August 1995, p. 15; Aderholt, audiotape, April 1997, p. 2; Aderholt, interview by Trest, 18 April 1996, p. 18.

19. Aderholt, interview by Trest, 15 August 1995, p. 15; Aderholt, audiotape, April 1997, p. 2; Aderholt, interview by Trest, 18 April 1996, p. 18.

20. Aderholt, interview by Ahmann, 12–15 August 1986, p. 54; Aderholt, interview by Trest, 18 April 1996, p. 16.

21. Aderholt, interview by Trest, 15 August 1995, p. 15.

22. Ibid., p 16; Aderholt, interview by Ahmann, 12–15 August 1986, pp. 60–61.

23. Aderholt, interview by Ahmann, 12–15 August 1986, pp. 60–61.

24. Colonel James W. Bothwell, Officer Effectiveness Report, Major Harry C. Aderholt, HQ USAFE, Aderholt Collection, AFHRA, 19 June 1957; Aderholt, interview by Trest, 15 August 1995, p. 14.

25. Aderholt, audiotape, April 1997, p. 2.

26. Ibid.

27. John Ranelagh, *CIA, A History* (London: BBC Books, 1992), 70, 71.

28. Ibid.

29. Nelson Lichtenstein, ed., *Political Profiles: The Kennedy Years* (New York: Facts on File, 1976), 496.

30. Futrell, *Ideas, Concepts, Doctrine*, 610–17; James, *Historical Highlights*, 40.

31. Futrell, *Ideas, Concepts, Doctrine,* 618–29.

32. Aderholt, official biography, 1 July 1975; Aderholt, interview by Trest, 15 August 1995, pp. 16–19.

33. Colonel Lawrence Ropka Jr., interview by Warren Trest, pp. 1–4, Aderholt Collection, AFHRA, 12 October 1996.

4. Shadow Wars and the Tibetan Airlift

1. Aderholt, interview by Ahmann, 12–15 August 1986, p. 27; Aderholt, interview by Trest, 15 August 1995, p. 17.

2. Aderholt, interview by Ahmann, 12–15 August 1986, p. 27; Aderholt, interview by Trest, 15 August 1995, p. 17; Willam M. Leary, ed., *The Central Intelligence Agency: History and Documents* (Tuscaloosa.: University of Alabama Press, 1984), 70.

3. Leary, *Central Intelligence Agency*, 55, 75, 76.

4. Mike Meserole, ed., *The 1994 Information Please Sports Almanac* (Boston: Houghton Mifflin, 1994), 97.

5. Aderholt, interview by Ahmann, 12–15 August 1986, p. 59.

6. Bothwell, Officer Effectiveness Report, Major Harry C. Aderholt, Aderholt Collection, AFHRA, 19 June 1957.

7. Aderholt, audiotape, April 1997, p. 2.

8. Bothwell, Officer Effectiveness Report, 19 June 1957; Bothwell, Officer Effectiveness Report, Major Aderholt, 2 February 1957; Lieutenant Colonel Robert O.

Fricks, Officer Effectiveness Report, Major Aderholt, 17 February 1956; Lieutenant Colonel John P. Remaklus, Officer Effectiveness Report, Major Aderholt, 20 October 1954. Aderholt Collection, AFHRA.

9. Ropka, interview by Trest, 12 October 1996, pp. 3, 4.
10. Colonel Carl E. Zeigler, recollections of Harry C. Aderholt, Aderholt Collecton, AFHRA, 20 June 1994.
11. Ibid.
12. Aderholt, interview by Ahmann, 12–15 August 1986, pp. 5, 6, 8.
13. Richard M. Bissell Jr., endorsement to Major Harry C. Aderholt's Officer Effectiveness Report, Aderholt Collection, AFHRA, 18 August 1959.
14. Aderholt, interview by Ahmann, 12–15 August 1986, pp. 75, 76, 79; Harry C. Aderholt interview by William M. Leary, Aderholt Collection, AFHRA, August 28–30, 1990, pp. 6, 7.
15. Lynn L. Bollinger, recollections of Harry C. Aderholt, Aderholt Collection, AFHRA, 7 March 1994.
16. Aderholt, interview by Trest, 17, 18 April 96, p. 15; Aderholt, audiotape, April 1997, p. 2.
17. Aderholt, interview by Ahmann, 12–15 August 1986, pp. 76, 80; Aderholt, interview by Leary, 28–30 August 1990, p. 6; Final report, operational test and evaluation U-10 in Republic of Vietnam, by HQ Second Air Division, Aderholt Collection, AFHRA, 1 June 1963; Aderholt, interview by Trest, 15 August 1995, pp. 17, 18.
18. Aderholt, audiotape, April 1997, p. 3; Aderholt, statement to Trest, 10 July 1998.
19. Aderholt statement to Trest, 10 July 1998.
20. Ibid.
21. Aderholt, audiotape, April 1997, p. 3; Aderholt, interview by Trest, 15 August 1995, pp. 18, 20.
22. Aderholt, interview by Trest, 15 August 1995, p. 12.
23. Aderholt, interview by Trest, 18 April 1996, p. 15; William M. Leary, "Robert Fulton's Skyhook and Operation Coldfeet," *Studies in Intelligence* (Spring 1994): 69 (Aderholt Collection, AFHRA).
24. Ranelagh, *CIA*, 105; Taylor, *Asia and the Pacific*, 543; Aderholt, interview by Trest, 18 April 1996, p. 35; William M. Leary, Notes on Indonesia, Aderholt Collection, AFHRA, 1993, p. 3.
25. Ranelagh, *CIA*, 105; Taylor, *Asia and the Pacific*, 543; Aderholt, interview by Trest, 18 April 1996, p. 35; Leary, Notes on Indonesia, 3.
26. Leary, Notes on Indonesia, 4, 7; Dan Hagedorn and Leif Hellstrom, *Foreign Invaders: The Douglas Invader in Foreign Military and U.S. Clandestine Service* (Leicester, UK: Midland Publishing, 1994), 124.
27. Aderholt, interview by Ahmann, 12–15 August 1986, pp. 62, 63.
28. Aderholt, interview by Ahmann, 12–15 August 1986, pp. 63, 92, 93; Aderholt, interview by Trest, 18 April 1996, p. 35.
29. Aderholt, interview by Trest, 15 August 1995, p. 17.

30. Ibid.; Ranelagh, *CIA*, 82–91.
31. Aderholt, interview by Trest, 15 August 1995, p. 17; Aderholt, interview by Trest, 11 October 1997.
32. Aderholt, interview by Ahmann, 12–15 August 1986, p. 59.
33. Aderholt, interview by Trest, 18 April 1996, p. 34.
34. Ropka, interview by Trest, 12 October 1996, p. 1; Aderholt, interview by Ahmann, 12–15 August 1986, p. 65.
35. Ed Smith, interview by Dr. William M. Leary, Aderholt Collection, AFHRA, undated, p. 3.
36. Colonel Robert White, audiotape, Aderholt Collection, AFHRA, undated, pp. 1, 2.
37. Aderholt, interview by Trest, 11 October 1997, p. 2.
38. White, audiotape, 2.
39. Ropka, interview by Trest, 12 October 1996, p. 1.
40. Ibid.; Aderholt, interview by Trest, 11 October 1997, pp. 1, 2; Aderholt, interview by Ahmann, 12–15 August 1986, p. 65.
41. Aderholt, interview by Trest, 11 October 1997, pp. 1, 2; Haas and Robinson, *Air Commando!* 30–31.
42. Ropka, interview by Trest, 12 October 1996, p. 2.
43. Ibid.
44. Aderholt, interview by Trest, 11 October 1997, p. 1.
45. Ibid., pp. 1, 2.
46. Ibid., pp. 2, 3.
47. Ibid., p. 1.
48. Ibid., p. 3.
49. Ibid.; White, audiotape, 3.
50. Aderholt, interview by Trest, 11 October 1997, pp. 1, 2.
51. Ibid.
52. Haas and Robinson, *Air Commando!* 28, 29; Ropka, interview by Trest, 12 October 1996, pp. 29, 30; Evan Thomas, *The Very Best Men* (New York: Simon and Schuster, 1995), 275–78.
53. Ropka, interview by Trest, 12 October 1996, pp. 29, 30.
54. Ibid.
55. Thomas, *Very Best Men*, 275–78.
56. Ibid., Haas and Robinson, *Air Commando!* 30–31.
57. Thomas, *Very Best Men*, 275–78; Haas and Robinson, *Air Commando!* 30–31.
58. Aderholt, interview by Ahmann, 12–15 August 1986, pp. 65, 66; Aderholt, interview by Trest, 11 October 1997, p. 4.
59. Aderholt, interview by Trest, 11 October 1997, p. 5; Ropka, interview by Trest, 12 October 1996, p. 5.
60. Aderholt, interview by Trest, 11 October 1997, p. 5; Ropka, interview by Trest, 12 October 1996, p. 5; Major General Baginski, recollections of Harry C. Aderholt, Aderholt Collection, AFHRA, 12 July 1994; Brigadier General Theodore Kershaw,

official Air Force biography, Secretary of the Air Force Public Affairs, July 1962; Major General James I. Baginski, official Air Force biography, Secretary of the Air Force Public Affairs, November 1981.

61. Ropka, interview by Trest, 12 October 1996, p. 6; Aderholt, statement to Trest, 7 February 1998; William M. Leary, "Secret Mission to Tibet" *(Smithsonian) Air & Space* (January 1998): 62–71 (Aderholt Collection, AFHRA).
62. Smith, interview by William M. Leary, Aderholt Collection, AFHRA, undated, p. 4.
63. White, audiotape, 4.
64. Ropka, interview by Trest, p. 6; Aderholt, interview by Trest, 11 October 1997, p. 9; Kershaw, official biography, July 1962.
65. White, audiotape, 5.
66. Ropka, interview by Trest, 12 October 1996, p. 6; Aderholt, inerview by Trest, 11 October 1997, p. 10.
67. Ibid.
68. Ibid.
69. Ibid.
70. Aderholt, interview by Leary, 28–30 August 1990, p. 10; Aderholt, statement to Trest, 15 April 1997.
71. Ropka, interview by Trest, 12 October 1996, p. 5.
72. Thomas, *Very Best Men*, 278; Aderholt, interview by Ahmann, 12–15 August 1986, pp. 106, 107.
73. Aderholt, interview by Trest, 11 October 1997, pp. 3, 10; Haas and Robinson, *Air Commando!* 30, 31.

5. The Secret War in Laos

1. Kenneth Conboy, *Shadow War: The CIA's Secret War in Laos* (Boulder, Colo.: Paladin Press, 1995), 25.
2. *Brief History*, p. 3; George F. Lemmer, *The Laos Crisis of 1959* (Washington, D.C.: USAF Historical Division Liaison Office, 1961), 9.
3. Lemmer, *Laos Crisis*, 16–18, 37–39; Roger Warner, *Back Fire: The CIA's Secret War in Laos and Its Link to the War in Vietnam* (New York: Simon and Schuster, 1995), 7.
4. Lemmer, *Laos Crisis*, 39–49.
5. Ibid., 52, 53, 61.
6. Aderholt, interview by Trest, 11 October 1997.
7. Ibid.
8. Conboy, *Shadow War*, 21; Shelby L. Stanton, *Green Berets at War: U.S. Army Special Forces in Southeast Asia, 1956–1975* (Novato, Calif.: Presidio Press, 1985), 3, 17.
9. Aderholt, interview by Trest, 11 October 1997.
10. Fact Sheet on Takhli Royal Thai Air Force Base, by History Office, HQ 13AF, Aderholt Collection, AFHRA, 12 August 1976; Hagedorn and Hellstrom, *Foreign Invaders*, 132, 133; *A Brief History*, 4.

11. Ropka, interview by Trest, 12 October 1996, p. 4.

12. Aderholt, interview by Trest, 11 October 1997, p. 7.

13. White, audiotape, 7; Aderholt, interview by Ahmann, 12–15 August 1986, pp. 99, 100.

14. Aderholt, interview by Trest, 11 October 1997, p. 5.

15. Ibid.; Conboy, *Shadow War,* 25.

16. Aderholt, statement to Warren Trest, 15 November 1997; Conboy, *Shadow War,* 26; Harry Clay Aderholt, Pilot Individual Flight Record, March, April, May 1960.

17. Aderholt, interview by Ahmann, 12–15 August 1986, pp. 76, 77; Harry Clay Aderholt, Pilot Individual Flight Record, February 1960.

18. Aderholt, interview by Ahmann, 12–15 August 1986, pp. 76, 77; Aderholt, statement to Warren Trest, 7 February 1998.

19. Ropka, interview by Trest, 12 October 1996, p. 6.

20. Aderholt, statement to Trest, 11 July 1998.

21. Ibid.

22. Conboy, *Shadow War,* 31–35; Castle, *At War in the Shadow of Vietnam,* 20–22; Captain Peter A. W. Liebchen, *MAP Aid to Laos, 1959–1972* (Tan Son Nhut AB, Republic of Vietnam: Project CHECO study, HQ 7AF, 25 June 1973), AFHRA File K717.0141-40, pp. 9,10; Arthur C. O'Neill, *Fifth Air Force in the Southeast Asia Crisis of 1960–1961* (Fuchu AB, Japan: HQ 5AF History Division, 8 June 1961), AFHRA File K730.04- 22, p. 3.

23. Conboy, *Shadow War,* 37, 38; Castle, *At War in the Shadow of Vietnam,* 23; Roger Warner, *Shooting at the Moon: The Story of America's Clandestine War in Laos* (South Royalton, Vt.: Steerforth Press, 1996), 8.

24. Conboy, *Shadow War,* 47–50; Castle, *At War in the Shadow of Vietnam,* 24, 25; Liebchen, *Map Aid to Laos,* 11–13; O'Neill, *Fifth Air Force,* 5–7.

25. Conboy, *Shadow War,* 47–50; Castle, *At War in the Shadow of Vietnam,* 24, 25; Liebchen, *Map Aid to Laos,* 11–13; O'Neill, *Fifth Air Force,* 5–7.

26. Conboy, *Shadow War,* 54, 55; Castle, *At War in the Shadow of Vietnam,* 41, 42.

27. Conboy, *Shadow War,* 35, 36.

28. Conboy, *Shadow War,* 45, 47, 48, 49, 51; Castle, *At War in the Shadow of Vietnam,* 25, 29.

29. Conboy, *Shadow War,* 51; Hagedorn and Hellstrom, *Foreign Invaders,* 132, 133.

30. Conboy, *Shadow War,* 51; Hagedorn and Hellstrom, *Foreign Invaders,* 132, 133.

31. Ropka, interview by Trest, 12 October 1996, p. 6.

32. Smith, interview by Leary, undated, p. 13; John L. Plaster, *SOG: The Secret Wars of America's Commandos in Vietnam* (New York: Simon and Schuster, 1997), 21.

33. Smith, interview by Leary, undated, p. 13; Plaster, *SOG,* 21.

34. White, audiotape, 9, 13; see Roger Warner's *Shooting at the Moon,* 46, 47, for a more detailed account of this incident.

35. Aderholt, interview by Ahmann, 12–15 August 1986, p. 67.

36. Ibid.

37. Ibid., 68.

38. Ibid.; General Emmett O'Donnell Jr., official USAF biography, Secretary of the Air Force Public Affairs, undated.
39. Lieutenant Colonel Warren Aderholt, interview by Warren Trest, Aderholt Collection, AFHRA, 10 October 96, p. 4; Aderholt, interview by Trest, 15 August 1995, pp. 21, 22.
40. Haas and Robinson, *Air Commando!* 33; Aderholt, interview by Ahmann, 12–15 August 1986, pp. 84, 85.
41. Aderholt, interview by Trest, 15 August 95, pp. 21, 22.
42. Conboy, *Shadow War*, 52; Castle, *At War in the Shadow of Vietnam*, 35; Hagedorn and Hellstrom, *Foreign Invaders*, 134.
43. Conboy, *Shadow War*, 52; Castle, *At War in the Shadow of Vietnam*, 35; Hagedorn and Hellstrom, *Foreign Invaders*, 134.
44. Conboy, *Shadow War*, 52; Castle, *At War in the Shadow of Vietnam*, 35; Hagedorn and Hellstrom, *Foreign Invaders*, 134.
45. Haas and Robinson, *Air Commando!* 32–37; David L. Langford, "Pilot Recalls Futility of Air Battle," *Las Vegas Review-Journal*, 13 April 1986.
46. Haas and Robinson, *Air Commando!* 32–37; Langford, "Pilot Recalls"; Aderholt, interview by Ahmann, 12–15 August 1986, p. 86; Hagedorn and Hellstrom, *Foreign Invaders,* 126–33.
47. Haas and Robinson, *Air Commando!* 32–37; Langford, "Pilot Recalls"; Aderholt, interview by Ahmann, 12–15 August 1986, p. 86; Hagedorn and Hellstrom, *Foreign Invaders,* 126–33.
48. Lieutenant Colonel Warren Aderholt, interview by Trest, 10 October 96, p. 5.
49. Conboy, *Shadow War,* 61, 62; Christopher Robbins, *The Ravens: The Men Who Flew in America's Secret War in Laos* (Atlanta: EAPLS, 1995), 100; Aderholt, interview by Ahmann, 12–15 August 86, p. 81. Robbins's book and the interview with General Aderholt both state that the message ordering the airdrop of weapons came on Christmas Day, 1960. Conboy's book places the date of the airdrop in early January, which General Aderholt agrees is probably correct.
50. Warner, *Shooting at the Moon*, 16, 17.
51. Ibid., 26–31; Conboy, *Shadow War*, 60.
52. John M. Newman, *JFK and Vietnam* (New York: Warner Books, 1992), 24–41; Conboy, *Shadow War,* 62, 65.
53. Conboy, *Shadow War,* 65, 66, 88, 90, 91.
54. Aderholt, interview by Ahmann, 12–15 August 1986, p. 91.
55. Conboy, *Shadow War,* 63; Aderholt, interview by Ahmann, 12–15 August 1986, pp. 77, 78, 94.
56. Conboy, *Shadow War,* 63; Aderholt, interview by Ahmann, 12–15 August 1986, pp. 95, 96, 125.
57. Conboy, *Shadow War,* 63; Aderholt, interview by Ahmann, 12–15 August 1986, pp. 95, 96, 125.
58. Castle, *At War in the Shadow of Vietnam*, 45, 46.

59. King, audiotape, 3, 4.
60. Robert F. Futrell, *The Advisory Years to 1965* (Washington, D.C.: Office of Air Force History, 1981), 79; Futrell, *Ideas, Concepts, Doctrine*, vol. 2, p. 257.
61. Futrell, *Advisory Years,* 79; Futrell, *Ideas, Concepts, Doctrine*, vol. 2, p. 257.
62. Lichtenstein, *Political Profiles,* 496; Futrell, *Ideas, Concepts, Doctrine*, vol. 2, p. 447; Aderholt, interview by Ahmann, 12–15 August 1986.
63. Colonel Bob Gleason, recollections, Aderholt Collection, AFHRA, 28 March 1994.
64. White, audiotape, p. 10.
65. Ibid.
66. Gleason, recollections, 28 March 1994.
67. Aderholt, interview by Ahmann, 12–15 August 1986, pp. 117, 124; Major General Rollen H. Anthis, official USAF biography, Secretary of the Air Force Public Affairs, 15 October 1972.
68. Aderholt, interview by Ahmann, 12–15 August 1986, p. 124; Gleason, recollections.
69. Aderholt, interview by Ahmann, 12–15 August 1986, p. 70.

6. The Air Commandos: A Breed Apart

1. Aderholt, interview by Ahmann, 12–15 August 1986, p. 144.
2. John R. Alison, biographical sketch, Aderholt Collection, AFHRA, AO 328165, undated; Chinnery, *Any Time, Any Place,* 17–58.
3. Aderholt, interview by Ahmann, p. 225.
4. Aderholt, interview by Trest, 15 August 1995, p. 24; Brigadier General Gilbert L. Pritchard, endorsement to Officer Effectiveness Report, Colonel Aderholt, Aderholt Collection, AFHRA, 30 March 1964; Officer Military Record, Colonel Aderholt, Aderholt Collection, AFHRA, 30 May 1967.
5. Herbert H. Kisling, *An Air Commando and Special Operations Chronology, 1961–1991* (Hurlburt Field, Fla.: n.p., n.d.), 26 (Aderholt Collection, AFHRA); "Air Commando Force to Be Increased," *Air Force News Service,* 11 January 1963.
6. "Air Commandos Have Busy Year," *Journal & Register,* 21 December 1963; Commander's Appraisal in History, Special Air Warfare Center, July-December 1963, AFHRA File K417.0731, pp. 1–3.
7. Kisling, *Air Commando,* 31; Momyer, *Air Power in Three Wars,* 13; Futrell, *Ideas, Concepts, Doctrine*, vol. 2, p. 259.
8. Aderholt, interview by Ahmann, 12–15 August 1986, pp. 208, 209.
9. Ibid.
10. Charles H. Hildreth, *USAF Counterinsurgency Doctrines and Capabilities, 1961–1962* (Washington, D.C.: USAF Historical Division, 1964), 39.
11. Charles H. Hildreth, *USAF Special Air Warfare Doctrines and Capabilities, 1963* (Washington, D.C.: USAF Historical Division, 1964), 1–16.

12. Aderholt, interview by Ahmann, 12–15 August 1986, p. 126; Kisling, *Air Commando,* 34, 37.
13. Kisling, *Air Commando,* 24, 51; Aderholt, interview by Ahmann, 12–15 August 1986, p. 133.
14. Kisling, *Air Commando,* 39.
15. Hildreth, *USAF Special Air*, 51; Aderholt, interview by Ahmann, 12–15 August, p. 145.
16. Kisling, *Air Commando,* 9–15; Gleason, recollections, 28 March 1994.
17. Brigadier General Benjamin H. King, official USAF biography, Secretary of the Air Force Public Affairs, 15 March 1969; Aderholt, interview by Ahmann, 12–15 August 1986, p. 148.
18. King, audiotape, June 1994.
19. Colonel William C. Thomas, recollections of Harry C. Aderholt, Aderholt Collection, AFHRA, 10 February 1997.
20. Ibid.
21. Aderholt, interview by Ahmann, 12–15 August 1986, pp. 82, 83, 147, 148. For coverage of the Howze Board, see Lieutenant General John J. Tolson, *Airmobility, 1961–1971* (Washington, D.C.: Department of the Army, 1973), 20–24.
22. Aderholt, interview by Ahmann, 12–15 August 1986, pp. 126, 127, 146; J. Farmer and M. J. Strumwasser, *The Evolution of the Airborne Forward Air Controller: An Analysis of Mosquito Operations in Korea* (Santa Monica: Rand Corporation, 1967), 79, 84; Major James B. Overton, *FAC Operations in Close Air Support Role in SVN*, HQ PACAF, Project CHECO, AFHRA File K717.0413-45, 1969, p. 1.
23. Farmer and Strumwasser, *Evolution of the Airborne*, 79; Aderholt, interview by Ahmann, 12–15 August 1986, pp. 126, 127, 146.
24. Lieutenant General James H. Ahmann, official USAF biography, Secretary of the Air Force Public Affairs, April 1982; Kisling, *Air Commando*, 25, 33; Aderholt, interview by Ahmann, 12–15 August 1986, pp. 119, 120; Aderholt, interview by Trest, 15 August 1995, pp. 25, 26.
25. Ahmann, official biography; Kisling, *Air Commando*, 25, 33; Aderholt, interview by Ahmann, 12–15 August 1986, pp. 119, 120; Aderholt, interview by Trest, 15 August 1995, pp. 25, 26.
26. Aderholt, interview by Trest, 15 August 1995, p. 26; Major General Richard V. Secord, interview by Warren Trest, Aderholt Collection, AFHRA, 14 October 1996.
27. Aderholt, interview by Trest, 15 August 1995, p. 26.
28. History of Special Air Warfare Center, January-June 1964, AFHRA File K417.9731, pp. 3, 84; Major General Pritchard to HQ TAC (DPLMO), General Officer Job Description, 16 April 1964; Major General Gilbert L. Pritchard, endorsement to Officer Effectiveness Report, Colonel Aderholt, Aderholt Collection, AFHRA, 17 August 1965.
29. Aderholt, interview by Trest, 15 August 1995, p. 27; Major General Leroy W. Svendsen Jr., official USAF biography, Secretary of the Air Force Public Affairs,

undated; Major General L. W. Svendsen Jr., recollections of Harry C. Aderholt, Aderholt Collection, AFHRA, 21 March 1994.

30. Major General Richard V. Secord, official USAF biography, Secretary of the Air Force Public Affairs, February 1982; Aderholt, interview by Trest, 15 August 1995, p. 26; Sid Marshall, recollections of Harry C. Aderholt, Aderholt Collection, AFHRA, undated.

31. Secord, official biography; Aderholt, interview by Trest, 15 August 1995, p. 26; Marshall, recollections.

32. Aderholt, interview by Trest, 15 August 1995, p. 26; Secord, *Honored and Betrayed*, 393.

33. Aderholt, interview by Trest, 15 August 1995, p. 28.

34. Ibid., 29.

35. Ibid., 204, 205.

36. Chief Master Sergeant Roland H. "Hap" Lutz, interview by Warren Trest, Aderholt Collection, AFHRA, 17 February 1997.

37. Ibid.

38. Colonel Jimmy A. Ifland, interview by Warren Trest, Aderholt Collection, AFHRA, 18 February 1997.

39. Ibid.

40. Ibid.

41. Kisling, *Air Commando*, 53; Aderholt, interview by Ahmann, 12–15 August 1986, pp. 167, 168.

42. Aderholt, statement to Warren Trest, 24 January 1998.

43. Conboy, *Shadow War*, 99–102, 105–8.

44. Newman, *JFK and Vietnam*, 388–415, 451–60.

45. Conboy, *Shadow War*, 108; Aderholt, statement to Trest, 24 January 1998; Kisling, *Air Commando*, 46.

46. Kisling, *Air Commando*, 46; Operation Order 4-64 (Revised), Water Pump, Special Air Warfare Center, Eglin AFB, Fla., 25 November 1964; History of Special Air Warfare Center, July-December 1964, AFHRA File K417.0731, p. 62; Aderholt, interview by Ahman, 12–15 August 1986, p. 272.

47. Lieutenant Colonel Drexel B. Cochran, interview by Captain R. B. Clement, USAF Oral History Collection, Maxwell AFB, Ala., AFHRA File K239.0512-217, 20 August 1969; Conboy, *Shadow War*, 159.

48. Cochran, interview by Clement, 20 August 1969.

49. Ibid.

50. Conboy, *Shadow War*, 108–59; Jacob Van Staaveren, *Interdiction in Southern Laos, 1960–1968* (Washington, D.C: Center for Air Force History, 1993), 23, 24.

51. Cochran, interview by Clement.

52. Lutz, interview by Trest, 17 February 1997.

53. History of Special Air Warfare Center, January-June 1965, AFHRA File K417.0731, p. 76.

54. Lieutenant Colonel Drexel B. Cochran, interview by William Leary, Aderholt Collection, AFHRA, 17 November 1990.

55. Van Staaveren, *Interdiction*, 25–27; John Schlight, *The Years of the Offensive, 1965–1968* (Washington, D.C.: Office of Air Force History, 1988), 4, 5.

56. Farmer and Strumwasser, *Airborne Forward Air Controller*, 79, 84.

57. Aderholt, interview by Ahmann, 12–15 August 1986, p. 127.

58. Ibid., 162.

59. Ibid.

60. Ibid.

61. Ibid., 163, 164.

62. Ibid., 128; Charles Jones, interview by Warren Trest, Aderholt Collection, AFHRA, 17 February 1997.

63. Aderholt, interview by Ahmann, 12–15 August 1986, p. 128; Jones, interview by Trest, 17 February 1997.

64. Major General Charles R. Bond Jr., official USAF biography, Secretary of the Air Force Public Affairs, 15 October 1967; Ropka, interview by Trest, 12 October 1996, p. 11.

65. Ropka, interview by Trest, 12 October 1996, pp. 11, 39; History of Special Air Warfare Center, July-December 1964, AFHRA File K417.0731, p. 84.

66. History of Special Air Warfare Center, July-December 1964, pp. 81, 82.

67. Ropka, interview by Trest, 12 October 1996, p. 37.

68. Ibid., p. 38.

69. Ibid.

70. Ibid.; History of Special Air Warfare Center, July-December 1964, p. 83.

71. Ropka, interview by Trest, 12 October 1996, p. 39.

72. History of Special Air Warfare Center, July-December 1964, p. 84.

73. Lutz, interview by Trest, 17 February 1997; History of Special Air Warfare Center, July-December 1963, AFHRA File K417.0731, p. 99.

74. History of Special Air Warfare Center, July-December 1964, pp. 86, 87.

75. Colonel Joseph W. Kittinger, audiotape, Aderholt Collection, AFHRA, undated; Ropka, interview by Trest, 12 October 1996, pp. 8, 9.

76. Kittinger, audiotape; Ropka, interview by Trest, 12 October 1996, pp. 8, 9.

77. Kittinger, audiotape; Ropka, interview by Trest, 12 October, pp. 8, 9.

78. Kittinger, audiotape.

79. Aderholt, statement to Warren Trest, 3 April 1998.

80. General David M. Shoup, "The New American Militarism," *The Atlantic Monthly*, April 1969, pp. 51–56.

81. H. R. McMaster, *Dereliction of Duty* (New York: Harper Collins, 1997), 82, 83; General Jacob E. Smart, official USAF biography, Secretary of the Air Force Public Affairs, undated; General Hunter Harris, official USAF biography, Secretary of the Air Force Public Affairs, 15 December 1965; General Jacob E. Smart, interview by Lieutenant Colonel Arthur McCants and Dr. James Haasdorf, USAF Oral History Collection, AFHRA file K239.0512-1108, 27–30 November 1978, pp. 313, 314

82. Aderholt, interview by Ahmann, 12–15 August 1986, p. 121; Secord, interview by Trest, 14 October 1996, p. 4.
83. Aderholt, interview by Ahmann, 12–15 August 1986, pp. 121, 211; W. B. Graham and A. H. Katz, "SIAT: The Single Integrated Attack Team: A Concept for Offensive Military Operations in South Vietnam," RAND Corporation, AFHRA File K146.003-69, December 1964.
84. Secord, interview by Trest, 14 October 1996, p. 5.
85. Colonel John A. Doonan, recollections of Harry C. Aderholt, Aderholt Collection, AFHRA, undated.
86. Ibid.
87. Ifland, interview by Trest, 18 February 1997, pp. 6, 7.
88. Aderholt, interview by Ahmann, 12–15 August 1986, p. 194; Aderholt, interview by Trest, 15 August 1995, p. 30.
89. Kisling, *Air Commando*, 64; Aderholt, interview by Ahmann, 12–15 August 1986, p. 194.
90. Aderholt, interview by Ahmann, 12–15 August 1986, p. 194.
91. Major General Gilbert L. Pritchard to Colonel William C. Thomas, Aderholt Collection, AFHRA, 18 April 1966.
92. Aderholt, interview by Ahmann, 12–15 August 1986, p. 226.

7. Faces of a Misbegotten War

1. General Hunter Harris, official USAF biography, Secretary of the Air Force Public Affairs, 15 December 1965; HQ PACAF, Hickam AFB, Hawaii, background paper on General Hunter Harris, January 1967.
2. Aderholt, interview by Ahmann, 12–15 August 1986, pp. 196, 226; Aderholt, interview by Trest, 15 August 1995, p. 31.
3. Aderholt, interview by Ahmann, 12–15 August 1986, pp. 196, 226; Aderholt, interview by Trest, 15 August 1995, p. 31; Lieutenant General James W. Wilson, official USAF biography, 30 January 1968. In his autobiography, General Chuck Yeager said that General Wilson was effective, but "everyone, including yours truly, was scared to death of him."
4. Aderholt, interview by Trest, 15 August 1995, p. 31.
5. Harry R. Fletcher, *Air Force Bases Outside the United States* (Washington, D.C.: Center for Air Force History, 1993), 24.
6. Aderholt, interview by Ahmann, 12–15 August 1986, p. 197.
7. Ibid.; Chronology of Thirteenth Air Force, 1965–1968, History Office, Clark AB, the Philippines, AFHRA File K750.01, undated, p. 149.
8. Major Arthur E. "Gene" Overton, recollections of Harry C. Aderholt, Aderholt Collection, AFHRA, 14 June 1994.
9. Ibid.; Aderholt, interview by Ahmann, 12–15 August 1986, p. 197; History of 6200th Combat Support Group, January-June 1966, Clark AFB, the Philippines, AFHRA File K-GP-6200-H1, pp. 121, 122.

10. Aderholt, interview by Ahmann, 12–15 August 1986, p. 198.

11. Ibid., 200.

12. Ibid., 198; History of 6200th Combat Support Group, January-June 1966, pp. 111–13.

13. Aderholt, interview by Ahmann, 12–15 August 1986, pp. 199, 200.

14. Ibid., 202, 203.

15. "A Demand for Heroes," *Time*, 7 January 1966, p. 26; "Crusade in Manila," *Time*, 4 February 1966, p. 27; Colonel Harry L. Waesche, Officer Effectiveness Report, Colonel Harry C. Aderholt, Aderholt Collection, AFHRA, 29 July 1966.

16. Waesche, Officer Effectiveness Report, Aderholt, 29 July 1966.

17. Chief Master Sergeant Roland H. "Hap" Lutz, audiotape, Aderholt Collection, AFHRA, undated.

18. Ibid.

19. Ibid.

20. Colonel William C. Thomas, recollections of Harry C. Aderholt, Aderholt Collection, AFHRA, 10 March 1997.

21. Ibid.

22. Aderholt, interview by Ahmann, 12–15 August 1986, p. 226; Aderholt, interview by Trest, 15 August 1995, p. 32.

23. Aderholt, interview by Ahmann, 12–15 August 1986, p. 226; Aderholt, interview by Trest, 15 August 1995, p. 32; Plaster, *SOG*, 23.

24. Aderholt, interview by Ahmann, 12–15 August 1986, p. 227; Aderholt, interview by Trest, 15 August 1995, p. 32; George J. Veith, *Code-Name Bright Light* (New York: Free Press, 1998), 104. Veith's book gives John's rank as brigadier general. According to his official biography, John was not promoted to brigadier general until three years later, in 1969.

25. Waesche, Officer Effectiveness Report, Aderholt, 29 July 1966.

26. Aderholt, interview by Trest, 15 August 1995, p. 32; Veith, *Code-Name Bright,* 105.

27. Aderholt, interview by Trest, 15 August 1995, p. 32; Veith, *Code-Name Bright,* 105; Peter Braestrup, *Big Story* (Novato, Calif.: Presidio, 1994), 94.

28. Aderholt, interview by Trest, 15 August 1995, p. 32; Veith, *Code-Name Bright,* 105; Braestrup, *Big Story*, 94.

29. Aderholt, statement to Trest, 24 January 1998.

30. Ibid.; Aderholt, interview by Ahmann, 12–15 August 1986, pp. 135, 210.

31. Aderholt, statement to Trest, 24 January 1998; Aderholt, interview by Ahmann, 12–15 August 1986, pp. 135, 210; Veith, *Code-Name Bright*, 105.

32. Veith, *Code-Name Bright*, 105; History of Joint Personnel Recovery Center, 1966, Appendix 5 to History of HQ U.S. Military Assistance Command Vietnam, Aderholt Collection AFHRA, 1966, p. 117; Edward P. Brynn and Arthur P. Geesey, *Joint Personnel Recovery in Southeast Asia*, HQ PACAF, Project CHECO, AFHRA File K717.0414-58, 1 September 1976, p. 7.

33. Aderholt, statement to Trest, 24 January 1998; General William W. Momyer, offi-

cial USAF biography, Secretary of the Air Force Public Affairs, 1 May 1971; Momyer, *Air Power in Three Wars*, 107, 108.

34. General William W. Momyer to Major General R. H. Ellis, Momyer Corona Harvest Files, Maxwell AB, Ala., AFHRA, 22 July 1969; "7th AF Rules out Special Headgear," *Air Force Times*, 5 October 1966, p. 5; "Airmen Reconciled to Aussie Hat Ban," *Air Force Times*, 3 May 1967, p. 16; General William W. Momyer to Brigadier General Robert L. Cardenas, Momyer Corona Harvest Files, Maxwell AFB, Ala., AFHRA, 17 December 1968.

35. Colonel Gordon F. Bradburn, "Air Commandos' Successors," *Air Force Magazine*, October 1992, p. 6.

36. Personal observations by the author, who was a civilian historian at HQ 7AF in Vietnam during the two years (1966–68) General Momyer was commander.

37. Lieutenant General John P. Flynn, official USAF biography, Secretary of the Air Force Public Affairs, February 1977; Lieutenant General John P. Flynn, interview by Lieutenant Colonel Arthur W. McCants Jr., USAF Oral History Collection, AFHRA File K239.0512-1187, 28–31 January and 1 February 1980, pp. 256, 257.

38. Flynn, interview by McCants, p. 258.

39. Aderholt, statement to Trest, 24 January 1998.

40. Lieutenant Colonel Lester Hansen, recollections of Harry C. Aderholt, Aderholt Collection, AFHRA, undated.

41. Ibid.

42. Plaster, *SOG*, 30,31; Veith, *Code-Name Bright*, xv.

43. Veith, *Code-Name Bright*, 109; Joint Personnel Recovery Center, 119.

44. Veith, *Code-Name Bright*, 109; Joint Personnel Recovery Center, 119.

45. Veith, *Code-Name Bright*, 109; Joint Personnel Recovery Center, 119; Plaster, *SOG*, 30, 31; on page 60 of *SOG* the USN pilot's name appears as Lieutenant Dean Woods, though his name is given as Lieutenant Robert Woods in Veith, *Code-Name Bright*, 109.

46. Veith, *Code-Name Bright*, xiii, xiv; Plaster, *SOG*, 63; Aderholt, statement to Trest, 24 January 1998.

47. Veith, *Code-Name Bright*, xiii, xiv; Plaster, *SOG*, 63; Aderholt, statement to Trest, 24 January 1998; Joint Personnel Recovery Center, 118.

48. Veith, *Code-Name Bright*, xii; Aderholt, statement to Trest, 24 January 1998.

49. Aderholt, interview by Ahmann, 12–15 August 1986, p. 228; Plaster, *SOG*, 64.

50. Aderholt, interview by Ahmann, 12–15 August 1986, p. 228; Plaster, *SOG*, 64; Joint Personnel Recovery Center, 118.

51. Veith, *Code-Name Bright*, xvi; Aderholt, statement to Trest, 24 January 1998.

52. Aderholt, audiotape, 15 April 1997; Aderholt, interview by Trest, 15 August 1995, p. 34.

53. Veith, *Code-Name Bright*, xvi; Plaster, *SOG*, 65.

54. Veith, *Code-Name Bright*, xvi; Plaster, *SOG*, 65; Joint Personnel Recovery Center, 118.

55. Plaster, *SOG*, 65, 66.
56. Ibid.; Veith, *Code-Name Bright*, 161–63.
57. General William C. Westmoreland, *A Soldier Reports* (Garden City, N.Y.: Doubleday, 1976), 309.
58. Aderholt, interview by Ahmann, 12–15 August 1986, pp. 229, 230. For a discussion of short rounds, see John Schlight's *The Years of the Offensive*, pp 258-61.
59. Ibid.
60. Momyer, *Air Power in Three Wars*, pp 65-99; Schlight, *Years of the Offensive*, 139–65.
61. Momyer, *Air Power in Three Wars*, 107, 108.
62. Aderholt, interview by Ahmann, 12–15 August 1986, pp. 252, 253.
63. Ibid.; Aderholt, statement to Trest, 24 January 1998.
64. Aderholt, interview by Ahmann, 12–15 August 1986; Aderholt, statement to Trest, 24 January 1998.
65. General Chuck Yeager and Leo Janos, *Yeager: An Autobiography* (New York: Bantam Books, 1985), 379–81, 386–89.
66. Lieutenant General John A. Heintges, Officer Effectiveness Report, Colonel Harry C. Aderholt, Aderholt Collection, AFHRA, 10 July 1967.

8. The Tigers of Nakhon Phanom

1. Warren Trest, *Lucky Tiger Special Air Warfare Operations*, HQ PACAF, Project CHECO, AFHRA File K717.0413-15, 31 May 1967, pp. 8, 9; Aderholt, interview by Ahmann, 12–15 August 1986, pp. 182, 183.
2. Aderholt, interview by Ahmann, 12–15 August 1986, p. 183; Colonel Lee Volet, recollections of Harry C. Aderholt, Aderholt Collection, AFHRA, 23 February 1994.
3. Aderholt, interview by Ahmann, 12–15 August 1986, p. 183; Aderholt, interview by Leary, 28–30 August 1990, p. 16; "Welcome to Nakhon Phanom Royal Thai Air Force Base, Thailand," undated brochure, Aderholt Collection, AFHRA.
4. Aderholt, interview by Ahmann, 12–15 August 1986, p. 183; Aderholt, interview by Leary, 28–30 August 1990, p. 16; "Welcome to Nakhon"; Aderholt, statement to Trest, 24 January 1998.
5. Aderholt, interview by Trest, 18 April 1996, p. 17; Aderholt, interview by Trest, 10 October 1996, p. 5.
6. Aderholt, interview by Ahmann, 12–15 August 1986; Brigadier General Aderholt, statement to Warren Trest, 3 April 1998.
7. Colonel Bill Keeler, recollections of Aderholt, Aderholt Collection, AFHRA, 23 July 1994.
8. Hildreth, recollections, undated.
9. Volet, recollections, 23 February 1994.
10. Aderholt, interview by Trest, 15 August 1995, p. 29.

11. Kittinger, audiotape.
12. Aderholt, interview by Ahmann, 12–15 August 1986, pp. 191, 192; Aderholt, interview by Leary, 28–30 August 1990, p. 16.
13. Aderholt, interview by Ahmann , 12–15 August 1986, pp. 183, 184.
14. Ibid., 193.
15. Hildreth, recollections; Brigadier General Aderholt, statement to Warren Trest, 13 May 1998.
16. Ibid., 207.
17. Ibid., 191; Aderholt, interview by Leary, 28–30 August 1990, p. 15; Ropka, interview by Trest, 12 October 1996, p. 12; Trest, *Lucky Tiger*, pp. 2, 3.
18. Van Staaveren, *Interdiction in Southern Laos,* 44, 45; Ambassador William H. Sullivan, recollections of Aderholt, Aderholt Collection, AFHRA, 17 April 1994.
19. Sullivan, recollections.
20. Ibid.
21. Ibid.
22. Robbins, *Ravens,* 50.
23. Ambassador William H. Sullivan, interview by Major S. E. Riddlebarger and Major. R. B. Clement, USAF Oral History Collection, AFHRA File K239.0512-258, 15 April 1970, pp. 1–5.
24. Ibid., 8, 9.
25. Ibid., 11–19.
26. Ibid.
27. Trest, *Lucky Tiger*, pp. 11–13.
28. Ibid., 13, 14.
29. Sullivan, recollections.
30. Aderholt, interview by Ahmann, 12–15 August 1986, pp. 128, 129; Robbins, *Ravens,* 49, 50.
31. Aderholt, interview by Ahmann, 12–15 August 1986, p. 129; Aderholt, statement to Trest, 3 April 1998.
32. Aderholt, interview by Ahmann, 12–15 August 1986, p. 129; Aderholt, statement to Trest, 3 April 1998; Captain Timothy Bailey, "Air Commando! A Heritage Wrapped in Secrecy," *Airman*, March 1997, pp. 6–11.
33. Trest, *Lucky Tiger*, pp. 19, 20.
34. Aderholt, interview by Ahmann, 12–15 August 1986, pp. 242, 243.
35. Ibid.
36. Ibid., 244.
37. Ibid., 245.
38. Trest, *Lucky Tiger*, 20, 21.
39. Ibid., 7, 14, 19, 26.
40. Aderholt, interview by Trest, 15 August 1995, p. 37.
41. Trest, *Lucky Tiger*, 38–41; Van Staaveren, *Interdiction in Southern Laos*, 240; Momyer, *Air Power in Three Wars*, 204.

42. Trest, *Lucky Tiger*, 38–41; Van Staaveren, *Interdiction in Southern Laos*, 240; Momyer, *Air Power in Three Wars*, 204.

43. Trest, *Lucky Tiger*, 38–41; Colonel Michael E. Haas, "Aderholt's Air Commandos: Props vs. Jets Over Ho Chi Minh Trail," *Soldier of Fortune*, August 1966, pp. 52–55.

44. Trest, *Lucky Tiger*, 22, 23; Aderholt, interview by Ahmann, 12–15 August 1986, p. 26.

45. Aderholt, interview by Ahmann, 12–15 August 1986, pp. 186, 187; Trest, *Lucky Tiger*, 26.

46. Aderholt, interview by Ahmann, pp. 184, 185.

47. Aderholt, interview by Ahmann, 12–15 August 1986, pp. 179, 180; Major General Charles R. Bond Jr., Officer Effectiveness Report, Aderholt, Aderholt Collection, AFHRA, 1 June 1967.

48. Aderholt, interview by Ahmann, 12–15 August 1986, pp. 179, 180.

49. Ibid., 182.

50. David Corn, *Blond Ghost: Ted Shackley and the CIA's Crusades* (New York: Simon and Schuster, 1994), 138, 139; Robbins, *Ravens*, 121; Secord, *Honored and Betrayed*, 61.

51. Aderholt, interview by Ahmann, 12–15 August 1986, p. 187; Aderholt, statement to Trest, 3 April 1998.

52. Aderholt, interview by Ahmann, 12–15 August 1986, p. 187; Aderholt, statement to Trest, 3 April 1998.

53. Aderholt, interview by Ahmann, 12–15 August 1986, p. 187; Aderholt, statement to Trest, 3 April 1998; Aderholt, interview by Trest, 18 April 1996, p. 23.

54. Aderholt, interview by Ahmann, 12–15 August 1986, p. 187; Aderholt, statement to Trest, 3 April 1998; Aderholt, interview by Trest, 18 April 1996, p. 23.

55. Aderholt, interview by Ahmann, 12–15 August 1986, p. 187; Aderholt, statement to Trest, 3 April 1998; Aderholt, interview by Trest, 18 April 1996, p. 23; Van Staaveren, *Interdiction in Southern Laos*, 162, 191, 192.

56. Aderholt, interview by Ahmann, 12–15 April 1986, p. 189; Aderholt, interview by Trest, 18 April 1996, p. 24.

57. Sullivan, recollections.

58. Aderholt, interview by Trest, 18 April 1996, p. 24.

59. Colonel Walter B. Forbes to Colonel Butler, Aderholt Collection, AFHRA, 31 July 1997.

60. Marshall, recollections.

61. Aderholt, interview by Ahmann, 12–15 August 1986, pp. 189, 190.

62. Marshall, recollections.

63. Major General Charles R. Bond Jr., Officer Effectiveness Report, Aderholt, Aderholt Collection, AFHRA, 1 June 1967.

64. Aderholt, interview by Ahmann, 12–15 August 1986, p. 257.

65. Ibid., 258.

66. Ibid., 260, 261; Yeager and Janos, *Yeager*, 378, 379. For a full account, see Jack Broughton, *Going Downtown: The War against Hanoi and Washington* (New York: Pocket Books, 1988).
67. Aderholt, interview by Ahmann, 12–15 August 1986, pp. 260, 261; Yeager and Janos, *Yeager*, 378, 379.
68. Aderholt, interview by Ahmann, 12–15 August 1986, p. 263.
69. Aderholt, interview by Trest, 15 August 1995, p. 40.
70. Aderholt, interview by Ahmann, 12–15 August 1986, p. 166.
71. Ibid., 279.
72. Ibid., 167.
73. Major General W. C. Lindley Jr., Officer Effectiveness Report, Aderholt, Aderholt Collection, AFHRA, 15 December 1967.
74. Colonel Harry C. Aderholt, Commander 56th Air Commando Wing, End of Tour Report, AFHRA file K717.131.19, November 1967.
75. Ibid.
76. Aderholt, interview by Ahmann, 12–15 August 1986, pp. 277, 278.
77. Ibid.
78. Aderholt, interview by Trest, 15 August 1995, p. 41; Colonel Michael E. Haas, "Aderholt's Air Commandos," *Soldier of Fortune*, August 1996, pp. 52–55.
79. Aderholt, End of Tour Report, November 1967.
80. Aderholt, interview by Ahmann, 12–15 August 1986, p. 286.
81. Ibid.; Van Staaveren, *Interdiction in Southern Laos,* 278, 279.
82. Aderholt, statement to Trest, 16 May 1998.
83. Aderholt End of Tour Report, November 1967.
84. Ibid.
85. Ibid.
86. Ibid.
87. Ambassador William H. Sullivan to General J. P. McConnell, CSAF, Aderholt Collection, AFHRA, 29 November 1967.
88. Lieutenant General James V. Edmundson to Brigadier General Harry C. Aderholt, Aderholt Collection, AFHRA, 21 March 1967.
89. Aderholt, statement to Trest, 3 April 1998.
90. Ibid.

9. Weathering the Storm

1. Aderholt, interview by Ahmann, 12–15 August 1986, p. 268; Aderholt, statement to Trest, 3 April 1998.
2. Aderholt, interview by Ahmann, 12–15 August 1986, p. 268; Aderholt, statement to Trest, 3 April 1998.
3. Aderholt, interview by Trest, 15 August 1995, p. 42.
4. Aderholt, interview by Ahmann, 12–15 August 1986, p. 269.

5. Kissling, *Air Commando*, 83; Jack S. Ballard, *Development and Employment of Fixed-Wing Gunships, 1962–1972* (Washington, D.C.: Office of Air Force History, 1982), 57, 58, 89.

6. Ballard, *Development*, 89, 90.

7. Ibid., 8, 9, 163, 164.

8. Ibid., 92–97, 105.

9. Secord, interview by Trest, 14 October 1996, p. 14; Ropka, interview by Trest, 12 October 1996, p. 12; Ifland, interview by Trest, 18 February 1997, p. 7; Kittinger, audiotape, p. 6.

10. Kissling, *Air Commandos*, 85, 86; Brigadier General Robert L. Cardenas, official USAF biography, Secretary of the Air Force Public Affairs, 1 September 1973; Secord, interview by Trest, 14 October 1996, p. 14.

11. Aderholt, statement to Trest, 3 April 1998; General John D. Ryan, official USAF biography, Secretary of the Air Force Public Affairs, 1 April 1973; Futrell, *Ideas, Concepts, Doctrine*, vol. 2, pp. 318–22.

12. General William W. Momyer, "Observations of the Vietnam War, July 66-July 68," AFHRA File K740.131, November 1970.

13. General William W. Momyer, Commander TAC, to Brigadier General Robert N. Ginsburgh, Commander Aerospace Studies Institute, AFHRA file 168.704123, October 1969.

14. General William W. Momyer, Commander TAC, to General William C. Westmoreland, Chief of Staff, U.S. Army, AFHRA file 168.7041, 3 January 1969.

15. General William W. Momyer to General John D. Ryan, AFHRA file 168.7041, 3 January 1969.

16. Momyer to Ryan, 3 January 1969.

17. General William W. Momyer to Lieutenant Colonel J. D. Moore, AFHRA file 168.7041-33, 17 October 1970.

18. General William W. Momyer to Major General George J. Keegan Jr., AFHRA file 168.7041-43, 17 August 1971.

19. General William W. Momyer to General G. P. Disosway, AFHRA file 168.7041-59, 13 December 1972.

20. General William W. Momyer, Corona Harvest Report, Corona Harvest Files, AFHRA, 18 July 1974, chap. 3, p. 14.

21. Cardenas, recollections.

22. Brigadier General Robert L. Cardenas to General William W. Momyer, AFHRA file 168.7041, 12 December 1968.

23. General William W. Momyer to Brigadier General Robert L. Cardenas, AFHRA file 168.7041, 17 December 1968.

24. Lieutenant General Joseph G. Wilson, official USAF biography, Secretary of the Air Force Public Affairs, 1 June 1975; Aderholt, interview by Ahmann, 12–15 August 1986, p. 268.

25. Lieutenant General Joseph G. Wilson, official USAF biography, Secretary of the Air

Force Public Affairs, 1 June 1975; Aderholt, interview by Ahmann, 12–15 August 1986, p. 268; Aderholt, statement to Trest, 13 August 1998.

26. Aderholt, interview by Ahmann, 12–15 August 1986, p. 269; Kisling, *Air Commandos*, 87, 88.

27. Futrell, *Ideas, Concepts, Doctrine,* vol. 2, pp. 310, 492; Tactical Air Command to Chief of Staff, Air Force, 20 January 1970.

28. Brigadier General Harry C. Aderholt, "Terrorism and Bright Ideas" (letter to the editor), *Air Force Magazine*, December 1976, p. 10; Captain Timothy Bailey, "Air Commando! A Heritage Wrapped in Secrecy," *Airman*, March 1997, pp. 6–11.

29. Aderholt, interview by Ahmann, 28–30 August 1990, p. 18; Ballard, *Development,* 127–29.

30. Ballard, *Development,* 142.

31. Aderholt, interview by Leary, 28–30 August 1990, p. 18; Secord, interview by Trest, 14 October 1996, p. 16.

32. Ropka, interview by Trest, 12 October 1996.

33. Momyer, *Air Power in Three Wars,* 211; Laurie R. Dick, "AC-130 Spectre Earns Its Wings," *Vietnam,* June 1997, pp. 30–36.

34. Excerpts from *History of the People's Army of Vietnam,* vol. 2 (Hanoi: People's Army Publishing House, 1994), 359–62, attachment to letter, Merle L. Pribbenow to Colonel Harry G. Summers, Aderholt Collection, AFHRA, 20 April 1997.

35. Wilson, official biography; Aderholt, interview by Ahmann, 12–15 August 1986; Aderholt, statement to Trest, 13 August 1998; Ropka, interview by Trest, 12 October 1996.

36. Secord, *Honored and Betrayed,* 70.

37. Aderholt, interview by Ahmnann, 12–15 August 1986, p. 269; Major General Peter R. DeLonga, official USAF biography, Secretary of the Air Force Public Affairs, 19 August 1974; General Louis T. Seith, official USAF biography, Secretary of the Air Force Public Affairs, 1 August 1977; Lieutenant General LeRoy J. Manor, official USAF biography, Secretary of the Air Force Public Affairs, February 1977; Aderholt, statement to Trest, 12 July 1998.

38. Thomas, recollections; Manor, recollections.

39. Aderholt, interview by Ahmann, 12–15 August 1986, 294; Seith, official biography; Colonel William C. Thomas, Trip report, Seventh Air Force Tactical Liaison Officer, Aderholt Collection, AFHRA, 6 October 1970; Saras Taverrungsenykl, interview by Trest, Aderholt Collection, AFHRA, 18 February 1997.

40. Aderholt, interview by Ahmann, 12–15 August 1986, p. 294.

41. Ibid., 293.

42. Ibid.

43. Ibid., 292; Aderholt, interview by Trest, 18 April 1996, p. 32.

44. Aderholt, interview by Trest, 18 April 1996, p. 32.

45. Major General James J. Gibbons, Officer Effectiveness Reports, Aderholt, Aderholt Collection, AFHRA, 13 March 1972, 2 July 1972.

46. Aderholt, interview by Trest, 15 August 1995, p. 44.
47. William H. Sullivan to Lieutenant General Robert J. Dixon, Aderholt Collection, AFHRA, 1 July 1971.
48. Ibid.
49. Kittinger, audiotape.
50. Aderholt, interview by Ahmann, 12–15 August 1986, pp. 294, 295.
51. Ibid.
52. Ibid.; Secord, official biography; Ropka, interview by Trest, 12 October 1996.
53. Aderholt, interview with Ahmann, 12–15 August 1986, p. 297.
54. Ibid., 298.
55. Ibid.
56. Ibid., 300; Air Force Special Order AB-1854, 4 October 1973.
57. History of the USMACTHAI/JUSMAGTHAI, 1973, pp. 1–10; Aderholt, interview by Ahmann, 12–15 August 1986, p. 300; "October 14, 1973: The Black Sunday," *The Nation*, Bangkok Sunday edition, 21 October 1973 (Aderholt Collection, AFHRA).
58. History of the USMACTHAI/JUSMAGTHAI, 1973, pp. 1–10; Aderholt, interview by Ahmann, 12–15 August 1986, p. 300; "October 14, 1973: The Black Sunday," *The Nation*, Bangkok Sunday edition, 21 October 1973 (Aderholt Collection, AFHRA).
59. Aderholt, interview by Ahmann, 12–15 August 1986, pp. 301, 302.
60. Foisie, "U.S. Air Force Retiree."
61. Aderholt, interview by Trest, 15 August 1995, p. 41.

10. Mission Accomplished

1. *Brief History,* pp. 42, 43; Carl Berger et al., *The United States Air Force in Southeast Asia, 1961–1973* (Washington, D.C.: Office of Air Force History, 1977), 147, 221.
2. Lieutenant General Leroy J. Manor, official USAF biography, Secretary of the Air Force Public Affairs, February 1977; Major General James R. Hildreth, official USAF biography, Secretary of the Air Force Public Affairs, June 1979.
3. William Shawcross, *Sideshow: Kissinger, Nixon, and the Destruction of Cambodia* (New York: Simon and Schuster, 1979), 15, 16, 190, 191, 312.
4. History of the USMACTHAI/JUSMAGTHAI, 1974, pp. 18, 180; History of the USMACTHAI/JUSMAGTHAI, 1975, pp. 33, 218.
5. Representative Patricia Schroeder to Secretary of Defense James R. Schlesinger, Aderholt Collection, AFHRA, 10 December 1973.
6. John O. Marsh Jr. to Patricia Schroeder, 19 January 1974.
7. Aderholt to von Marbod, Aderholt Collection, AFHRA, undated.
8. Ibid.

9. Ibid.
10. Hildreth, recollections.
11. Ibid.
12. Aderholt, interview by Trest, 18 April 1996, p. 31.
13. Ibid.
14. Ibid.
15. Ibid.
16. Aderholt, interview by Ahmann, 12–15 August 1986, pp. 309, 310. For statistics on U.S. military personnel in Southeast Asia, 1960–1968, see John Schlight's *Years of the Offensive*, 5.
17. Ibid., 311, 312.
18. Hildreth, recollections.
19. Aderholt, statement to Trest, 12 July 1998.
20. Tactical Air Improvement Plan, Cambodia, AFHRA file K143.054-4, 20 November 1973.
21. Ibid., 1–3.
22. Tony Koura, *The Cambodian Airlift, 1974–1975* (Hickam AFB, Hawaii.: Office of PACAF History, 1976), 3.
23. Tactical Air Improvement Plan, Cambodia; Aderholt, statement to Trest, 12 July 1998; Aderholt, interview by Leary, 28–30 August 1990.
24. Koura, *Cambodian Airlift*, 3–5; Ray L. Bowers, *Tactical Airlift* (Washington, D.C.: Office of Air Force History, 1983), 625, 626.
25. Koura, *Cambodian Airlift*, 3–5.
26. Aderholt, statement to Trest, 12 July 1998.
27. Koura, *Cambodian Airlift*, 6; Bowers, *Tactical Airlift*, 627; Aderholt, statement to Trest, 3 April 1998.
28. Koura, *Cambodian Airlift*, 6, 7; Colonel Donald K. Cole, HQ USAF, to PACAF/XOA, Contract Airlift Operations in Cambodia, Aderholt Collection, AFHRA, 20 June 1975.
29. Koura, *Cambodian Airlift*, 12, 13. Brigadier General Aderholt to General Brown, Admiral Gaylor, and von Marbod, DTG 130935Z, August 1974; Brigadier General Aderholt to General Brown et al., DTG 211700Z, August 1974; Brigadier General Aderholt to General Brown, DTG 261030Z, August 1974 (Aderholt Collection, AFHRA).
30. Bowers, *Tactical Airlift*, 627. Brigadier General Aderholt to General Brown, DTG 270904Z, September 1974; General Brown to Brigadier General Aderholt, DTG 281540Z, September 1974 (Aderholt Collection, AFHRA).
31. Koura,*Cambodian Airlift*, 5.
32. Aderholt, interview by Ahmann, 12–15 August 1986, p. 320; Ralph Wetterhahn, "Escape to U Taphao," *Air & Space*, December 1996/January 1997, pp. 36–43.
33. Ibid.

34. Tobin et al., *Last Flight from Saigon*, p. 14; General David C. Jones, interview by Lieutenant Colonel Maurice Maryanow with Dr Richard H. Kohn, AFHRA File No. K239.0512-1664, August and October 1985, January and March 1986, pp. 139,140.
35. Aderholt, interview by Ahmann, 12–15 August 1986, pp. 137, 323.
36. Ibid., 138, 324.
37. Ibid.
38. Koura, *Cambodian Airlift*, 27; General Burns to General Brown and Admiral Gaylor, DTG 141110Z , January 1975.
39. Koura, *Cambodian Airlift*, 30–36; Aderholt, interview by Trest, 18 April 1996, p. 28.
40. Aderholt, statement to Trest, 12 July 1998.
41. Ibid.
42. Aderholt, interview by Trest, 18 April 1996, p. 28; Baginski to Aderholt, 12 July 1994; Aderholt, interview by Leary, 28–30 August 1990, p. 19.
43. Brigadier General Aderholt to Eric von Marbod, DTG 111230Z, Aderholt Collection, AFHRA, February 1975.
44. Ibid.
45. Ibid.
46. Ibid.
47. Koura, *Cambodian Airlift*, 35, 40, 41; Aderholt, statement to Trest, 12 July 1998.
48. Ibid., 41, 42.
49. Aderholt, interview by Ahmann, 12–15 August 1986, p. 357.
50. Koura, *Cambodian Airlift*, 53, 55–57.
51. Ibid., 63, 64, 66, 67, 69; Tobin et al., *Last Flight from Saigon*, 45.
52. Koura, *Cambodian Airlift*, 1, 2.
53. Ibid., 75.
54. Wayne G. Peterson et al., *Fall and Evacuation of South Vietnam* (Hickam AFB, Hawaii: Office of PACAF History, 1978), 191–93 (AFHRA File No. K717.04-16).
55. Aderholt, interview by Ahmann, 12–15 August 1986, pp. 327, 328.
56. Peterson et al., *Fall and Evacuation of South Vietnam*, 116.
57. Ibid., 326.
58. Ibid., 339; Brigadier General Harry C. Aderholt, paper on Hmong evacuation, Aderholt Collection, AFHRA, undated.
59. Peterson et al., *Fall and Evacuation of South Vietnam*, 116; Aderholt, paper on Hmong evacuation. See Conboy, *Shadow War*, 415, for a brief description of the Hmong evacuation and the fall of Laos to the communists.
60. Aderholt, interview by Ahmann, 12–15 August 1986, pp. 305, 306.
61. Ibid., 306, 307.
62. Ibid., 307, 308; History of USMACTHAI/USMAGTHAI, 1975, p 33; Aderholt, statement to Trest, 12 July 1998.
63. "Greeting from General. Aderholt," *A-l Skyraider Association Newsletter*, February 1976, p. 1 (Aderholt Collection, AFHRA).
64. CINCPAC Command History, 1975, Appendix 6, *The SS Mayaguez Incident*,

AFHRA File No. K712.01, pp. 1, 21–23, 27; Aderholt, interview by Ahmann, 12–15 August 1986, p. 317; "Whitehouse May Replace Kintner," *The Nation*, Bangkok, 26 February 1975, p. 1.

65. John Burlage, "Pentagon's Second Shot at Special Operations Slot," *Army Times*, May 1988 (Aderholt Collection, AFHRA).

66. William D. Toomey, recollections of Harry C. Aderholt, Aderholt Collection, AFHRA, 26 April 1994.

67. Ambassador Charles S. Whitehouse to General Aderholt, 2 December 1975; Chief of Mission's Evaluation of Performance on Brigadier General Harry C. Aderholt, 26 November 1975. Aderholt Collection, AFHRA.

68. "Greeting from General Aderholt," 1.

69. Ibid.

70. Brigadier General Aderholt, COMUSMACTHAI, to Admiral Gaylor, CINCPAC, DTG 091100Z, Aderholt Collection, AFHRA, March 1976.

71. Ibid.

72. Aderholt, interview by Ahmann, 12–15 August 1986, p. 354.

73. Ibid.

74. L. H. Tifverman, Memorandum of Conversation with General Kriangsak, 25 March 1976; Brigadier General Aderholt, Debriefing report, May 1975-July 1975, p. I-52. Aderholt Collection, AFHRA.

75. Tifverman, Memorandum; Aderholt, Debriefing report, p. I-52.

76. Tifverman, Memorandum; Aderholt, Debriefing report, p. I-52.

77. Tifverman, Memorandum; Aderholt, Debriefing report, p. I-52; "MACTHAI's Last Parade," *Bangkok Post*, 26 June 1976; Brigadier General Aderholt to Admiral Gayler, DTG 070635Z, Aderholt Collection, AFHRA, April 1976.

78. Aderholt, interview by Ahmann, 12–15 August 1986, p. 356.

79. Colonel Michael E. Haas, *Apollo's Warriors: United States Air Force Special Operations during the Cold War* (Maxwell AFB, Ala.: Air University Press, 1997), xiii.

80. Haas, "Aderholt's Air Commandos," 53.

81. Aderholt, interview by Ahmann, 12–15 August 1986, p. 358.

82. Brigadier General Aderholt to Truck Killers, Aderholt Collection, AFHRA, 23 January 1975.

83. Aderholt, interview by Ahmann, 12–15 August 1986, p. 337.

84. Ropka, interview by Trest, 12 October 1996, p. 37.

85. Brigadier General Harry C. Aderholt, "Terrorism and Bright Ideas," *Air Force Magazine*, December 1976, p. 10.

86. Aderholt, interview by Ahmann, 12–15 August 1986, p. 129.

Epilogue

1. Manor, recollections.

2. Ibid.

3. Brigadier General Harry C. Aderholt, audiotape, Aderholt Collection, AFHRA, July 1998.
4. Ibid.
5. Ibid.
6. Ibid.; UPI press release, Fort Walton Beach, Fla., 27 March 1985; Robert Timberg, "Retired Air Force General Deals in Rattan Furniture—and Sometimes Other Things," *Baltimore Sun*, 22 March 1987. Aderholt Collection, AFHRA.
7. Aderholt audiotape, July 1998; UPI press release, Fort Walton Beach, Fla., 27 March 1985.
8. Ibid.; Robert Timberg, "Alleged Iran-Contra Players No Strangers," *Baltimore Sun*, 27 December 1986; Brigadier General Aderholt to *Newsweek*, Aderholt Collection, AFHRA, 4 November 1986.
9. "Guatemala Thanks A.C.A.," *Air Commando Newsletter*, May 1987, pp. 1, 3.
10. Aderholt, audiotape, July 1998; Thomas Goltz, "The Great Azeri Oil Scam," *Soldier of Fortune*, November 1994, pp. 33–37.
11. Aderholt, audiotape, July 1998; Goltz, "Great Azeri Oil Scam," 33–37.
12. Aderholt, statement to Trest, 12 July 1998.
13. Ibid.; Ropka, interview by Trest, 12 October 1996.
14. Major General Bruce L. Fister to Brigadier General Aderholt, 29 June 1993; Major General Bruce L. Fister to Brigadier General Aderholt, 26 August 1993. Aderholt Collection, AFHRA.
15. Aderholt, statement to Trest, 12 July 1998; "Fallout from a Media Fiasco," *Newsweek*, 20 July 1998, pp. 24, 25.
16. Brigadier General Aderholt, "Hmong National Recognition Day," *Air Commando Association Quarterly Newsletter*, September 1995, p. 11.
17. Ibid.; Aderholt, audiotape, July 1998.
18. Aderholt, statement to Trest, 12 July 1998.
19. Ibid.; "Lao-Hmong Recognition," *Air Commando Newsletter*, September 1996, p. 12; Yang Chee, President Lao-Hmong American Coalition, to Brigadier General Aderholt, Aderholt Collection, AFHRA, 10 March 1996.
20. "McCoskie Threshold Foundation," *Air Commando Newsletter*, June 1998, p. 14.
21. Ibid.; Aderholt, audiotape, July 1998.
22. Aderholt, audiotape, July 1998; *Quarterly Newsletter*, September 1995, p. 11.
23. James A. Taylor, "'Old Man' Supported U.S. by Actions, Not Words," *Cass County Democrat, Missouri*, 6 June 1996.
24. Ibid.

SELECTED BIBLIOGRAPHY

Brigadier General Harry C. Aderholt's personal papers are located at the Air Force Historical Research Agency, Maxwell AFB, Alabama. These papers, supplemented by material (written recollections, tapes, interviews, and so on) gathered for this biography, are referenced in the notes as the Aderholt Collection, AFHRA. Unit histories housed at the Research Agency provided useful information on General Aderholt's military assignments. The histories and the extensive oral history collection at AFHRA filled research gaps with nuggets of information that were not available elsewhere. Two comprehensive interviews with General Aderholt in 1986 and 1995 by Hugh N. Ahmann, the Research Agency's oral historian, served as indispensable road maps to the general's Air Force career. An earlier interview in 1970 by Major Samuel E. Riddlebarger for Project Corona Harvest fills out the portrait.

In addition to holdings at the Maxwell AFB repository, the Office of the Air Force Historian at Bolling AFB, D.C., oversees a comprehensive book program and a dynamic monographic effort extending throughout the major command field programs. These published histories and studies are invaluable sources for authors conducting research into military aviation. Particularly helpful to the preparation of General Aderholt's biography were monographs and studies prepared during the Vietnam War era by the Office of Air Force History (a blue-cover monograph series), Project CHECO (a special historical program in Southeast Asia), and the historians at HQ PACAF, Hickam AFB, Hawaii. Background and anecdotal material from a wide range of books and magazine articles helped glue the story together. A selected bibliography follows.

Books

Appleman, Roy E. *United States Army in the Korean War. South to the Naktong, North to the Yalu*. Washington, D.C.: Office, Chief of Military History, 1961.

Ballard, Jack S. *Development and Employment of Fixed-Wing Gunships, 1962–1972*. Washington, D.C.: Office of Air Force History, 1982.

Berger, Carl, ed. *The United States Air Force in Southeast Asia, 1961–1973*. Washington: Office of Air Force History, 1977.

Broughton, Jack. *Going Downtown: The War against Hanoi and Washington*. New York: Pocket Books, 1988.

Castle, Timothy N. *At War in the Shadow of Vietnam*. New York: Columbia University Press, 1993.

Chinnery, Philip D. *Any Time, Any Place: A History of USAF Air Commando and Special Operations Forces*. Annapolis: Naval Institute Press, 1994.

Conboy, Kenneth. *Shadow War: The CIA's Secret War in Laos*. Boulder, Colo.: Paladin Press, 1995.

Corn, David. *Blond Ghost: Ted Shackley and the CIA's Crusades*. New York: Simon and Schuster, 1994.

Davis, Benjamin O. *Benjamin O. Davis, Jr., American: An Autobiography*. Washington: Smithsonian Institution Press, 1991.

Futrell, Robert F. *Ideas, Concepts, Doctrine: Basic Thinking in the United States Air Force, 1907–1960*, 2 vols. Maxwell AFB, Ala.: Air University Press, 1989.

———. *The United States Air Force in Korea, 1950–1953*. Washington: Office of Air Force History, 1983.

———. *The United States Air Force in Southeast Asia: The Advisory Years to 1965*. Washington, D.C.: Office of Air Force History, 1981.

Goldberg, Alfred, ed. *A History of the United States Air Force, 1907–1957*. Princeton, N.J.: D. Van Nostrand, 1957.

Gropman, Alan L. *The Air Force Integrates, 1945–1964*. Washington, D.C.: Office of Air Force History, 1978.

Haas, Colonel Michael E. *Apollo's Warriors. United States Air Force Special Operations during the Cold War*. Maxwell AFB, Ala.: Air University Press, 1997.

Haas, Colonel Michael E., and TSgt Dale K. Robinson. *Air Commando! 1950–1975: Twenty-Five Years at the Tip of the Spear*. Hurlburt AFB, Fla.: HQ SOFC, undated.

Hagedorn, Dan, and Leif Hellstrom. *Foreign Invaders: The Douglas Invader in Foreign Military and U.S. Clandestine Service*. Leicester, UK: Midland Publishing, 1994.

Hamilton-Merritt, Jane. *Tragic Mountains. The Hmong, the Americans, and the Secret Wars for Laos, 1942–1992*. Bloomington: Indiana University Press, 1993.

Kelly, Orr. *From a Dark Sky: The Story of U.S. Air Force Special Operations*. Novato, Calif.: Presidio Press, 1996.

Kohn, Richard H., and Joseph P. Harahan, ed. *Air Superiority in World War II and Korea*. Washington: Office of Air Force History, 1983.

Leary, William M., ed. *The Central Intelligence Agency: History and Documents*. Tuscaloosa: University of Alabama Press, 1984.

Momyer, General William W. *Air Power in Three Wars*. Washington: HQ United States Air Force, 1978.

McMaster, H. R. *Dereliction of Duty*. New York: HarperCollins, 1997.

Newman, John M. *JFK and Vietnam*. New York: Warner Books, 1992.

Plaster, John L. *SOG: The Secret Wars of America's Commandos in Vietnam*. New York: Simon and Schuster, 1997.

Robbins, Christopher. *The Ravens: The Men Who Flew in America's Secret War in Laos*. Atlanta: EAPLS, 1995.

Schlight, John. *The United States Air Force in Southeast Asia: The Years of the Offensive, 1965–1968*. Washington, D.C.: Office of Air Force History, 1988.

Schnabel, James F. *United States Army in the Korean War. Policy and Direction: The First Year*. Washington, D.C.: Office, Chief of Military History, 1972.

Secord, Richard, with Jay Wurts. *Honor and Betrayed: Irangate, Covert Affairs, and the Secret War in Laos*. New York: John Wiley and Sons, 1992.

Shawcross, William. *Sideshow: Kissinger, Nixon, and the Destruction of Cambodia*. New York: Simon and Schuster, 1979.

Stanton, Shelby L. *Green Berets at War: U.S. Army Special Forces in Southeast Asia, 1956–1975*. Novato, Calif.: Presidio Press, 1985.

Tilford, Earl H. Jr. *SETUP: What the Air Force Did in Vietnam and Why*. Maxwell AFB, Ala.: Air University Press, 1991.

Van Staaveren, Jacob. *The United States Air Force in Southeast Asia: Interdiction in Southern Laos, 1960–1968*. Washington, D.C.: Center for Air Force History, 1993.

Veith, George J. *Code-Name Bright Light*. New York: Free Press, 1998.

Warner, Roger. *Back Fire: The CIA's Secret War in Laos and Its Link to the War in Vietnam*. New York: Simon and Schuster, 1995.

Warner, Roger. *Shooting at the Moon: The Story of America's Clandestine War in Laos*. South Royalton, Vt.: Steerforth Press, 1996.

Yeager, General Chuck, and Leo Janus. *Yeager: An Autobiography*. New York: Bantam, 1985.

Articles

Bailey, Captain Timothy. "Air Commando! A Heritage Wrapped in Secrecy." *Airman*, March 1997, 6–11.

Haas, Colonel Michael E. "Aderholt's Air Commandos. Props vs. Jets Over Ho Chi Minh Trail." *Soldier of Fortune*, August 1996, 52–55.

Leary, William M. "Secret Mission to Tibet." (*Smithsonian*) *Air & Space*, January 1998, 62–67.

Wetterhahn, Ralph. "Escape to U Taphao." (*Smithsonian*) *Air & Space*, December 1996–January 1997, 36–43.

Monographs and Studies

Farmer, J., and M. J. Strumwasser. *The Evolution of the Airborne Forward Air Controller: An Analysis of Mosquito Operations in Korea*. Santa Monica, Calif.: RAND Corporation, October 1967.

Graham, W. B., and A. H. Katz. *SIAT: The Single Integrated Attack Team. A Concept for Offensive Military Operations in South Vietnam*. Santa Monica, Calif.: RAND Corporation, December 1964.

Hildreth, Charles A. *USAF Counterinsurgency Doctrines and Capabilities, 1961–1962*. Washington, D.C.: USAF Historical Division, February 1964.

Hildreth, Charles A. *USAF Special Air Warfare Doctrines and Capabilities, 1963*. Washington, D.C.: USAF Historical Division, 1964.

Kisling, Herbert H. *An Air Commando and Special Operations Chronology, 1961–1991*. Hurlburt Field, Fla.: History Office, undated.

Koura, Tony. *The Cambodian Airlift, 1974–1975*. Hickam AFB, Hawaii: HQ PACAF Office of History, October 1976.

Lemmer, George F. *The Laos Crisis of 1959*. Washington, D.C.: USAF Historical Division Liaison Office, May 1961.

Liebchen, Captain Peter A. W. *MAP Aid to Laos, 1959–1972*. Tan Son Nhut AB, RVN: HQ 7AF Project CHECO, June 1973.

O'Neill, Arthur C. *Fifth Air Force in the Southeast Asia Crisis of 1960–1961*. Fuchu AB, Japan: HQ 5AF Historical Division, June 1961.

Overton, Major James B. *FAC Operations in Close Air Support Role in SVN*. Tan Son Nhut AB, RVN: HQ 7AF Project CHECO, 1969.

Peterson, Wayne G., et al. *The Fall and Evacuation of South Vietnam*. Hickam AFB, Hawaii: HQ PACAF Office of History, April 1978.

Tobin, Thomas G., et al. *Last Flight from Saigon*. Washington, D.C.: Office of Air Force History, 1985.

Tolson, John J. *Airmobility, 1961–1971*. Washington, D.C.: Department of the Army, 1973.

Trest, Warren A. *Lucky Tiger Special Air Warfare Operations*. Tan Son Nhut AB, RVN: HQ 7AF Project CHECO, May 1967.

INDEX

A

Abrams, Gen. Creighton W., 179, 217–18

Aderholt, Brig. Gen. Harry C. ("Heinie"): and Bay of Pigs, 8–9, 113–15; and George S. Brown, 233, 242–43, 252; and Cambodian airlift, 242–52; on centralized control, 176–79, 198; on Claire Chennault, 260–61; as chief, Air Force advisory group, 225–30; as chief, JPRC, 10–11, 165–81; and CIA, 1, 5, 7–9, 13, 51–65, 75–124, 264; cleaning up Clark Air Base, 159–63; commands 1st Air Commando Wing, 9–10, 133–39; commands 56th Air Commando Wing, 3, 11, 24, 146, 180–212; commands black squadron, 18–24; commands detachment 2, 84–124; commands JUSMAG/MACTHAI, 252–58; commands Mill Pond, 109–16; commands special detachment in Korea, 29–52; commands Tibetan airlift, 242–52; on counter-insurgency warfare, 9–12, 102, 121–23, 132; cover name, Sakaffie, 103, 112, 120; crashes helio, 122–23; early life of, 2, 18, 78; at Eighteenth Air Force, 66–68; first C-47 napalm drop, 33; and gunships, 215–16, 220–23; and helio program, 78–81, 99–122; Ho Chi Minh Trail, interdiction of, 11, 188–99, 201, 203, 207–11, 213–14; as humanitarian, 15, 262, 264–65, 267–70; as Lao-Hmong adviser, 267–70; and Laos, secret war in 8, 99–104; leadership style, 2–5, 11, 56, 87, 137, 154, 184–87, 203, 228, 261–62; and Lima Sites, 8, 118–19; marries, 14, 18; at Maxwell field, 17–25; on military discipline, 44; promotions, 6, 15, 49, 96, 134, 235; recalled, 231–32; regular commission, 18; and special air warfare, 8, 55, 64, 103, 131; in USAFE, 6, 66, 68–72; Vang Pao, arming of, 116–20, 268; on Vietnam War, 12, 103, 152–56, 168, 212, 259–60; in World War II, 2, 17, 19

Aderholt, George (son), 14, 69

Aderholt, Janet (daughter), 14, 69

Aderholt, Jessie (Mrs. Harry C.), 14, 18, 25, 52, 68, 70, 84, 157, 166, 212, 229, 259

Aderholt, Robert (brother), 19

Aderholt, Warren (brother), 19, 52, 83, 112–15, 183–84

Ahmann, Lt. Gen. James H., 133, 153–54, 216

Air America, 8, 80, 85, 99, 104–7, 110, 114, 118–22, 140–42, 145–46, 193, 199, 206, 230, 242, 247, 252, 255

air bases (U.S. and overseas): Andrews, 125, 232; Ashiya, 26–27, 50, 52; Bien Hoa, 111, 113, 120, 127, 130, 133, 155, 174–76, 193, 251–52; Brady, 28; Cannon, 110; Chaumont, 71; Clark, 10, 53, 81, 93, 155, 158–66, 204–205, 225, 239, 245, 247, 252; Donaldson, 4, 62, 66–68; Eglin, 9, 13, 79, 112, 122–34, 152–55, 215–16, 219–222, 232, 235; England, 155; Hamilton, 131;